ABBREVIATIONS

CD   *Church Dogmatics* (Barth)
CO   *Ioannis Calvini opera quae supersunt omnia* (CR XXIX-LXXXVII)
CR   *Corpus Reformatorum;* Philippi Melanchthonis, *Opera quae supersunt omnia* (CR I-XXVIII)
CCSL   *Corpus Christianorum, Series Latina*
Clemen   Otto Clemen, *Luthers Werke in Auswahl. Studienausgabe*
DBW   *Dietrich Bonhoeffer Werke*
DS   Denzinger-Schönmetzer, *Enchiridion symbolorum, definitionum et declarationum de rebus fidei et morum*
EA   *Dr. Martin Luther's Sämmtliche Werke* (*Erlanger Ausgabe*)
Inst.   *Institutio* (Calvin)
KD   Karl Barth, *Die kirchliche Dogmatik*
MA   Martin Luther, *Ausgewählte Werke* (*Münchener Ausgabe*)
OS   Joannis Calvini, *Opera Selecta*, vol. I - V
PL   *Migne, Patrologia, series latina*
PRE   *Realencyklopedie für protestantische Theologie und Kirche*, in *dritter Auflage*
St.A.   *Studien Ausgabe* (Melanchthon)
S.Th.   *Summa Theologica* (Thomas Aquinas)
Th.E.h.   *Theologische Existenz heute*
Th.St.   *Theologische Studien*
WA   *D. Martin Luthers Werke. Kritische Gesamtausgabe* (Weimarer Ausgabe)
WA Br.   *Weimarer Ausgabe. Briefe*
Zw.d.Z.   *Zwischen den Zeiten*

EDITORIAL PREFACE

The Dutch theologian Frans Hendrik Breukelman (1916-1993) was not a writer. Not only during his years as a church minister, but also during the time he taught at the theological faculty of the University of Amsterdam (from 1968 onwards) he was accustomed to gathering an *audience*. In brilliant oral improvisation he would carry his listeners along the discoveries he had made in his study of the Bible, Rabbinics or the doctrinal traditions of the church. All of this in full agreement with his insight that we need to rediscover the book which we call 'the Scriptures' as *Miqra*, 'that which is called out, proclaimed'. We need to become 'hearers' of the Word instead of being just readers. Breukelman had learned this from the Jewish philosophers Martin Buber and Franz Rosenzweig. Their German translation of the Bible was printed colometrically, in breathing-units. Breukelman put this principle into practice far beyond the strict territory of biblical exegesis.

It was not easy, therefore, to elicit from this man a coherent written presentation of his theological findings and expositions. His publisher (Gerrit Brinkman of the publishing house Kok in Kampen) managed with great difficulty to convince him to finish three monographs (called 'cahiers') in the final years of his life. However, he left behind the bulk of his work to be published by a later generation of students.

Being a perfectionist, Breukelman made numerous corrections to his initial design of the series of cahiers. The series was to bear the name of *Biblical Theology*, referring to the hermeneutical discipline which in his view had to reproduce the implicit theology of the 'first witnesses' (i.e., the prophets and apostles). As such, Breukelman claimed, biblical theology is an indispensable conversational partner of dogmatic theology. In the opinion of Breukelman, dogmatic theology is the critical reflection of the church on its own proclamation, which should be in line with the message of the first witnesses.

Part I of his series, *Toledot,* was to concern itself with the theology of the book of Genesis. Breukelman rejected the common historical-critical division of this book into a 'primeval history' followed by a 'patriarchal history'. Instead, he posited the unity of the book. Referring to Gen 5:1, Breukelman used to call Genesis the 'Book of the Generations of Adam, the Man'. As he saw it, the book of Genesis deals with the generation of Israel as the firstborn of many brothers and sisters (the *goyim*, i.e., the non-Jews). The task of biblical theology, therefore, is to bring to light the universal scope of the particular history of Israel.

Part II was to deal with biblical keywords distinguishing the witness of Israel from the worldview of the *goyim*. To Breukelman's mind, the *goyim* characteristically tend toward metaphysical thought. The *goyim* think in 'essences', whereas Israel thinks in 'names' (*shemot*). Also, the *goyim* tend to focus on 'works', whereas in Israel's witness the stress is on 'words' (*debarim*). A further opposition concerns the biblical concept of the 'days' (*yamim*) in contrast to thinking in terms of 'time and eternity'. Finally,

Breukelman opposes the biblical concept of 'the earth below the heavens' *(ha'arets tahat hashamayim)* to thinking in terms of the 'kosmos'. To be sure, Breukelman did not so much as attempt to sketch the central content of a biblical theology. Rather, he tried to outline the framework within which the various theologies we meet in the Bible find their place.

Part III of the series was to focus on the theology of Matthew the evangelist. Canonically situated at the beginning of the 'New Testament', Matthew starts with a 'Book of the Generation of Jesus Christ' (Mat 1:1). In doing so, he follows the example of Gen 5:1. Just as Genesis deals with the birth and growth of Israel among the nations, so Matthew's book deals with the birth and growth of the Messiah among his people Israel. As one of Breukelman's many poignant sayings would have it: 'Just as we do not speak humanistically about Israel, but rather Israelitically about humanity, so we do not speak Israelitically about the Messiah, but Messianically about Israel'.

The fourth and final part was to confront the findings of the first three parts with a study of the 'structure of sacred doctrine in the theology of the church'. The central question here was to be: To what extent did this structure preserve the Israelite-Messianic characteristics of the biblical witnesses? The study of 'the structure of sacred doctrine in the theology of Calvin' was intended to be a component of this fourth part of Breukelman's envisaged series of cahiers.[1]

The initial impetus to this study of Calvin's theology[2] came from the remarkable Dutch theologian K. H. Miskotte, Breukelman's inspirer and mentor. Miskotte suggested that Breukelman contributed to the *Festschrift* to be published on the occasion of Karl Barth's seventieth birthday. It would be entitled *Antwort* (Answer). Barth – an unexpected presence in Buber's and Rosenzweig's company – was one of the chief sources of inspiration for Breukelman's theological project, although this project was construed quite independently from Barth.[3]

In his contribution to the *Festschrift*, Breukelman planned to confront the 'structure of biblical witness', as he thought he had discovered it, with the 'structure of sacred doctrine' in the history of Christian doctrine. In particular, he wanted to focus on the works of Thomas Aquinas, John Calvin, Francis Turrettini, and Karl Barth. He aimed to arrive at the conclusion that only Barth's dogmatics could be reconciled with the biblical structures (cf. the final words in this volume, chapter V §2).

Of course, the program for this article was far too pretentious, and the article was not published in the *Festschrift*.[4] However, Breukelman did not give up on his project. In the 1960s he tried to write a book in German, in which he wanted to expound his thesis. Chapter I of the present book, written in German, dates back to this phase of his activities (1962-1969). Shortly after his appointment as a lecturer at the University of Amsterdam, Breukelman returned to this study, this time writing in Dutch. The introduction, plus chapters II and III, of the present book derive from this period (they were for the most part ready by January 1974).[5] In the winter of 1975/76, Breukelman was invited, through the intercession of Friedrich-Wilhelm Marquardt, as a visiting lecturer at the Institute for Evangelical Theology of the Free University (West) in Berlin, where the retirement of Hellmut Gollwitzer had left a vacancy. Here, Breukelman composed a German syllabus for a seminar on Calvin's *Institutes*. Chapter IV of the present publication is to a large extent based on this syllabus. During the twenty years following

1976 Breukelman never finished his study. We do have traces of lectures and seminars on Calvin and the reformed doctrinal tradition, including improvements made by Breukelman in the chapters he had already written. Yet none of these texts point to a completion of the study. As a result, chapter V of the present book had to be compiled on the basis of a series of monographs which had come into being separately. This chapter, therefore, has the fragmentary character of a 'collage'.

It should be noted that the editor alone is responsible for the compilation of chapter V as well as for all other editorial interventions in the present publication. This is also true for the decision to cite Calvin's works only in translation. Breukelman was (even by continental European standards) thoroughly grounded in old-fashioned, solid philology, and did not hesitate to confront his students with the Latin and French original texts. This was usually followed by a brief summary that served as a translation (traces of this habit may be found in the published texts). When Breukelman himself recited the original texts, Calvin's words became much more easily understood to his audience. However, this effect cannot be imitated in script, though an attempt has been made to maintain the colometric transcription, facilitating oral presentation.[6]

It is not the editor's task to be the first reviewer of the book he has edited himself. Nevertheless, it might be appropriate to justify why this study – posthumously and in edited form – is now submitted to an international forum of Calvin-lovers and Calvin-researchers. After all, as is shown in §3 of the introduction, Breukelman undertook this study more than half a century ago. He was prompted by the simultaneous publication (in 1952) of two studies on the knowledge of God in the theology of Calvin. The authors, Edward A. Dowey Jr. and Tim H. L. Parker, arrived at contradictory conclusions. This led Breukelman to speak of an 'impasse' in the field. He wished to break this stalemate by a close reading of Calvin's texts.

The background of Dowey's and Parker's disagreement is formed by the controversy between Karl Barth and Emil Brunner on the natural knowledge of God. This debate, however, is no longer the context within which Calvin studies move. On the contrary, a leading scholar such as Richard A. Muller vehemently opposes everything that he views as an accommodation of the historical Calvin to the systematic-theological needs and interests of the present, be they Barthian, Schleiermacherian, or otherwise.[7] Calvin, Muller claims – and many researchers with him – must be placed back in his own time, and ought to be interpreted within the context of the issues and scientific methods of his age. Although the theology of Karl Barth has given an important impulse to Calvin study in the past, this phase is now behind us. Seen from this vantage point, isn't the present publication hopelessly out of date?

To answer such objections we may in the first place point to the fact that Breukelman, in spite of evident differences, also *shares* a number of interests with a man like Richard Muller. Indeed, Breukelman in a certain sense was ahead of his time by calling attention to aspects in the approach to Calvin, which had theretofore been neglected and would only later demand attention. Consider the following examples:

a. Breukelman notes that many formal differences between the various editions of the *Institutes*, such as differences in style, can be explained by differences in literary genre and corresponding audience;

b. Breukelman gives much attention to the way the first generations after Calvin published his works, and how these early editorial practices can nurture our understanding of his texts (cf. chapter IV §2 II on the *argumenta* of Olevianus);

c. Breukelman observes that the content of what Calvin said can hardly be detached from the form in which it was said. Breukelman was sensitive to what recent studies call the 'rhetorical' element in Calvin. This element was given special attention by him through the colometric presentation of Calvin's texts.

Secondly, we may add that Breukelman not only anticipated later tendencies in research, but also made discoveries which – as far as we can see – have not yet been discussed elsewhere. Here we could point out the following:

a. Breukelman concurs with Paul Wernle's thesis that the first pages of the first chapter of the *Institutes* of 1536 form an introduction. Then, however, Breukelman provides his own interpretation of this introduction. To his mind it serves as an indication of the entire *ordo docendi* of the first three subsequent chapters in these *Institutes*, following the example of Luther's *Enchiridion piarum precationum* (chapter I, §§ 1 and 2);

b. Breukelman offers a new explanation of the familiar observation that Calvin, in the *Institutes* of 1539, had replaced the title *summa doctrinae* (essence of doctrine) with *summa sapientiae* (essence of wisdom). Breukelman points out that Calvin did not throw out the expression '*summa doctrinae*' but placed it at the beginning of the seventh chapter. It functions as a key to understanding the structure of this second edition (chapter III § 1);

c. Breukelman deals with the age-old discussion as to how much weight should really be accorded to Calvin's arrangement of the final Latin edition of the 1559 *Institutes*. According to his own words, Calvin based it on the Apostles' Creed. Breukelman asks what happens when the intent of this edition is understood from the introduction of the Apostles' Creed as presented in earlier editions (Inst. 1543-54, chapter VI.1-5). Remarkably enough, this introduction was scrapped in 1559 for architectural reasons (see among others, introduction § 2 and chapter IV §§ 1 and 2.III).

Finally, one may wonder whether the resistance of scholars such as Muller to 'accommodating' Calvin should really be the last word on the subject. If it should be regarded as the final wisdom of historical theology, one might ask how one could honor the confession of the *communio sanctorum*? Aren't earlier and later generations placed in the communion of saints among the witnesses of Christ, in a common space and in a common hope? Aren't they placed in mutual conversation, since they all find themselves in conversation with the Scriptures and with the Messiah proclaimed by those Scriptures? Indeed, 'being in Christ' means 'being in conversation'.

Needless to say, a certain distance must be respected in that conversation. This applies not only to our conversation with Calvin but also to our conversation with Karl Barth. (Of course, being his younger contemporary, Breukelman kept much less distance with regard to Barth than we are able to keep.) Yet we should not abandon every attempt at conversation. That Breukelman has ventured into such a conversation – in this case starting from the theology of Karl Barth – with the theology of John Calvin, may be seen as a shortcoming as far as historical distance is concerned, but also as a virtue. It is a promise and a task for all those who will, in the communion of saints, continue the conversation between the generations with the speaking Scriptures in their midst.

Rinse H. Reeling Brouwer

NOTES

1. The Dutch edition of Breukelman's *Biblical Theology*, as it has been published so far, consists of ten volumes: I.1. *Schriftlezing. Een verhandeling over de kolometrische weergave van bijbelse teksten als hulp bij het lezen en als grondslag voor de exegese* [Scripture Reading. A Treatise on the Colometric Presentation of Biblical Texts as an Aid to Reading and as a Foundation for Exegesis], Kampen 1980; I.2. *Het eerstelingschap van Israël* [Israel as the First-Born], Kampen 1992; I.3. *Ouvertures van Genesis* [Overtures on Genesis] (in preparation); II.1. *Debarim* [Words], published in German, Kampen 1992; II.2. *Sjemot: De eigen taal en de vertaling van de Bijbel [Shemot/Names: The Own Language and the Translation of the Bible]* (Kampen, 2009); III.1. *De ouverture van het evangelie naar Matteüs. Het verhaal over de genesis van Jezus Christus* [The Overture of the Gospel according to Matthew. The Narrative of the Origin of Jesus Christ], Kampen 1984; III.2. *De Koning als Richter. Het evangelie naar Matteüs als 'Heilsbotschaft vom Königtum'*, hoofdstuk I [The King as Judge. The Gospel according to Matthew as 'Message of Kingship'. Chapter I], Kampen 1996; III.3, *Idem*, hoofdstuk II [Idem, chapter II] (in preparation)' IV.1. *De structuur van de heilige leer in de theologie van Calvijn* [The Structure of Sacred Doctrine in the Theology of Calvin], Kampen 2003; IV.2. *Theologische opstellen* [Theological Essays], Kampen 1999. Breukelman personally has only been able to take care of cahiers I.1 (1980), III.1 (1984) and I.2 (1992).
2. The Dutch edition of the present study (*Bijbelse Theologie* IV.1, Kampen 2003, 540 pages) was published by Rinse H. Reeling Brouwer, who teaches The History of Christian Doctrine at Kampen Theological University. The edition was based on fragments left behind by Breukelman. Reeling Brouwer has utilized many successive versions, which can be found in the Breukelman archives, and are stored under number 674 in the *Historisch Documentatiecentrum voor het Nederlands Protestantisme (1800-present)*, a research institute of the Free University of Amsterdam. Also, in the Dutch edition a 'second' apparatus of notes is provided, clarifying the origin of certain textual fragments. This textual apparatus has been left out of this English edition, as well as (not all, but many) duplications, which are the result of the complicated genesis of the text.
3. It may be suggested that Breukelman – completely independently – envisaged to some extent a similar elaboration of the theology of Karl Barth as the so-called New Yale School in the United States.
4. Miskotte himself wrote the article, entitled 'Erlaubnis zu schriftgemässem Denken'. It inspired Breukelman immensely. See: W. Wolf (ed.), *Antwort*, Zurich 1956, 29-51.
5. A chapter on 'Karl Barth and the Tradition of Theological Dualism', which also stems from this period, is not included in the present work, except for some fragments from this chapter, such as chapter V §1.11 on Jean Alphonse Turrettini.
6. Particularly in chapter I, this meant that the English translation of the *Institutes* of 1536 by Ford Lewis Battles (Revised Edition, Grand Rapids MI 1986), in spite of all its merits, could not be used.
7. Richard A. Muller, *The Unaccommodated Calvin. Studies in the Foundation of a Theological Tradition*, New York/Oxford 2000.

INTRODUCTION

'Although I did not regret the labor which I dedicated to this work, I was never satisfied, until I arrived at the order and arrangement in which the *Institutes* are presently offered. I now trust to have given it a form you will all agree with.'

'I promise that it may serve as a key and entrance to the Holy Scriptures, so that all of God's children may hear it properly and directly. I urge all who respect the Word of the Lord to read it and to carefully remember it, if they wish to possess a summary of Christian doctrine, and gain entrance into both the Old and the New Testament.'

John Calvin

In this study we aim to describe the structure of the theology of John Calvin. We do so in order to point at a potential heresy[1] in early Reformation theology. This often developed into a real heresy in later Protestant theology. The structure of Calvin's theology can be most clearly seen in the composition of his main dogmatic work, the *Institutio Christiane religionis*. Therefore, our study will mainly consist of a careful analysis of this work. Calvin kept editing and reediting his *Institutes* from 1535 to 1560. Only in 1558/59 he found the form which completely satisfied him. If we wish to describe the structure of Calvin's theology, we will have to describe the entire genesis of the Institutes. As a result, the present study will be occupied with (1) the potential heresy of early Reformation theology; (2) the structure of Calvin's theology; (3) the composition of the *Institutio Christianae religionis*; (4) the genesis of the Institutes.

§1. THE EDITIONS OF CALVIN'S *INSTITUTES*

The Institutes came into being over a period of twenty-five years. Beginning with the Latin edition of 1535 (which was published in 1536) up to the French edition of 1560, Calvin repeatedly edited and published the book. The Latin edition was usually rapidly followed by a French edition.

From 1536, the year in which the *Institutes* were published for the first time,[2] until 1564, the year of Calvin's death, we distinguish three forms, five recensions and twenty-five editions in the genesis of this book:

	10 Latin editions:	15 French editions:
I. Catechism *1537 Catechism*	1st recension 1536 (6 chapters)	1537 ?
II. Loci *1542 Catechism*	2nd recension 1539 (17 chapters)	1541
	3rd recension 1543 (21 chapters) 1545	1545

	4th recension 1550 (divided into
	                                   paragraphs)
	                        1553
	                        1554
		1551
		1553
		1554
		1557

III. Apostolicum	5th recension 1559 (four books,
	                                   80 chapters)
	                        1561 (twice)
		1560
		1561 (twice)
		1562 (four times)
		1563
		1564

Jacques Pannier offers the following classification of the various editions:	Peter Barth and Wilhelm Niesel label the five recensions in their introduction as follows:
Latin editions French editions	
1536 Basel ?	I. Recensio 1536
1539 Strasbourg 1541 Geneva	II. Recensio 1539
1543 Strasbourg	III. Recensio 1543
1545 Strasbourg 1545 Geneva	IV. Recensio 1550
1550 Geneva 1551 Geneva	V. Recensio 1559
1553 Geneva 1553 Geneva	
1554 Geneva 1554 Geneva	With each recension they offer:
1557 sine loco	A. Latin editions
1559 Geneva 1560 Geneva	B. French versions.[3]
1561 Geneva 1561	
Geneva (twice)	
Strasbourg	
1562 Geneva and 3 elsewhere	
1563 Lyons	
1564 Geneva	

Between 1863 and 1900, the Strasbourg theologians Wilhelm Baum, Eduard Cunitz, and Eduard Reuss published the *Ioannis Calvini opera quae supersunt omnia* in 59 volumes. These volumes make up volumes XXIX to LXXXVII of the *Corpus reforma-*

torum.[4] Two other Latin editions of Calvin's complete works had preceded their edition, the Geneva edition of 1617 in seven volumes, and the Amsterdam edition of 1671 in nine volumes.[5] These two editions only include the *Institutes* of 1559, i.e. the *Institutes* in its definitive form, whereas the Strasbourg theologians included the earlier versions of the *Institutes* as well.

Let us take a closer look at how these fifty-nine volumes of Calvin's collected works were published by these three theologians:

The *Ioannis Calvini opera quae supersunt omnia* in 59 volumes:		
1863–1866	*Institutio religionis christianae* Four volumes i. The Latin text of 1536, 1-252 The Latin text of 1539-1554, 253-1152 ii. The Latin text of 1559 iii-iv. The French text of 1560	i–iv
1866-1871	Shorter theological tracts Six volumes (a total of 94 writings) v-ix 51 short writings ix 9 confessions, 11 prefaces, 4 speeches x.1 11 texts on ecclesiastical order, 7 counseling texts, 1 apology	v–x.1
1872-1879	Letters (1530–1564) Twelve volumes containing in total 4271 letters, of which around 1200 by Calvin; volume xxi contains the biographies of Beza and Colladon; *Annales calviniani*	x.2–xxi
1880	The French version of Calvin's first catechism; indices of the xxi volumes published so far	xxii
1882–1897	Exegetical and homiletical works (published according to the order of the books of the Bible) 35 volumes; the final two volumes lvi – lvii contain 'La Bible francaise de Calvin'	xxiii–lvii
1900	Supplement Registers from vol. XXIII, catalogues of works and bibliographical catalogues	lviii lix

The first volume of the *Opera omnia* of 1863 included the Latin *Institutio* of 1536 in columns 1 to 252, as well as the *Institutio* of 1539 (1543, 1550 and 1554) in columns 253 to 1152. The definitive Latin text of 1559 followed in the second volume of 1864. Finally, the years 1865 and 1866 witnessed the publication of the definitive French text of 1560 in the third and fourth volumes.

At the conclusion of the *Prolegomena* of the first volume, these editors printed a 'Synopsis of the editions of the *Institutes*' on eight pages (li-lviii). In five columns it shows us how Calvin up to four times used the material of a previous edition in a newer version of the book (1536, 1539, 1543-45, 1550-54, 1559ff.). This synopsis provided, as it were, the invitation to write the genesis of Calvin's *Institutes*. The Lutheran J. Köstlin accepted this invitation by writing two comprehensive articles on 'The historical development of Calvin's *Institutio*' for the journal *Theologische Studien und Kritiken* of 1868.[6] In the first of these two articles, Köstlin analyzes the genesis of Calvin's main dogmatic work in sixty-six pages. Virtually all later authors on Calvin's theology refer to this analysis by Köstlin whenever they discuss the genesis of the *Institutes* in their studies. They rightly show their appreciation for Köstlin's study. Werner Krusche, too, in his splendid study about *Das Wirken des Heiligen Geistes nach Calvin* talks about of 'die gründlichen Analyses von Köstlin' (Köstlin's thorough analyses).[7]

Köstlin's opinion of the definitive edition of the *Institutes* during the winter of 1558-59 is of great importance.[8] This is because we will take Köstlin's verdict as a starting point for our study. First, however, we need to say something about the various forms in which Calvin's book appeared during this twenty-five year period (from 1536 to 1560).

§2. THE PROBLEM OF THE *ORDO DOCENDI* IN CALVIN'S *INSTITUTES*

The work appeared in three different forms.

1. The 1536 edition of the book followed Luther's example by taking the form of a catechism, intended for Calvin's French fellow believers.[9] It consisted of six chapters:

I.	The Law	(with the explanation of the Ten Commandments)
II.	Faith	(with the explanation of the Apostles' Creed)
III.	Prayer	(with the explanation of the Lord's Prayer)
IV.	The Sacraments	
V.	The Five False Sacraments	
VI.	Christian Freedom, Ecclesiastical Power, and Political Administration	

2. In 1539 Calvin completely reshaped the book. Following the example of the *Loci Communes* of Melanchthon, Calvin turned it into a theological textbook for students containing seventeen chapters:

Doctrina: 1. The knowledge of God
            2. The knowledge of man
            3. The Law (the old first chapter)

            4. Faith (the old second chapter)
            5. Penance
            6. Justification

Aspects: 7. Similarities and differences between Old and New Testament
            8. Predestination and providence
            9. Prayer (the old third chapter)

            10. The sacraments
            11. Baptism   } (the old fourth chapter)
            12. The Lord's Supper

            13. Christian freedom
            14. Ecclesiastical power   } (the old sixth chapter)
            15. Political administration

            16. The five false sacraments (the old fifth chapter)
            17. The life of a Christian

The French translation was published two years later. In this French edition of 1541 the chapter on the five false sacraments came directly after chapters 10-12 on the sacraments. Chapters 13-15 of the Latin edition became chapters 14-16 of the French edition of 1541.

Note how the new book of 1539 evolved out of the old one. Calvin created the first three chapters of the new book out of the first chapter 'The Law' of the old book. Next, he turned the second chapter 'Faith' of the old book into the second set of three chapters of the new book. Then, in the first sentence of the seventh chapter, Calvin provides a retrospect on these first six chapters:

'Above I have, to the best of my abilities, explained the essence of sacred doctrine. From the true knowledge of God and of ourselves we arrive at the communion of salvation'.[10]

Thus, the first six chapters of the 1539 *Institutes* contain Calvin's *summa doctrinae* (summary or essence of doctrine). The theme of this *summa doctrinae* is: How do we arrive 'from the true knowledge of God and of ourselves at the communion of salvation'?

In the second sentence of the seventh chapter Calvin offers a preview of what he will discuss in the next two chapters. To begin with, Calvin writes, 'I will attach an appendix to these six chapters. This appendix is of no small importance. It confirms the truth of this doctrine'. This appendix consists of two chapters. Chapter 8 (on providence and predestination) deals with 'all those whom God elected to belong to his people from the beginning of the world'. Chapter 7 (on the similarities and differences between the Old and the New Testament) deals with the 'covenant through the law and through the bond of this doctrine'. In chapters 7 and 8 Calvin discusses two closely related aspects of the *summa doctrinae*. Events in time ('from the beginning of the world and after Christ's birth') are events which originate from God's eternity, i.e. from God's will.

Calvin rewrote the old chapters 3, 4, 5, and 6 and inserted them after the eighth chapter of the new version (chapters 9 to 16). He adds a final seventeenth chapter, on Christian living. In this chapter Calvin again reveals a very important aspect of the entire doctrine. Ultimately, it points to the 'life of a Christian'.

In 1543 Calvin divided the material of the fourth chapter 'Faith' into four chapters, because of the enormous expansion of the part on the church. He also inserted a new chapter 'The monastic vows' after the third chapter 'The Law'. The new book (in the five Latin editions of 1543, 1545, 1550, 1553, and 1554, and in the French editions of 1545, 1551, 1553, 1554, and 1557) came to contain twenty-one chapters, instead of the seventeen chapters of the editions of 1539 and 1541.

In his 'Word to the reader' of the 1539 edition, Calvin describes his intentions in publishing this work. After briefly expressing his gratitude for the fact that the first edition of the work (of 1536) 'was received favorably by all pious folk', he continues with the words:

'Furthermore, I wrote this work for those who commenced the study of sacred theology. I wanted to prepare them and instruct them in reading the divine Word, so that they might have an easy access to it and might continue studying it without many problems. I believe to have summarized the essence of religion, showing how the different aspects of it are related to each other, and how they should be arranged. I have put them in such an order (*eo ordine digessisse*) that it will not be difficult for those who have correctly understood this summary to see what is most important in Scripture, and how it should be applied'.[11]

Calvin wishes to provide students of theology with a tool for reading Holy Scripture. He wanted to make it easy for them to see what Scripture is all about, and what it is aimed at (the 'scopus'). Like Melanchthon's *Loci communi*,[12] Calvin meant his *Institutio Christianae religionis* to be a hermeneutics for the church, the *ecclesia audiens* (a hearing congregation). We must pay special attention to the words '*eo ordine digessisse*'. By the 'digerere', the arranging of the material, Calvin expressed his aim to offer what we call 'the structure of sacred doctrine'.

Calvin continues that he plans to publish a few commentaries on the Scriptures. By publishing the *Institutes* 'detailed explanations on dogmatic issues' can be avoided in these commentaries.[13] 'This way the pious reader will be spared much trouble and torment, that is, if he approaches these commentaries with the work presented here as is an indispensable tool (*quasi necessario instrumento*).'[14] The first commentary was published in 1540 and concerns Paul's letter to the Romans, 'because, when someone understands this letter, he holds the key to understanding all of the Scriptures'.[15] Though Calvin added some lines to this preface in 1559, his words on the purpose of his *Institutes* remain the key passage of his 'word to the reader' in the definitive edition of the *Institutes*.

He says the same thing even more emphatically in the preface to the French editions of 1541 up to 1551. The reader of Holy Scripture needs 'a rule (reigle) to measure all that is present in the Scriptures'.[16] Through his Institutes, Calvin wishes to provide the reader with nothing but this 'reigle'. He does not wish to say too much about his own work to avoid the impression that he might want to praise his own work. 'However, I promise that it may serve as a key and entrance to the Holy Scriptures, so that all of God's children may hear it properly and directly'.[17] Here, too, he announces the planned publication of his commentary of the Scriptures. (The first French commentary appears in 1542). He then continues to say of his Institutes: 'I urge all who respect the Word of the Lord to read it and to carefully remember it, if they wish to possess a summary of Christian doctrine, and gain entrance into both the Old and the New Testament.'[18] This, then, is what Calvin wants his *Institutes* to be before all else: an 'instrument', a 'reigle' for reading the Holy Scripture. He wants it to be a hermeneutic tool, an entrance both the Old and the New Testament.[19]

3. The 1539 *Institutes* was a meaningfully composed work. However, by 1543 it had become a chaotic book. In the winter of 1558/59, therefore, Calvin decided to reshape the book. This time it found its definitive form. At the beginning of the 'Word to the reader', Calvin informs us of his motives:

'Although I did not regret the labor which I dedicated to this work, I was never satisfied, until I arrived at the order and arrangement in which the Institutes are presently offered. I now trust to have given it a form you will all agree with'.[20]

First we hear the words *tunc* (then) and *nunquam* (never), followed twice by the word *nunc* (now). *Now*, Calvin says, I have finally been able to give the book the form which satisfies me completely. Again, Calvin mentions the words *ordo* and *digerere* in this passage. Calvin was never satisfied with this work '*donec in hunc ordinem qui nunc proponitur digestum fuit* (until I arrived at the order and arrangement in which it is presently offered)'. Indeed, Calvin believes to have expressed the structure of sacred doctrine in this edition much more convincingly than in the old ones.

In the 'Word to the reader' of the 1559 *Institutes,* Calvin mentions the words *digerere* and *ordo* at another place as well. The second instance stems from 1539, whereas the first instance was written in 1559. When Calvin translated this 'Word to the reader' in French in 1560, he rendered these passages as 'ie pense (…) l'avoir digérée en tel ordre, que…' (1539), and 'iusques à ce que ie l'ay eu digérée en l'ordre que vous y verrez maintenant' (1559).[21] These passages show us that Calvin has been looking for the right *ordo docendi* (order of instruction) all these twenty-five years, ever since he began to write the *Institutes* in 1534.

The new form Calvin gave to his *Institutio Christianae eligionis* of 1559, and thus to his entire summary of sacred doctrine, is an *Explicatio symboli*, a commentary on the 'Apostles' Creed'. He arranges the *Apostolicum* into four articles and divides his dogmatic material into four books accordingly. The twenty-one chapters of the old

Institutes (from 1543 to 1554) are now spread over four books with a total of 18 + 17 + 25 + 20 = 80 chapters:[22]

Book I	The knowledge of God the creator	18 chapters
Book II	The knowledge of God the redeemer in Christ, which was first revealed to the fathers under the law, and then to us in the gospel	17 chapters
Book III	How the grace of Christ is appropriated, the fruits that result from this, and the effects which follow from it	25 chapters
Book IV	The external means, through which God invites us to communion with Christ, and keeps us in it	20 chapters

Each of the titles of books II, III and IV contains the word 'Christ'. Calvin gave his Institutes the definitive form of an *Explicatio symboli* in order to express the Christological concentration – a distinctive feature of his theology – as powerfully as possible. He explains the Apostles' Creed as a translation of the salvation we are given in Christ. He himself confirms this in the introduction to the *Explicatio symboli* of the Institutes in its earlier forms.[23] Two quotes from that introduction – the beginning and conclusion of the first two paragraphs – will serve to illustrate the point.[24] After describing in the previous paragraphs the way *fides* (faith) should be understood, Calvin continues as follows:

'It is true that the power of faith shows itself most clearly when its explanation is directed to the gospel as its goal. On the other hand, it is only in the gospel that the essentials of faith are to be found in the first place. We already noted this in passing when we discovered how the essence of the gospel is summarized in Jesus Christ. (...) The goal of our faith is the gospel, and the goal of the gospel is Christ. Hence it is in Christ himself that all our riches lie – everything He has done and suffered for our salvation. In order to receive a complete explanation of faith, therefore, we need to consider the way Christ reveals it. For after having explained the contents of the Creed,[25] it will be easier to recognize its characteristics, like in a painting. Thus, the Apostles' Creed will assume for us the place of such a painting, because it demonstrates in a few words the entire economy of salvation bit by bit without omitting even the smallest part.'

Calvin himself tells us here how he wants us to understand his *Explicatio symboli*. He does so by citing a number of core concepts in a certain order: faith → gospel → Christ → our salvation → the Apostles' Creed. In 1559 the *Explicatio symboli* was no longer a component of the *Institutes,* but had itself become the framework of the entire *Institutes.* As a result, this introduction to the *Explicatio symboli* of the old Institutes was deleted.[26] It is almost the only part of the old *Institutes* which was not included in the definitive form of the *Institutes*. However, it is precisely this introduction that we need to listen to, if we want to understand Calvin's goal when in 1559 he gave the book as a whole the structure of an *Explicatio symboli*.[27]

We must also call attention to a second aspect of the definitive form of the *Institutes*. In order to focus on this second aspect we have to pay attention to a certain series of insertions which Calvin added to the existing texts, with the aim of justifying its new form from the perspective of biblical theology. The series begins with the newly composed second chapter of the first book, 'Quid sit Deum cognoscere' (what does it mean to know God?) and culminates in the completely rewritten sixth chapter of the second book, 'Homini perdito quaerendam in Christo redemptionem esse' (sinful man should seek his redemption in Christ). Further on in this study we shall look at this series of insertions in more detail. They deal with the relationship between the *cognitio Dei creatoris* (the knowledge of God the creator), discussed in book I, and the *cognitio Dei redemptoris* (the knowledge of God the redeemer), discussed in book II.

Right at the beginning of this series, Calvin presents us with the entire *Institutes* in its new form. He does so in just one sentence:

'Because the Lord first appears simply as creator (both in the making of the world and in the general doctrine of Scripture) and then as redeemer in the face of Christ, there is a twofold knowledge of God. The first will be discussed now' – in book I, FB – 'and the latter will follow later in due time' – in books II, III, and IV, FB.[28]

Calvin distinguishes between two doctrines: a *generalis scripturae doctrina* (a general doctrine of Scripture)[29] and a *propria fidei doctrina* (a true doctrine of faith).[30] The *generalis scripturae doctrina* deals with the *apparere* (the appearance) of God as creator and the *propria fidei doctrina* with the appearance of God as redeemer. As he put it in the sentence cited above, God appears *primum* (first) as creator and *deinde* (then) as redeemer in the face of Christ (*in Christi facie*). If man had not fallen, the original *simplex Dei cognitio* (simple knowledge of God) would have sufficed for man to obtain eternal salvation.[31]

Therefore, there are two aspects we need to pay attention to when analyzing the definitive form of the *Institutes*. First, in order to express the Christological concentration[32] of his theology as forcefully as possible, Calvin presents his main dogmatic work in the form of *Explicatio symboli* in 1558/59.[33] Second, he bases this *Explication symboli* on the duality of the knowledge of God. These two aspects determine the structure of Calvin's theology. How these two aspects are evaluated is decisive for the interpretation of Calvin's theology.

§3. THE CONTROVERSY IN CALVIN RESEARCH

It is interesting to see how Calvin studies, particularly over the past fifty years (1925-1975, ed.), has resulted in two totally different pictures of Calvin's theology. This is because the two structural elements of Calvinian doctrine discussed above contradict each other. Some scholars focus on the duality of Calvin's theology (e.g., Joh. Köstlin, Emil Brunner, Günter Gloede, E. A. Dowey), whereas others stress the Christological concentration (e.g., Peter Brunner, Karl Barth, Pierre Maury, Wilhelm Niesel, T. H. L. Parker, and Werner Krusche).

In his analysis presented above, Köstlin asserts that the form of *Explicatio symboli* does not agree with the true intent of the entire dogmatic argument. According to Köstlin, the concept of the duality of the knowledge of God completely dominates the *Institutes* of 1559. He thinks Calvin should have expressed that in the form of his book:[34]

'The path Calvin really followed in the Institutes, instead of identifying it with the path of the Creed, can be summarized as follows. Calvin first discusses the subject of God, Father, Son, and Spirit, and of creation and its government in a general way, apart from sin and the subsequent revelation of salvation. In the same way he talks about mankind, apart from sin and the need for salvation (first book). Second, he discusses the historical revelation and activity of God for the salvation of sinners. This includes: (1) the salvation through the Son who became man, already prepared in the Old Testament (second book); (2) the appropriation of salvation through the Holy Spirit. This appropriation is discussed in two ways: (a) the inner process of salvation through the Spirit until the final completion at the resurrection (third book); and (b) the external means, used by God for these works of his Spirit (fourth book). We are presented with a clear structure here. The material is presented very clearly and sharply. However, this is not because the book is divided into four parts, or because of Calvin's reference to the Creed, as many have thought.'

How one evaluates Köstlin's judgment on the definitive form of the *Institutes* is decisive for the interpretation of Calvin's theology. In the fourth part of his great work on Calvin, *Jean Calvin, les hommes et les choses de son temps*, E. Doumergue mentions Köstlin's opinion on Calvin's *Institutes* in a footnote.[35] However, Doumergue does not deal with the issue of whether Köstlin is right or not. It seems of no importance to Doumergue. More puzzling is the fact that François Wendel in his book *Calvin, sources et evolution de sa pensée religieuse* quotes the Köstlin text cited above without saying that it stems from Köstlin's article.[36] Neither does Wendel question Köstlin's assessment of the definitive form of Calvin's book. If Köstlin was right in his contention that the duality of the knowledge of God dominated Calvin's unfolding of doctrine, we should agree with him that Calvin was wrong in choosing the form of the *Explicatio symboli*.

In his judgment on the *Institutes* of 1559, Köstlin follows the lead of the Protestant doctrinal tradition in the post-Reformation era. The duality of creation and redemption, law and gospel, nature and grace, reason and revelation started to play an increasingly important role in this development.[37] Theologians talked about a dual order (i.e., natural and supernatural) and a dual revelation (i.e., a general and a particular). We will discover later on in this study how older Protestantism via the transitional phase of 'rational orthodoxy' turned into neo-Protestantism. Emil Brunner, in his little book *Natur und Gnade. Zum Gespräch mit Karl Barth* of 1934, continues to interpret Calvin along these lines.[38] Brunner published the book in the same year as the confessing church in Germany published the Barmen Declaration on 'the one word of God, which we need to hear'. In the preface to the second edition (1935), Brunner specified the theme of his little book as follows:

'There is one God who reveals himself in the works of creation, in the law which was written in the human conscience, and in Jesus Christ. It is therefore a Christian natural theology, not a pagan or rational one, that concerns us here. Indeed, *in the context of the Christian knowledge of God*, we are dealing with the general revelation of God. This revelation is visible in all his works and in his law, which is written in the hearts of *all men*'.[39]

Of this 'double revelation of creation' Brunner says:

'This little book is concerned with this biblical doctrine. This doctrine seems insignificant, but it is of great importance for church and theology. It is as valid today as it was in the first century'.

The evidence on which Brunner based his interpretation was furnished by a study of his student Günter Gloede, *Theologia Naturalis bei Calvin*. This study was written in Zurich from 1932 to 1934 and published in 1935.[40] Using the as yet unpublished work of his student, Brunner stated in a special paragraph that his thoughts were good Reformation theology. He referred to Calvinian theology to prove this.

In the same year (1934) that Brunner published his short book, Barth published his short reply *Nein! Antwort an Emil Brunner*.[41] In this booklet Barth says 'no' to Brunner's 'Christian *theologia naturalis*'.[42] However, in the same booklet Barth also says 'no' to Brunner's interpretation of the theology of Calvin.[43] 'Brunner has made a Jean Alphonse Turrettini out of Calvin',[44] Barth writes. After Barth had said *Nein* to Brunner's *Natur und Gnade* in 1934, he was forced one year later to substantiate this 'no', by changing the traditional order of 'law and gospel' into 'gospel and law'.[45]

Contrary to Brunner's and Gloede's interpretation of Calvin's theology, Wilhelm Niesel gave a different interpretation to Calvin's theology. He did so in his 1938 book *Die Theologie Calvins*.[46] Niesel said that we encounter more or less the same Christological concentration in Calvin's unfolding of sacred doctrine as we do in the theology of Karl Barth.[47]

As we said earlier, however, we are dealing with two factors in Calvin's theology. In addition to the Christological concentration, we are also concerned with the dualistic concept of the knowledge of God. The relationship between these two factors in Calvin's theology was still not accounted for in any satisfactory way. This became clear after World War II, when two students of Calvin's theology – Edward Dowey and T. H. L. Parker, the former being a student[48] of Brunner and the latter a follower of Barth – published two profound studies in the same year (1952) and on the same subject, the *cognitio Dei* in the theology of Calvin. They did so independently of each other.[49] Both studies were based on an analysis of the *Institutes* in its definitive form of 1559. The title of Dowey's book reads *The Knowledge of God in Calvin's Theology*,[50] and of Parker's *Calvin's Doctrine of the Knowledge of God*.[51]

Dowey agrees with Köstlin that Calvin gave his book a form in 1559 that does not agree with its content. Dowey, too, is of the opinion that Calvin in the entire process of the unfolding of sacred doctrine meant to express the content of a *duplex Dei cognitio*, similar to what Emil Brunner did in the twentieth century.[52] Dowey's book contains five chapters. In the first preparatory chapter, Dowey discusses the 'General characteristics of the knowledge of God'. In the brief second chapter, on the *Duplex cognitio Dei*, we are shown the program according to which Dowey will develop the theme of his book (the knowledge of God in Calvin's theology). After quoting Köstlin's comments on the 1559 *Institutes,* which we cited at the beginning of this paragraph,[53] he continues:

'I wish to maintain with Köstlin, although in greater detail and with more emphasis upon its importance, what was clear to me before consulting Köstlin: that the really significant ordering principle of the Institutes in the 1559 edition is the *duplex cognitio Domini*, not the Apostles' Creed.'[54]

To prove he was right, Dowey gives a list of the all the instances where Calvin formulates his thesis of the dualistic character of the knowledge of God in the first book of the *Institutes.* He then comments on these sayings. 'The distinction (i.e., of the *duplex cognitio Domini*) is nowhere clearly formulated by Calvin before the 1559 edition', Dowey says. Nevertheless, Dowey was right in claiming hat it was also present in the old *Institutes,* though not described *expressis verbis*.[55] At the end of the chapter, Dowey formulates his program:

'Calvin's final plan, which from the epistemological point of view follows the *duplex cognitio* and not the Creed, is simply the systematic arrangement most compatible with his concept of the knowledge of God. We shall now examine this twofold concept, considering the origin and contents of the parts and their mutual relation. First, the knowledge of God the Creator, in Chapter III, then the knowledge of God the Redeemer in Chapter IV, followed by an analysis of their systematic relationship in Chapter V.'[56]

The final section of Dowey's book is called *The Dialectical Relationship*. It explains the dialectical relationship between the two revelations of God (in his *opera* and *in Christi facie*). In Dowey's view, the theology of Calvin was basically the same as the theology of Emil Brunner.

Concerning this latter point we can safely say that Werner Krusche, in the third chapter of his dissertation, has thoroughly disproved the statements of Emil Brunner and of his student Günter Gloede. As a result, this interpretation of Dowey should be rejected as well.

However, this does not mean we are rid of Dowey yet! Calvin, in his *Institutes* of 1559, did distinguish between a *generalis scripturae doctrina* and a *propria fidei doctrina*, a divine revelation in his *opera* and *in Christi facie*. Calvin did formulate in those *Institutes* the thesis of the duality of the knowledge of God. Guided by this thesis he composed the first two books of the final edition. There are indeed two elements which determine its structure. Dowey was right in perceiving this. The question is whether we can, or indeed should, follow Dowey's interpretation of this fact. Dowey himself felt compelled to say 'the really significant ordering principle of the *Institutes* in the 1559 edition is (...) not the Apostles' Creed'. This gives us a hint that Dowey's interpretation of Calvinian theology was not on the right track.

The book by T. H. L. Parker, published in the same year (1952), contains two parts. Part one is concerned with the knowledge of God the creator. Part two with the knowledge of God the redeemer. In the seven chapters contained in these two parts, Calvin's basic ideas on the *cognitio Dei* theme are clarified by Parker in an illuminating way. Parker follows the order in which Calvin's ideas on this theme are found in the *Institutes* of 1559. However, the entire sequence of comments inserted by Calvin in the text of his first book on the duality of the knowledge of God, is not considered by Parker at all! He mentions them, but does not take them into account.

Many years later, both scholars issued new editions of their books. Dowey reissued his book in 1965, largely unchanged ('with some minor corrections'[57]). While he praises Krusche in the preface to the second edition, he is inappropriately disparaging about Parker.

Not doubting the accuracy of his exposition, he once again briefly summarizes his thesis in this preface, saying:

> 'The most inclusive thesis in the present volume continues to reflect, in the mind of the writer, a sound analysis of Calvin. That is to say that the "two-fold knowledge of God" as Redeemer and Creator, the latter dependent on the former, the two in dialectical relationship, and the whole rooted in faith, is basic to Calvin's mode of thought in all its branches.'[58]

We certainly cannot deny that Dowey's thesis is right in that Calvin indeed bases his *Explicatio symboli* on the duality of the knowledge of God in the final edition of his Institutes.

Four years later (1969) Parker, too, published a new edition of his book. He did not change the structure of his study. However, the first part was largely rewritten. In an elaborate Introduction[59] he reacted to Dowey's thesis. Dowey had claimed that the form Calvin gave to his book in 1559 does not correspond to its content, and that the concept of the *duplex cognitio Domini* forms the basis of the entire exposition of Calvin. Therefore, Dowey claimed, all of Calvin's theology ('in all his branches') should be interpreted from this concept of the *duplex cognitio Domini*. With regard to this thesis, Parker writes:

> 'Professor Dowey, of course, like Köstlin before him, is well aware that the 1559 *Institutio* corresponds to the fourfold division of the Creed. (...) He re-arranges the *Institutio* because he regards it as a statement and exposition of the *duplex cognitio Dei*'
>
> — for Dowey postulates a dual division instead of a division into four books: 1. Inst. I.1 – II.5, and 2. Inst. II.6 – IV.20, FB. —

'Such a reordering of the material must be regarded as illegitimate textual criticism because in assessing the nature of the subject, it does not take the order itself into account (a necessary step, above all, when you are dealing with a master of method) but imposes upon the order what is in fact a presupposition.'[60] (...) 'The *Institutio* is not to be divided arbitrarily into a form that Calvin did not give it. The form which Dowey imposes on it does not correspond to the general theme, but takes one methodological distinction made in the work and magnifies it into the leading principle to interpret the whole. (...) It is highly significant that Dowey has a final chapter in his book entitled "The Relation between the Knowledge of God the Creator and the Knowledge of God the Redeemer". Plainly, if a *duplex cognitio Dei* is put forward as the heart of a theology, such a relating and reconciling is necessary. That Calvin himself not only did not have this relating to do, but did not need to, is owing to the fact that the *duplex cognitio* Dei is not the theme of his work.'[61]

Parker had voiced this critique before in a review of Dowey's book in *The Evangelical Quarterly*. Dowey's reaction in 1965 was:

'The claim that problems of the *duplex cognitio Domini* arise from my "rearranging" of the *Institutes* is made so irresponsibly as to cast doubt on Parker's desire to be taken seriously.'[62]

We note that the two scholars stand over against each other. Dowey says: 'the really significant ordering principle of the *Institutes* in the 1559 edition is the *duplex cognitio Domini*, not the Apostles' Creed'. (...) 'Calvin's final plan from the epistemological point of view follows the *duplex cognitio* and not the Creed'. Parker says: 'the duplex cognitio Dei is not the theme of this work'.

Dowey and Parker reproach each other sharply, but do not wish to learn from each other. Parker's question whether it is reasonable to suppose that a man such as Calvin – 'a master of method'[63] – was unable to adequately express what he really wished to say, is not seriously answered by Dowey. In turn, Dowey based his interpretation in on the series of insertions, in which Calvin turned the idea of the duality of the knowledge of God into the foundation of his *Explicatio Symboli*. Parker, in the second edition of his book, should have examined Dowey's question why Calvin did this. Unfortunately, Parker did not.

How is it possible that there are two very different structural elements of Calvinian theology in the *Institutes* of 1559? This question remains unanswered. We have to conclude that the study of the structure of sacred doctrine in Calvin's theology is in an impasse. This is a pity, because this subject – i.e., the problem of theological epistemology[64] – is very important.

Usually, when a summary of the theology of Calvin is given, the themes of his theology are dealt with in the same way Calvin had discussed them in the 1559 Institutes (and often also in the same order). For example, Seeberg writes:[65] 'Our presentation of the doctrine of Calvin essentially follows the final edition of the *Institutio*, for it was this edition that has made the most impact historically'.[66]

Schellong correctly states:[67] 'One encounters the systematizing reductions of Calvin's thought mostly there (...) where his exegetical work and the historical genesis of the *Institutes* have not been taken into account, but where Calvin is merely seen as a builder of a system, from the sole perspective of the 1559 *Institutes*.'[68]

If we wish to answer the question about the relationship between the two very different structural elements of Calvinian theology[69] as they appear in the final edition of the *Institutio*,[70] we need to earnestly reflect on the historical genesis of this work. Therefore, we need to describe from scratch the entire development of Calvin's *Institutes*.

To overcome the impasse in Calvin studies, this study will describe the structure of sacred doctrine in the theology of Calvin. It will analyze the composition of his main dogmatic work in its definitive form, as he presented it in 1558/59. However, in order to support this analysis we will have to describe the entire genesis of the book. Our analyses of the *Institutes* will have to be much more thorough than those presented by Köstlin more than a century ago. They will be more thorough in that we plan to describe in far greater detail how the *Institutes* were formed. With each edition, we shall have to ask which theological motives led Calvin to make the changes he made. According to François Wendel, such a study has never been done before. 'It would be very interesting to study in detail how Calvin divided the material of preceding editions among the four books of the 1559 edition, and to understand his motives for the way he divided it.'[71] This would indeed be 'a very interesting study'. By constantly following Calvin in the formation of each of the *Institutes*, Calvin himself will show us the way to a correct interpretation of his theology.

We heard Calvin express his satisfaction with the form he had given the book in the winter of 1558/59: 'I was never satisfied with the work, until it was ordered and arranged in the way in which it is now offered.'[72] In the course of our study, we will discover why only the definitive composition of the *Institutes* could satisfy him. We will come to see that in none of the previous editions Calvin was able to fully express the Christological concentration, which was characteristic for his theology. He could only express it as beautifully and completely as he did by giving the work the form of an *Explicatio symboli*. However, although this Christological concentration was indeed the determining factor for the structure of Calvin's theology, the duality of the knowledge of God also contributed to this structure. Indeed, it was a potential heresy.

At the end of our description of the genesis of the *Institutes*, we will be able to conclude that, on the one hand, in the definitive form of the *Institutes* we are dealing with the final grandiose summary of all of Reformation theology, and that, on the other hand, this work was at the same time the starting point for the further development of Protestant theology.[73] The two factors in Calvin's theology which determine its structure will prove to be mutually contradictory. Where the concept of the duality of the knowledge of God begins to dominate – as was increasingly the case in post-Reformation Protestant dogmatics – the Christological concentration can no longer function as the sole determining factor for the structure of the whole. We see this in the development of later Protestant theology. In the theology of the so-called rational orthodoxy the neo-Protestantism of the eighteenth and nineteenth centuries is born. Its roots are the old Protestantism of the sixteenth and seventeenth centuries. We see how 'modernism' emerged out of orthodoxy itself.[74]

In the theology of Karl Barth, however, this process was radically reversed. The Christological concentration completely dominates the unfolding of sacred doctrine. The concept of a twofold knowledge of God does not play any role in Barth's theology. Here, then, after many centuries we see the biblical simplicity clearly reflected in the structure of sacred doctrine, as the church must unfold it in its teachings.

§4. THE STRUCTURE OF THIS STUDY

Calvin is a *homo unius libri*, a man of just this one book. Everything he writes, in sermons and in commentaries, in confessions, tracts, and letters, he writes against the background of this book. If it is true that the structure of Calvin's theology is completely reflected in the composition of this main work, it seems reasonable to sketch the structure of Calvin's theology on the basis of an analysis of this composition.

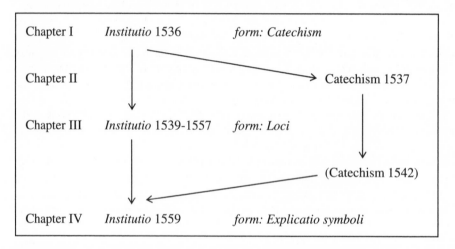

This study is organized as follows: in chapter I we will describe how Calvin went about shaping the first edition of his *Institutes,* as a catechism. In chapter III we will describe how he proceeded in 1539 with the new edition of the work, which he now organized as a traditional textbook with different *Loci*. And finally, in chapter IV, we will see how he composed the definitive form of the work in 1558/59, as an *Explicatio symboli*. By describing how Calvin from 1535 to 1560 worked for 25 years on the structure of his main work, the *Institutio Christianae religionis*, we will be able to grasp the structure of his theology.

In 1534-35 Calvin wrote the *Institutes* in its first form as a catechism. However, it was not suitable for the instruction of children. When he became 'professor' in Geneva in July 1536, therefore, he wrote a new catechism (just as Luther's Large Catechism was followed by the Small Catechism). This was published in French in 1537. A year later it was published in Latin as well, to serve as a Confession of Faith for the church of Geneva. After discussing the *Institutes* of 1536 in the first chapter, we will proceed to discuss the Catechism of 1537 in chapter II, as this constitutes the transition from the 1536 *Institutes* to the *Institutes* of 1539.[75]

In our concluding remarks of chapter V, we will show how the entire Reformed doctrinal tradition has proceeded along the lines of the duality of the knowledge of God. In contrast to that development, Karl Barth called the Calvin of the Christological concentration the real Calvin.

NOTES

1. For the concept of 'potential heresy' see Karl Barth, *Die kirchliche Dogmatik* (Zurich 1932-1967) I.2, §23.1, particularly pages 902-908 (*Church Dogmatics*, Edinburgh 1956-1975, I.2, 807-812).

2. There may have been a French version of the oldest edition of the *Institutes* as well, though no such text has been found as yet. See Jean Calvin, *Epitre à tous amateurs de Jésus Christ, 1535. Préface à la traduction francaise du Nouveau Testament pas Rovert Olivetan (1935) – le plus ancient texte francais de Calvin qui ait été imprimé – avec Introduction sur: Une edition francaise de l'Institution dès 1537?* by Jacques Pannier, Paris 1929. Thus, the oldest form of the French *Institutio* known to us is the edition of 1541 as a rendering of the Latin *Institutio* of 1539. The Strassbourg theologians did not include this French text of 1541 in the *Calvini Opera* either. However, a beautiful edition of this text in two volumes was prepared by Abel Lefranc, Henri Chatelain, and Jacques Pannier in 1911: Jean Calvin, *Institution de la Religion Chrestienne*, Texte de la première edition francaise (1541) réimprimé sous la direction de Abel Lefranc, Henri Chatelain et Jacques Pannier, Paris 1911. The pages and letters of this edition are identical to the original edition. In 1935-1939, this same text was republished in four volumes by Jacques Pannier (Paris, Soc. des Belles-Lettres). In Wilhelm Niesel's *Calvin-Bibliographie* 1901-1959 (Munich 1961), these two editions are referred to by the numbers 39 and 40.

3. See for the genesis of the *Institutes:* 1. Jacques Pannier, Jean Calvin, *Epitre au roi*, Préface de la première édition française de l'Institution de la religion chrétienne (1541), Paris 1927, Introduction I-XXXIV; 2. Jacques Pannier, Jean Calvin, *Epitres a tous amateurs de Jésus-Christ*, 1535, Paris 1929 (see above, note 2), Introduction, 1-30. The diagram included here may be found there under number 18; 3. Joannis Calvini, *Opera selecta*. Ediderunt Petrus Barth & Guilelmus Niesel (vol. I – V, Munich 1926-1936), Vol. III, Munich 1928, the description and the history of the French and Latin editions, published during Calvin's life, leaves VI-L; 4. The *Corpus Reformatorum*, Vol. I, Brunswick 1863, Prolegomena XXI-L (see below); 5. Joh. Köstlin, 'Calvins Institutio nach Form und Inhalt in ihrer geschichtlichen Entwicklung', in: *Theologische Studien und Kritiken*, 41. Jahrgang, Gotha 1868, 7-62 and 410-486 (see below); 6. Joh. Wilh. Marmelstein, *Etude comparative des texte latins et français de l'Institution de la religion chrétienne*, Groningen/The Hague 1921; 7. Paul Wernle, *Der evangelische Glaube nach den Hauptschriften der Reformatoren*, Band III. Johann Calvin, Tübingen 1919 (see below, note 35).

4. For the significance of the publication of this edition see also KD I.2, 683-684 (CD, 612).

5. See *La France protestante* by MM. Eugène and Emile Haag (10 vols., Paris 1846-1859), first edition Paris 1852, Vol. III, 162; second edition Paris 1881, Vol. III, 632. See also B. B. Warfield, 'The Literary History of Calvin's "Institutes"', in *The Presbyterian and Reformed Review* 38 (April 1899), (193-219) 209-210.

6. J. Köstlin, op. cit. (See above, footnote 3, point 5.)

7. W. Krusche, *Das Wirken des Heiligen Geistes nach Calvin*, Göttingen 1957, 70 (footnote 230).

8. Köstlin, op. cit. 57-58. (See below, footnote 33.)
9. In 1536 the title is: 'The Christian religion. An instruction, *containing virtually the entire essence of piety and all that is necessary to know in the doctrine of salvation; a work which is more than worthwhile to read for all students in piety and recently published.*' With a preface 'to the most Christian king of France, to whom this book is offered by way of a confession of faith by the author, Johannes Calvin, of Noyon', Basel 1536 (CO I, 1; OS I, 1). In this title, the words in italics must be by Platter. The book was published (in the spring, in Frankfurt) and needed to be sold. Such words of praise for his own work were totally foreign to Calvin. The title of 1539 may be conceived as a reaction of the printer of this edition, Wendelinus Rihelius of Strassbourg, to the way in which the publishers of 1536 had recommended this work. 'Instruction in the Christian religion, that truly lives up to his title' (CO I, XXXII). Calvin himself also appears to express himself critically in the beginning words of the preface of 1539 (about the unexpected success of the first edition) with regard to the subtitle of 1536, which was altogether too pretentious. On the four first publishers of the *Institutes* (Platter, Oporin, Lasius, and Winter) see Albert Autin, *l'Institution chrétienne de Calvin*, Paris 1929, Ch. IV, 47-57: 'Les éditeurs de l'Institution Chrétienne, de 1536.'
10. CO I, 801.
11. OS III, 6 ll. 18-25.
12. Cf. the 'Epistola dedicatoria', in which Melanchthon dedicates his *Loci communes* in 1521 to Tileman Plettener: 'Concerning the material as a whole, the most important points of Christian doctrine are described here, so that the youth may understand..., which main questions to ask in the Scriptures.' CR I, 510 and CR XXI, 81; Melanchthon's *Werke in Auswahl*, Studienausgabe II,1. Edited by Hans Engelland. Gütersloh 1952, 8-22.
13. OS III, 6 ll. 27-28.
14. OS III, 6 ll. 29-31.
15. CO X (402-406) 403, epistola 191 Calvinus Simoni Grynaeo 15.11.1539.
16. Cited in OS III, 7 ll. 35-36. Cf. Jacques Pannier's reissue of the French *Institutes* of 1541, Paris 1911, vol. I (pp. II-IV) II ll. 26-28.
17. OS III, 8 ll. 4-7, resp. Pannier op. cit., III ll. 12-15.
18. OS III, 8 ll. 16-20, resp. Pannier op. cit., III ll. 28-33.
19. These words of Calvin on what he aimed to achieve with his *Institutio* correspond to Barth's words in the *Kirchliche Dogmatik* in both closing paragraphs of its Prolegomena (§23 and §24) in relation to the dogmatic assignment: 1. 'Dogmatics as a Function of the Hearing Church' ('The Formal Task of Dogmatics'), and 2. 'Dogmatics as a Function of the Teaching Church' ('The Material Task of Dogmatics').
20. OS III, 5 ll. 13-15.
21. CO III, 6.
22. Cf. below, Chapter IV §1.
23. Inst. 1539 Chap. IV; 1541 ed. Pannier (1911) 212 ll. 9 and 215 l. 29; 1543-1554 Chap. VI, sections 1-5.
24. Inst. 1543-1554, Cap. VI, sections 1 and 2; CO I, 477 and 478.
25. French 1541: 'la matière et la substance'.
26. We encounter the first part of the old introduction, paragraphs 1-2, again in the Institutes of 1559: III.2.1 resp. III.2.6 (but not in its entirety) and the second part (paragraph 3 of paragraphs 3-5) in II.16.18 (again, not in its entirety). The first part is about *quid sit vera fides* (what the true faith may be). The second part is on Christology.
27. Characteristic for the way in which sacred doctrine is unfolded in this *Explicatio symboli* is the trinitarian structure and the Christological concentration within the framework of this structure. What would the *Institutes* have looked like if Calvin in 1558/59 had made the

above quoted introduction to the *Explicatio symboli* of 1539 the introduction of the entire *Institutes*?

28. OS III, 34 ll. 21-25: quia ergo Dominus primum simpliciter creator tam in mundi opificio, quam in generali Scripturae doctrina, deinde in Christi facie redemptor apparet: hinc duplex emergit eius cognitio: quarum nunc prior tractanda est, altera deinde suo ordine sequetur (mark: 'suo ordine', FB).

29. Inst. I.2.1 and I.10.3; resp. OS III, 34 ll. 23 and III, 87 l.20. Otto Weber (Johannes Calvin, *Unterricht in der christlichen Religion*, translated by Otto Weber, Neukirchen-Vluyn [1]1955, [2]1963) translated the words *generalis Scripturae doctrina* in I.2.1 correctly with 'the general doctrine of Scripture.' It misunderstands Calvin, however, when he renders the words *summa generalis doctrinae* at the beginning of I.10.3 as 'the main contents of the entire doctrine.'

30. Inst. I.6.1; OS III, 61 l. 10; cf. III, 61 ll. 24-25: *illa doctrinae pars (quae) in Christo fundata est*, that part of doctrine that is grounded in Christ.

31. See II.6.1, OS III, 320 ll. 13-15: 'This was indeed the given order that the edifice of the world should be our school to learn to respect for God, so that from there we might move to eternal life and complete bliss; but after the fall...'.

32. The expression 'Christological concentration' is used by Karl Barth for the first time in the 'Parergon', which he wrote for *The Christian Century* at the end of 1938 ('How My Mind has Changed', 1928-1938), reprinted in: K. Barth, *Der Götze wackelt*. Zeitkritische Aufsätze, Reden und Briefe von 1930 bis 1960, published by K. Kupisch, Berlin 1961, (181-190) 186.

33. See, in the edition of 1590, an overview of the Institutes by Caspar Olevianus with the title *Institutionis Christianae Religionis Methodus & Disputatio: seu, Totus operis Argumentum* (for example to be found in: *Joannis Calvini magni theologi Institutionem Christianae Religionis, libri quatuor*, Editio Postrema. Amstelodami apud Joannem Jacobi Schipper, MDCLXVII). Olevianus opens this *Argumentum* as follows: 'The goal of the author in this Christian instruction is twofold: first he aims to discuss the knowledge of God, which leads us to blissful immortality, second he wishes to discuss the knowledge of ourselves, which prepares us for the former. To lead us to this goal, he uses the method of the Apostolic Creed, with which all Christians are very familiar. Insofar as that confession consists of four parts, of which the first one deals with God the Father, the second with the Son, the third with the Holy Spirit, the fourth with the church, the author, in order to reach the first of his stated goals, proceeds to a division into four books, of which the first corresponds to the first part of the confession, the second to the second, the third to the third, and the fourth to the fourth. This needs to be elaborated upon piece by piece.'

34. Köstlin, op. cit., 57ff.

35. E. Doumergue, *Jean Calvin. Les hommes et les choses de son temps*. Tome quatrième. *La pensée religieuse de Calvin*. Lausanne 1910, 1, note 3 and 22 note 2 (See K. Barth on Doumergue, *Das Wort Gottes und die Theologie*. Vorträge 1. Munich 1924, 192: 'Heroenkultus').

See also Otto Ritschl, *Dogmengeschichte des Protestantismus* III. Göttingen 1926, 161 note 11: 'A penetrating discussion of the various editions of the *Institutes* was published by J. Köstlin's first article on form and content of Calvin's *Institutes* in its historical development and in Wernle's book on Calvin' (see above, note 3, point 7).

In the framework of the trilogy of Wernle's *Der evangelische Glaube nach den Hauptschriften der Reformatoren*, the heading of the third book reads as follows: 'Calvin'. But in the table of contents the heading reads: 'Calvin's instruction in the Christian Religion' (four volumes: 1536, 1539, 1543, 1559). In accordance with the way in which Wernle describes the progress of the *Institutes* in his book, he writes in the preface: 'It was not easy at all to work on the *Institutes* of Calvin in such a way, that the living part of it, the Reformational faith, leaps out of the immense theological material. Calvin himself, as he got older, encapsulated his faith more and more in an ever more complete system of biblical theology. *To pull him out from there was my main task*' (italics added). 'The precondition for this was, that an opportunity was given, to grasp his ideas on faith as they had appeared in their first and fresh form, and to place them in front of the reader and then to present the most important of the later revisions. The first *Institutes* of 1536 with its Christian elementary truths must come first, followed by the Pauline core doctrines of 1539, to conclude with the biblical and early Catholic church law of 1543 and the completed theological system of 1559. This train of thought could not be carried through without any division of the parts that belong together; but I hope that one thing has succeeded: that one reads the thoughts of Calvin in flux, as they flowed each time through his pen. Besides, I was committed, to the best of my ability, to highlight everywhere what is religiously alive, and to omit the mere theological, particularly the polemical parts' (pp. III – IV).

Wernle's book comes to 407 pages. The fourth part, 'Das fertige theologische System von 1559' contains only seventeen pages (301-406). To investigate the structure of Calvinian theology by means of an analysis of Calvinian systematics in the respective composition of his dogmatic main work, is a task which fully lies outside of Wernle's view, because something like that belongs, in his view, to the 'mere theological' and not to the 'religiously alive.' Schellong has called Wernle's book 'akin to a biography of Calvin's theology' (Dieter Schellong, *Calvins Auslegung der synoptischen Evangelien*, Munich 1969, 38). Lacking in this biography is one element, however, which for Calvin the theologian (in indissoluble connection with his piety) was of great importance: the question as to the right *ordo docendi* (see above, the preface of the *Institutio*).

36. F. Wendel, *Calvin, sources et évolution de sa pensée religieuse,* Paris 1950, 87: 'It would be very interesting to study in detail how Calvin divided the material of preceding editions among the four books of the 1559 edition, and to understand his motives for the way he divided it.' (This work is presently done by us, FB.) 'Let us limit ourselves to the remark that the plan of the catechism had prevailed until it was definitively abandoned for the benefit of an account which reproduced the four-part division of the Creed. Calvin had adopted this plan since his 1543 edition.' (This is incorrect, see below, Chap. IV, FB.) 'There are also divergences which are important enough. The third part which normally would have had to be devoted to the Holy Spirit, in reality only treats his action in the inner part of man. On the other hand, Calvin speaks of the resurrection before he approaches the problem of the church, which does not conform any longer with the ideas imprinted in the Creed. In spite of appearances, the rapport between the final edition of the Institutes and the traditional plan of the Creed thus remain external and formal' (= Köstlin = Otto Ritschl, FB). And now hear Köstlin: 'In fact, the dogmatic exposition comprises two great parts under his novel aspect. The first is constituted by the first Book, and concerns the doctrine of God (Trinity, Creation, Providence), scriptural revelation, and man (independent of guilt and the need for salvation). The second part extends to the three other books and treats historical revelation and the work of salvation. It can in turn be subdivided into two parts: 1. The preparation of the work of salvation of the old covenant and its fulfillment in the Incarnation of the Son of God (Book II); 2. The conferring and application of salvation by the Holy Spirit: a. the interior operation of the Holy Spirit in the believer, until its completion in the future life (Book III); b. the exterior means, which the Holy Spirit utilizes to complete, and to bring to a proper, end that interior operation (Book IV).'

37. This development continues to this century. Regin Prenter entitled his dogmatics *Schöpfung und Erlösung*. Dogmatik. Göttingen 1960. See also the 'Theologie der Existenz' by Fritz Buri: *Dogmatik als Selbstverständnis des christlichen Glaubens*, I. 'Vernunft und Offenbarung (Prolegomena zur Dogmatik)', Bern 1956, II. 'Der Mensch und die Gnade', Bern 1962.

38. E. Brunner, *Natur und Gnade. Zum Gespräch mit Karl Barth.* Zurich 1934.
39. Brunner, op. cit., IV. Italics by EB.
40. G. Gloede, *Theologia naturalis bei Calvin*, Stuttgart 1935 (see Brunner, op. cit., 23, n. 1). The book by Gloede was strongly refuted by Werner Krusche (explicitly for example in Krusche, op. cit., 61, 85, 87). In the second edition of his book *Die Theologie Calvins*, Munich 1957, 20, Wilhelm Niesel writes however: 'Today the author knows (i.e., Gloede) that his first work can no longer be thus defended. – Meanwhile, see his beautiful book: *Calvin, Weg und Werk*, Leipzig 1953.'
41. K. Barth, 'Nein! Antwort an Emil Brunner', *Theologische Existenz heute* Heft 14, Munich 1934.
42. On the topic of this 'Christian Natural Theology' see also KD II.1, 149-158 (CD, 134-142) and KD I.1, 25-30 (CD, 26-31).
43. K. Barth, 'Nein!', op. cit., 32-45, point 4: 'Brunner and Calvin.'
44. Barth, o.c., 'Nein!', 41. Compare Calvin's saying cited above, from *Institutes* I.2.1, on the duality of the knowledge of God with the second thesis of the *Theses de Theologia naturali in genere* of Jean Alphonse Turrettini. See below in Chapter V §1.11.
45. K. Barth, 'Evangelium und Gesetz' (1935), *Th.E.h.* Heft 32.
46. W. Niesel, *Die Theology Calvins*, ¹Munich 1938.
47. However, Barth himself has never turned Calvin into a Karl Barth. See e.g. what he says in KD IV.1, 406 (CD, 367) relative to the book of T. F. Torrance, *Calvin's Doctrine of Man* (London 1948) and in KD III.3, 34 (CD, 30f.) on Niesel's *Die Theologie Calvins*. See also KD II.2, 92 and 369 (CD, 86 and 335).
48. Indeed, a 'student', not a 'disciple', oral remark by Edward Dowey to Rinse H. Reeling Brouwer, January 15, 1999.
49. In the preface of his book *Das Grundverständnis der Theologie Calvins. Unter Einbeziehung ihrer geschichtlichen Abhängigkeiten*, Neukirchen-Vluyn 1963, Karl Reuter says: 'Calvin may not appear in the light of a later era.' We ask: But why not? When Reuter himself had Calvin appear 'in the light of an earlier era', it brought very little clarification. 'The outcome consists of many suspicions (…) and of few sure results' (thus Dieter Schellong, op. cit., 38). The one *verbi divini ministerium* (service of the divine Word) which must be accomplished by the ecclesia from Israel in the midst of the goyim, makes people of very different eras into contemporaries without ceasing to be also, and foremost, children of their own time.
50. E. A. Dowey Jr., *The Knowledge of God in Calvin's Theology*, ¹New York 1952, ²1965.
51. T. H. L. Parker, *Calvin's Doctrine of the Knowledge of God*, ¹Edinburgh 1952, ²Edinburgh 1969.
52. See e.g. section 81-86 (in the second edition): 'Calvin's evaluation of the Revelation in Creation.' This revelation has 'a definite eristic function. Wrong ideas must be cleared away to make room for the truth', 84. (…) 'Then, after this clearing away of the bad, the gospel is to be preached', 85. (…) 'The man of faith, then, who knows from the word the inexcusability of mankind, can bring that consciousness to the pagan unbeliever by argumentation based on the revelation in creation. This does not lead directly to faith, but to awareness of the insufficiency of this or that heathen creed. After this, the gospel is introduced', 86 ('Emil Brunner's concept of responsibility as the essence of man agrees well with Calvin', note 196).
53. Dowey, op. cit., 42.
54. Contrary to Dowey, Parker viewed the Institutes as *Explicatio symboli*. The Christocentric aspect in Calvin's theology thus came to look quite differently from Dowey's.
55. Dowey, op. cit., 46-49.
56. Dowey, op. cit., 49.
57. Dowey, ²1965 (also the Expanded Edition, Grand Rapids 1994), XII.

58. Dowey, [2]1965 (1994), XV.
59. Parker 1969, op. cit., 1-12.
60. Parker 1969, op. cit., 6-7.
61. Parker 1969, op. cit., 11.
62. Dowey, op. cit., XV–XVI, directed against 'the polemics of T. H. L. Parker in an appendix of the American reprint of his book.'
63. See above, the citation from the 'Introduction' of 1969, 7.
64. Karl Barth, in his answer to Emil Brunner in 1934, formulated his view sharply: 'They [the Reformers] have indeed seen and attacked the possibility of an intellectual justification by works in the core of theological thought, but did not see and attack it in the same breadth, sharpness and fundamental nature [Grundsätzlichkeit] as the moralistic justification by works in the basis of Christian life.' ('Nein!', op. cit., 38). But this now happens in Barth's *Kirchliche Dogmatik,* immediately after the doctrine of the Word of God in the Prolegomina in the fifth chapter 'The Knowledge of God', particularly in the section on 'The Readiness of Man' in the paragraph on 'The Knowability of God' (KD II.1 §26.2).
65. R. Seeberg, *Lehrbuch der Dogmengeschichte*, Vierter Band, Zweiter Teil, Die Fortbildung der reformatorischen Lehre und die gegenreformatorischen Lehre, Erlangen/Leipzig [3]1920, §94: 'Die Theologie Calvins in ihrer dogmengeschichtlichen Bedeutung', 560-61, footnote 2.
66. Parker states at the end of his 'Introduction' (1969, op. cit., 12): 'As the chief source for our understanding of Calvin's doctrine of the knowledge of God is the 1559 *Institutes,* the plan of our present book will follow the arguments of the first two books and part of the third. Comparison with the earlier editions is sometimes fruitful.'
67. Schellong, op. cit., 35.
68. The heading of the fourth and final part of Wernle's book on Calvin (see above, note 35) says: 'The finished theological system of 1559' (only seventeen pages).
69. See what Karl Barth says: 'What, however, if there should be (…) *more* than one Luther…?' KD IV.3, 428 (CD, 371). Italics by KB. See also KD I.2, 340 (CD, 311).
70. But also in Calvin's exegesis. See e.g. how we find the entire chapter of Inst. 1559 I.5 in Calvin's exegesis of Psalm 113. F. H. Breukelman, 'Psalm 113', in *Om het levende Woord* 2/3 – 1968, 212-250, particularly 212-213 and 246-249.
71. Wendel, op. cit., 87.
72. See above, note 20.
73. For this point see below. Chapter V §1.
74. In his book *De Richtingen in de Nederlandsche Hervormde Kerk*, Wageningen 1934, Prof. Th. L. Haitjema starts from the Enlightenment: 'Starting from the Enlightenment we must now try to understand our religious schools [richtingen] of the 19th and 20th centuries', he says on page 16. It is better to view the Enlightenment as a catalyst in a process that has its origins in the theology of the reformers, as it was processed in Protestant scholastics by the theologians of the 'orthodoxy.'
75. However, this little book – a brief summary of the *Institutes* of 1536 – was not suitable to serve as a study book for children. From 1538 to 1541 Calvin was banned from Geneva, and he became pastor of the small French exilic congregation at Strasbourg. As soon as Calvin returned to Geneva, he wrote another Catechism around the turn of the year of 1541/42, the definitive edition, in questions and answers: the *Catechism of Geneva* (*Catechismus ecclesiae genevensis*, CO VI). This Catechismus of 1542 (1545) forms the transition from the *Institutes* of 1539 to the *Institutes* of 1559.

CHAPTER I

THE *CHRISTIANAE RELIGIONIS INSTITUTIO* OF 1536

§1. CALVIN AS A STUDENT OF LUTHER IN THE *INSTITUTES* OF 1536

> Luther cannot be understood without Calvin,
> Calvin can only be understood through Luther.
>
> Karl Barth[1]

When Calvin committed his *Institutes* to paper for the first time in the years 1534-1535 (he may have started writing early 1534 in Angoulême), he wished to present the 'essence of sacred doctrine' in the form of an interpretation of the four constituent parts of the catechism: *de lege – de fide – de oratione – de sacramentis* (the law, faith, prayer, the sacraments). At the start of the first chapter he speaks of a *summa sacrae doctrinae*[2] (the essence of the sacred doctrine), and opening the sixth chapter he mentions the *summa evangelicae doctrinae* (the essence of evangelical doctrine).[3]

Calvin thus writes his *Christianae Religionis Institutio* in the form of a catechism (3 + 3 = 6 chapters) following the example of Luther's *Small Catechism*. Calvin used Luther's oft reprinted *Betbüchlein* (Little Prayer Book) of 1522[4] in the 1529 Latin translation. This translation, which is not included in the Weimar edition,[5] also contained the first Latin translation of the Small Catechism, which had been published a short time earlier in 1529.

Prior to his exposition of this catechetical material, Calvin writes an introduction to the book as a whole, in which he confronts us in advance with the entirety of the subsequent description of the *summa doctrinae*.[6] This will remain Calvin's modus operandi: he first briefly announces what he will talk about, after which the exposition follows. Just like Luther in the introduction to his *Betbüchlein*,[7] Calvin in the introduction to this Institutes shows the connection between the first three parts: the law – faith – prayer.

Let us first of all read the introduction to Luther's *Betbüchlein*:

'By divine providence the ordinary Christian, who is not capable of reading the Scriptures, can now learn and know the Ten Commandments, the Faith (i.e., the

Creed) and the Lord's Prayer. These three parts indeed contain everything which is written in the Scriptures, which is suitable to be preached at all times, and which a Christian needs to know. They are composed with such conciseness and simplicity that no one has a reason to complain. The things they say about what we need for our salvation are not too much or too difficult to remember.

In order to be saved, man needs to know three things. First, he must know how he should act. Next, upon realizing that he is incapable of doing this by his own strength, he should know where he can obtain this strength. Thirdly, he should know how to seek it. To use an analogy: man is just like a person who is ill. Somebody who is ill must first of all know what his sickness is. Then he must know where his medication is to be found. And thirdly, it must be his desire to seek that medicine or to have it brought to him.

Thus, the commandments teach man to know his illness, so that he may have insight as to how he should act. It teaches him that he is a sinner and an evil man. Secondly, faith stands before his eyes, teaching him where he may find the medicine. This medicine is divine grace which helps him to be devout and to keep the commandments. In Christ, God's compassion is offered to him.[8] Thirdly, the Lord's Prayer teaches him how he may desire that medicine, obtain it and have it brought to him. By means of orderly, repentant and comforting prayer it is given to him. Thus, he receives salvation by fulfilling God's commandment. These are the three central teachings of Scripture.'

In his introduction, Calvin confronts us with the entirety of the subsequent exposition of sacred doctrine. He introduces us to the dominant theme of his teachings (not only the dominant theme of his teachings in its original form of 1536, but also his teachings in all later forms). As we shall see in the third chapter, Calvin will shape his new Institutes of 1539 on the model of this old introduction as well. Therefore, we are simply obliged to proceed from this introduction if we wish describe the structure of Calvinian theology. We must hear it, and comment on it, in its entirety.

§2. THE INTRODUCTION

The opening sentence of the 1536 *Institutes* reads:

'The essence of sacred doctrine consists almost entirely of these two parts: the knowledge of God and of ourselves.'

From the perspective of biblical theology, the *sacra doctrina* (sacred doctrine) should deal with the history of the relationship between God and man. In this study of the structure of the theology of Calvin, we shall attempt to answer the question, to what extent Calvin's biblical perspective is a Christological concentration.

The first part of the Introduction consists of an explication of the opening sentence.[9] First, the question: 'what does *cognitio Dei* (the knowledge of God) mean?' is answered. Then the question: 'What does *cognitio hominis* (knowledge of man) mean?' is answered.

'Without doubt, we must first learn the following things about God.'

§2.1.1 THE KNOWLEDGE OF GOD[10]

Now, four things are said about God:

> 'First,[11] we may firmly hold, with the certitude of faith,
> that He is infinite wisdom, righteousness, goodness,
> compassion, truth, virtue and life.
> There is absolutely no other wisdom, righteousness, goodness,
> compassion, truth, virtue and life (Baruch 3:12-14; James 1:17).
> And all of these virtues, wherever they may be seen, derive from him (Prov 16:4).'

Whoever says 'God' says: infinite riches in perfections and abundant goodness. And if goodness exists outside of God, it derives exclusively 'from him'. Secondly, Calvin says about God that he is the creator:

> 'Further, that all beings which exist in heaven and on earth
> are created for his honor (Psalm 148, Daniel 3).
> And it is right that everyone, each according to his own nature,
> should serve him,[12]
> attend to his commandments,
> accept his majesty,
> and acknowledge him as Lord and King, by obeying him (Rom 1:20).'

The doctrine of creation is a very practical matter. That all beings in heaven and on earth have been created 'for his honour' and – being God's creatures – are obliged to serve him and obey him in complete servitude is one of Calvin's important principal ideas.

In conclusion, two expressions about God's relationship to his creation are presented here. The first expression relates to God's righteousness *(iustitia)* and the second to his compassion *(misericordia)*. They concern two of the above mentioned seven divine perfections. God's entire behavior towards his creation is shaped by these two perfections.

The next two remarks concerning God's righteousness and his compassion hind to the entire content of the first two chapters, 'The Law' and 'Faith'.

The Law	'Thirdly,
	that He is a righteous judge,
	and that He will therefore severely punish those,

>>> 1. who have deviated from his prescriptions,
>>> 2. who have not followed his will in everything,
>>> 3. who have thought, said, and done other things,
>>>> than those that bring him glory (Psalm 7, Romans 2).'

God commands us (1) not to deviate from his 'prescriptions'. This means (2) to obey his 'will'. To obey his will means (3) to live and act 'to his glory'. Those who fail to do this will meet God as the 'righteous judge'. God will punish them severely. That includes us all, as Calvin will explain in the chapter 'The Law'. Here, the righteousness of God is characterized as God's judgment on those 'who have thought, said, and done other things than those that bring him glory'.

It must be noted here that the Latin term *iustitia* (*iustitia vindicatrix*, punitive righteousness) is far removed from the biblical *tsedaka,* which always means *iustitia alutifera* (redeeming righteousness),[13] even if it sometimes functions as 'punitive' righteousness.

Alongside the *iustitia Dei* (righteousness of God), the *misericordia Dei* (compassion of God) is now introduced:

Faith   'Fourthly,
        Compassion   that He is compassionate and merciful,
             Favour   a God who will favorably receive
    and faithfulness   the miserable and the poor
          toward the   who take refuge in his favour
miserable and the poor   and put their trust in his faithfulness;

        Justification ⎫   ⎧ who is prepared to save them and to forgive
                             ⎪   ⎪   if they ask him for forgiveness,
      Sanctification ⎬   ⎨ who will rush toward them and offer aid
                             ⎪   ⎪   when they call for help,
         Protection   ⎭   ⎩ who will protect them
                                              when they put all their trust on him
                                              and cleave to him.
                                  (Psalm 103; Isa 55:6ff.; Psalm 25; Psalm 85.)'

The first line 'fourthly, that He is compassionate and merciful' is followed by a sentence which puts this line into action as well as summarizes it: 'who will favorably receive the miserable and the poor / those who take refuge in his favour / and put their trust in his faithfulness'. According to this sentence, God's compassion is about his favour and faithfulness towards the miserable and the poor. In other words, it concerns God's *chèsèd we èmèd*, his grace and truthfulness, for the *anawiem we-èwjoniem*, the miserable and the needy.

The exposition of all that is contained in the compassion of God follows in the last three sentences, each starting with 'who...'. In these sentences, Calvin tells us that God is gracious, good and faithful, and that he justifies, sanctifies and protects.[14]

Calvin mentions here what he will later call (after 1539) the *duplex gratia* (twofold grace – justification and sanctification).[15] Justification is expressed by the words 'who is ready to save and to forgive, when they ask forgiveness of him'. Sanctification is expressed by the words 'who will rush toward them and offer aid when they call for his help'. In addition, the protection is expressed by the words 'who will protect them, when they put their trust in him, and cleave to him'.

The single term *compassion* is thus clarified by many expressions. All salvation is summed up in the compassion of God.[16] For Christians of the Latin West it was not an easy thing to identify the term 'righteousness of God' with the consolation offered by the gospels.[17] Therefore, the great evangelical principle of the Institutes is the concept of mercy.

Calvin says four things about God's relationship to mankind: He is rich in perfections, he is the creator, he is the just judge, and he is the merciful God. The concept 'rich in perfections' is crucial. It cannot be said of mankind that riches, fullness, blessedness, and glory are found there. Concerning man we hear of poverty, emptiness, misery and shame, nothing more.

§2.1.2 THE KNOWLEDGE OF MAN[18]

Answering his second question, 'what does the knowledge of man signify?', Calvin first writes the following:

'If we wish to come to a sure knowledge of ourselves,
we need first of all to affirm
that our ancestor Adam was created
in the image and likeness of God (Gen 1:26),
that is,
he was endowed with wisdom, righteousness and holiness.
If only he would have clung to God with these gracious gifts,
and would have remained in the purity of nature which God had given him
he would have lived forever in God.
However, since he fell into sin (Genesis 3),
this image and likeness of God was destroyed and erased,
that is,
he has lost all goods of divine grace,
by which he could have been led on the way of life.'

Twice we hear the words 'that is'. We will meet them often further on (e.g., during the explanation of the fourth part of the Apostles' Creed).[19] The tone of these words is that of a teacher.

Whoever speaks about 'us', about mankind, speaks first of all about 'our ancestor Adam'. It is clear that Calvin reads the biblical testimony of Christ – God's covenant with mankind – historically as well. That is to say, he takes it as an account of a linear history, moving in one direction, from the beginning to the end.

The following applies to 'our ancestor Adam': he was 'created in the image of God'; that is: as a created being he shared in the riches of the divine perfections ('he was endowed with wisdom, righteousness and holiness'). Through this relationship with God he could have lived forever – as we, his descendants, could have done as well, if only Adam 'would have remained in the purity of nature which God had given him'.

By *imago Dei* (image of God, see Genesis 1) Calvin, like many others, means the initial *status integritatis* (the state of paradise in Genesis 2). He does not mean man's original destiny of being in covenant with God. This destiny, which according to the testimony of Genesis 1 distinguishes man from all other creatures, could never be lost.[20]

However, our father Adam did fall into sin. The image of God became concealed and was lost, that is: 'he has lost all goods of divine grace, by which he could have been led on the way of life.' This thought – that man lost all goods by which he could have lived forever in God, and that by his sinful estrangement from the God of riches he plunged himself in abysmal poverty – is now underlined by phrases describing the resulting *status corruptionis* (the state of corruption):[21]

> 'Moreover, he is separated from God and totally estranged from him.
> The result of this
> is that he is stripped of all wisdom, righteousness, virtue and life
> – virtues which one cannot possess except in God, as said above.[22]
> Therefore nothing was left to him
> except ignorance, unrighteousness, powerlessness, death and judgment (Rom 5:12ff.):
> These are the fruits of sin.'

The expression 'nothing was left to him' is used several times in the *Institutes*.[23]

Because of his sin man fell from the *status integritatis* into the *status corruptionis*, from closeness to God into remoteness to God, from heights into depths, from riches into poverty, from life into death.

Thus, in the *Institutes* the entire doctrine of mankind falls under the heading: 'but into sin Adam fell'. This is opposed to the anthropology of medieval dogmatic theology. For the moment (until 1559)[24] Calvin's teaching concerning mankind is completely marked by the *peccatum originale* (original sin) as *peccatum haereditarium* (inherited sin) and the radical and total *corruptio naturae* (corruption of nature):

> 'This tragedy did not only strike him,
> but us as well, his seed and descendants.
> And so all of us, being born of Adam,
> are ignorant of God and estranged from him.
> We are corrupt and depraved, lacking all good.'

The fact that man lost all goods of divine grace does not lead to just a neutral emptiness, but to the reign of evil:

> 'Our heart in particular is inclined to all evil,
> filled to the brim with evil desires
> and rebellious against God (Jer 17:9).'

Calvin says two more things concerning the fall of man. First he addresses the question whether man in spite of his sins can still do good things, in which he could take pride. Calvin denies this possibility. God looks at the heart, he says, and the human heart is evil.

Justification	'And first,
(forgiveness	when, trusting Him, we beg Him to turn away His wrath
of sins)	and ask for forgiveness,
	then – without doubt – He will grant us this kindness,
	remove what our sins had merited
	and accept us in grace.
Sanctification	Further,
	when we call for His help
	and the intervention of His powerful hand,
	– we, who by then have been convinced
	that under His protection we can do anything –
	we will be granted a new heart (Ezek 36:26),
	because of His benevolence.
	Then we will want to follow His commandments,
	and find the strength to follow them.'

By now, Calvin has announced everything he will discuss in the first chapter 'The Law' in advance. The fact that he concludes the first chapter 'The Law' (1534) with the doctrine of justification and sanctification is significant. It shows us to what extent the entire order of 'the knowledge of God – the knowledge of man – the Law' in the Institutes is composed with regard to 'God's mercy in Christ'. For already here Calvin mentions the 'benefits of Christ', while he will mention Christ himself only in the second chapter, 'Faith'.

One can only properly speak of Jesus Christ – according to Calvin – when one has a clear idea of the distance separating God and man, and of man's abysmal need of God's mercy. Now that Calvin has made this clear he is able to proceed to the second part of the introduction, and announce the content of the second chapter 'Faith' in advance as well.

§2.3 FAITH[51]

Two sections follow, both beginning with the words *haec omnia* (all these things), thus connecting the sections to was said about justification and sanctification.

1. 'All of these things are given to us generously for the sake of Jesus Christ our Lord... .'
2. 'All of these things are offered to us by God and given in Christ our Lord (...) when we embrace them with a firm faith... .'

Let us first of all listen to the beautiful words of the first paragraphs in which Calvin tells us that 'all these things' are granted us 'for the sake of Jesus Christ our Lord':

(1) 'And all these things are given to us generously
    for the sake of Jesus Christ our Lord,

who, though He was one God together with the Father (John 1:1ff.)
has assumed our flesh,
by which He entered into a covenant with us,
and has attached us closely to God again,
although sin had removed us at a great distance from Him (Isaiah 53).

Also, through the merit of His death,
He has paid what we owed to the righteousness of God,
and soothed His wrath,
by redeeming us from the curse and the judgment,
to which we were subjected.
He has borne in His body the punishment of sin,
so that He might relieve us from it (Eph 2:4-6; Col 1:13).

All of the riches of heavenly blessings
He brought with Him when He descended to earth
and distributed them to us with a generous hand (John 1:17; 7:29; Rom 8:32).
For these are the gifts of the Holy Spirit:

through this Spirit we are reborn,
released from the power and the bonds of the devil,
accepted through grace as children of God,
sanctified for every good deed;

also, as long as we are stuck in this mortal body
through this Spirit the evil groanings within us,
the desires of the flesh, and whatever grows out of our nature
which is distorted and spoiled
are put to death;

through this Spirit we are renewed day by day,
to walk in newness of life and to live for righteousness.'

The further development of these thoughts in the second chapter (when explaining the Apostles' Creed) proceeds in the same way. 'Things would have been most miserable if the majesty of God himself had not come down to us, since we were no longer able to rise up to Him'.[52] Through Jesus Christ there is proximity again instead of distance, and riches instead of poverty in the relationship of man to God. The *longum intervallum* (the great distance, in time and space) has been annulled. It should be noted that – again – in this first paragraph beginning with the words 'all these things', both graces (justification and sanctification) are mentioned together.

Let us now pay attention to the second paragraph in which Calvin tells us that 'all these things' are granted to us 'in Jesus Christ our Lord, when we embrace them with a firm faith':

(2) 'All these things are offered to us by God in Christ our Lord,
    namely, the free forgiveness of sins,
    peace and reconciliation with God,
    the gracious gifts of the Holy Spirit.

These things are given to us
when we embrace them with a firm faith and accept them,
and with great trust lean on the divine goodness,
and do not doubt whether the Word of God, which promises us all these things,
is indeed strength and truth (Rom 3:21; Rom 5:1ff.).'

With this discussion of the theme *Christus – verbum – promissio – fides – fiducia* (Christ – Word – promise – faith – trust) Calvin opens the second chapter 'Faith', as an introduction to the explanation of the Apostles' Creed.[53]

We need to pay attention to the fact that, in both of these *haec omnia* texts, Calvin labels the 'heavenly treasures' we possess 'in Christ' as 'gracious gifts of the Holy Spirit'. He will do the same thing in the following text. Here he repeats what he had already said in both *haec omnia* references, but this time in such a way that the main concept of the entire introduction – and thus also the main concept of the entire *Institutio* – is pointedly expressed. This central concept is (1) we possess all of our riches only in Christ and (2) therefore we possess all of our riches only in faith:

(1) 'To put it briefly: when we are in fellowship with Christ,
    we possess *in Him* all heavenly treasures and gifts of the Holy Spirit,
    which lead us to life and salvation'.[54]
(2) 'We can never acquire this except through genuine and living faith,
    recognizing that all of our good rests *in Him*,
    and that we, if we are not *in Him*, are nothing at all.
    It is only *in Him* that we become children of God
    and heirs to the kingdom of heaven (John 1:12; Rom 8:14).'

We hear the words 'in Him' four times. Because we are 'in Him' we are 'in faith'. In order to emphasize that all of our riches are in Christ and therefore in faith, Calvin concludes this paragraph:

'Conversely, those who have no share in Christ,
whoever they may be, whatever they do or undertake,
they will meet their ruin and shame, indeed the judgment of eternal death,
rejected by God and excluded from any expectation of salvation
(John 3:18; 1 John 5:16).'

At the end of this discussion of the *Institutes* of 1536 (see below, §4) we shall return to this central idea that 'all of our good rests in Him, and that we, if we are not in him, are nothing at all'.

After Calvin has revealed – in this second part of the introduction – the content of the first chapter, 'The Law', and then also announced in advance the content of the second chapter, 'Faith', he concludes the introduction with another sentence in which he reveals to us the content of the third chapter, 'Prayer'.

§2.4 Prayer[55]

In this sentence Calvin recapitulates everything that was said in the introduction, while at the same time offering us a foretaste of the entire 'essence of doctrine', to be presented in the three chapters 'The Law' – 'Faith' – 'Prayer':

	And because	
The law	1.	'this knowledge of our neediness – indeed, our disaster – by which we are taught

> – that is, to know ourselves means to know our neediness, FB –

to humble ourselves and to cast ourselves down before God and to seek His mercy,'

> – which, as we saw, the law has taught us,[56] FB –

Faith	2.	'and because this faith, which gives us a foretaste of the divine goodness and mercy (Jer 31:20-22), by which He deals with us in His Anointed,'

> – the word 'mercy' appears here for the second time, FB –

'indeed, because neither of these two
find their origin in us nor are they within our power,'

> – i.e., neither 'the law' nor 'faith', FB –

Prayer	3.	'we must ask God that He

(1) leads us to such knowledge of ourselves through honest repentance,
(2) and to the knowledge of His mercy, by unyielding trust,
      and of His sweetness, which He shows us in His Anointed One,
that we may be led to eternal bliss with Him as our guide,
who is the only way to the Father
(Phil 1; John 14:6; Rom 1:1-2).'

Again, the word 'mercy' is mentioned two times in the final sentence of the introduction. The law taught us to seek the mercy of God in Christ. It is in faith that we can taste it.

The opening sentence of the introduction reads: 'The essence of sacred doctrine consists of these two parts: the knowledge of God and of ourselves.' The final sentence of the introduction takes up the same theme. However, the order has been reversed. According to this final sentence, prayer is summed up by (1) prayer for the right knowledge of ourselves so that we might become aware of our misery and (2) prayer for the right knowledge of God, leading us to divine mercy in Christ.

This reversal shows us that the *Institutes* of 1536 move from knowledge of ourselves to the knowledge of God. In the section following upon the opening sentence,

Calvin writes a brief summary and at the same time complete description of the content of the knowledge of God, culminating in the mercy of God. This was followed by a description of the knowledge of self, as it is awakened in man by the law. In the remainder of his book Calvin intends to explain how man arrives at the knowledge of God's mercy in Christ, through this knowledge of self which is brought about by the law in faith. Put in simple words, how does God lead his people to Christ?[57]

After highlighting once more the scope of this 'essence of the doctrine' in the final sentence of the introduction, Calvin introduces the theme of the first chapter 'The Law' by stating that 'the Ten Commandments of the law are divided into two tables'.[58]

In the introduction to the *Institutes* of 1536 we have encountered Calvin's characteristic working method. He always reveals in advance what he plans to discuss in more detail later on. However, the ensuing discussion of what was announced in advance never becomes longwinded. Calvin's ideal of *perspicua brevitas* ('transparent brevity'), which he mentioned in the preface of his first published commentary, is masterfully and consistently realized in his work as dogmatician.[59]

As we saw, in the second part of the introduction (§2.2 – 2.4) the content of the entire 'sacred doctrine' which Calvin will expound in the three chapters 'The Law' – 'Faith' – 'Prayer', is announced in advance. This announcement is summed up in the final sentence, in which Calvin once more unfolds the totality of 'sacred doctrine'.

Because in this study it is our task to describe the *structure* of Calvin's theology (and then in particular the change of this structure in 1559), we need only to discuss the content of the *Institutes* in their three forms (1536, 1539-1554, 1559) insofar as it pertains to our enquiry.

In chapter three we will describe the *Institutes* of 1539, which were published in an entirely new form. As we will see, in this new edition Calvin does not do away with the introduction of the 1536 *Institutes* commented on above. The six chapters of the 1536 *Institutes* are copied in the new 1539 *Institutes* as well. However, this old material is significantly expanded. It is also put into a different order, because of a different *series docendi* (succession of the instructional themes).[60] In order to describe how Calvin deals with the old material in his new composition, we need to briefly look at the first edition, the booklet published in March 1536 by Platter and Lasius in Basel.

§3. THE SIX CHAPTERS OF THE *INSTITUTES* OF 1536

§3.1 CHAPTER I. The Law. Including an explanation of the Ten Words.[61]

The first chapter 'The Law' opens with the introduction to the entire book, discussed above. Then follow two parts.[62]

FIRST PART[63]
In the first part, Calvin aims to show us that all who live under the law are under the curse. First, an explanation of the Decalogue is given.[64] 'In explaining the Ten Commandments, Calvin follows Luther's Small Catechism. Each commandment is formu-

lated as follows: "We are to fear and love God in such a way that we should not...". In each case Calvin moves from acts to underlying attitude.'[65]

Immediately after this explanation, the law of God is characterized as *lex spiritualis* (spiritual law). That is to say, the law does not only concern the external side of man. It first of all addresses man's inner life and thus the whole man.[66] It is important to see that Christ, being the *novus legislator* (new lawgiver), has not just supplemented the *lex mosaica* (law of Moses) by a *lex evangelica* (evangelical law). Rather, as *legis interpres* (interpreter of the law) he wished to show us the *sensus spiritualis* (spiritual sense) of the law. Therefore, the distintion between *mandata legis* (commandments of the law) and *consilia evangelica* (evangelical counsels) should be rejected.[67]

Man does not keep the law. Not just a part of him is sinful; he is a sinner with every inch of his being. The *satisfactiones* (reparations) of the sacrament of penance and *opera supererigationes* (superfluous good works) cannot make him more righteous. He is a total sinner, who is totally under control of the *maledictio legis* (curse of the law).[68] Thus, the climactic conclusion of the first part of chapter one runs as follows:

'Further, you have heard it before',

– in the introduction,[69] FB –

'that a heavy and terrible judgment has been pronounced by the Lord
on all those who have trespassed His law in any way
and have not fulfilled it in its entirety.
However, it is not within the reach of our powers to fulfill it.
Thus, we are all regarded as transgressors of the law.
And the curses of the law
threaten not just this one or that one among us
but all of us.
Thus, when we fix our eyes on the law
we can do nothing but lose our courage, become confused, indeed despair,
because we all are judged and damned (Gal 3:10-13).
This is what Paul says:
"All who are under the law are under the curse" '.

SECOND PART.[70]

In the second part, Calvin describes how man can be liberated from the law, and what such a liberated life looks like. It opens with the paragraph we mentioned in the commentary on the introduction:[71]

'Thus, the entire human race is accused by the law,
subjected to the curse and the wrath of God.
To be released from this curse,
it is necessary for us to be pulled away
from the power of the law
and as it were solemnly to be declared
no longer to belong to slavery but to freedom.
Not the freedom of the flesh, to be sure,

which keeps us from observing the law,
inviting us to lawlessness in all things,
and allowing us to be swept away by our desires,
but a spiritual freedom,
which raises up our frightened conscience,
telling us that we are no longer under the curse and damnation of the law.
We obtain this liberation from the law, this freeing from slavery,
when by faith we grasp the mercy of God in Christ.
Then we can be assured that our sins are forgiven,
and we are no longer held captive to the law.'[72]

Now follows the description of the doctrine of justification,[73] which Calvin repeatedly calls 'forgiveness of sins'.[74] After this section, Calvin mentions the *triplex usus legis* (the threefold use of the law). The so-called *usus elenchticus* (the accusing use) is not the only function of the law.[75] This discussion ends with the following words:

'Put briefly,
those who believe are encouraged by the law,
not to bind their conscience with the curse,
but to shake off their lethargy,
and to tear off their incompleteness.
Indeed. many have said that to be liberated from the curse of the law
means that the law is abolished for those who believe;
not because it does not contain any indications for them as to what is right,
but because it is no longer for them what it used to be.
That is, it no longer confuses their consciences
or terrifies them by the announcement of death.
It no longer causes us to be lost and damned.
Just so, approached from the opposite side,
justification should be cut loose from good works.
This is not to stop us from doing good works, or to deny them,
but to prevent us from relying on our works
and taking pride in them;
we ought not expect salvation from our works.
Rather, we should believe that Christ, the Son of God, is ours.
He has been given to us,
so that we may be in Him and become children of God,
heirs to the kingdom of heaven (Isa 9:6; 1 Thes 4:14),
called by God's benevolent grace and not by our own efforts
to the hope of eternal salvation.
However, we are called, not to uncleanness and unrighteousness,
but to be clean and unspotted before our God, in love (Eph 1:4).'

Our 'good works' therefore 'cannot be counted as righteousness before God or even a part of it'.[76] This does not mean that evangelicals no longer wished to speak or hear about *bona opera* (good works) and their *merces* (reward); to the contrary. Yet they did not wish to connect them with 'merit'. 'Truly, those who use the word "merit", raise blasphemy against the grace of God. Surely, this is full of arrogance and raging vanity toward God'.[77] With the discussion of this topic, Calvin ends the first chapter of 'the Law'.[78]

Thus, in the first chapter 'The Law', Calvin did what he announced he would do in the introduction. While in the second chapter, 'Faith', he will speak on the Apostles' Creed concerning Christ, he already in the first chapter spoke of 'God's mercy in Christ' and the 'mercies of Christ', as we grasp it by faith. He did this so that he could contast the 'righteousness by the works of the law' with the 'justification by faith'. Thus, in Calvin's theology the framework within which 'grace' is mentioned is no longer the description of the *motus rationalis creaturae in Deum* (the movement of the rational creature toward God), as in Thomas Aquinas.[79] Rather, it consists in the *Dei nostrique cognitio* (the knowledge of God and of ourselves) of man under the law. Calvin only mentions 'grace' in the context of the knowledge of sin. Justifying and sanctifying grace[80] no longer in the first place serves to help nature in its upward movement to reach its supernatural goal, eternal *beatitudo* (blessedness) in God. Rather, it is grace for *sinners* through the 'mercy of God in Christ'.

§3.2 CHAPTER II. Faith. Including an explanation of the Apostles' Creed.[81]

Looking back to what he discussed in the first chapter of 'The Law', and looking ahead at what he will now deal with, Calvin begins the second chapter, 'Faith', with a paragraph in which he renders visible the *series docendi*:

Summary of the first part of chapter one, 'The Law'	1. 'The previous exposition has made it sufficiently clear what the Lord want us to do according to the law. If we should fail to fulfill even the least part of it, His wrath and the terrible judgment of eternal death will come upon us. Moreover, it is not just that it is difficult to fulfill the law as He demands it, it exceeds our powers completely. It lies beyond our strength. Thus, if we only look at ourselves, and what we are capable of, we have no good reason for hope. Rejection by God, death, and most certain ruin await us.
Summary of the second part of chapter one, 'The Law'	2. However, we also noticed that there is a way out of this disaster. The mercy of the Lord can restore us.[82] When we accept it with a firm faith we will undoubtedly experience it. It will give us shelter.

> The chapter   3. It remains to be discussed
> 'Faith' is   how this faith must be understood.
> announced.   We will easily learn this from the Creed,
>   also called 'apostolic',
>   which briefly summarizes what faith is all about,
>   and what the catholic church assents to.'[83]

Next follows a paragraph which distinguishes between two *fidei formae* (forms of faith).[84] The *vera fides* (true faith) is contrasted to a purely 'historic' faith.[85] Of this second form of faith Calvin says 'that it carries no weight whatsoever'. It is 'unworthy of the name of "faith".' By contast, 'true faith' is described by Calvin as

> 'not only believing that God and Christ exist,
> but really putting our trust in them,
> acknowledging God to be our God
> and Christ to be our savior.
> This, then, means that we not simply affirm
> what has been written or said about God and Christ.
> Rather, it means that we put all our hope and trust on God and Christ.
> This trust strengthens us,
> so that we no longer doubt God's benevolence toward us.'[86]

Here we have the source of the later definition (1539): '... faith is the firm and sure knowledge of God's benevolence toward us, grounded in the truth of the promise in Christ by grace, which the Holy Spirit both reveals to our minds and seals in our hearts.'[87]

This 'true faith' bases itself on the promises of the Bible. With absolute certainty it expects God to bring to pass all the things he has committed himself to in his Word.[88]

Calvin points out that this 'true faith' cannot be and remain in us 'except by God's grace'. Further, it is this 'true faith' which God demands from us in the first commandment of the law.[89] Calvin ends this paragraph concerning the question 'what is true faith?' with the words:

> 'We now plan to consider this faith in more detail.
> Our instruction is summarized by the creed,
> which consists of four parts.
> The first three are devoted to the three persons of the holy Trinity:
> the Father, the Son and the Holy Spirit;
> the eternal and almighty God in whom we believe.
> The fourth part explains what this faith in God means for us
> and what we may expect.'[90]

Next follows a discussion of the doctrine of the Trinity.[91] Here Calvin disputes those who are of the opinion that the formation of a theological concept needs to keep within the boundaries of the biblical vocabulary. These people reject each *novitas verborum* (using new words).[92]

'When someone criticizes newly coined words,
he rejects the light of truth,
because he does not want the truth to be expressed clearly and distinctly.
However, it is precisely to protect the truth
against blasphemers who try to walk past it
that new words are needed.'[93]

After this discussion of the Trinity, 'the four parts of the Creed' are expounded.[94] This exposition is introduced with the words 'let us now hear the simple confession of the truth'.

This chapter on the locus *de fide* (faith) began with a brief paragraph unfolding the essence and character of the *vera fides* (true faith). It now concludes with a paragraph exlaining that this *vera fides* is never a *fides otiosa* (idle faith):

'This living faith, consisting of trust in God and Christ alone,'

    – here Calvin refers back to the beginning part of this chapter, FB –

'can never be idle,
since its companions are hope and love.'[95]

The chapter ends with a brief explanation of this subject.[96] For Calvin, faith always means 'to embrace Christ as He is offered to us by the Father'.[97] This idea is key to Calvin's thinking. At the same time, however, Calvin never fails to mention that 'faith cannot be inactive'.

One thing still needs to be pointed out in this context. The concept of predestination is not mentioned in the introduction. Calvin does not touch on the subject until he comes to speak about the church in the second chapter (at the beginning of the discussion of the 'fourth part' of the Creed).[98] 'First of all, we believe in a holy catholic church, which is to say, the full number of the elect...'. The discussion of this *credimus ecclesiam* (we believe in the church) is at the same time a discussion of predestination.

Why is predestination not discussed in the introduction? Why is it not mentioned earlier? The answer is simple. For Calvin predestination never formed the main subject of sacred doctrine. Rather, it was merely an aspect of it. The main subject is salvation in Christ for lost sinners through the mercy of God (and the 'double grace' of justification and sanctification it contains). Nevertheless, predestination does form an important aspect of this subject. Calvin therefore paid much attention to it. In the various forms of his *Institutes* (1536, 1539-1554, 1559) and his Catechism (1537, 1542), however, he discusses the concept at very different places.[99]

§3.3 CHAPTER III. Prayer. Including an explanation of the Lord's Prayer.[100]

Just as Calvin opened the second chapter, 'Faith', with a retrospect of the previous and a prospect of the following chapter, so he opens the third chapter, 'Prayer', with a paragraph in which he again unfolds the *series docendi*. In this section he once again expounds the theme of the entire book as summarized in the introduction, the poverty of sinful man and the riches of God's mercy offered to him in Christ.

	'From the things which we have discussed thus far, we have clearly seen,
Summary of the first chapter, 'The Law'	1. to what extent man is needy, devoid of all goods and lacking all means of salvation. If therefore he seeks help, he must look for it outside of himself.[101]
Summary of the second chapter, 'Faith'	2. It was then explained to us how the Lord shows himself to us freely and generously in His Christ, in whom He offers us happiness instead of misery and riches instead of poverty. In Christ He gives us His heavenly treasures, so that all of our faith would be focused on Christ as God's beloved Son, and all of our expectation would depend on Him, and all of our hope would cleave to Him and rest in Him. This is a secret and hidden philosophy which is not based on syllogisms. But surely those whom God opened the eyes, so that in His light they would see the light (Ps 36:10), will come to know it.
The third chapter, 'Prayer', is announced	3. Having thus learned to understand that our need can only be filled by God and by our Lord Jesus Christ, in whom the Father revealed the fullness of His riches (Col. 1; John 1), we have to seek Him and come to Him in prayer. In our prayers we ask to receive from God what – as we have learned – He alone can give. If we only know that God is the Lord and the giver of all goods, but do not actually go to Him in prayer to receive what He has to give us, this knowledge would not help us in the least. We would be like someone who found a treasure but dug a hole in the ground and hid it there. This last point, which up to now was only mentioned in passing, we will now deal with in a more detailed way.'[102]

In the above retrospect we hear Calvin say – against the scholastics – that the 'secret and hidden philosophy' of faith does not originate out of logical deduction, but is given by divine illumination. It should be noted that faith and hope are named beside each other.[103] As justification is not without sanctification, so faith is not without hope. Christian faith, which trusts on the truth of divine promises – *fides* as *fiducia* (faith as trust) – provides the ground for Christian expectation and hope (*fides – expectatio – spes*; faith – expectation – hope).

The introduction to the third chapter, 'Prayer', which consists of three parts, corresponds with the final sentence of the introduction of the entire book, which also consists of three parts: law, faith, prayer.[104] The theme 'prayer', which was only touched upon *antea* (up to now, in the final sentence of the introduction of the entire book), will *nunc* (now; in this third chapter) be 'dealt with in a more detailed way'.

The *lex* or *ratio orationis* (the law or the rule of prayer) is discussed first,[105] followed by the *forma orationis* (the form of the prayer), the Lord's Prayer.[106]

§3.4. CHAPTER IV. The Sacraments.[107]

The final sentence of the beginning part of the third chapter reads, 'This last point, which up to now was only mentioned in passing, we will now deal with in a more detailed way'. By way of conclusion the topic of prayer has to be discussed in detail, Calvin says. Indeed, as far back as the introduction to the entire book, the three chapters constituting *all* of sacred doctrine were indicated as: 'The Law – Faith – Prayer'.

There is no doubt, however, that Calvin had intended his book from the outset to have four chapters, 'Law – Faith – Prayer – the Sacraments'. Yet he does not mention the fourth chapter in the introduction. Why not? This is because sacred doctrine itself is comprehensively summed up in the first three chapters. According to Calvin God added the sacrament of the proclaimed *promissio* (promise) to the gospel. Calvin correspondingly adds the fourth chapter 'the Sacraments' to the three previous chapters of his catechism. This chapter opens as follows:[108]

'We must now discuss the topic of the sacraments.
It is of the greatest importance that we receive reliable instruction
concerning this topic.
We should learn both for what purpose the sacraments have been instituted
and how we are to use them.[109]
To begin with, we need to consider what a sacrament is.
It is an outward sign,
by which the Lord actualizes and demonstrates His benevolence toward us,
in order to sustain our weak faith.
It may also be defined as a witness of God's grace,
given to us by an external sign.
This makes us realize
that a sacrament is never without a preceding promise.
Rather, it is a kind of appendix,
strengthening and sealing the promise (as a testament),
and making it even more persuasive for our sake.
God does this because He is well aware

of our ignorance and the weakness of our flesh.
The promise itself, however, does not need the sacrament.
It is we who need it.
The truth of God is in itself sufficiently clear
and does not need a stronger confirmation from elsewhere.'

The 'sacraments' are thus 'added', not for the sake of the 'promise' of the gospel, 'the fixed and certain truth of God in itself', but for our sake, to help us be more confident.

The proclaimed word is understood as 'promise'. Correspondingly *fides* is described as 'trust – expectation – hope'.[110] Note that the expressions which in chapter 2[111] were connected to 'true faith' – 'God's benevolence toward us' and 'promise' – are connected to the 'true sacrament' in the fourth chapter.[112]

In this chapter, Calvin explores the nature of the sacraments, which he describes as 'mirrors reflecting the riches of God's grace',[113] and explains why they were instituted. He then discusses baptism and closes off with a section on the Lord's Supper.

§3.5 CHAPTER V.   In which the other five sacraments are revealed not to be sacraments at all, although they are commonly held to be so. Their true nature is shown.[114]

In the first four chapters (following Luther's example) the material of the Catechism is treated. This may be heard already in the superscriptions:

I. The Law	Including an explanation of the Ten Words
II. Faith	Including an explanation of the Apostles' Creed
III. Prayer	Including an explanation of the Lord's Prayer
IV. The Sacraments	

Unlike the first three chapters, the fourth does not bear any semblance to a chapter from a catechism. It contains almost twice as many pages (45 pages) as the previous chapters (The Law, 27 pages;[115] Faith, 28 pages; Prayer, 21 pages). Also, the style has changed from didactic to polemic.

This change of style is even more apparent in the two chapters – *De falsis sacramentis* (the false sacraments) and *De libertate Christiana* (the Christian freedom) – which Calvin added when he finally edited the booklet in Basel, in 1535. (The letter to King Francis at the beginning of the book is dated August 23, 1535.)[116]

In 1534 Calvin had begun to write the *Christianae Religionis Institutio* as an instructional booklet for his French fellow believers. At the end of 1534 he had left France. He arrived in Basel at the beginning of 1535, via Strassburg (to study theology; he was jurist). There news reached him that King Francis I had sent a memoir to the German Protestant princes, with whom he had an alliance. In it, the king explained to them that the people he persecuted in France were the same kind of folk as the revolutionary zealots in Germany, who were active in Münster. And just as the German princes were slaughtering the zealots in their country, Francis intended to destroy the revolutionaries in his own country.

When Calvin heard this, he took his 'Catechism' (consisting of the four chapters 'Law – Faith – Prayer – the Sacraments') and supplemented it with the two very extensive polemical chapters 'The False Sacraments' (61 pages) and 'Christian Freedom' (58 pages) mentioned above. Thus, Calvin did not only publish a catechism, but a polemic treatise, with the aim of freeing his fellow believers from imminent death. He tried to move the king to more worthy policies (see the letter to Francis I, 'Preface to the very Christian king of France, to which this book is dedicated as a confession of faith';[117] see also the significant foreword of the commentary on the Psalms of 1557).[118] We now turn briefly to these two final chapters of the *Institutes* of 1536.

The detailed superscription of the first of these chapters already testifies to the polemical character of it. Calvin wrote it in Basel in 1535. 'In which the other five sacraments are revealed not to be sacraments at all, although they are commonly held to be so. Their true nature is shown.' Like the other chapters, this fifth chapter begins with a brief introduction as well. This introduction distinguishes the *duo vera sacramenta* (two true sacraments), from the *quinque falsa sacramenta* (five false sacraments). It begins with the following words:[119]

'The explanation of the sacraments we offered above
should persuade receptive and thoughtful people not to be too curious.
Apart from the two sacraments which they know to be instituted by the Lord
they should not embrace any other sacraments
which are not based on the Word of God.'

The difference between *verum sacramentum* ('instituted by the Lord') and *falsum sacramentum* ('not based on the Word of God') is elaborated as follows:

'To begin with, we need to hold firmly
to the unshakeable observation we made earlier on.
The power to institute a sacrament rests with no other than the Word of God.'

This fact is implied by the description of the 'true sacrament' given in the previous chapter. It follows then (note again the expressions 'God's benevolence toward us' and 'promise'):

'A sacrament aims to raise up and comfort the conscience of believers,
who will never accept their certainty from the hands of a human being.
Therefore, a sacrament is a testimony of God's benevolence toward us,
which no human being or angel can give, since none has been God's counselor.'

Now follows the cardinal sentence:

'Through his Word the Lord gives us a testimony of himself.'

Applied to the teaching of the sacraments:

'The sacrament is a seal,[120]
by which the testament or the promise of God is sealed.

Physical entities and things of the world cannot seal it,
if they were not formed and singled out by the power of God.
Therefore, no human being can institute a sacrament.
Causing such divine mysteries to be present in the base things of the world –
surely, this lies outside the power of a human being.'

As in the definition of 'true sacrament'[121] we hear the words *testimonium – testis – testificari* (testimony – witness – giving witness). No created being has the power to cause God ('such divine mysteries') to be present amongst us. Created beings can only be 'designated' by the Word of God to be a vehicle for God's revelation, and so to serve him. The Word of God always comes first. The church must humbly follow after it.[122]

Next, the 'five false sacraments' are discussed: confirmation – penance – the so-called extreme unction – ordination – marriage. More than half of this long chapter of sixty-one pages is taken up by the discussion of *poenitentia* (thirty-three pages!).[123] This is hardly surprising. Since the earliest times of the church, penance has played a significant role. Indeed, the proclamation of the gospel is at the same time a call to 're-pentance'.[124] The Reformation can be seen as an evangelical reaction against the practice and teaching of penance in the sixteenth century. This practice dates back to the early church, but was for the most part developed in the Middle Ages.[125]

§3.6 CHAPTER VI. Christian Freedom, Ecclesial Power and Civil Government.[126]

The chapter begins as follows:

'We must now go on to disuss Christian freedom.
In a summary of the essence of evangelical doctrine
this subject cannot be omitted.

– Again we hear the words 'essence of evangelical doctrine' as in the opening sentence, FB –

'This freedom is very important.
Without it, our conscience does not dare touch anything without hesitation.
Often it wavers and shrinks back,
being inwardly divided and anxious.
We have hinted to this subject above.
Now we will give it a more elaborate treatment.'[127]

'We have hinted to this subject above', Calvin states. He is refering to the second part of the first chapter, where the issues of justification and sanctification are discussed. Already at this point the contrast is made between 'justification by faith' and 'right-eousness by the works of the law'. This discussion began with the remark that the 'mercy of God in Christ' liberates us from the 'curse' of the law, which torments our 'conscience'.[128]

Calvin now sets out to explore in more detail what this means in practice. For without knowledge of this freedom 'our conscience does not dare touch anything without hesitation. Often it wavers and shrinks back, being inwardly divided and anxious.'[129]

Hence, Calvin's ultimate aim in writing this chapter is to reassure our conscience, which 'wavers and shrinks back, being inwardly divided and anxious'. At the same time, however, we saw that this final chapter was occasioned by the memoir of Francis I. This secondary motive comes to the fore again in the following passage:

'As soon as Christian freedom is mentioned,
either sinful desires are enflamed or resistance arises.
These lawless passions will ruin the very best there is
in the worst way possible,
if they are not opposed at the right time.
Under the pretense of this freedom,
some people no longer obey God.
They relish in unbridled sin.
Others are upset about this freedom,
because they fear it will destroy public order and ruin healthy relationships.
What must we do, surrounded by such distress?'[130]

Calvin's answer to this question is as follows. Basing oneself solely on the Word of God, one must explain as clearly as possible what Christian freedom ('this so necessary part of the teaching'[131]) amounts to, neither fearing the left-wing party of progressives nor the right-wing party of worried conservatives.

The development of this theme of the final chapter begins with these words:

'Christian freedom consists, at least in my view, of three parts.
First, the consciences of those who believe,
seeking justification before God,[132]
raise themselves above the law,
and do not count on the righteousness of the law.'[133]

Thus Calvin proceeds from what he already discussed in the second part of the first chapter, 'The Law', which is here summarized as follows:

'Therefore, as far as justification is concerned,
all mention of the law should be abandoned,
and every thought of works disregarded.
We should only embrace the mercy of God,
turning away from ourselves and looking upon Christ.
Justification is not about trying to become righteousness.
That would never do, since we are unrighteous and unworthy.
Rather, it is about how we may be regarded as righteous, even though we're not.[134]
In this, the law will not give our consciences any certainty.'[135]

Just as in the introduction of the book and in the second part of the first chapter, justification is directly followed by sanctification:

'However, one cannot conclude from this
that the law is superfluous for those who believe.
It does not cease to instruct them and urge them towards the good.
Yet, before God's judgment seat in our concience,[136]
there is no room for the law.
These are, after all, two very different things,
which we need to distinguish carefully.
In a sense, all of Christian life should be a meditation on piety,
since we are called to sanctification (Eph 1:4).
Here, the law has a function.
It urges us to the practice of holiness.
It tells us how we, being justified, should behave.
Yet if our consciences are worried as to how they should win God's favour,
and how they should be able to stand when judgment comes,
we should not subject ourselves to what the law demands.
Instead, we should look at Christ. He is our righteousness.
He exceeds every perfection of the law.'[137]

In his 1536 Catechism, Calvin is very much a student of Luther, but the distinctive features of his own thought are visible at the same. From the outset, his theology is characterized by the idea that justification and sanctification are on the one hand strictly distinct, but on the other hand indissolubly connected. This notion will receive its most elegant expression in the 1559 Institutes, where Calvin speaks about the *duplex gratia Christi* (twofold grace of Christ), which is bestowed on us by the hidden works of the spirit in faith.

Christian freedom, Calvin continues, leads to genuine obedience:

'The second part',

     – that is, of the three parts of Christian freedom mentioned earlier, FB –

'depends on the first.
Having been freed from the yoke of the law,
we no longer follow it out of compulsion, but voluntarily.
We wish to obey the will of God.'[138]

This freedom of genuine obedience, however, means freedom in the *res indifferentes* (the things which are not essential to salvation).[139]

'The third part consists of the following.
Living before the face of God
we are not bound to external things
which in themselves have no real importance.
It makes no difference whether we use them, or not.'[140]

The essence of Christian freedom ('the three parts of which Christian freedom consists') is summarized in one sentence. Once again we have to admire Calvin's transparent conciseness:[141]

	'We need to pay careful attention to the fact that Christian freedom is, in all of its parts, a spiritual matter. It gives peace to anxious consciences before the face of God,
Freedom from the curse of the law	1. when they are worried about the forgiveness of sins,
Freedom for genuine obedience	2. or fearful that their imperfect works, defiled by the flesh, might not please God,
Freedom in the *'Mitteldingen'*	3. or disturbed by questions concerning the use of things which do not really matter.'[142]

The sixth chapter consists of three parts. First the basis and essence of Christian freedom is discussed, under the heading of (1) *De libertate Christiana* (Christian freedom).[143] Then follows a discussion on the right way of putting this Christian freedom into practice. First in relation to ecclesiastical 'authority' (*regimen spirituale*, the spiritual realm), under the heading of (2) *De potestate ecclesiastica* (ecclesiastical power).[144] And then also with reference to worldly authority (*regimen politicum*, the political realm), under the heading of (3) *De politica administratione* (the political government).[145]

The *libertas Christiana* (Christian freedom), Calvin argues, is not something man possesses by virtue of his *liberum arbitrium* (free will). Nor does he take hold of it in a revolutionary manner. No, it is the gift which God's justifying and sanctifying grace bestows on man. It is the gift of the *misericordia Dei in Christo* (God's mercy in Christ).[146]

For a better understanding of the entire booklet, we must point to the way Calvin repeatedly uses the concept of *conscientia* (conscience) in the final chapter. In the cited sentences from the last chapter we often came across this term. In the original text, all these passages have a plural (*conscientiae* – see above all the last citation, which expresses the entire theme of this last chapter). In the previous chapters we met this word at significant points as well.

(1) In the introduction, we read that the the law which the Lord has written on our hearts 'is in truth nothing but the conscience, which is the internal witness in us of the things that we owe to God. It shows us what is good and what is evil, it accuses us and considers us guilty when we have not fulfilled our duty in an appropriate manner.'[147]

(2) In the second part of the first chapter, there is mention of freedom from the curse of the law: 'Thus, the entire human race is accused by the law, subjected to the curse and the wrath of God. To be released from this curse, it is necessary for us to be pulled away from the power of the law and as it were solemnly to be declared no longer to belong to slavery but to freedom. Not the freedom of the flesh, to be sure, which keeps us from observing the law, inviting us to lawlessness in all things, and allowing us to be swept away by our desires, but a spiritual freedom, which raises up our frightened conscience, telling us that we are no longer under the curse and damna-

tion of the law. We obtain this liberation from the law, this freeing from slavery, when by faith we grasp the mercy of God in Christ. Then we can be assured that our sins are forgiven, and we are no longer held captive to the law.'[148]

(3) When there was mention of the 'threefold use of the law', Calvin wrote: 'Put briefly, those who believe are encouraged by the law, not to bind their conscience with the curse, but to shake off their lethargy, and to tear off their incompleteness. Indeed many have said that to be liberated from the curse of the law means that the law is abolished for those who believe; not because it does not contain any indications for them as to what is right, but because it is no longer for them what it used to be. That is, it no longer confuses their consciences or terrifies them by the announcement of death. It no longer causes us to be lost and damned.'[149]

(4) In the second chapter it was said that those who believe 'receive this forgiveness, when they, touched by their conscience and pressed by their sins, pained and confused, are dismayed by the prospect of divine judgment...';[150]

(5) In the fifth chapter there is mention of what the sacrament accomplishes. 'A sacrament aims to raise up and comfort the consciences of believers...'.[151]

By repeating time and again this word 'conscience' in the beginning section of the final chapter, 'Christian freedom', Calvin makes abundantly clear what the 'essence of evangelical doctrine' is really all about. In 1536, Calvin's main concern is 'to raise up, comfort and bring peace to downtrodden and anxious consciences, brought into confusion (by the law)' with the gospel of 'God's mercy in Christ'.

In most passages we hear the plural *conscientiae*. While writing his *Institutes* Calvin is consistently concerned with 'consciences'. It is clear that he is writng a pastoral dogmatics. This pastoral character is expressed in an inward as well as outward movement. Calvin not only as an exegete of Scriptures points to God's way, he also wards off everything which from the outside might drive his flock (his fellow believers in France) from this path.[152]

The memoir of King Francis I was what moved Calvin in 1535 to complete his four-chapter *catechism* with the two long final chapters 'The false sacraments' and 'Christian freedom'. This was prefaced by a 'Foreword to the most Christian King of France, to which this book is dedicated as a confession of faith'.

We will see the same thing happening when we look at the subsequent editions of the *Institutes*. The battle Calvin had to fight is reflected in the different phases of this book. He is a *homo unius libri*, a man of one book; indeed he is the man of *this* one book. Everything he says and writes in his sermons, commentaries, letters and treatises, is done against the background of this book.

Calvin's battle, however, is not what we have set out to explore in this study. It is our task to describe the structure of his theology, basing ourselves on the composition of his *Institutes*. And that is why we are discussing the original structure of his theology, first the one of 1536, then the one of 1539, and finally the edition of 1558/59.

§4. THE STRUCTURE OF CALVINIAN THEOLOGY IN THE *INSTITUTES* OF 1536

In order to get an idea of the original structure of Calvin's theology, we began our study with a detailed commentary on the introduction of the *Institutio* of 1536, the knowledge of God – the knowledge of man / the Law – Faith – Prayer. From the perspective of the introduction we obtained a good overview of the entire book, first the four catechetical chapters, 'The Law' – 'Faith' – 'Prayer' – 'The Sacraments', and then the two extensive closing chapters, 'The False Sacraments' – 'Christian Freedom'. These chapters turned the catechism into a *professio fidei* (account of faith).

We saw that the 'mercy of God in Christ' is the central concept of the *Institutes*.[153] Indeed, the entire doctrine is dominated by a very strong Christological concentration. Even the first chapter, 'the Law', is written from the vantage point of God's mercy in Jesus Christ. However, in this chapter the content of the law is identical to the 'law of nature'. This raises the question: To what extent and in which way did the Christological focus determine the contents and particularly the structure of the 1536 edition? There is a short section in the first chapter which can answer this question. Before turning to this section, let us remind ourselves of the conclusions we drew from our discussion of the first chapter.

We saw that the first chapter consists of two parts. In the first Calvin aimed to demonstrate that all men, as long as they are under the law, are under the curse. 'This is what Paul says: all who are under the law, are under the curse.'[154] In the second part of this chapter Calvin described the way man is liberated from the law and its curse, and what this liberated life looks like.

In the first part Calvin said that the law leads us *Domini misericordiam quaerere* (to seek the mercy of God).[155] However, we also saw that this 'accusing function', as it was later called, is not the only function of the law. In the second part Calvin describes the 'threefold use of the law'. At the end of this discussion we heard Calvin say:

'Just so, approached from the opposite side,
justification should be cut loose from good works.
This is not to stop us from doing good works, or to deny them,
but to prevent us from relying on our works
and taking pride in them;
we ought not expect salvation from our works.
Rather, we should believe that Christ, the Son of God, is ours.
He has been given to us,
so that we may be in Him and become children of God,
heirs to the kingdom of heaven (Isa 9:6; 1 Thes 4:14),
called by God's benevolent grace and not by our own efforts
to the hope of eternal salvation.
However, we are called, not to uncleanness and unrighteousness,
but to be clean and unspotted before our God, in love (Eph 1:4).'[156]

As we saw, the first chapter is rounded of with a discussion on the *bona opera* (good works) and their reward. In it, Calvin strongly underlines the last quotation.

Let us now turn toward the section I mentioned above. In this passage Calvin strongly expresses the way in which the Christological concentration came to determine his entire theology:[157]

'Haec si quo oportuerat ordine tractata digestaque essent anteactis saeculis, nunquam tantum turbarum ac dissensionum ortum esset.

Paulus ait (1 Cor. 3),
in architectura Christianae doctrinae
retinendum fundamentum, quod posuit,
et praeter quod nullum aliud poni potest,
quod est Jesus Christus.

Quale autem istud est fundamentum?

An quod Jesus Christus initium fuit nostrae salutis
et quod viam nobis aperuit, cum nobis meruit occasionem merendi?

Minime.

Sed quod in eo electi ab aeterno sumus ante mundi constitutionem,
  nullo nostro merito,
   sed secundum propositum beneplaciti Dei,
quod eius morte ipsi a mortis damnatione redempti ac liberati a perditione sumus,
quod in ipso adoptati a patre sumus, in filios et haeredes,
quod per ipsius sanguinem patri reconciliati,
quod illi a patre in custodiam dati sumus ne unquam pereamus aut excidamus,
quod ita illi inserti iam vitae aeternae quodammodo sumus participes, in regnum Dei per spem ingressi (Eph. 1. Rom. 9. 2 Tim. 1. Ioan. 1. Eph. 1.3. Rom. 5.8. 2 Cor. 5. Ioan. 10.17).

Hoc parum est:
quod *talem eius participationem adepti,*
  ut simus adhuc in nobis stulti,
   ipse nobis coram Deo sapientia est;
  ut peccatores simus,
   ipse est nobis *iustitia*;
  ut immundi simus,
   ipse est nobis *sanctificatio*
  ut infirmi simus, ut inermes et satanae expositi,
   ipsi tamen data est potestas in coelo et in terra,
  ut pro nobis satanam conterat et inferorum portas confringat;
  ut corpus mortis adhuc nobiscum circumferamus,
   ipse tamen nobis vita est. (1 Cor.1. Matth.ult. Col. 1.3. Rom. 8. Eph. 2.4).

Breviter,
quod omnia illius nostra sunt et nos in eo omnia, in nobis nihil.

Super hoc fundamentum aedificari nos convenit,
si voluimus crescere in templum sanctum Domino.'

TRANSLATION:

'If in previous centuries these things had been presented in the right order,
there would never have been such confusion and disunity.

In 1 Cor 3:11 Paul says
that the foundation of Christian doctrine
can never be replaced by something else.
This foundation is Jesus Christ.

What kind of foundation is that?
Is it that Jesus Christ was merely the beginning of our salvation,
and by His merit opened the way for us to acquire merit on our own?

Certainly not!

Rather, it means that in Him we are chosen in eternity,
even before the foundation of the world,
without any merit of our own,
because it pleased God

that   by His death we are saved from the judgment of death and ruin,

that   in Him we are adopted as children and heirs of the Father,

that   by His blood we are reconciled to the Father,

that   to His care the Father has given us, so that we will never be lost or perish,

that,   incorporated in Him, we have somehow been given eternal life already,
       and have already entered the kingdom of God through hope
          (Eph 1:4; Rom. 9; 2 Tim 1:9; John 1:12; Eph 1:7; Eph 3:15; Rom 5:2; Rom
          8:17; 2 Cor 5:19; John 10:28; John 17:12).

However, this is not all. It also pleased God

that   we have gained such a close *communion* with Him that
       though we are foolish in ourselves,
         He is our wisdom before the face of God;
       though we are sinners,
         He is our *righteousness*;
       though we are unclean,
         He is our *sanctification*;
       though we are weak and defenseless and delivered to diabolic violence,
         to Him all power is given in heaven and on earth,
         so that He can crush Satan for us and demolish the gates of hell;
       though we carry the body of death with us,
         He is our life
         (1 Cor 1:30; Mat 28:18; Col 1:22; Col 3:4; Rom. 8; Eph 2:14; Eph 4:24).

Put briefly:
That   all His possessions are ours. In Him we have everything, in ourselves nothing.

It is fitting that we should be built on this foundation,
if we wish to grow into a holy temple for the Lord.'

When Calvin says that according to Paul, Jesus is the foundation of Christian doctrine, he asks the question: 'What kind of foundation is that?' Of course, all Christian theologians would agree that Jesus Christ is the foundation of Christian teaching. However, the question 'in what way' needs to be answered. The answer theologians 'in previous centuries' gave to this question, is expressed by Calvin in a question.

'Is it that Jesus Christ was merely the beginning of our salvation,
and by His merit opened the way for us to acquire merit on our own?'

Is Jesus Christ the foundation of Christian doctrine in this way? Calvin answers: *minime!* Certainly not. But then, how else should we understand it? In what follows, we hear the answer the reformers posited in lieu of the old answer of medieval scholastic theology. The answer comes in six clauses, all of which begin with 'that'.

Jesus Christ as the foundation of Christian teaching means (1) that we are chosen in him; (2) that we by his death are redeemed from the judgment of death; (3) that in him we are adopted by the Father as sons and heirs; (4) that we are reconciled to the Father by his blood; (5) that the Father has given us in his protection; and (6) that in him we are partakers of eternal life. The sixh clause sums up the entire line of reasoning.

The words 'however, this is not all' temporarily interrupt the progress of the clauses beginning with 'that' to prepare us for the following climax. The seventh clause beginning with 'that' is: 'that we have gained such a close communion with Him that'. In this clause, Calvin repeatedly opposes the words 'though we are (…)' to 'He is'. He does this so as to make it as clear as possible that our salvation lies in Christ. As the apostle Paul puts it in 1 Cor 1:30: 'Christ has become for us God's wisdom, righteousness, sanctification and redemption'. Calvin had this text constantly in mind when he wrote the *Institutes* of 1536.

While the words 'however, this is not all' prepare us for the surprising accentuation which follows, the words 'we have gained such a close communion with Him that' point back to what was said in the six previous clauses beginning with 'that'. After the fivefold 'though we are – He is', the eighth and last clause beginning with 'that' summarizes the entire argument.[158]

'Put briefly:
That all his possessions are ours. In him we have everything, in ourselves nothing.
It is fitting that we should be built on this foundation,
if we wish to grow into a holy temple for the Lord'.

We have seen how Calvin in the entire book constantly underlines the words 'everything' and 'nothing' – 'we in Him *everything*, in ourselves *nothing*' – and 'in Him' and 'in ourselves' – 'everything in *Him*, nothing in *ourselves*'. With this the thought that Christ 'by His merit opened the way for us to acquire merit on our own' is radically rejected in any form.

The paragraph discussed above forms the introduction to the discussion of 'the good works' and their 'merit' with which Calvin closes the first chapter 'the Law'. We can see the underlying principle of this discussion in the following words:

'We do not say that man is justified because of his works before the face of God. To the contrary, we hold that every-one who belongs to God is reborn and becomes a new creation.' [159]

Our opponents lie when they claim that we have a low esteem of 'good works', Calvin says. It is not that we have a low esteem of good works, but that they have a low esteem of God's grace, the blood of Christ and the forgiveness of sins. To Calvin, *sanctificatio / regeneratio / renovatio* (sanctification / rebirth / renewal) are indissolubly linked to *iustificatio* (justification). Moreover, *iustificatio impii* (justification of the godless) excludes any thought of *meritum* (merit): 'whoever uses the word "merit" is insulting God', Calvin says at the conclusion of 'The Law'.[160] Note that at the beginning of the paragraph we discuss above Calvin does not say:

'If in previous centuries these things had been presented
there would never have been such confusion and disunity.'

He said:

'If in previous centuries these things had been presented *in the right order*
there would never have been such confusion and disunity'.

By 'order' in the sense of *ordo docendi* (order of instruction) Calvin means: the way the separate parts are arranged so that their function within the whole of the 'sacred doctrine' becomes apparent. In every new edition of the *Institutes* we can see how Calvin was preoccupied with the question concerning the right 'order of instruction'.[161] He is deeply convinced of the importance of what Karl Barth called 'the theological method demanded by the Holy Scriptures'. Thinking and speaking in obedience to the Bible, Barth asserted, resists all selfmade theology. 'A particular ontological order (...) calls for a corresponding epistemological order.'[162]

Calvin uses the word 'order' not only in the sense of epistemological order (= 'order of instruction'), but also in the sense of ontological order. For example, exlaining the words of the creed 'we believe in the forgiveness of sins' in the second chapter, he says:

'This is the order in which God has deemed it right to show himself to man: he must put aside all pride by acknowledging his poverty. Only by rejecting himself completely and esteeming himself to be totally worthless, will he begin to taste the sweetness of God's mercy in Christ.'[163]

This 'ontological order' of divine and human activity was expressed as follows in the introduction:

'After we have sunk into humiliation and subjugation, the Lord will make His face shine upon us, and show himself to be accommodating, obliging, merciful, and mild.'[164]

In the final sentence of the introduction, Calvin shows how this 'ontological order' calls for a corresponding 'epistemological order'. Or to put it differently: how the order of divine and human interaction is reflected in Calvin's own 'order of instruction'.

In this sentence Calvin gives a summary of the entire 'sacred teaching'.

'And because

The law	1.	this knowledge of our need, indeed our misery, by which we are taught to humble ourselves, to cast ourselves down before God's face and to seek His mercy,
Faith	2.	and also this faith, which gives us a foretaste of the divine goodness and mercy, offered to us in Christ, his Anointed One – indeed, because these do not come from out of ourselves, nor do they lie in our power,
Prayer	3.	therefore we need to ask God himself to lead us to such knowledge of ourselves by unfeigned repentance and by a firm trust. We also need to ask Him to lead us to the knowledge of His benevolence, the sweetness which He shows us in His Anointed One, so that we may be led to eternal bliss with Him as our guide. He is the only way to the Father.' [165]

We saw how Calvin at the beginning of the third chapter, 'Prayer' – reminding us of this final sentence of the Introduction – once more presents this 'order of instruction'.[166]

According to Calvin, the essence of prayer consists in praying for the right knowledge of ourselves and the right knowledge of God by means of 'law and gospel'. All of our salvation lies in 'Christ alone'. It is 'by faith alone' that we become partakers of this salvation.

In sum, the 'order of instruction' in the *Institutes* of 1536 is law and then gospel. This order functions as the frame within which Calvin's teaching concerning salvation in Christ is unfolded. So even though Calvin take great pains to show that all salvation is contained in Christ alone,[167] and that he alone is the *fundamentum sacrae doctrinae* (foundation of the sacred doctrine), this salvation is nevertheless discussed within the framework of law – gospel.

This will prove to have fatal consequences, already in Calvin's theology (for example in his exegesis), but even stronger in the development of his theology during the period of 'orthodoxy'.

Those who with Karl Barth say 'no' against the age-old 'nature and grace' (as old as the church since the second century), will likewise with Karl Barth have to reverse the 'order' of law and gospel, which was deemed to be irreversible. They will have to speak of gospel and law instead.[168] Such a theologian will not only, like the reformers, interpret the Tanakh from the perspective of Paul's letters. They will do the reverse as well, and interpret Paul from the persepective of the Tanakh. Barth has tried to do this in the twentieth century.

However, if one wishes to maintain Calvin's order of law – gospel (even if it is in conflict with the basic structure of the Tanakh), one will be forced to discuss the relationship between 'nature and grace', with all the ensuing consequences.

It goes without saying that these apodictic pronouncements do not suffice. They are only intended to alert the readers to the problems which in our opinion are at stake here. For the moment, we need to continue our exploration of Calvin's *Institutes* in the next three chapters in order to see how Calvin constantly struggled with the problem of the right 'order of instruction', until in 1559 he could write the following remark in the Word to the Reader:

'Although I did not regret the labor which I dedicated to this work' – namely from 1539 to 1554, FB – 'I was never satisfied, until I arrived at the order and arrangement in which the *Institutes* are presently offered. I now trust to have given it a form you will all agree with.'[169]

Calvin asks for our approval. Or rather, he counts on it. In the following chapters we will see to what extent we can give it, or not.

NOTES

1. Karl Barth, 'Die Kirche und die Kirchen', *Th.E.h.*, Heft 28, in an 'appendix' on 'Gott erkennen, Gott ehren, Gott vertrauen nach Calvins Katechismus' (Protocol of a team of the Ecumenical Seminar, held in Geneva in July 1935, on the beginning of Calvin's Catechism).

2. OS I, 37.

3. OS I, 223.

4. M. Luther, *Betbüchlein*, WA (*D. Martin Luthers Werke. Kritische Gesamtausgabe*. Weimarer Ausgabe) 10^2, 331-501. Cf. also 'Eine kurze Form der zehn Gebote, eine kurze Form des Glaubens, eine kurze Form des Vaterunsers' (1520), WA 7, 195-229.

5. The Latin translation of Luther's *Betbüchlein* had as its title *Enchiridion piarum precationum*. Cf. WA 10^2, 343 and 361 (sub *m*). Calvin must have known this little Latin book.

6. OS I, 37-41 l. 23.

7. WA 10^2, 376 ll. 11-377 ll. 13. Cf. WA 7, 204-205.

8. The pair of concepts *Morbus et medicina* may already be found in Augustine, *De doctrina Christiana* I.XIV.13. For a comparison of 'Law and Grace' with 'sickness and medicine' (*Morbus et Remedium*) see also Luther's sermon on Matthew 15:21-28 on Sunday Reminiscere 1525 (WA 17^2, 201 ll. 8ff.) and *De servo arbitrio* (WA 18, 766). Cf. further in this study in Chapter V, note 12 (Melanchthon, *Loci Communes* 1521), 41 (Johann Gerhard, *Loci Theologici* 1610-1622) and 49 (the Leiden *Synopsis purioris Theologiae* 1625).

9. OS I, 37-39, l. 7.

10. OS I, 37, ll. 2-23.

11. Italics are, unless indicated otherwise, added to Calvin's text.

12. By an *aberratio oculi*, eight words have dropped out in the edition of Barth-Niesel: 'deberi, ut singula pro naturae suae ratione illi.' These erroneously deleted words should be inserted.

13. See in our study on the structure of the biblical theology the description of 'Being in the Act as a being in the *sedaqa*,' F. H. Breukelman, *Biblische Theologie II. Debharim. Der biblische*

Wirklichtkeitsbegriffs des Seins in der Tat. Kampen, 1998, Chap. 4, §4, 88-168. Compare: 'Righteousness contains a brilliance in the Bible, not of a sharp judgment, but of goodness, of mildness, of victorious power, which disentangles things, which softens what is rigid and which reveals the hidden essential beauty of things. Righteousness in the Bible is more or less identical with grace; indeed, it is not the same, but not a contrast either.... No, it is the necessary reverse of it.' K. H. Miskotte, *In de Waagschaal. A selection of articles of the first five years*, Verzameld Werk I. Kampen, 1982 (40-43) 41.

14. Cf. OS I, 69, ll. 18-19, the beginning of the chapter 'Faith': forgiveness of sins, sanctification, salvation.

15. Inst. 1539: VI = Inst. 1554: X.1 = Inst. 1559: III.11.1; OS IV, 182 ll. 4-5.

16. See also *Breukelman*, Debharim, Chap. 5, 'Being in the Act as a Being in Faithfulness'.

17. We may contrast Luther's famous preface in the publication of his Latin writings of 1545, where he expresses the kernel of his Reformational discovery. Paul's concept of 'justice' which he originally hated became the concept that he came to love the most. WA 54, 185 ll. 14–186 l. 16.

18. OS I, 37 ll. 24–39, l. 7

19. OS I, 86-96. Already 86 l.11 in the description of the ecclesia.

20. Cf. the views of Barth in KD III.2 §45, 'Der Mensch in seiner Bestimmung zu Gottes Bundesgenossen' (Man in His Determiniation as the Covenant Partner of God), against the background of Barth's exegesis of Gen 1:26, cf. KD III.1, 204-231.

21. The expressions *status integritatis* and *status corruptionis* are not used by Calvin himself.

22. See above, note 11, the first statement that Calvin made about God.

23. See OS I, 56 ll.40-42 and 67 ll.11-12.

24. Cf. *Institutes* of 1559, chapter I.15 (OS III, 173ff). See below, Chapter V §2.II.

25. OS I, 55ff, resp. 56 ll. 46–57 l. 1 and 56 ll. 39-40.

26. Note that Calvin often used the language of the jurist.

27. OS I, 39 l. 7 until 41 l. 23.

28. OS I, 39 l. 7 until 40 l. 16

29. See Barth's brochure 'Evangelium und Gesetz' (1935) and further the entire KD volume II/2.

30. Cf. Barth, KD IV.1 §60.1, 'Der Mensch der Sünde im *Spiegel des Gehorsams des Sohnes Gottes*' (The Man of Sin in the Light of the Obedience of the Son of God).

31. See below, the citation of n. 39.

32. See above, 'About the knowledge of God': 3.

33. See Inst. 1559 III. 6.1. At the beginning of his treatise concerning the Christian life in the final edition of his Institutes (in connection with the tractate on the rebirth or sanctification), Calvin speaks of a *symmetria* and a *consensus* between the righteousness of God and the obedience of man.

34. OS I, 41-53.

35. OS I, 53-58.

36. OS I, 56 l. 5. See note 70.

37. OS I, 58, ll. 31-61.

38. OS I, 58 ll. 32-44.

39. OS I 39 ll. 42-45. Cf. Joh. Wollebius, *Christianae Theologiae Compendium*, Basiliae 1626 (re-issued by Ernst Bizer, Neukirchen 1935), Caput XIII §1, Canon I: 'The divine law which was handed down by Moses differs from the law of nature which was planted into the first man, and of which the remnants can still be seen with the pagans, not according to the substance but according to our understanding of it.'

40. Cf. Inst. 1559: II.6.I, OS III, 321 l. I. See Chapter V §1.1.

41. Inst. 1554: Chap. III.1-4.

42. Inst. 1559: II.8.1-3; see OS III, 343-345.

43. See above, Introduction §2.
44. Cf. Joh. Wollebius, o.c. Caput XIII, §1 (colometry by FB):
    '3. The Redeemer is known from the Law and from the Gospel;
        from the Law, the necessity of redemption,
        but from the Gospel, the truth of it.
     4. The Law is the teaching by which God
        under threat of eternal death
        and with the promise of eternal life,
        shows what He wants us to do
        so that we, where we feel incompetent to do His bidding,
        will be obliged to seek Christ.'
45. OS I, 60 ll.11-13 in the discussion of the doctrine of justification.
46. See above at the conclusion of the first quote from §2.1.2.
47. OS I, 92 ll. 34-38.
48. Melanchthon, *Loci communes* 1521. See below, Chapter II, n. 165.
49. OS I, 37 ll. 17-23. See above, n. 15.
50. OS I. 60 ll. 36-61 l. 8; here also he says again: 'First...subsequently'.
51. OS I, 40 l. 21 until 41 l. 12.
52. OS I, 78 ll. 10-12; cf. Inst. 1559; II.12.1, OS III, 437 ll. 15-17.
53. OS I, 68 ll. 36-70 l. 31.
54. Cf. above, at the conclusion of the first citation from §2.1.2: 'Adam has lost all goods of divine grace, that might have led him on the way of life'.
55. OS I, 41 ll. 12-23.
56. See above, note 44.
57. The Introduction to the *Institutes* of 1536 which we have discussed, is summarized by Paul Wernle in five pages (Wernle, op. cit., 3-7). He claims that in the 'Einleitung' and in the 'Anhang' of chapter 1 *De Lege* we have to do with 'probably two essays of Calvin written at a different time.' After his summary he writes (p. 8): 'One is surprised, at the climax of this book, before the discussion of the decalogue, to meet with such a summary of the essence of Christendom (cf. Feuerbach and Harnack, FB.) which in a brief space omits no central point. Calvin as a Christian thinker does not endure tarrying with the law as an independent entity; he rushes hastily forward to Christ and to salvation and interprets the law as the pedagogue to Christ, the Savior. That shows that he does not know another but a moral redemption. Forgiveness of sins and a new heart with a new power for good, both always together in the closest relation – that is for him the meaning of the coming of Christ in the world.' On the basis of our analysis of the text it should be noted concerning these words of Wernle that the tendency of Calvin's Introduction is not, as Wernle claims, that Calvin as a Christian thinker simply cannot tolerate remaining with the law as an independent entity, and therefore rapidly rushes to Christ and salvation. The meaning of the Introduction must be indicated as showing the *ordo docendi* (order of instruction) in advance.
58. OS I, 41 l. 24.
59. See the preface to the commentary on Romans (1540), 'Johannes Calvinus Simoni Grynaeo', CO X, (402-406) 402 infra.
60. 'Series docendi': Inst. 1554: Chap. II.4; Inst. 1559: II.1.3, OS III, 231 l. 13.
61. OS I, 37-68; CO I col. 27-55.
62. OS I, 41 ll. 24–58 l. 30 and 58 ll. 31–68 l. 15.
63. OS I, 41 ll. 14–58 l. 30.
64. OS I, 41-53.
65. Wernle, op. cit. 8f. Luther: 'We should fear and love God, so that...not...(debemus Deum timere et diligere, ne...).' See *Die Bekenntnisschriften der evangelisch-lutherischen Kirche,*

¹Göttingen 1930, 507ff. Calvin, loc. cit.: 'Quandoquidem timeri Deum a nobis atque amari oportet, ne...' ('since we should fear and love God, we may not...').

66. OS I, 54 ll. 6-39.

67. OS I, 54 ll. 40–55 l. 35.

68. OS I, 55 ll. 36–58 l. 30.

69. OS I, 40 ll. 4-5: 'that all are ultimately worthy of the curse, the judgment, eternal death.' See above §2.2.

70. OS I, 58 ll. 31–68 l. 15.

71. OS I, 58 ll. 31-44.

72. In the original text, Calvin uses the word 'bit'. Compare this with Luther's translation of Job 27:6: 'Of my righteousness which I have / I will not let go / My conscience does not bite me for any of my days.'

73. Tjarko Stadtland says in his much too short text concerning 'Die Stellung von Rechtfertigung und Heiligung in den verschiedenen Ausgaben der Institutio': 'In the first edition of the Institutes of 1536 the Lutheran...doctrine of justification pervades all of Calvin's work.' – That is correct, FB – 'It has no particular place.' – That is incorrect, FB – 'It does, however, has a small space within this work (therefore, the many repetitions).' – That is incorrect; see chapter II of this work, in the schema with paragraphs 16-19 of the Catechismus of 1537, the arrows, FB – 'This undoubtedly relates to the fact that the *Institutes* of 1536 follows the Apostles' Creed much closer than the 1559 edition' (T. Stadtland, *Rechtfertigung und Heiligung bei Calvin*. Neukirchen-Vluyn, 1972, 109). The last sentence shows that Stadtland lacks insight in the genesis of the *Institutes*.

74. OS I, 59 ll. 1–61 l. 31.

75. OS I, 61 ll. 32–63 l. 14.

76. *The Heidelberg Catechism*, Q. 62.

77. OS I, 68 ll. 4-7.

78. OS I, 63 ll. 15–68, l. 15.

79. Thomas Aquinas, *Summa theologica*, 'pars secunda', according to the brief description of the content at the beginning of S. Th. I Q. 2.

80. S. Th. Ia IIae Q. 113: de effectibus gratiae (concerning the working of grace, that is concerning justification); Q. 114: de merito, quod est effectus gratiae cooperantis (concerning merit, which is a work of cooperative grace).

81. OS I, 68-96; CO I col. 56-81.

82. See the beginning of the second main part of 'The Law', above.

83. OS I, 68 ll. 20-35.

84. OS I, 68 ll. 36-70. See in Luther's *Betbüchlein* the beginning of the part 'Der Glaube' (op. cit., WA 7, 215): 'Here may be noted / the two kinds of faith...'.

85. Cf. Buber, *Two Types of Faith*.

86. OS I, 69 ll. 7-14.

87. In 1543 at the conclusion of V.6; in 1559 at the conclusion of III,2.7; OS IV, 16 ll. 32-35.

88. OS I, 69 ll. 31-32.

89. OS I, 70 ll. 17-21.

90. OS I, 70 ll. 25-31.

91. OS I, 70 ll. 32–75, l. 36.

92. See what Karl Barth says concerning the *novitas verborum* which *he* introduced ('das Nichtige', 'die unmögliche Möglichkeit', 'die ontologische Unmöglichkeit') in his conversation with Berkouwer in §60.3 ('Jesus ist Sieger!') of the Kirchliche Dogmatik, KD IV.3 (198-206) 203, CD IV.3 (173-180) 177.

93. OS I, 74 ll. 8-14.

94. OS I, 75 ll. 37-93 below.

95. OS I, 93 ll. 42–94, l. 2.
96. OS I, 93 below – 96.
97. Cf. the second *haec omnia* from the passage n the Introduction (§2.3), which announces the chapter 'Faith.'
98. OS I, 86-91, l. 16, l. 29.
99. See K. Barth, KD II.2, §32.3, 'Die Stellung der Erwählungslehre in der Dogmatik' (The Place of the Doctrine in Dogmatics).
100. OS I, 96-117; CO I, col. 81 to 101.
101. For this *quaerere* (to seek) see above, n. 44 'another way of salvation must be sought' and n. 56: 'and to seek for His mercy.'
102. OS I, 96 ll. 9-35.
103. See above, n. 85.
104. See above, n. 55.
105. OS I, 97-104.
106. OS I, 104-117.
107. OS I, 118-162; CO I, col. 102-140. According to the table of contents, OS I, 20, the complete title of this chapter is: 'The Sacraments. In which Baptism and the Lord's Supper are discussed.'
108. OS I, 118 ll. 3-19.
109. With 'both ... and' Calvin indicates how this chapter is organized. First he discusses what the sacrament is and how it is organized (OS I, 118, ll. 6-124, l. 17) and then follows a discussion how we are to use them, first *generaliter* (in general), OS I, 124 l. 18, and then (OS I, 125 l. 19) *particulariter* (in particular), of both sacraments instituted by the Lord: Baptism (OS I, 127, ll. 4-136, l. 35) and the Lord's Supper (OS I, 139 ll. 36-162).
110. Cf. the *Heidelberg Catechism*, Q. 22, 21.
111. See above, n. 86.
112. Cf. also the later *definitio*, namely the one of 1543 (Inst. 1554: XVI.1) in the *Institutes* 1559: IV.14.1 (OS V, 259 ll. 3-8 + 8-10).
113. OS I, 119 l. 25. Calvin treats as images for the sacraments successively *sigilla* (seals), *exercitia* (exercises), *columnae* (pillars) and *specula* (mirrors).
114. OS I, 162-223; CO I col. 141-195.
115. Counting the number of pages in OS I, deducting the Introduction of ca. 4 pages.
116. OS I, 36 ll. 19.
117. This the title page, OS I, 19.
118. CO 31 (13-26) 23-24.
119. OS I, 162 ll. 13–163, l. 8.
120. Compare with this *sigillum* (seal) above, in the beginning citation of Chapter IV *signum* (sign).
121. See above, n. 108.
122. For more on the 'doctrine of the Word of God' with Calvin, see below, Chapter III §3-c.
123. OS I, 169-202.
124. Cf. KD IV.2 §66.3 'Die Ruf in die Nachfolge' (The Call to Discipleship), §66.4 'Die Erweckung zur Umkehr' (The Awakening to Conversion).
125. Luther's very radical *Disputatio contra scholasticam theologiam* (against the scholastic theology) of Sept. 4, 1517, did not bring this about (WA 1, 224-228), but his *Disputatio pro declaratione virtutis indulgentiarum* (for announcement of the power of the indulgences) of Oct. 31, 1517 (WA 1, 233-238).
126. OS I, 223-280; CO I, col. 195-248.
127. OS I, 223 ll. 15-22.
128. See above: the discussion of the second main part of the second chapter.

129. Calvin expressed himself in the same way in the discussion on the doctrine of justification (OS I, 59 ll. 32-36): 'Believing is after all not to be drifting about, to be internally divided, letting oneself be led up and down, wavering, leaving undecided, finally despairing, but it is: strengthening the soul with a steadfast certainty and a firm realization of safety and having a place where you can rest and where your foot also finds a resting place.'

130. OS I, 223 ll. 22-30.

131. OS I, 224 ll. 2-3: adeo necessaria doctrinae pars.

132. For this *quaerere* (seek) see above, notes 44, 56 and 101.

133. OS I, 224 ll. 5-9.

134. See how K. Barth, concerning this *simul iustis et peccator* (simultaneously justified and sinner), answers the question, to what extent such justification 'is not a nominalist "as if".' KD IV.1, 576-577 (CD IV.1, 517).

135. OS I, 224 ll. 15-21.

136. See *Dei tribunal*, likewise OS I, 58 l. 21.

137. OS I, 224 ll. 21-35

138. OS I, 225 ll. 3-226 l. 29: *altera pars*; the cited sentence in 225 ll. 3-5.

139. Otto Weber translates the expression in his German translation (Inst. 1559, III.19.7) as 'die Mitteldinge.'

140. OS I, 226 ll. 30-227 l. 44: *tertia pars*; the cited sentence in 226 ll. 30-32.

141. See above, n. 59.

142. OS I, 227 ll. 45-228 l. 6.

143. OS I, 223-232. In 1559 (III.19) Calvin will close the doctrine of justification with this section as a separate chapter with the same heading.

144. OS I, 232-258.

145. OS I, 258-280.

146. Cf. Karl Barth's lecture 'Das Geschenk der Freiheit. Grundlegung evangelischer Ethik' (1953), *Theologische Studien*, Heft 39.

147. See above, n. 28.

148. See above, n. 70.

149. See above, n. 74. In this sentence we hear the word first in the singular and then in the plural.

150. OS I, 92, ll. 25-27.

151. See above, the conclusion of the series of citations under n. 119.

152. Karl Holl spoke of Luther's religion as a 'religion of conscience.' See: 'Was verstand Luther under Religion?' (1917); in '*Gesammelte Aufsätze zur Kirchengeschichte*, Band I. Luther, Tübingen, ⁴1927, 35-110. In his inaugural lecture in the aula of the Berlin University on July 31, 1930, on 'Die Frage nach dem Menschen in der gegenwärtigen Philosophy und Theologie' (published in: *Dietrich Bonhoeffer Werke*, Band 10, Munich 1991, 357-378) Bonhoeffer writes (pp. 369-370): 'Man understands himself from the reflection of himself, on his possibilities. If man can only understand himself in context with the transcendent, here with God, then God must somehow reveal himself, otherwise he would not have any relationship to God. The place, where God testifies to himself, must be the place from which man understands himself and where the unity of man is founded. This place, however, is obviously the conscience. Here man knows himself called, drawn toward responsibility, judged and suitably addressed. Here is God's gateway to man, here is given the direct relationship to God. Man is the man of conscience. He understands himself out of the reflection on his conscience, in which he encounters God. When we hear the name of Karl Holl, we have named an impressive representative of the overwhelming majority of contemporary theologians.' (With the addition, likely not said by Bonhoeffer): 'Holl has called Luther's religion a religion of conscience. Coupled with this, as will shortly be noted, went a remarkably small evaluation of Christology with Luther. Man finds God somehow in himself, God exists in his reflection of

himself. Because man can hear God in his conscience and have him, he therefore understands him out of his conscience as his own possibility to be man' (end of the note). 'Yet, Holl experienced here the most vivid contradiction by the so-called dialectical theology...'.

153. See above, n. 16, above n. 27, ad notes 38, 47, above notes 56, 72, ad n. 82, above n. 134.

154. See above, notes 36, 70.

155. See above, n. 55.

156. See above, below n. 75.

157. OS I, 63 ll. 15-44.

158. Comparable to Luther's *simul peccator et iustus* (both sinner and righteous). M. Luther, *Vorlesung über den Römerbrief 1515-16,* herausgegeben von Johannes Ficker (Zwei Teile), Leipzig 1908 (WA 56, 222-304), Teil II, 108 r. 12 (WA 56, 272) en 176 r. 12 (scholia bij resp. Rom. 4:7 en Rom. 7:25).

159. OS I, 64 ll. 30-32. Cf. Luther, 'Von den Konziliis und Kirchen' (1539), WA 50 (509-563), 599-600.

160. OS I, 68 ll. 4-5. See above, n. 77.

161. See the following five passages; 1. OS III, 5 ll. 14-15: Joannes Calvinus ad Lectorem, passage of 1539; 2. OS III, 6 ll. 21-21: Johannes Calvinus Lectori, passage of 1559 (both of these passages are discussed above in §2 of the Introduction); 3. OS III, 34 l. 2: Inst. 1559 I.1.3 final sentence (this passage of 1539 is discussed below in Chapter III §2); 4. OS III, 34 l. 25: Inst. 1559 I.2.1 (see for this passage below, Chapter IV *passim*); 5. OS II, 61 l. 14: Inst. 1559: I.6.1; for this passage see below, Chapter V §1.1.

162. KD I.2, 6 (CD I.2, 5).

163. OS I, 92 ll. 34-38. See above, n. 47.

164. OS I, 40 ll. 10-12. See n. 46 (again *se exhibere* [show oneself]).

165. OS I, 41 ll. 12-23. See above, n. 5.

166. This passage repeatedly returns in later editions of the *Institutes*. In 1559, in Inst. III.20.1; OS IV, 296 ll. 33-297 ll. 19 + ll. 26-28.

167. By *haec* Calvin means the immediately preceding ('justification') – 'the threefold use of the Law'), but at the same time all that was discussed before and thus the entire teaching as he presents it to us.

168. In KD II.2 (1942) this became 'God's gracious choice [Gnadenwahl] and Command.' See the leading sentences of paragraphs 32 and 36.

169. OS III, 5 ll. 13-16. See above, the Introduction §2, n. 20.

CHAPTER II

THE *INSTRUCTION ET CONFESSION DE FOY* OF 1537

§1. BRIEF DESCRIPTION OF THE HISTORY AND THE VARIOUS EDITIONS OF CALVIN'S GENEVAN CATECHISM

In the final part of the sixth chapter of his 1536 *Institutes,* Calvin expounds the subject of *De politica administratione* (civil government). This theme is described in the back of the book (in the 'list of remarkable key words which are dealt with in this book'), as: 'Civil order is necessary for the church congregation'.[1] Civil administration must see to it 'that among Christians a public form of religion should exist and that there is charity and compassion among the people', as the briefest description of its task has it.[2] The Articles,[3] which the ministers submitted to the Geneva City Council on November 10, 1536, show us the application of the ideas Calvin had developed in that final part of the *Institutes* concerning the task of government.

In the second half of the introduction to the Articles we read that the government has a responsibility to obey the Word of God. Its first task is to ensure that the church can serve the Word amongst the people without hindrance.

In the first half of the introduction, four points are put forward by the ministers. Here, we recognize Calvin's orderly mind.[4] After briefly defining these points in the introduction, they are discussed in full detail in the ensuing articles. The new way of celebrating the Lord's Supper is used as the point of departure for building up church life. Then follows a discussion on the maintaining of discipline surrounding this new celebration of the Lord's Supper, and on the singing of Psalms. The third point of discussion, which particularly interests us right now, is the catechesis.[5] This means the handing down of sacred doctrine 'from hand to hand and from father to son', as the introduction puts it. The articles have the following to say on the subject:[6]

'The third article concerns the instruction to the children, who undoubtedly owe the congregation a confession of their faith as well. For this reason, people used to have a certain Catechism at their disposal, which was meant to teach everyone the foundations of the Christian religion. It was a sort of summary which everyone could use to declare whether he or she was a Christian. Particularly the children were taught by means of this Catechism, so that they might give witness to their faith in the congregation, since in their baptism they had been unable to bear such witness themselves. For we see that Scripture always connects the confession with faith, and tells us that if we truly "believe with our hearts towards righteousness, with our mouths we will confess what we believe" (Rom 10:10). Indeed, while this prescription was always fitting and appropriate, it is now more necessary than ever, given the contempt for the Word of God we see everywhere and the negligence on the part of parents to instruct their children in the way of God, resulting in an enormous ignorance which cannot be tolerated in any manner in the congregation of God.

In order to get things right again, we propose to a give a brief and easy summary of the essence of the Christian faith, which is to be taught to all children. The children will then at certain times of the year have to appear before the ministers of the Word in order to be questioned and examined and to receive further explanation, according to the abilities of each of them individually, until one may be sure that they have been adequately taught. But it is up to you to have the parents make this effort and ensure that their children learn this summary and appear before the ministers at the appointed times.'

Thus, the ministers propose to use 'a brief and easily understood summary of the Christian faith, to be taught to all children'. The 'essence of sacred doctrine'[7] discussed in the previous chapter, which Calvin had written as a 'Catechism' for his French fellow believers, was not suitable to serve as instruction for children. Therefore, he wrote a new Catechism entitled *Instruction et Confession de foy, dont on use en leglise de Genève*.[8]

The Latin text of this Catechism, however, does not carry the title *Instructio et confessio fidei*, but *Catechismus sive Christianae Religionis Institutio* (Catechism or Instruction in the Christian Religion). In the passage cited above, we can recognize both titles. In the first sentence, the title of the Catechism in its French form, *Instruction and Confession of Faith,* is recognizable: 'The third article concerns the instruction of the children, who undoubtedly owe the congregation a confession of their faith'. The second sentence reads: 'for this reason, people used to have a certain Catechism at their disposal, which was meant to teach everyone in the foundations of the Christian religion'. In this sentence we recognise the title of the Catechism in its Latin form: '*Catechismus sive Christianae Religionis Institutio*'.

It can be no accident that in these two initial sentences of the discussion on the Catechism in the Articles we encounter the titles of both the French and the Latin text of the new Catechism. Calvin contributed to the drafting of the Articles in the fall of 1536. At the same time he was engaged in composing the Catechism in its two forms. Already in February 1537 it was cited verbatim in its Latin form as *confessio nostra* (our confession) in a letter written by Calvin. In this letter to their fellow workers in Bern, the Genevan ministers insisted on convening a synod to refute P. Caroli, who had accused Geneva of Arianism.[9]

Wigand Koeln published the French text of the Catechism in Geneva in the spring of 1537.[10] Only a full year later (March 1538) was the Latin text published in Basel by the same printer who produced the *Institutes* of 1536.[11]

The complete title of the Latin text of the Catechism, published in the spring of 1538, reads as follows:

> *Catechism, or Instruction in the Christian religion*, unanimously accepted by the church in Geneva – having been reborn through the proclamation of the gospel –, which was initially published in the vernacular, but now also in Latin, so that other churches may persuade themselves of the sincerity of the faith of this church as well. Written by John Calvin. Basel, 1538.[12]

We may deduce from the passage in the Articles cited above that the title of the Latin manuscript contained only the words italicized above: 'Catechism, or Instruction in the Christian religion'. Thus, all the subsequent words were added by Calvin when he published the text in Basel one year later. Twice we hear the word *etiam* (also, as well). The text is *also* published in Latin, in order that it may be studied in all other (German speaking) churches *as well*, and that others, everywhere and anywhere, may be able to persuade themselves of the sincerity and purity of the faith which the church of Geneva professes. The Latin edition of the Catechism contained a preface by Calvin, explaining in detail this reason for publication.[13]

The elaborate title of the Latin edition shows that the Genevan church made itself know to the outside world through the publication of this work. It invites the following remarks:

1. In the title of the Latin edition, Calvin is mentioned as the author of this Catechism.
2. In various letters Calvin – and others – called the *Christianae Religionis Institutio* of 1536 a 'Catechism'.[14] By now adding the title *Christianae Religionis Institutio* in its Latin form, Calvin points out that this small Catechism presents a brief summary of the *Institutes* of 1536. Therefore, the Institutes of 1536 and the *Instruction and Confession of Faith* of 1537 can be called 'the large and the small Catechism' of Calvin. This differs from the 'large and small Catechism' of Luther in that both Calvin's works, unlike those of Luther, were replaced by other books. The Institutes of 1536 was replaced by the great textbook, which after a number of different editions (of 1539, 1543, 1550, 1554) would find its definitive form in the 1559 edition; and the *Instruction et Confession de Foy* was replaced by the small textbook which would become the 'Geneva Catechism'. This textbook was written in 1541, when Calvin returned to Geneva after his exile (1538-1541) and again took up the work of serving the congregation in that city.
3. The *Christianae Religionis Institutio* of 1536 opened with a 'Preface to the most Christian king of France, to whom this book is dedicated as a confession of faith'.[15] The *Institutes* of 1536 therefore served both as a Catechism and as a 'confession of faith'. The small textbook of 1537, too, had this dual character of instruction and confession. However, the fact that Calvin called this little book in its Latin form

Christianae Religionis Institutio means that by now it had become a *confessio nostra*, a confession of faith for the whole Genevan church.

4. Already in the fall of 1536 the Articles asked the City Council for cooperation in order to ensure that all citizens of Geneva should personally confess the faith – just for once, 'only this one time'. Apparently, what had happened in May 1536 was not good enough. On that occasion, the citizens of Geneva had collectively sworn to God – by raising their hands – that they would aim to live 'according to the gospel and the Word of God'. This was deemed unsatisfactory. As we saw, the passage in the Articles dealing with catechesis began with the words: 'the third article concerns the instruction of the children, who undoubtedly owe the congregation a confession of their faith'. The title of the small Catechism which Calvin wrote on the basis of the *Institutes* was therefore called *Instruction and Confession of Faith*, as we saw as well. After their instruction the children had to confess their faith. However, the Reformation of the congregation required that this time ('only this one time') not only the children, but all inhabitants of Geneva should confess their faith after having been instructed. 'Everyone for himself', the Articles stated, 'because it is not clear yet which doctrine each person follows'. This alone could be 'the correct start of a church'.[16] All citizens of Geneva, therefore, were assembled in St Peter's. Here, they had to confess their faith in small groups of ten, so that they could belong to the Christian congregation and remain citizens of the city. For this occasion, a brief text was used and presented as a 'summary' of the 'instruction'. It was entitled 'Confession of faith to which all citizens and inhabitants of Geneva as well as the subjects of the lands (belonging to it) must swear to adhere; also an abstract of the instruction which is being used in the churches of this city'.[17]

5. The Latin title also tells us why the text, published in French in 1537, was published in Latin the following year. That was done, we are told, 'so that other churches may persuade themselves of the sincerity of the faith' of the Genevan congregation. This was extensively commented on by the Genevan pastors in the preface, which was written by Calvin.

6. The first two sentences of the passage in the Articles concerning the catechesis contained the titles of both the French and the Latin text of the small Catechism. From this we deduced above that Calvin, while cooperating with the composition of the Articles, was at the same time engaged in writing this Catechism in both forms.[18] Since most of Calvin's works were written first in Latin and then in French, it would be reasonable to assume that this was also the case with this Catechism, even if we had no indications to this effect. There are, however, a few passages in the letters of 1537 which point in this direction. In a letter by Calvin which we already referred to we find a literal citation of the Latin text of this Catechism, and in a letter to Grynaeus written in June 1537 in Basel we read: 'Some time ago we wrote a Catechism which was also published in the French language'.[19] The words '*gallice etiam editus*' do not mean that the text was published in French in addition to being published in Latin. It means that it was not only written, *but also* published in French. This gives as a clue. Whereas the Latin text was written but not published, the French text was both written *and* published.

The publication of the Latin text in 1538 provided the 1537 Catechism with a triple function: (1) It was an 'instruction' for the children; (2) it was a 'confession of faith', to which all Genevan citizens had to swear; and (3) it was a 'confessio' by means of which the church of Geneva wanted to communicate to all other churches of the region (particularly Bern, Zurich, Basel, Strasbourg) what she confessed as her faith.

Excursus
a. So far, we have described the genesis and the various versions of Calvin's first Genevan Catechism. We now will have to briefly discuss the modern editions of these texts. In the *Calvini Opera* of the *Corpus Reformatorum*[20] we find the works in the following locations. The *Articles bailles par les prescheurs* of late 1536 are printed in Vol. X.1, 5-14 as the first of the *Ordonnances ecclésiastiques et autres* under the heading of 'Articles concernant l'organisation de l'église et du culte à Genève, proposés au conseil par les ministres'.
b. The 1538 Latin text of the Catechism (*Praefatio, Catechismus, Confessio Fidei*) is found in Vol. V, 317-362.
c. The *Confession de la Foy laquelle tous bourgeois et habitans de Genève et subiecetz du pays doyuent iurer de garder et tenir extraicte de linstruction dont en use en leglise de la dicte ville* can be found in Vol. IX, 693-700 (as the first of the nine 'Confessiones' printed there).
d. The French text of both the *Instruction et Confession de Foy, dont en use en leglise de Geneve,* and of the *Confession de Foy laquelle tous bourgeois etc.* are found in Vol. XXII, 33-74 and 79-96.

Thus, the Latin text of the Catechism and the confession of faith was printed in the fifth volume, published in 1866. The French text, however, appears in the twenty-second volume, published in 1880. The French text was published only in 1880 because the text of the Catechism in its French form had been lost. It was rediscovered, however, in 1877 in the 'Collection Dupuy' (Vol. 940) of the 'Bibliothèque Nationale' in Paris, and published in 1878 by Albert Rilliet and Théophile Dufour: '*Le Catéchisme français de Calvin*, publié en 1537, Réïmprimé pour la première fois d'après une exemplaire nouvellement retrouvé, et suivi de la plus ancienne confession de foi de l'église de Genève. Avec deux Notices, par Albert Rilliet et Théophile Dufour' (Geneva 1878).

In the first part of the *Joannis Calvini Opera Selecta*, Peter Barth printed the Articles, the French text of the Catechism and of the confession of faith, as well as the preface of the Latin edition on pages 369-434.[21] However, in our discussion of the 1537-1538 Catechism in the following paragraph we will need – in addition to the French text – the Latin text as printed in the fifth volume of the Strasbourg edition as well. Just as Peter Barth's edition of the French Catechism is based on that of the *Corpus Reformatorum*, the Catechism of the *Corpus Reformatorum* is based on the edition of Rilliet and Dufour (not mentioned by P. Barth).[22]

Calvin's first stay in Geneva till April 24, 1538, was dominated by the *Instruction et Confession de Foy*.[23] This is lucidly described by Albert Rilliet in the first introduction to the book mentioned above (1878).[24]

At the end of his 'Notice' Rilliet points to the connection between the words Calvin spoke when told, on April 23, 1538, to leave the city in three days – 'we serve a greater master who will reward us'[25] – and the words with which the Catechism concludes in the final paragraph 'Du magistrat' – 'one must obey God rather than people' (Acts 4:19).[26] 'If it is by affirming this rule' – he says at the close of his statement – 'that the instruction used in the church of Geneva comes to a close, it is by applying it that the first stay in Gevena of him (i.e., Calvin, FB) who has restored it to its full glory comes to an end.' He adds, however: 'It is an excellent maxim, which might be infallible, if one would always be sure that it is truly God whom one obeys. – As concerns himself, Calvin seems never to have doubted this.'[27]

We understand why Rilliet concludes his 'Notice' in this way. It was right to assume that only those who have confessed their faith should belong to the Christian congregation and take part in the Lord's Supper. It was wrong, however, to follow in the footsteps of the medieval *corpus Christianum*, and to identify the Christian congregation simply with 'all citizens and inhabitants of Geneva as well as the subjects of the lands belonging to it' (cf. the title of the above cited brief 'Confession de la Foy'). The confession of faith was not used anymore – says Rilliet – 'as a means of admitting in the church only those who received the doctrines which had been most legitimate and very natural, but as a means of chasing from the country, for one reason or another, those who would refuse to take an oath on that faith, in order to arrive at a religious unity of the population by the purification of exile.'[28] Excommunication from the Christian congregation meant at the same time banishment from the territory of the city.

Karl Barth

In the conclusion of the first part of the doctrine of reconciliation, Karl Barth in his *Kirchliche Dogmatik* (§62) deals with 'The Holy Spirit and the Gathering of the Christian Community' (in faith). He then, at the conclusion of the second part of the doctrine of Reconciliation (§67), deals with 'The Holy Spirit and the Upbuilding of the Christian Community' (in Love). Finally, at the conclusion of the third part of the doctrine of reconciliation (§72), he deals with 'The Holy Spirit and the Sending of the Christian Community' (in hope). This final paragraph first mentions 'The People of God in World Occurrence', and then 'The Community for the World' (and thereafter 'The Task of the Community' and 'The Service of the Community'). In the section just mentioned (§72.2), Barth says that the Christian community should behaves like a 'Community for the World'. Barth calls this 'a proper *nota ecclesiae*' (characteristic of the church).[29] In the Genevan *corpus Christianum*, however, in was the other way around. The community was not a 'community for the world', but the world was 'world for the community'. This radical change in the structure of the whole of sacred doctrine has had considerable consequences for the theology of Karl Barth, for instance for the way in which he develops the doctrine of the *locus de ecclesia* (the doctrine of the church).

In this introductory paragraph on the genesis and the various editions of Calvin's first Genevan Catechism we have seen how all of Calvin's work for the congregation during his first stay in Geneva was dominated by this *Instruction and Confession of Faith which is used in the church of Geneva*. We now need to describe the significance of this work as a phase in the development of Calvin's theology, namely as a link between the *Christianae Religionis Institutio* of 1536 and the *Institutio Christianae Religionis* of 1539.

§2. THE 1537 CATECHISM AS A LINK BETWEEN THE *INSTITUTES* OF 1536 AND THE *INSTITUTES* OF 1539.

Just as the Confession of Faith of 1537 was an extract of the Catechism of 1537, so the 1537 Catechism, in its turn, as we said,[30] is a brief summary of the *Institutes* of 1536: 'le premier Catéchisme francais (1537) n'est q'un résumé de l'Institution' (Jacques Pannier).[31]

1536				Instruction and Confession of Faith used in the Church of Geneva
(Knowledge of God)	I.	1.		All men are born to know God.
		2.		The difference between true and false religion.
		3.		In which our knowledge of God must consist.
(Knowledge of Man)	II.	4.		Man.
		5.		Free will.
		6.		Sin and death.
I. The Law	III.	7.		How we are recreated to salvation and life.
		8.		The law of the Lord. Exodus 20.
		9.		The summary of the law.
		10.		What it is that only the law gives us.
		11.		That the law is a step forward in coming to Christ.
II. Faith	IV.	12.		That we receive Christ through faith. ← The Gospel
		13.		Election and predestination.
		14.		What is true faith? ← The Gospel
		15.		That faith is a gift of God.
		16.		That we are justified in Christ through faith.
		17.		That we are sanctified by faith, to obey the law.
		18.		Penance and rebirth.
		19.		How the righteousness of good works and of faith belong together.
		20.		The Creed.
		21.		What is hope?
III. Prayer	V.	22.		Prayer.
		23.		What needs to be borne in mind in prayer.
		24.		Exposition on the Lord's Prayer.
		25.		Perseverance in prayer.
IV. The Sacraments	VI.	26.		The Sacraments.
		27.		What is a Sacrament?
		28.		Baptism.
		29.		The Lord's Supper.
VI. Christian Freedom, Ecclesial Power and Civil Government		30.		The shepherds of the church and their authority.
		31.		Human traditions.
		32.		Excommunication.
		33.		Magistracy.

If this Catechism were nothing but 'just' a summary of the *Christianae Religionis Institutio* of 1536, we would not have had to dedicate a separate chapter to it. It is, however, something else as well. It is also an announcement of the *Institutio Christianae Religionis* of 1539, that is, the Institutes in its second form (1539-1554). As a summary of the *Institutes* of 1536 and as announcement of the 1539 *Institutes*, the 1537 Catechism is a link between both editions of the *Institutes*. That will be the topic of discussion in this second paragraph of chapter two.

The Catechism of 1537 contains – not in Calvin's numbering, but in ours, FB[32] – thirty-three paragraphs, each with their own heading. In order to be able to describe how the entire *Institutio* is constructed, we give an overview of the thirty-three paragraphs, which shows how the parts and components cohere within the whole of the new composition. To the left, in the margin, we see the titles of the chapters of the *Institutes* of 1536, of which this Catechism is the summary.

When the Strasbourg publishers pinted the Latin text of the 1537 Catechism in the fifth volume of their edition, they marked in italics everything which Calvin had copied word for word from the 1536 *Institutes* into this new Catechism: 'In this Catechism are printed in italics or so-called cursive letters those parts of the text which the writer without alteration has copied from his Institutes and transferred into this text.'[33] When we look at the thirty-two columns of this fifth volume (columns 323-354) it is striking that the italicized part appears exclusively in the second half of the work, in columns 338-354. In the first half of the work, in columns 323-337, we only meet seven italicized lines in column 328 containing the exegesis of the second commandment. The reason why in all of the first half of the Catechism, up to paragraph 20 – which concerns the explanation of the creed – we solely encouter new formulations of the themes is that the theme of *De Lege – De Fide* (law – faith) is unfolded in a completely new way in this Catechism. We discern the contours of the new form Calvin will give the *Institutes* in 1539.[34] Two new things happen in the 1537 Catechism:

1. In the 1536 *Institutes*, the chapter on 'The Law' began with an introduction, containing firstly a brief description in two parts of the contents of the 'knowledge of God' and the 'knowledge of man', and subsequently an announcement in three parts of the contents of the three subsequent chapters, which in 1536 together formed the 'essence of doctrine': 'The Law – Faith – Prayer'.[35] In 1537 these last three parts of the old Introduction were omitted and a new form was given to the first two parts on the knowledge of God and of ourselves. 'The knowledge of God' and 'the knowledge of man' take first place independently and in two groups of three paragraphs, followed by the five paragraphs on 'The Law'. This 1937 sequence of two leading groups of three paragraphs on 'the knowledge of God and the knowledge of man', and the five paragraphs on 'the Law' that follow, prefigures the outline of the first three chapters of 1539: *De cognitione Dei – De cognitione hominis – De lege* (the knowledge of God – the knowledge of man – the law).

2. Everything which was said in the first chapter, 'The Law' of the 1536 *Institutes* – in the second half of that chapter to be precise – is removed in 1537 from 'The Law' and moved to 'Faith'. This concerns the *beneficia Christi* (benefits of Christ): justification by faith alone, the threefold use of the law, sanctification and good

works. Calvin did this because he discusses the 'present' of faith (paragraphs 16-19) immediately after the two paragraphs (14-15) on true faith as a gift of God. Thus, this combination of paragraphs 16-19 with paragraphs 14-15 prefigures already in 1537 the second cluster of three chapters of the 1539 version: *De Fide –De Poenitentia – De Justificatione* (Faith – Penance – Justification; the reverse order 'sanctification – justification' will be the new order of 1539, though that reversal, too, reveals itself in 1537).

Now we understand that in the first half of the 1537 Catechism, up to paragraph 20, we encounter only new formulations, and why in the second half from paragraph 20 onwards we find predominantly texts that are borrowed from the 1536 *Institutes*. In the first half we are dealing with a new construction. A provisional one, but still a new one. We will encounter the definite new construction later in the *Institutes* of 1539 (although even that one will be provisional as well).

Comparing the Catechism of 1537 with the *Institutes* of 1536, Albert Rilliet writes: 'Between the two texts, only the beginning differs. All of the rest of the summary is an extract and even, in the second half, a literal copy of the main work'.[36] He also writes: 'At the beginning he reveals the order which he will adhere to in the new editions of the *Institutes*. For the remainder of the Catechism, he follows the structure he had already adopted for his great work'.[37] For Rilliet the 'beginning' both times only refers to the first six paragraphs on the knowledge of God and of man. However, we have seen that not only in the first six paragraphs, but in the entire first half of the work up to paragraph 20, we are dealing with the foreshadowing of the *Institutes* of 1539. In the rendering of the Reformed doctrines 'The Law – Faith' everything has changed compositionally in 1537, and in this respect the Catechism of 1537 already presents us with the renewal of 1539.

After this broad description of the 1537 Catechism, we must now investigate how Calvin develops the entire subject matter of Reformational preaching in the thirty-three paragraphs of this work. In doing so, we will again repeatedly pay attention to those textual elements that are of importance for the understanding of the structure of Calvin's theology.[38] The Catechism begins with:

I. THE KNOWLEDGE OF GOD
in three paragraphs:
1. All men are born to know God.
2. The difference between true and false religion.
3. In which our knowledge of God should consist.

The *Institutes* of 1536, too, began with a very brief section on 'the knowledge of God'. However, what Calvin develops more elaborately in these three paragraphs reveals to us an outline of what will be discussed more broadly in the first chapter of the 1539 Institutes. The 1537 Catechism and later on the 1539 *Institutes* open with the 'exposition on true and false religion', which is lacking in the 1536 *Institutes*.[39] An awareness of God is implanted in the souls of all people.[40] This awareness becomes true knowledge of God when God is recognized by man as he made himself known through his *opera* (works). That only happens, however, when man, blinded by sin, allows himself to be instructed in the *vera religio* (true religion) by the Word:

> 'Therefore, one needs to come to the Word of God, in which God is described very adequately by his works, since these works are not valued here according to our failing judgment, but according to the rule of eternal truth.'[41]

This key sentence in which the first three paragraphs of the 1537 Catechism culminate will reapppear in the first chapter of the 1539 Institutes[42] and will also be included in the definitive Institutes of 1559.[43] Our conversation with Calvin will particularly deal with the difference between the biblical *ma'asim* as the history of God's 'acts' and the *opera*, the 'works', of dogmatic tradition.

II. THE KNOWLEDGE OF MAN
also in three paragraphs:
4. Man.
5. Free will.
6. Sin and death.

This second group of three paragraphs offers a preview of what will be developed more extensively in the second chapter of the 1539 Institutes. Compared with Calvin's 1536 writings on the knowledge of ourselves, this is a new statement about *liberum et servum arbitrium* (the free and bound will).[44] The central paragraph begins with the statement: 'Scripture often testifies that man is a slave to sin'. It concludes with the words: 'man is unable to freely choose either good or evil, there is no free will'. In 1539 this theme will form the main subject of the second chapter.

The three paragraphs on the knowledge of God and the three paragraphs on the knowledge of self are now followed by:

III. THE LAW
in five paragraphs:
7. How we are recreated to salvation and life.
8. The law of the Lord.
   Exodus 20.
9. The summary of the law.
10. What it is that the law gives us.
11. That the law is a step forward in coming to Christ.

The first paragraph

7. How we are recreated to salvation and life.

constitutes the transition from the knowledge of self as described in the previous three paragraphs to the discussion of the law. This paragraph begins as follows:

'This knowledge of ourselves shows us our insignificance. When it has seriously entered our hearts we gain more easily access to the true knowledge of God.'

This opening sentence of 'The Law' informs us that the direction of his teachings is mainly from the knowledge of self to the knowledge of God, even though Calvin spoke first about the knowledge of God and only then about the knowledge of self. The scheme 'The Law – Faith' implies this direction, and it will not change as long as this framework is not abandoned. It is only in the 1559 *Institutes* that things change. Here, Calvin abandons this scheme. He no longer explains the Creed within the framework of 'the Law – Faith'. Instead, in book II.6-11 he treats *lex et evangelium* (law and gospel) as *explicatio symboli* (exposition of the Creed). When God gives us access to true knowledge of him, based on our true knowledge of self, he opens, as it were, the first door to his kingdom:

'He himself has opened a first door for us to His kingdom, by destroying those two most pernicious evils: our false feeling to be safe from His vengeance and our false trust in ourselves.'

Thus, a first door has already been opened in to God's kingdom, when two pernicious things have been destroyed, to wit: self-assuredly not fearing God's judgment, and its cause, a deceptive trust in ourselves and our own goodness. How this door opens (being brought from the true knowledge of self to the true knowledge of God) is now described in two sentences. The first sentence describes this event from our human perspective:

'From that moment on we begin to raise our eyes, which had been fixed on earthly things, to heaven. We who had put our trust in ourselves begin to sigh and call for the Lord.'

Seen from God's perspective, opening that first door to his kingdom is described as follows:

'And simultaneously the Father of mercy shows himself to us who were oppressed. We are amazed at this, because we did not deserve it because of our sins. Yet God calls us out of His unspeakable goodness and out of His own will. With the aid of whatever He deems suitable for our weakness He calls us from the wrong path to the right path, from death to life, from ruin to salvation, from the realm of the devil to his kingdom.'

The final sentence of this paragraph reveals why God first shows us his law:

'The Lord puts His law in front of us as a first step towards Him, so that all those whom He wants to recreate to inherit celestial life – according to His good pleasure – would become deeply saddened by their conscience and the burden of their sins, and would be stimulated to fear Him.'

The right knowledge of self needs to be awakened first, if we are to arrive at a true knowledge of God. Therefore the law comes first, followed by faith, as a first and a second 'door' or as a first and a second 'degree' (Latin: *gradus*).[45] It is the *ordo docendi* (order of instruction) of the *Institutes* of 1536, which in turn will be the 'order of instruction' of the *Institutes* of 1539.[46] Later, we shall describe the fatal results this initial 'order of instruction' will have for the unfolding of sacred doctrine, even when in 1559 the 'order of instruction' has changed into an 'explanation of the Creed'.

This transition of 'the knowledge of man' to 'the law' in paragraph seven is followed by the actual introduction to 'the Law' in the eighth paragraph.

8. The law of the Lord.

The introduction reads as follows:

'In the law of God we were given an absolute rule of all righteousness, which for good reasons may be called the eternal will of the Lord...'.

Karl Barth
Now that we hear Calvin call the law of God the absolute rule of all righteousness, we cannot help but think of the use Karl Barth makes of this expression when he speaks of 'The eternal will of God in the election of Jesus Christ' in §33.2 of the *Kirchliche Dogmatik*.[47] In the 'Doctrine of God', as the first of four 'main loci,'[48] 'The Election of Grace' is discussed first in KD II.2 in chapter VII, after which he speaks of 'The Command of God' in chapter VIII (as 'Foundation of Theological Ethics'). Similarly, the remaining three main loci (the third, fourth, and fifth volumes) each time conclude with a chapter on ethics, in which God's commandment is discussed: 'The Commandment of God the Creator' (KD III.4, Chap. XII) – 'The Command of God the Reconciler' (KD IV.4, Chap. XVII – fragments) – 'The Command of God the Redeemer' (planned, but unwritten conclusion of KD V). 'The eternal will of the Lord' becomes known primarily in what God does himself and – resulting from this – in what He commands us (in accordance to what He does himself). When Barth in 1935 discussed the theme 'Law and Gospel', he did so under the title of 'Gospel and Law'.

As 'absolute rule of the entire righteousness' the law is thus the expression of the 'eternal will of God',

'(...:) for He included on two tablets everything He demands of us completely and clearly. On the first tablet He prescribed for us in a few commandments what service of His majesty is pleasing to Him; on the second, the acts of love we owe to our neighbor are prescribed.'

The explanation of the decalogue in 1536 opened in the same way.[49] The introduction is now concluded with a sentence announcing what will follow with regard to theme of 'The Law':

Explanation of the law in §§8-9	'Let us now pay more attention to this.' – this will be done in the following explanation of the decalogue, which closes with the ninth paragraph 'The summary of the law', FB –
Answer to a first question in §10	'After this, we will see which doctrine we should derive from that' – the answer to this first question will be given in the tenth paragraph: 'What it is that the law gives us', FB –
Answer to a second question in §11	'and similarly which fruits we will gain from that'. – the answer to this second question will be given in the eleventh paragraph: 'That the law is a step in coming to Christ', FB –

After the *explicatio legis* (explanation of the law) in paragraphs 8 and 9, we first encounter the question: 'which doctrine should we derive from that?' The answer is given in the tenth paragraph:

10.　　What it is that only the law gives us.

In 1539, the explanation of the Decalogue is again followed by a discussion of the *triplex usus legis* (threefold function of the law).[50] However, in this 1537 Catechism – and on precisely this location in the Catechism – Calvin exclusively speaks about the *usus elenchticus* (the accusatory function). The *usus in renatis* (function in the lives of the reborn) will be discussed separately and much later in this Catechism, when Calvin in the section concerning faith, speaks about sanctification by faith in the seventeenth paragraph, after justification by faith. Here he writes 'that we are sanctified by faith in order to obey the law'. At the conclusion of that paragraph he writes:

'Thus, the use of the law among Christians is very different from what it was able to be without faith:
for where the Lord has written in our hearts the love for His righteousness, the outward teaching of the law (which *previously* could only accuse us of our weakness and our transgression), has *now* become[51]
　a lamp
　　to guide our feet,
　　that we might not stray from the right path (Ps 119:105),
　our wisdom,
　　by which we are shaped, taught, and encouraged to righteousness
　our discipline,
　　that does not tolerate that we – through vile lawlessness – lose our dignity.'[52]

Concluding the seventeenth paragraph, Calvin sings 'the joy of the law', for now the *externa legis doctrina* (the outward teaching of the law) is no longer – as it used to be – an accuser, but 'a lamp..., our wisdom..., our discipline...' for those who were renewed internally by the Spirit. In 1539 Calvin will call this *usus tertius legis* (third function of the law) the *praecipuus usus* (the most important purpose).[53] However, just as the scheme 'The Law – Faith' inevitably entails that the direction in which we move is mainly from the knowledge of self to the knowledge of God, so too this scheme inevitably entails that the 'accusing function of the Law' is the 'main function'. It is for both these reasons that Calvin is less and less satisfied with this scheme as a framework within which to unfold the 'essence of doctrine'.

Thus, due to the scheme 'The Law – Faith', the 1537 Catechism speaks exclusively of the 'accusing function'. For at this point in the Catechism, man is not coming from Christ, but rather driven to Christ by the law. This last point, i.e., how man is chased by the law out of all hideaways and driven to Christ,[54] is introduced at the conclusion of the section 'The Law' in the last of its five paragraphs (the eleventh paragraph), where Calvin begins to discuss the second question, 'which fruits we may gain':

11. That the law is a step forward in coming to Christ.

Calvin posited at the beginning of this paragraph that God brings us to the knowledge of ourselves through the law (that is to say: to the knowledge of our unrighteousness, adversity, and our being lost) not in order to drive us to despair, but that he might have mercy on us. He continues:

'After the Lord has reproaches us through His law with regard to our weakness and sinfulness, He comforts us because we can trust in His power and His mercy, that is to say, we can trust in Christ, His Son, through whom He shows himself benevolent and loving towards us.'[55]

In this final paragraph we hear, again, that the right knowledge of self needs first to be awakened in order to reach true knowledge of God. Therefore, first 'The Law' is discussed; then comes 'Faith'. This is motivated as follows in the final words of the paragraph on 'The Law':

| (The Law) | 'For the law makes clear that He rewards perfect righteousness. However, this righteousness is totally lacking in us. The law tells us that God is the impeccable and stern judge of our sins.' |
| (Faith) | 'But in Christ His face is full of grace and benevolence towards miserable and unworthy sinners. When He gave us His Son, He gave us a wonderful example of His infinite love, opening up all the treasures of His kindness and goodness.'[56] |

When we hear these words, we are automatically reminded of the scheme in the *Institutes* of 1559: 'Because of a twofold appearance of the Lord, there is a twofold knowledge of God.'[57] The 1539-1554 *Institutes* point in the same direction. In particular we must pay attention to how the first paragraph of 'The Law' in the composition of the 1537 Catechism – 'How we are re-created to salvation and life' (§7) – corresponds to the final paragraph of this section – 'That the law is a step forward in coming to Christ' (§11). We encountered this word 'step' (Latin: *gradum*) in the first paragraph as well:

> 'The Lord puts His law in front of us as a first step towards Him, so that all those whom He wants to recreate to inherit celestial life – according to His good pleasure – would become deeply saddened by their conscience and the burden of their sins, and would be stimulated to fear Him.'

The title of the last paragraph of 'The Law' calls this step a 'degré pour venir a Christ' (a step to come to Christ).

Paragraphs 7 and 11, framing the chapter on 'The Law', tell us how Calvin and other reformers thought of the law (in the accusatory function). When the law is discussed first, this is only to prepare the way for the next topic, the mercy of God in Christ. If the law had not been discussed first, we would not have been able to speak about Christ correctly. We are talking here about the core of early Reformation preaching. It is expressed in the scheme 'Law – Faith', as we discovered in the previous chapter in the final sentence of the introduction to the 1536 *Institutes*.[58] This sentence summarized all of the doctrine. We also saw it in the sentences 'first – then...', which we cited early on in that chapter.[59] Explaining the words 'we believe in the forgiveness of sins' in the *Institutio* of 1536, Calvin said:

> 'The Lord intended to show himself to humanity in this order. Those who discard all pride, being aware of their own poverty, reject themselves completely and deem themselves totally worthless, will begin to taste the sweetness of God's mercy in Christ. And when they have received it, they breathe more freely and are comforted, because they may be sure of the promise of both forgiveness of sins and salvation. Conversely, those who do take these steps to come to God will never enter the heart of salvation, which is the forgiveness of sins.'[60]

Thus, Calvin used the word *gradus* (step) as far back as 1536. It is used in the plural ('these *steps* to come to God'). The 'order' of divine dealing with humanity consists of two successive 'steps': first, that we come to the knowledge of ourselves as sinners through the law; second, that we accept Christ in faith. This corresponds to the *ordo docendi* 'Law – Faith'. Moving up along these two 'steps' we receive the *remissio peccatorum* (forgiveness of sins), which encompasses our entire life. This means that we share in the *justificatio* (justification) as *cardo salutis* (heart of salvation).

Thus, in paragraphs 7 and 11 of the section concerning the law, Calvin establishes several points of transition. Firstly, in paragraph 7, the transition of the knowledge of man to the law, and secondly, in paragraph 11, the transition from the law to faith. If we omit this framework, we are left with the third chapter, 'The Law' of 1539: 'explanation of the law' followed by the discussion of 'the function of the law' (which will be the 'threefold function of the law' again in 1539).

Thus, the last paragraph – corresponding to the first paragraph – of 'The Law' is meant to be a transition from the section concerning the law to the subsequent section:

IV. FAITH

    in ten paragraphs

12.	That we receive Christ through faith.
13.	Election and predestination.

14.	What is true faith?
15.	That faith is a gift of God.
16.	That we are justified in Christ by faith.
17.	That we are sanctified by faith to obey the law.
18.	Penance and rebirth.
19.	How righteousness of good works and of faith belong together.
20.	The Creed.
21.	What is hope?

Refering to the conclusion of the section on the law– 'that the law is a step forward in coming to Christ' – this section on faith opens with a brief introductory paragraph:

    12. That we may receive Christ by faith.

The first sentence reads as follows:

> 'As the merciful Father[61] offers us His Son by the word of the gospel, we embrace Him in faith and acknowledge Him as given to us.'[62]

In addition to the word 'foy' (faith) we also encounter the word 'évangile' (gospel). In the fourteenth paragraph Calvin will once more use the word 'évangile'. We did not come across the word *evangelium* in the *Institutes* of 1536. Calvin did not express the theme of Reformation preaching in the words 'The Law – The Gospel' (as in Melanchthon's *Loci communes*),[63] but in the words 'The Law – Faith' (which was more in agreement with Pauline usage).[64]

    In the two remaining sentences of this brief paragraph, Calvin points to a 'fact of experience': there are people who believe, but there are also quite a few who do not:

> 'It is true that the word of the gospel calls on all people to embrace Christ, but several (Latin: the majority), blinded and hardened by unbelief, reject this extraordinary grace. Only those who believe partake in the joy of Christ. They receive Him as the one who was sent to them. They do not reject Him but follow the one who calls them.'

Noting this fact of experience is the reason for Calvin to discuss the topic of predestination in the thirteenth paragraph.

    13. Election and predestination.

In 1536 the locus *de Praedestinatione* (predestination) still coincided with the locus *de Ecclesia* (the church). This is because in the first *Institutes* Calvin discussed the topic in conjunction with the explanation of the words 'We believe in the church'.[65] However, he did not discuss 'the election of the community' in the sense of the *Kirchliche Dogmatik* of Karl Barth.[66] Calvin then also dealt with the election of the many individuals, the *ecclesia* as *populus electorum Dei* (God's people of God). The doctrine of election, concerned exclusively with the election of individuals, could thus be separated easily from ecclesiology. This happened in 1537, when Calvin, as a result of the fact of experience that not all are believers, separately discussed predestination, right at the beginning of the section on faith.

Calvin's sketch of the doctrine of election in the thirteenth paragraph will reappear in the *Institutes* (and also in the 1552 polemics against Bolsec and Pighius).[67] We therefore need to listen to it carefully. Calvin opens the paragraph with a description of the doctrine of election. The fact of experience that not all people believe, Calvin says, points us to the great mystery of God's eternal counsel.

'Confronted with this fact, one must reflect on the great mystery of God's counsel. The seed of God's word only bears fruit in those whom the Lord, in His eternal election, has predestined to be His children and heirs to the heavenly kingdom. All others are rejected before the foundation of the world by the same will of God. For them, the clear and plain preaching of the truth can only be a "scent of death" (2 Cor 2:16).'

In the introductory paragraph to his 'Doctrine of the Election of Grace', Barth discusses 'The Foundation of the Doctrine of Election'.[68] Before he moves on to his own christological foundation, Barth first rejects four wrong motives for talking about election.

1. The argument that we should discuss the doctrine of election because it is an imposing and respectable church tradition. We should not want to be a 'Calvinist without reserve', as Loraine Boettner puts it.[69]
2. The argument that it should be discussed because of its practical worth, 'its pedagogical usefulness in the curing of souls'.
3. The argument that we would have to discuss this doctrine on account of 'a fact of supposed or real experience'.
4. The argument that this doctrine should be discussed because of a certain 'necessity of thought'. This argument would refer to 'the concept of God as an omnipotent will, governing and irresistibly directing each and every creature according to His own law, and thus disposing also of the salvation and perdition of men'.[70] The theme of election is then a *pars providentiae* (a part of providence).[71]

To Barth's mind, we should take the last two arguments seriously insofar as they show us that the doctrine of election deals both with chosen man and the electing God. Yet we must reject the idea of basing the doctrine of election either on a 'fact of experience' or on a 'necessity of thought', because if we would, we would be talking about man and God in the abstract (and *latet periculum in generalibus*, danger lurks in generalities!).[72]

It is clear that Calvin introduces the topic of election with reference to the 'fact of experience' that not all believe. That is his starting point. It is small wonder, then, that Barth, when discussing the third argument, has a few words to say on Calvin.[73] Barth starts as follows:

'I would not say that he really founded his doctrine of predestination on conscious experience. However, he put so much emphasis on this experience that it can hardly be denied. As a result, a good deal of emotion is involved in his discussion. This must have objectionable consequences for the argumentation.'

At the beginning of paragraph thirteen Calvin formulates the dogma of predestination. In the remainder of the paragraph he tells us what we are to do if our thinking on predestination is to be beneficial. The first thing, he says, we must not want to do, is to try to understand the hidden, eternal will of God. We can never grasp the 'why' of God's decisions. God's will is holy and righteous. It is pure light – but we cannot endure the sight of it. It is pure wisdom – but we cannot fathom it.

'The reason why the Lord extends His mercy toward one group of people, while judging others, is only known to Him. He wants this to be hidden from us, for a good reason. The stubbornness of our spirit cannot tolerate such great clarity. We, being so small, cannot understand such great wisdom. All who are unwilling to temper the hubris of their spirit will experience the truth of Solomon's words: 'those who want to investigate his majesty will be cast down by his magnificence' (Prov 25). Let us simply affirm that this decision of the Lord is holy and righteous, even tough its motives remain hidden. If He had wanted to damn the entire human race, He would have had the right to do so. It is out of his sheer goodness that He has chosen to save some. Let us therefore acknowledge that the elect are vessels of His mercy (which they truly are), and the lost are vessels of His wrath – which is totally righteous (Rom 9:22-23).[74] Both the saved and the lost are a reason to give Him honor.'

We are not allowed to construct a perilous *theologia gloriae* (theology of glory).[75] The text that contains this term is Proverbs 25:27 in the Vulgate (therefore, also in the *Institutes* of 1536 and 1539-54;[76] in 1559 Calvin changed the quotation of this text).[77]

In the third and last part of the paragraph, Calvin states that we need to keep ourselves to Christ, in whom we are granted security with regard to our salvation and our election, when we through faith receive and embrace him:

'No, we do not attempt to gain an absolute certainty of our salvation (as has become a habit of many), by climbing up the heavens and penetrating into God's eternal plans. Such a thought can only bring us into a state of excitement, i.e., anxiety and confusion. To the contrary, we content ourselves with the witness by which He gives us sufficient and generous confirmation of our certainty. All who were chosen in Christ were destined to life before the foundation of the world. When we receive and embrace Christ in faith, we are given the pledge of our election in Him. What else do we seek in election but to have a share in eternal life? Indeed, we possess this in Christ, for He was life from the beginning. He is presented to us as our life, so that all who believe in Him should not be lost but enjoy eternal life (John 3:16). Thus, if we have Christ in faith, and likewise in Him have life, we need not further investigate God's eternal counsel; for Christ is not only a mirror revealing to us the will of God, but also a pledge by which His will to us is sealed and confirmed.'

With regard to this last thought – Christ as *speculum electionis* (mirror of the election; based on Eph 1:4f.) – Barth writes:

'Yet something of this very practical and important reference remains unsatisfactory in all such texts (with Luther and the Lutherans, as well), because the following question remains: Is this proposition – that is, it is in Jesus Christ that we meet divine election – really taken seriously by these teachers on a theological level? (...) Is it possible to affirm election in Christ noetically, without also affirming it ontically – i.e., that there is in reality no electing God outside of Christ? Or is the proposition of these preachers nothing more than a pastoral matter, a practical instruction as to how one should hold *rebus sic stantibus* with regard to the question of election, in order not to be cast into doubt and despair?'[78]

Put briefly: 'Is the basis of recognizing predestination also its real basis?'[79] Barth's own christology is founded on an affirmative answer to this question.[80]

In the second and third parts of the paragraph Calvin told us what we must adhere to when we speak about predestination. In the 1536 *Institutes* he expressed this as follows:

'It is in Christ alone that we find the benevolence of God the Father toward us. We find life, salvation, and finally the kingdom of heaven itself in Him. Therefore, He alone must be sufficient for us, indeed, more than sufficient. (...) Those who are not content with Christ, however, are calling for God's wrath. Because they try to penetrate the abyss[81] of His majesty, they will be cast down by His glory (Prov 25).'[82]

When discussing predestination Calvin does not start from a 'necessity of thought', but from a 'fact of experience'. However, this thirteenth paragraph made us understand that this 'experience' contains much more than simply the observation that not all people believe. In his doctrine of predestination, too, Calvin starts from what he often calls the *experientia* (experience), which is *practica notitia* (practical knowledge) in contrast to all *otiosa speculatio* (useless reflection).[83] This experience thus entails a process of becoming aware of the *benevolentia* (benevolence) and *misericordia* (mercy) of God through faith. This is the starting point of his doctrine of predestination. For example, speaking on 'church and election' in the *Institutes* of 1536, he states:

'Although humanity has been depraved from the beginning of time due to Adam's sin, God has taken from this defiled multitude a few sanctified vessels for His glory, so that there would not be a single generation which would not experience His mercy.'[84]

Calvin does not proceed from a necessity of thought, but from experience, conceived as practical knowledge. He describes predestination not as a *pars providentiae* (part of providence), as Thomas and many subsequent Reformed theologians did. For them, the topic of predestination came immediately after the doctrine of God within the framework of the eternal will of God. The *providentia aeterna* (eternal providence) regarding the *genus humanum* (human family) was particularized to *praedestinatio* (predestination), and then (in the seventeenth century) to the *pactum salutis patrem inter filiumque* (covenant of salvation between Father and Son) for the *electi* (elect).[85]

That does not mean that the concept of *providentia Dei* (providence of God), which had played a large role in Augustine and the scholastics, had not been a key concept in the theology of Calvin (and in his exegesis). Neither does it mean that Calvin did not use the word *providentia* when he spoke of predestination. For example, he uses it twice when speaking about the church as *universus electorum numerus* (the entire number of the elect) in the *Institutes* of 1536: 'She is also holy, because those who are chosen by the eternal providence of God to be members of the church, are all sanctified by the Lord'.[86] With regard to the issue that Scripture often speaks of calling and justification without mentioning 'election', Calvin says: 'Here Scripture does not look upon the one and unchangeable providence of God, but describes such children of God, as can be known by us' – and therefore experienced by us – 'who are led by the Spirit of God'.[87]

Yet we must say that in his discussion on predestination Calvin does not start from the *providentia aeterna immutabilis* (eternal, unchangeable providence), but from the witness of Christ, the rebirth through the Holy Spirit, and the justification by faith. In all of this he starts from the experience of the mercy of God. Calvin mentions predestination in close connection to the providence of God, but does not start from the providence of God when he talks about predestination. This will be shown to us in the eighth chapter of the *Institutes* of 1539, *De Praedestinatione et providentia Dei* (predestination and providence of God), where he first devotes twenty-eight columns to predestination and only then fourteen columns to providence.[88]

Thus, in his unfolding of sacred doctrine, Calvin first discusses the themes of law and faith, which examine how the merciful God deals with his people through law and gospel. Proceeding from there, Calvin discusses predestination (with regard to providence). But now – in 1537 – the locus 'on predestination' at the start of the section on faith, is not yet in its correct place. Calvin recognized this as well. In 1539, therefore, he moves the discussion of this theme further to the end. Calvin's view is constantly focused on how God deals with mankind ('the people') and on what mankind ('the people') experiences in God's dealings. So much so that in 1539 – after unfolding the theme of 'The Law – Faith' as the main summary of sacred doctrine in chapters I-VI – he starts out by discussing the unity of God's covenant in chapter seven, 'agreement and difference between the Old and the New Testaments'. Only then he discusses pre-destination and providence in chapter eight.

Wilhelm Niesel turns Calvin into a 'Barthian'.[89] This leads him to distort Calvin's theology. It does not serve the theology of Karl Barth well either. After discussing – in the chapter on Calvin's doctrine of election – the place Calvin gave to the locus on predestination in the different editions of his Institutes (and Catechisms),[90] Niesel con-tinues as follows:

> 'Calvin did not manage to express in a satisfying formal way the idea that the doc-trine of election does not have a fundamental character for theology, in the sense that other doctrines were to be developed from it. We must consider election within the total framework of theology in its appropriate place, but we should not give more attention to it than other issues.'[91]

In the third and final section of the introductory paragraph of his 'Doctrine of the Elec-tion of Grace', Barth adds a correction by reacting as follows to Niesel's comments (in 1942):

> 'Can we really say that Calvin discussed the election at the appropriate place, "but not more than other issues?" Is not the proper place, where he mentions it, and what he says with regard to it, far too important and far too prominent for us to be able to say that this doctrine should not be used, and that Calvin did not mean it to be used to shed a decisive light on all that precedes and follows? Between a basic tenet (as Calvin undoubtedly did not understand or treat the doctrine of election) and a proposition like all others, there might be a third one, and even this third one Calvin appears to have discerned in the doctrine of election: a final (and at the same time a first) word on the entire reality of the Christian life: that the continuance and the future of that life are wholly and utterly of the free grace of God. But all Chris-tian doctrine, even when it mentions God at the beginning and the Church later on, deals substantially with this reality of the Christian life: with the life of man whom God has claimed for himself in Jesus Christ. And if this is the case, then how can we avoid thinking of the doctrine of election as the last or first word of the entire Christian doctrine? When we consider the place given to the doctrine of election in the later forms of Calvin's *Institutes* and especially in the definitive edition', – Barth means the *Institutes* after 1539, FB – 'it seems to me that the total picture presented in that work drives us irresistibly to the conclusion that at this point Cal-vin did intend to find and to say something particularly significant both in its sub-stance and in its consequences.'[92]

As to the function of the doctrine of election within the whole of sacred doctrine, Barth appears to entirely agree with Calvin. Barth, too, is of the opinion that this doctrine must be understood 'as the last or the first word of the entire Christian doctrine'. At the conclusion of the first introductory paragraph entitled 'The Task of the True Doctrine of God's Gracious Choice', Barth – reviewing everything he discussed in the three sections of this paragraph – expresses this as follows:

'In the first section of this paragraph' – on 'The Orientation of the Doctrine of Election' §32.1, FB – 'we established the fact that inasmuch as the doctrine deals with this decision it contains and expresses the sum of the Gospel. It does so because it is the good news, the best news, the wholly salvific news, that from all eternity God has decided to be God only in this way, moving towards man. Then, in the second section' – on 'The Foundation of the Doctrine of Election', §32.2, FB – 'we established the fact that the basis of our knowledge of this doctrine cannot be any other than its basis in actuality, i.e., Jesus Christ Himself, and no other, because He is the head of Israel and the Church is the content of this primal decision of God, and as such He is its authentic revelation. We summarize the doctrine' – in this final section about 'The Position of the Doctrine of Election in Dogmatics', (§32.3), FB – 'combining the thus understood doctrine of election with the doctrine of God, and as its integrating component we put it at the head of all other doctrines. Thus placed, in relation to all that follows, a necessary witness is given to the fact that all God's works and ways have their origin in His *grace*.'[93]

16-19. Justification and sanctification within the section on 'Faith'.

Progress in the unfolding of the theme 'The Law – Faith' was interrupted. For at the beginning of the section on faith, Calvin first called attention to predestination, as a result of the empirical fact that not all believe. Then he turned to discussing his thoughts on this theme, which he had already written down in the Institutes of 1536. However, paragraphs 14-21, following the thirteenth paragraph on predestination, now present the entire section on faith of the 1537 Catechism as both a summary of the 1536 Institutes and an announcement of the 1539 *Institutes*. We can see this clearly when we pay attention to the comparative overview below.

The part in which Calvin deals with justification, sanctification, and redemption – in other words with our participation in salvation, obtained for us by Christ – has been outlined four times in this comparative overview. In the previous chapter we learned that Calvin wrote the 1536 *Institutes* to discuss the ways in which we become participants in salvation through Christ. This was expressed in the structure of 'The Law – Faith'. Prayer, too, was described by Calvin as a means to acquire the correct knowledge of self and the correct knowledge of God through law and gospel. 'At the time, Calvin was, as was Melanchthon sixteen years prior, (...) preoccupied with the problems of the appropriation of salvation and not with its objective presuppositions.'[94] The problems surrounding the appropriation of salvation – being the foremost subject of the development of sacred doctrine – were so crucial, that Calvin discussed these as early as 1536 at the beginning of his book, in the first chapter on 'The Law' directly after the *explicatio legis* (the explanation of the law). When we follow the arrow in the comparative overview from the first column to the second, we will see that in 1537 he moves the discussion of these problems from 'The Law' to 'Faith'. But here, too, all attention is concentrated on these problems, so much so that he discusses these halfway through the section on 'Faith', immediately following the description of true faith as a gift of God. Only now the explanation of the confession of faith and the conclusion of the paragraph with *quid sit spes* (what is hope?) are given. When we follow the second arrow from the second to the third column, we notice that in 1539 Calvin moves the discussion of the problems surrounding the appropriation of salvation in the development of sacred doctrine still further back. He does this by discussing without interruption the theme 'Faith' in its entirety in chapter IV, before dealing with sanctification and justification in chapters V and VI against the backdrop of the explanation of the confession of faith.

1536	1537	1539
	§§1-3 The knowledge of God §§4-6 The knowledge of man	I. The knowledge of God II. The knowledge of man
I. The law	§§7-11 The law	III. The law

(OS I: 41-58) Explanation
    of the law
(58-68) Justification
    Sanctification
    (The three functions
    of the law)
    Good works		

II. Faith	§§12-21 Faith	IV. Faith

	(§12) That by faith we can
	    embrace Christ
	(§13) Election and
	    predestination	

(68-70) Definition of faith	§§14-15 Definition of faith	Definition of Faith

	§§16-19 Justification
	    Sanctification
	    Penance
	    Good works	

(70-75) The Trinity
(75-93) Explanation of the
    Creed
(93-96) Hope and love
	§20 The Trinity
	    Explanation of the Creed
	
	§21 Hope
		The Trinity
		    Explanation of the Creed
		
		Hope

		V. Penance
		VI. Justification
		VII. Comparison of Old
		    and New Testament
		VIII. Predestination and
		    providence.

III. Prayer (96-117)	§§22-25 Prayer	IX. Prayer
VI. The sacraments V. The false sacraments VI. Christian freedom Ecclesial power and civil government	*Institutes* 1559 III. 3-10 and 11-18: After the first brief chapter on the works of the Holy Spirit and after the lengthy second chapter on faith, the third book continues with the discussion on sanctification in chapters 3-10 and then the discussion on justification in chapters 11-18.	

Finally, we need to follow down the arrow in the third column. In 1559 Calvin drops the scheme 'The Law – Faith' as his starting point and develops the entire doctrine within the framework of the *Explicatio Symboli* (the explanation of the Creed). The appropriation of salvation is now described in the third book, under the heading 'on the manner in which the grace of God is received', after the knowledge of God the creator has been discussed in the first book and the knowledge of God the redeemer in the second. The appropriation of salvation is presented as the work of the Holy Spirit.

This third Book, containing 352 columns in the edition of the *Corpus Reformatorum,* is almost as voluminous as the first two books put together, which contain 144 + 218 = 362 columns. The fourth book (on the church) contains 374 columns.[95] Thus, much more space is alotted to the work of the Holy Spirit in the medium of the *verbi divini ministerium* (the service of the divine Word) and of the *ecclesia*, than to creation and redemption as the work *per appropriationem* (by way of appropriation) of the Father and of the Son. Of course, the 1559 *Institutes* still strongly focus on the problems of the appropriation of salvation. The entire unfolding of sacred doctrine culminates in book three: 'The manner in which the grace of Christ is received'. Nevertheless, a certain balance has been achieved in this definitive version of the Institutes between, on the one hand, the discussion in the first two books on the problems of the objective presuppostions of the salvation granted in Christ and, on the other hand, the discussion on the problems surrounding the subjective appropriation of this salvation in the final two books. The comparative overview above shows us how Calvin aimed to establish this balance. First, in 1537 he moves the description of the way we, through faith, participate in the salvation granted to us in Christ from the second goal of 'The Law' to the middle one of 'Faith'. Second, in 1539 he moves it from the center of 'Faith' to the two chapters following on 'Faith'. Finally, in 1559 he moves it to the third book entitled 'The manner in which we participate in the Grace of Christ'.[96]

Since the description of our justification and sanctification by faith was moved to the center, the section on 'Faith' – consisting of ten paragraphs in the 1537 Catechism – acquired the following format. After opening this section in paragraph 12, Calvin reserves the discussion of predestination to paragraph 13. After unfolding the *definitio fidei* (definition of faith) in paragraphs 14 and 15, he writes: 'faith is a strong and solid confidence of the heart, allowing us to rest assured in the mercy of God, as promised by the gospel'. This is what true faith as a gift of God entails.[97] Salvation, in which we partake through faith, is discussed in four paragraphs (16, 17, 18, and 19). Only then the explanation of the creed is given, in paragraph 20, because faith – as *fiducia*, trust in the truthfulness of God's promises – cannot exist without hope. The entire section on 'Faith' concludes with paragraph 21 on the theme of hope. We will need to consider this final paragraph of the 'Faith' section in more detail, since here the Catechism of 1537 again proves to be the link between the *Institutes* of 1536 and 1539.

21.   What is hope?

While Paul often discuss faith, love, or hope separately, on a few occasions the apostle mentions these three 'theological virtues' together (1 Thes 1:3; 5:8; 1 Cor 13:13; see also Col 1:4-5; Eph 1:15-18). Likewise, in 421 AD, Augustine gave his *Enchiridion* – the handbook of Christian faith, that a certain Laurentius had asked for – the title *De fide, spe et charitate* (on faith, hope, and love).[98] In the previous chapter we saw that in 1536 Calvin, too, dealt with hope and love as companions of faith at the end of the second chapter 'Faith' after the explanation of the Creed.[99] We need to discuss this final part of 'Faith' of 1536, dealing with 'hope and love', in some more detail in order to describe Calvin's treatment of the subject in the new edition of the 'Institutes' (i.e., the Catechism) of 1537. Its first lines read as follows:

1536	1539
1. 'Wherever this living faith is truly present, of which we have previously shown that it consists of trust in God alone and in Christ; it surely cannot be without effect (*otiosa*), since it is accompanied by hope and love.	'Wherever this living faith is truly present, it is accompanied by the hope for eternal salvation, which is its inseparable companion (*comitem individuam*). More precise, this hope is born out of living faith. If that hope is taken away, faith is also absent, regardless of any eloquent and beautiful arguments we may provide for it'.
Where these are totally lacking, faith is absent too, regardless of any eloquent and beautiful arguments we may provide for it. Not because faith is born in us out of hope and love, but because it cannot be otherwise than that hope and love always follow faith.'	– This sentence is continued in the next box, under 2, FB –

2. 'Let us now first state what hope is concerned with:

> Faith, as we heave heard, is a secure conviction concerning the truth of God, and therefore cannot lie, deceive, or provoke. Those who have received this certainty may surely also expect that God will keep His promises, for they are convinced that these promises cannot be anything else but true.

Therefore, hope is nothing but the expectation of the things which faith believes to be promised by God.

(a) faith   believes, that God is truthful /
    hope   expects, that He in his own time will prove His truthfullness;
(b) faith   believes, that He is a Father to us /
    hope   expects, that He will always show himself to us as such;
(c) faith   believes, that eternal live is granted to us /
    hope   expects that this will be revealed some day;
(d) faith   is the foundation on which hope rests /
    hope   feeds and nourishes faith.

For just as no one can expect anything from God,
if he had not at first believed His promises,
so, the weakness of our faith,
if it is not to collapse due to exhaustion,
has to be supported and protected by patient hope and expectation.

3. As far as love is concerned, the evidence is no less clear.

FAITH   Since faith embraces Christ as He is offered to us by the Father,
JUSTIFICATION   He is not only our forgiveness,
                righteousness, peace, and reconciliation with the Father,
SANCTIFICATION but also our sanctification and source of living water.
                Faith will surely find love in Him as the gift and fruit of the Holy
                Spirit and as the work of sanctification by Him (Gal 5:22).

4. Notice how hope and love are both born equally from faith, and emerge from it, and
    are united and bound to it by an inseparable bond (*individua copula*)!'

    – he moves this word *individual* in 1539 to 1, FB –

'Yet, we should not assess love in the same way as hope,
i.e, as if it would feed, protect, and maintain faith.
After all, by expecting the Lord quietly and patiently,
hope keeps faith from wavering or doubting the promises of God (Isa. 28).
The inner structure of love, however, is quite different and does not possess such
characteristics....'

Calvin formulated all segments of sacred doctrine with extreme care. He treated his
text for each new edition of the Institutes with great care and did not dispose of anything which he had formulated well.

Let us now look at what Calvin did in 1537 with this text of 1536. The text consists
of four parts (1-2-3-4). In the first part Calvin says that faith is never without hope and
love.[100] In the second part Calvin first proves this with regard to hope, and in the third
part with regard to love. However, in the fourth part Calvin states that the relationship

of love to faith is very different from that of hope to faith. Hope supports, confirms, keeps, and nourishes faith. None of this can be said of love. This being the case, does it make sense to treat 'hope and love' in such a parallel way in the instruction at the conclusion to the section concerning faith?

Added to this is the fact – which became a decisive argument for changing the composition – that what Calvin said in 1536 at the conclusion of 'Faith' about 'love' is in fact a repetition of what he had said in 1536 in the second part of 'the Law' about *sanctificatio* (sanctification). Indeed, in the third part of the text cited above he wrote: 'Since faith embraces Christ as He is offered to us by the Father, He is not only our forgiveness, righteousness, peace, and reconciliation with the Father, but also our sanctification and source of living water. Faith will surely find love in Him as the gift and fruit of the Holy Spirit and as the work of sanctification by Him (Gal 5:22).' Again, in just one sentence we encounter the characteristics of the essence of doctrine, as analyzed in the previous chapter:

1. Embracing Christ in faith is the same as becoming a participant in salvation, which he has gained for us. All attention is concentrated on becoming a participant in the salvation granted by Christ.
2. This salvation consists of justification, the *remissio peccatorum* (forgiveness of sins) as *cardo salutis* (heart of salvation); but justification is never without sanctification.
3. Christ sanctifies us by ruling us through his Holy Spirit.

As we have seen, in 1537 Calvin removed the comprehensive discussion of this theme from the first chapter, 'The Law', and placed it in the middle of the chapter on 'Faith' in paragraphs 16-19, right after paragraphs 14-15 dealing with the question of what true faith as a gift of God entails. Since he already discussed this theme in full detail in the middle of 'Faith', it would have been superfluous and interfering to repeat it at the end of the chapter on 'Faith'. Thus, in 1537, at the conclusion of 'Faith', he omits everything he had written in 1536 about love as the work of sanctification. Only the part about 'hope' remains.

The entire part outlined in the above citation is repeated word for word in the tentyfirst and closing paragraph of 'Faith' of 1537.[101] Thus, Calvin begins by saying:

> 'Faith, as we heave heard, is a secure conviction concerning the truth of God, and therefore cannot lie, deceive, or provoke.'

Calvin reminds us with the words 'as we have heard' of what he said in paragraph 14 on 'What is faith?'. In this way the final paragraph of the section on 'Faith' concerning 'What is hope?' corresponds with the third paragraph of this section concerning 'What is true faith'. Because *fides* (faith) is essentially *fiducia* (trust) – trust in the *veritas* (truthfulness) of God's promises, this *fides* cannot possibly exist without 'hope', which expects the fulfillment of these promises:

'Those' – i.e. those who trust in *fides* as *fiducia* (trust), FB – 'who have received this certainty may surely also expect that God will keep His promises, for they are convinced that these promises cannot be anything else but true.'

Now that he exclusively speaks about hope, Calvin also changes the *definitio fidei* (the definition of faith), with which, after a brief introduction, he opened the chapter on 'Faith' in 1536.[102] In that 1536 description true faith was defined as:

'not only believing that God and Christ exist,
but really putting our trust in them,
acknowledging God to be our God
and Christ to be our savior.
In reality this means that we not simply affirm
what has been written or said about God and Christ.
Rather, it means that we put all our hope and trust on God and Christ.[103]
This trust strengthens us,
so that we no longer doubt God's benevolence toward us.

Note that in 1536 *fides* (faith) and *credere* (to believe) were described as 'putting all hope and trust on God and Christ'. Later on, Calvin mentions *fides* (faith) *spes ac fiducia* (hope and trust) two times as well. However, in 1537 he no longer describes faith as 'hope and trust', but exclusively as 'trust'. *Credere in Deum* (believing in God) is to hold God as a man who is true to his word. In the *Confessio de Trinitate* of 1537 – to be discussed in the next paragraph – Calvin no longer speaks of 'to put all hope and trust on Christ', but rather the reverse: 'fixing all trust and hope on him'.[104] Thus, in 'What is true faith?' – the fourteenth paragraph of the 1537 Catechism – Calvin focuses all our attention on the *fides* as *fiducia*, as trust in the *veritas* (truthfulness) of God's promises. He does this in order to show – at the conclusion of the section on 'faith' in the twenty-first paragraph – that this true faith never exists without the hope which expects the fulfillment of these promises.

'Thus: (a) faith   believes, that God is truthful /
        hope   expects, that He in His own time will prove His truthfullness;
    (b) faith   believes, that He is a Father to us /
        hope   expects, that He will always show himself to us as such;
    (c) faith   believes, that eternal live is granted to us /
        hope   expects that this will be revealed some day;
    (d) faith   is the foundation on which hope rests /
        hope   feeds and nourishes faith.

For just as no one can expect anything from God,
if he had not at first believed His promises,
so, the weakness of our faith,
if it is not to collapse due to exhaustion,
has to be supported and protected by patient hope and expectation.'

The Reformational 'Theology of the Word' (Barth), as 'Theology of Promise' (Bizer),[105] is on all points a 'Theology of Hope' (Moltmann).[106]

We now have the full picture of Calvin's approach in 1537, from the text of 1536 to the reworking of the 'Faith' section in paragraphs 12-21 of the small Catechism:

1. As a result of his observation that not all people believe, Calvin has separated the locus 'on predestination' from ecclesiology by discussing it right at the beginning of the section on 'Faith' in the second paragraph (§13: 'Election and Providence').
2. The description of our participation in salvation granted by Christ is put in the middle of the section on 'Faith', instead of in the section on the law. This is because Calvin wanted to present – in paragraphs 16-19 – the discussion on justification by faith and sanctification by faith in direct connection with the description of the *vera fides* (true faith) as *donum Dei* (gift of God) in paragraphs 14-15. He placed the explanation of the Creed in the twentieth paragraph, closing the section with the twenty-first paragraph 'What is faith?' .
3. Since Calvin in the middle of the section 'Faith', in paragraphs 16-19, exhaustively described how justification by faith is never without sanctification, it would have been interfering and superfluous to discuss this theme again at the close of 'Faith'. Thus, he omitted the entire part on the relationship between love and faith.
4. Now that Calvin, at the close of 'Faith', exclusively discussess the relationship between hope and faith, he describes, in paragraphs 14-15, true faith as a gift of God. That is, he no longer describes it as 'hope and trust' but exclusively as 'trust'.

We stated above that Calvin in his newer versions of the Institutes never discarded anything that he had formulated well previously. This is proved, for example, when in 1537 he deletes the piece on the relationship between love and faith at the conclusion of 'Faith' (point 3). Here, Calvin says:

'Faith embraces Christ as He is offered to us by the Father.'

While Calvin omits the entire piece about the relationship between love and faith in 1537, he holds on to this senctence to introduce the entire section on 'Faith'. The first paragraph of this section – §12 'That we may receive Christ by faith' – opens with the following sentence:

'Just as the merciful Father offers us His Son by the word of the gospel, we embrace Him in faith and acknowledge Him as given to us.'[107]

Since at this point of our discussion we are interested in describing the Catechism of 1537 as a link between the 1536 and the 1537 *Institutes* we must not only show how Calvin, starting from the 1536 *Institutes*, approached the reformulation of the section on 'Faith', but also what will happen to this section when he recomposes the Institutes as the 'large Catechism' in 1539.

In our discussion of §13 we noted that the locus on predestination (given the function of that doctrine in Calvin's theology) in 1537 had not yet found its proper place within the whole of the unfolding of sacred doctrine. The same is true of the description in paragraphs 16-19 of how we can participate in the salvation bestowed by Christ. That description had not found its proper place in 1537 either. In 1537 that description was followed by the explanation of the Confession of Faith in paragraph 20:

20. The Creed

This paragraph began as follows:

> 'It was stated above' – i.e., in paragraphs 16-19, FB – 'that we receive Christ by faith. Now we need to be told what our faith must contemplate and consider in Christ in order to be confirmed. This is explained in what is called the *Symbolum* (Creed). This tells us how Christ, by the Father, has become for our sake wisdom, redemption, life, righteousness, and sanctification (1 Cor 1:30).'[108]

Thus, in 1537 the theme 'our participation in salvation offered by Christ' is mentioned first. Then only is Christ mentioned. It is explained how Christ became our salvation, indeed our 'wisdom, redemption, life, righteousness, sanctification'. However, should this order not be reversed? Should not the 'objective presupposition' of salvation – 'the way in which Christ has become for us wisdom, righteousness, sanctification, and redemption' by the Father – have been discussed first, only then to be followed by a discussion on the subjective 'appropriation of salvation', i.e., the way in which we participate in salvation by faith?[109] Here again (as with regard to the place of the doctrine of predestination within his summary) we must say that Calvin recognized this problem. In the 1539 *Institutes* he says so himself. In the fourth chapter, on 'Faith', the 'explanation of faith' is directly followed by 'the description of faith'. After this, Calvin introduces the explanation of the Creed as follows:[110]

> '[1.] It is true that the power of faith shows itself most clearly when its explanation is directed to the gospel as its goal. On the other hand, it is only in the gospel that the essentials of faith are to be found in the first place. We already noted this in passing when we discovered how the essence of the gospel is summarized in Jesus Christ. (...)
>
> [2.] Well then, the true knowledge of Christ means when we receive Him as He is offered to us by the Father.[111] In Him we find the inexhaustible fullness of heavenly riches, making Him our only treasure of happiness and goodness. However, in order to come into possession of this wealth, we need to know the way in which it was acquired for us. This is the obedience of Christ, which He has shown by doing and fulfilling all that was necessary for our salvation, according to the eternal will of God. The goal of our faith is the gospel, and the goal of the gospel is Christ. Hence it is in Christ himself that all our riches lie – everything He has done and suffered for our salvation. In order to receive a complete explanation of faith, therefore, we need to consider the way Christ reveals it. For after having explained the contents of the Creed' – in chapter V in 1543-1554, FB – 'it will be easier to recognize its characteristics, like in a painting. Thus, the Apostles Creed will assume

for us the place of such a painting, because it demonstrates in a few words the entire economy of salvation bit by bit without omitting even the smallest part.'

The French version of 1541 reads as follows: 'In order to come in possession of his wealth, we need to know first the way in which it was acquired for us.'[112] Thus, Calvin added the word 'premierement' (first) to the French text. First, the objective presuppositions must be discussed; first, the way salvation is acquired for us must be discussed. Then only how we come to participate in that salvation.

Calvin has now himself given us an explanation of the second arrow which we drew above, in the comparative overview concerning the discussion of paragraphs 16-19. This concerns the arrow pointing from the second to the third column, showing us how in 1539 Calvin postones the description of our participation in salvation even further. It no longer precedes the explanation of the creed, but follows it (in two separate chapters, namely chapters V and VI).

In 1539 Calvin also removes the locus on predestination from the section on 'Faith' and puts it back in chapter VIII. As a result, the chapter on 'Faith', following the first three chapters ('The Knowledge of God', 'The Knowledge of Man', 'The Law') simply looks like this in 1539:

	What is faith? The Creed (Introduction)		What is hope?
1541:[113]	187-212 25 pages	212-298 87 pages	298-299 2 pages

Thus, in the fourth chapter, 'Faith', of 1539, the explanation of the Creed is put in between the corresponding parts 'What is faith?' and 'What is hope?'.

Because the size of the explanation of the Creed greatly increased in the edition of 1543 (chiefly because so much was said about 'the church' in 1543), Calvin divided the material of the single chapter 'Faith' of 1539 into four chapters in the edition of 1543. Thus, in 1543 the chapter split up into the chapters V, VI, VII, and VIII.[114] This severed the correspondence between 'What is faith?' and 'What is hope?', which had constituted the framework for the explanation of the Creed in 1539. However, as we have seen, the relationship between faith and hope was of great significance to Calvin. He did not wish to sever the link between them. Therefore the paragraph 'What is hope?' was put directly after 'What is faith?'.

Thus, in the *Institutes* of 1543 (-1554), Calvin puts the paragraphs 'What is faith?' and 'What is hope?' first (in chapter V), to be followed by the explanation of the Creed in the three chapters VI to VIII (chap. VI, 'Explanation of the first part of the Creed'; chap. VII, 'Explanation of the second and third parts of the Creed'; chap. VIII, 'Explanation of the fourth part of the Creed').

In 1559 Calvin shapes the entire *Institutes* in the form of *Explicatio Symboli* (explanation of the Creed) and spreads out the material of the older edition of the *Insti-*

tutes over the four books of the new version (in accordance with his division of the Creed into four 'parts': on the Father, the Son, the Holy Spirit, and the Church).[115] Calvin placed the old fifth chapter, 'Faith', of the Institutes of 1543-1554 at the beginning of the 1559 book – immediately following the short first chapter on 'the hidden work of the Spirit'. We encounter the paragraphs 'What is faith?' and 'What is hope?' in the second chapter of the third book of the 1559 *Institutes:* 'Faith: in which a description is given and its characteristics are explained.'[116]

To summarize: we have outlined so far how Calvin put the passage on the relationship between faith and hope at the conclusion of the second chapter, 'Faith', in the 1536 Institutes. This passage was reproduced word for word in the twenty-first paragraph of the 1537 Catechism, concluding the entire section 'Faith' in this Catechism. However, we have also seen the reason for the appearance of this passage at the close of the second chapter of the third book of the 1559 *Institutes.*[117]

Regarding this passage we also stated that the Reformational 'theology of the Word' as a 'theology of promise' is at the same time a 'theology of hope'.[118] Therefore, we should not be surprised to see Jürgen Moltmann quote this passage from Calvin's *Institutes* with approval in his book *Die Theologie der Hoffnung* of 1964.[119] 'Faith binds man to Christ', Moltmann writes in the introductory paragraph called *Meditation über die Hoffnung.* 'Hope opens this faith to the all encompassing future of Christ. Hope is therefore the "inseparable accompaniment" of faith *(individua comes)'*, he continues.[120] Then he quotes Calvin on the relationship between faith and hope. Already in 1959 Barth had cited this passage of the *Institutes* in the first section of the paragraph entitled 'What is hoped for' at the conclusion of the Doctrine of Reconciliation in paragraph 73 of the KD.[121] Barth calls this passage from Calvin's book 'one of the most significant of his *Institutes'*. However, unlike Moltmann, Barth thinks that 'hope, so beautifully described' by Calvin is unfortunately not described as 'hope in him', i.e., 'hope in Jesus Christ' as 'the certain, patient, and joyful expectation of his second coming'. This second coming 'will complete the revelation of God's will which is being fulfilled in him'.[122] Back in 1953, Barth had said, with regard to the same passage from the *Institutes:* 'Like the other reformers, Calvin's treatment of eschatology is somewhat shaky.'[123]

We have now analysed the entire composition of the section on 'Faith' in paragraphs 12-21 of Calvin's 'small Catechism' of 1537. We have seen clearly how the early Reformation theme 'the Law → Faith' was unfolded by Calvin in the first twenty-one paragraphs. We remember that the entire Catechism consists of thirty-three paragraphs, arranged in seven parts. Of these, we already discussed the first four: I. The Knowledge of God (§§1-3); II. The Knowledge of Man (§§4-6); III. The Law (§§7-11) and IV. Faith (§§12-21). These are followed by:

V. Prayer,
    in four paragraphs (§§22-25).
VI. The Sacraments,
    in four paragraphs (§§26-29).
VII. Christian freedom, ecclesial power and civil government,
    in four paragraphs (§§30-33).

Our intention in writing this third chapter of our study was to show how Calvin's Catechism of 1537 constitutes the link between the 1536 *Institutes* and the one of 1539. It summarizes the first *Institutes*, we noted, and at the same time announces the second *Institutes*. It does so mainly in the first twenty-one paragraphs, in which the Reformation theme of 'the Law → Faith' is unfolded. The last three parts of this Catechism, containing twelve paragraphs, are almost exclusively summaries of the 1536 *Institutes* and to a much lesser degree announcements of the 1539 *Institutes*. We do not need to discuss these any further. However, in a third and final paragraph of this chapter we need to pay attention to an important aspect of Calvin's instruction, the connection between 'Scripture' and 'the experience of piety' .

§3. SCRIPTURE AND THE EXPERIENCE OF PIETY

Let us first read the introduction to the explanation of the Creed, at the beginning of the twentieth paragraph. Here we discover the function of the expression 'the experience of piety'.[124]

20.   The Creed

Faith,   I.   'It was said above, that we receive Christ by faith.'
Christs,
Creed   – See paragraphs 16-19, FB –

'Now we need to be told what our faith must contemplate and consider in Christ in order to be confirmed.'

> – I.e. how He has become our salvation in all that He accomplished. That will happen 'now' in the explanation of the Creed in this twentieth paragraph; for the text continues as follows, FB –

'This is explained in what is called the *Symbolum* (Creed). This tells us how Christ, by the Father, has become for our sake wisdom, redemption, life, righteousness, and sanctification.'

> – The Latin text adds: 1 Cor 1:30, FB[125] –

'It does not matter which author or authors composed this summary of the faith. This summary does not contain any human doctrine at all, but is derived from the scriptural witnesses which are reliable.'[126]

> – Three times we encounter the words *faith* and *Christ*. Faith is faith in Christ. This faith in Christ is summarized in the symbolum, composed from words solely derived from the Scriptures. This is of particular significance for us because in 1559 Calvin will turn the explanation of the Creed into the framework within which he will unfold all of sacred doctrine. This first general introduction to the explanation of the Creed is followed by a second, particular introduction, consisting of the locus on the Trinity. This is the case in the Institutes of 1536,[127] in the Catechism of 1537, and also in the Institutes of 1539. The God who mercifully grants us salvation in Christ, and whose Spirit causes us to own this salvation through faith – this God is the triune God. FB –

On the II. 'However, to prevent anyone from being disturbed by the fact that we
Trinity   confess our faith in the Father, the Son and the Holy Spirit, we need to
           add a few words. When we name the Father, the Son and the Holy
           Spirit, we do not imagine three gods. *Scripture along with the experi-*
           ence of piety shows us that God is both Father, Son and Holy Spirit in
           such a way, that we cannot understand the Father apart from the Son, in
           whom His image is revealed. Nor can we understand the Father apart
           from the Spirit in whom His strength and power are made known. Let
           us therefore, with our thinking hearts, be directed to the one God and let
           us at all times contemplate the Father together with the Son and His
           Spirit.'

> – The Latin *tota mentis cogitatio* (all the thinking of our spirit) is rendered by Cal-
> vin in French as *'toute la pensee de nostre coeur'* (all the thinking of our heart).
> Christian 'thinking' is, according to Calvin, a 'thinking with the heart' in a biblical
> way. Just as in the Bible, the heart is for Calvin the center of the integral human be-
> ing, where decisions are made and deeds are born. FB –

We need to speak about the Trinity to avoid being dismayed about the fact that we
confess to believe in the Father, the Son, and the Holy Spirit. This is how Calvin starts
out. He begins the discussion on God's Trinity in a similar vein in 1539:

'That in the one Deity there is truly a distinction between the Father, the Son and
the Holy Spirit is not easily recognized and has caused much difficulty and concern among many people' (French: 'has greatly upset the spirits', FB).[128]

It is quite obvious that Calvin, too, feels we should approach this subject with great
reticence, since we are dealing here with a mystery, impenetrable to our mind. In the
second sentence he mentions what should be our starting point and to what we need to
adhere to:

'When we name the Father, the Son and the Holy Spirit, we do not imagine three
gods. Scripture along with the experience of piety shows us' – note the singular
verb, FB – 'that God is both Father, Son and Holy Spirit.'

This is the phrase which we need to discuss in greater detail: 'Scripture along with the
experience of piety'. Because Calvin writes *et ... et* (and ... and) in the Latin text, the
unity of thee two terms is emphasized:

'(...), but in the simplicity and unity of God both Scripture and the experience of
piety itself show us that God is Father, Son, and Spirit.'[129] – Here, the verb is plural, FB.

First of all, Calvin mentions the Scriptures. Scripture speaks of God's *opera* (works).
This is always Calvin's starting point. Scripture tells us what God does. However, what
God does is directed towards us; it is something we experience. Thus, what Scripture
says, is at the same time something that our *pietas* (piety) experiences in faith.[130] In his

entire theological thought and speech, Calvin constantly sticks as closely as possible to what Scripture says and what faith experiences. As in all loci, this is also the case in the doctrine of the Trinity.

This explains why the traditional words of the dogma *Trinitas* and *Persona*, which appeared in the *Institutes* of 1536,[131] are not mentioned in this Catechism. As is well known, the Genevan reformers were able to speak in a very sober and simple way. As a result, 'the theological-ecclesiastical adventurer' (Barth)[132] Petrus Caroli of Lausanne, 'who was theologically a true chameleon' (Krusche),[133] accused Calvin and his colleagues of Arianism (first at a colloquy at Lausanne on February 17, 1537,[134] and later at another one held at Bern, from February 28 to March 1). This created quite a stir for Calvin during the year 1537. As appears from the letters of that year, Caroli's accusation made quite an impression in Bern, Zurich, Basel, and Strasbourg (and even at Wittenberg), calling in doubt the orthodoxy of Geneva.[135] Finally, on May 14, a Synod convened at Lausanne to resolve this issue. Basing itself on a confession, composed by Calvin on behalf of the Genevan pastors – the *Confessio de Trinitate propter calumnias P. Caroli* (Confession on the Trinity because of the charges made by Petrus Caroli)[136] – the Synod declared Caroli's accusation unfounded.[137] In this *Confessio de Trinitate* Calvin offers an explanation of the phrase 'both Scripture and the experience of piety' from the Catechism.

Calvin opens the confession with a very precise description of the demands pertaining to confessional speech in the church. The *regula cogitandi et loquendi* (the rule of thought, as well as the rule of speech) must be derived from Scripture. The opening of this introduction reads as follows:

> 'The human spirit in itself is altogether too blind to penetrate the majesty of God. It is capable of nothing but entangling itself in endless errors, to be caught in strange nonsense, and finally to sink in the deepest darkness when it tries to imagine God according to its modest powers of comprehension. Therefore we trust that all who are well-disposed towards us will forgive us when we seek God nowhere but in His Word. We only think of Him as He is revealed in His Word, and make no statements about Him except by means of His Word.[138]

Further on, Calvin describes the meaning of this general rule for the confession of the church in the following words:

> 'A confession of religion is nothing but a witness of faith, arrived at from within. To be well founded and of earnest intention it ought to be derived from the pure sources of Scripture. However, we do not accept a confession which is sewn together out of the words of Scripture in anxious superstition. We think it is possible to write words the meaning of which remains within the truth of Scripture, and at the same time contain as little crudity as possible, so that they might not offend pious ears and relate God to something unworthy of his majesty.'

Calvin, then, is not opposed to the use of words that are not derived from Scripture, whenever that should be necessary or desirable. In the Confession itself, Calvin says that we believe in – and pray to – one God 'whom we imagine to be as He is described to us in Scripture'. However, in the single being of God we acknowledge the Father alongside with his eternal Word and Spirit. We do not imagine three gods. Neither is this simply about three 'epithets'. Together with the fathers of the church 'it is our feeling that the simplicity and unity of God contain three hypostases or forms of existence which – though they have their existence in one being – are not to be confused'. Calvin does not use the word *persona* here, but the word *hypostasis*, meaning *substitentia*, which he prefers,[139] just as Barth prefers the word 'Seinsweise'.[140] Before discussing the *distinctio* (the difference) between the Father and the Word and between the Word and the Spirit, Calvin first discusses the deity of the Son and the deity of the Spirit. This passage reads as follows:

'The Son is also called Jehovah, the strong God (Isa 9:5), and the God who is to be praised for all eternity (Rom 9:5), by all the angels of God (Ps 97:7), and whose throne is established forever and ever (Ps 45:7). To Him are given various properties which cannot be ascribed in any way to anyone except to the one and eternal God. For as He is called Salvation, Righteousness, our Sanctification. We believe that all of our trust and our hope[141] rests in Him. We invoke His Name – a practical knowledge which undoubtedly is more certain than any useless reflection. Is it in practical knowledge that the pious soul discerns God to be most present. Indeed, when someone experiences being restored to life, enlightened, redeemed, justified, and sanctified, God becomes almost tangible. This practical knowledge is the source of our apprehending the deity of the Holy Spirit as well. For indeed, Scriture nowhere ascribes to created beings what it does ascribe to the Spirit. Our experience of piety confirms this. He is the one who is everywhere, supporting, strengthening, and enlivening all things. He lives in those who believe and leads them in all things. He causes them to be reborn, sanctifies them, and will some day bring them to full life. Therefore, Scripture does not refrain from calling Him God...'

Here we encounter Calvin's own explanation of the phrase 'showing us both the Scriptures and the experience of piety' from the Catechism. We should connect these terms with the *certa pietatis experientia* (the certain experience of piety) and the *practica notitia* (practical knowledge) being the opposite of all *otioso speculatio* (useless reflection) from this passage. In the commentary John Calvin says, commenting on John 1:3, that this 'practical knowledge' is of particular importance. 'He proves His deity (that is, the one of the Word) through His works. This is a practical knowledge, which is entirely suited for us to become used to Him.'[142]

In the locus on the Trinity of the *Institutes* of 1539[143] we again find the text of 1536 both at the beginning and the conclusion.[144] However, in between, we encounter the train of thought, and also some of the words, of the *Confessio de Trinitate* of 1537.[145] Thus, also by way of the *Confessio de Trinitate* – in the locus on the Trinity – the Catechism of 1537 provides the link between the *Institutes* of 1536 and 1539.

In the locus on the Trinity in the *Institutes* of 1539 Calvin uses only words borrowed from Scripture. This happens first in sections 8-15 on the deity of the Son and in sections 16-17 on the deity of the Spirit. Only after these section Calvin comes to discuss the dogma *(ousia, hypostaseis, essentia, personae)*, taking his cue from a quote of Gregory Nazianzus: 'As soon as I think about the one (God), I am immediately lit up by the glow of the three (hypostases); as soon as I distinguish the three, I am immediately led to the one'.[146] Calvin discusses the dogma in the sections 21-25 on the *distinctio* (the distinction) between the Father and the Word and between the Word and the Spirit.

This restraint by Calvin, which he respects in others as well, has its origin in the fear that we might step outside the boundaries of 'practical knowledge' and the 'experience of piety', i.e., outside the boundaries of what Scripture says and what faith experiences. 'The rules of thought and speech must most definitely be derived from Scripture.'[147] Heresy, however, needs *novitas verborum* (the coining of new words) and the use of so-called *exotica verba* (foreign words).[148] Calvin expresses this thought very aptly:

'Arius says that Christ is God – but he mumbles that He was made and had a beginning. He says, that Christ is one with the Father; but secretly he whispers in the ears of his people that Christ is united with God in the same way as other believers, albeit with special privileges. Say 'one in being', and you tear off his mask; yet, you do not add anything to the Scriptures. Sabellius says that the names Father, Son, and Holy Spirit do not express anything distinct in God. If you say that they are three, he growls that you call them three gods. If you say that in the one being of God there is a trinity of persons, then you express in one word what Scripture teaches, and you have put aside all that empty chatter.'[149]

Arianism and Sabellianism have made it unavoidable to use expressions such as *filius homoousios toi patri, consubstantialis patri* (the Son of one being with the Father) and *personarum trinitas in una Dei essentia* (a trinity of persons in the single being of God).

Calvin finds himself confronted by two extreme points of view. On the one hand, those who in *anxia superstitio* (anxious superstition) forbid him on account of *sola scriptura* (solely the Scriptures) each *novitas verborum* (usage of new words). On the other hand, people like Caroli want to force him to sign the three early church confessions (as formulas of unity) and to swear by all the traditional formulations of the dogma. The path Calvin takes is the one of *libertas Christiana* (freedom of a Christian), while at the same time dealing respectfully with the dogmatic traditions. Doumergue concludes his discussion of the *Confessio de Trinitate* with the words: 'without any exaggeration it may be concluded that a whole bit of spiritual and free biblicism animates all the great words of the Reformer, which we have been quoting'.[150]

Although the Synod of Waadt on May 14 at Lausanne had declared the accusation of Caroli unfounded, people were only completely reassured because of a synod in Bern in September (where Bucer and Capito from Strasbourg and Myconius and Grynaeus from Basel were also present). Here, Calvin did not refuse to add to the *Confessio de Trinitate* an explanation *de voce Trinitatis et de voce personae* (on the term 'Trinitatis' and the term 'Persona') stating categorically that he does not reject these words *Trinitatis* and *Persona*.[151] In the previous confession the words *Trinitas* and *Persona* did not appear.

When Calvin reshapes the *Institutes* in 1559 into its definitive form, he also changes the discussion of the locus on the Trinity.[152] The 'battle over words',[153] the discussion of traditional dogmatic terminology, is moved from the end to the beginning. Instead of using it to conclude the locus, we see Calvin opening the locus with it.[154] Then follows the entire part we mentioned above; the part on the deity of the Son and the deity of the Spirit and on the distinction between the Father and the Word and between the Word and the Spirit.[155]

However, the words with which Calvin had opened the locus on the Trinity in 1536 and then in altered form in 1539 are now moved to the back of the locus. They now serve as an introduction to its extensive polemic part, which concludes the locus on the Trinity.[156] When we compare the three versions of this text we note that the polemics came to play an increasingly important role (because of Servetus):

1536[157]	1539[158]	1559[159]
'When, however, some ungodly people, in order to tear out our faith by the roots, already at the outset make noises and ridicule us because we confess one God in three persons,	'However, because Satan, wishing to tear out our faith by the roots, partly because of the divinity of Christ and of the Spirit, and partly because of the distinction of the persons, has always generated enormous conflicts, and in almost all ages has encouraged unbelieving spirits to torture orthodox and pious spirits, and rebel against the words of Scripture,	'However, because Satan, wishing to tear out our faith by the roots, partly because of the divinity of Christ and of the Spirit, and partly because of the distinction of the persons, has always generated enormous conflicts, and in almost all ages has encouraged unbelieving spirits to torture orthodox teachers, and who at the present hour attempt to fan a new fire from old sparks –
	it is by far the best policy, it seems to me, to begin the explanation of the Creed by addressing this issue.	*it will be worthwhile to confront such perverse madness.*
one might expect me to put an end to their blasphemies in this place.		
However, because I plan to help honest seekers of truth and not to get in trouble with hooligans and rebels,	However, because I plan to help honest seekers of truth and not to get in trouble with hooligans and rebels,	Up to now it had been my purpose to help honest seekers of truth and not to get in trouble with the inflexible and combative.
I will not enter into an organized battle.	I will not enter into an organized battle, which the significance of the matter would call for.	

I will only indicate in a few words what this matter is about and what one needs to watch out for,	*Rather, I will attempt to point out what this matter is about and what one needs to watch out for, not in a combative way, but in such a way that the truth will be protected against all allegations of the wicked.*	*Now, however, the truth which formerly has been quietly explained, needs to be protected against all allegations of the wicked.*
in order that they, who wish to open their ears to the truth, may have something on which to firmly plant their feet'.	However, I particularly labor for those who wish to open their ears to the Word of God, so that they may have something on which to firmly plant their feet'.	However, I particularly labor for those who wish to open their ears to the Word of God, so that they may have something on which to firmly plant their feet'.

We see that the battle which in almost all centuries has been raging against the dogma prompted Calvin in 1539 to thoroughly discussing the doctrine of the Trinity, opening the explanation of the Creed with it. 'It is by far the best policy, it seems to me, to begin the explanation of the Creed by addressing this issue', he writes. As we noted above, in 1559 Calvin moves this entire passage to the end of the locus, as an introduction to the polemic part, which concludes his discussion on the doctrine of the Trinity. The battle against this doctrine is no longer just the occasion to address the issue thoroughly. It has become the reason to strongly defend it against all old and new attacks: 'it will be worthwhile to confront such perverse madness'.

How the polemics came to play an ever-increasing role we can see particularly in the second column (the 1539 text). In 1536 Calvin said: 'I will only indicate in a few words what this matter is about and what one needs to watch out for'. In 1539 this becomes: 'Rather, I will attempt to point out what this matter is about and what one needs to watch out for, not in a combative way, but in such a way that the truth will be protected against all allegations of the wicked'. When Calvin moves this entire passage from the beginning to the end of the secion on the Trinity in 1559, he writes: '*hactenus* (until now)... , *nunc autem* (now, however) the truth which formerly has been quietly explained, needs to be protected against all allegations of the wicked'.

Thus, we can see how Calvin not only increasingly defends the dogma, but also the traditional Greek and Latin formulations of the dogma. We agree with Werner Krusche who comments as follows:

'It is true that Calvin goes to battle using the old theological armory, but not – as Wernle thinks – because he could not prove his doubted orthodoxy except in that way, but because the doubt of the eternal true deity of the Son and the Spirit could (and can) best be confronted with these weapons. Taking up the ancient ecclesiastical trinitarian terminology ('jargon' as Wernle calls it) is not a lethargic repetition, but a fundamental theological decision. Calvin finds the doctrine of the trinity – the distinction of Father, Son, and Spirit and the attestation of their equal and eternal divinity – everywhere in the Scriptures.'[160]

In all the editions of the *Institutes* which unfold sacred doctrine according to the scheme 'Law – Faith' (1536-1557, including the Catechism of 1537), the locus on the Trinity was therefore the *exordium* (introduction) of the entire explanation of the Creed. 'It is by far the best policy, it seems to me, to introduce the explanation of the Creed by addressing this issue'. When Calvin in 1559 turned the explanation of the Creed into the framework for explaining the entire sacred doctrine, he does not, however, give precedence to the locus of the Trinity as the introduction to the entire *Institutes*. In this, he differs from Karl Barth, whose entire explanation of sacred doctrine in the Kirchliche Dogmatik begins with 'The Triune God' (first paragraph of the first chapter, entitled 'The Revelation of God').[161] Calvin does not do this. We find the locus on the Trinity (just as the locus on the Holy Scriptures) somewhere in the middle of the first Book 'the Knowledge of God the Creator' (in I.13). The reason for this shall be discussed in chapter 4 of our study.

At the end of this paragraph we need to briefly come back to the words used in the *Confessio de Trinitate* of 1537 concerning the *practica notitia* of the *pietatis experientia*, which were also included in the Institutes of 1539. Every time Calvin inserts a part from his other writings in the Institutes, this is indicated in the edition of Barth-Niesel in the first apparatus at the bottom of every page. Thus they note, for example, with regard to the text from the third paragraph of the Catechism, cited above:[162] 'this unit of text is almost literally quoted from the Catechism of 1538'.[163] They apparently missed the fact that there are two instances in which the Institutes of 1539[164] quotes from the *Confessio de Trinitate* of 1537, for the other quotation is not marked in their apparatus. Concerning the phrase: 'a practical knowledge which undoubtedly is more certain than any useless reflection' they refer in the second apparatus at the bottom of the page to Melanchthon.[165] This concerns Melanchthon's famous opening passage of 1521 to his *Loci communes,* the first Protestant dogmatics. We need to keep this passage in mind to understand the scheme and basic pattern of the oldest Protestant dogmatics, which had been Calvin's scheme in his *Institutes* until the 1559 edition as well. The passage reads as follows:

'These are more or less the main subjects theology concerns itself with:

God	Law	Predestination
The One	Promises	Sacramental Signs
The Trinity	Renewal through Christ	States of Man
Creation	Grace	Government
Man, Powers of Man	Fruits of Grace	Bishops
Sin	Faith	Damnation
Fruits of Sin, Slander	Hope	Bliss
Punishments	Love	

Although some of these main points are totally incomprehensible, there are also some which Christ wanted all Christian people to know very precisely. We had better worship than investigate the mysteries of the Godhead. Indeed, they cannot be investigated without the greatest danger, as even holy men have not infrequently experienced. God, the Highest and the Greatest, has cloaked the Son in flesh, so as to invite us not to reflect on His majesty but on our vulnerability. Paul, too, writes to the Corinthians that God wished to be known through the folly of preaching. This was without doubt a new way of knowing Him. It was needed, for He could not be known in wisdom through wisdom (1 Cor 1:21). Therefore, there is no reason why we should spend much effort on the above mentioned main themes: God, Unity, the Trinity of God, the mystery of Creation, the Incarnation.

I ask you, what have all the scholastic theologians accomplished in so many centuries, when they occupied themselves exclusively with these main themes? Have they not, as is said (Rom 1:21), become shallow in their views because all their lives they talked nonsensically about abstractions, formalities, general remarks, and other meaningless words? One could have ignored the folly of these people were it not for the fact that by those silly views they had obscured to us the gospel and the benefactions of Christ. If I were inclined to demonstrate my talent in a question without significance, I could easily overturn what they had advanced as proofs for the dogmas of the faith, and in this they seem to promote certain heresies rather than catholic dogmas.

'However, those who do not know the other subjects such as the power of sin, the law, and grace – I do not know how I might still call them Christians, for from these things we know Christ. Knowing Christ means to know His benefactions, and not – as the scholastics teach – to contemplate His natures and the different aspects of His incarnation. If you do not know for which purpose Christ took on flesh and was nailed to the cross, what use is it to know about His life? Is it sufficient for a physician to know the forms, colors, and shapes of the herbs? Should he not be much more interested in their powers to heal? We must know Christ in a different manner than the scholastics teach us. Christ has been given to us as a medicine, or – to use a word from Scripture – as the way to salvation. This, then, is Christian knowledge. It means to know what the law demands, where you might get the strength to fulfill it, where you can obtain the grace for the forgiveness of your sins, how you may raise your stumbling soul to confront the devil, the flesh, and the world, and how your wounded conscience can be comforted. Yet do the scholastics teach such things? Did Paul in his letter to the Romans, when writing a brief summary of Christian teaching, speculate about the mysteries of the Trinity, the Incarnation, or the "active" and "passive" creation? Not at all! What does he discuss? He talks about the law, sin, grace. These things alone constitute the knowledge of Christ. Indeed, how often does Paul declare that he wishes those who believe a rich knowledge of Christ! Apparently, he saw in advance that if we were to give up on the themes of salvation our souls would turn to useless debates, which are alien to Christ. For this reason, then, we will present to you the subjects which commend Christ to you, which strengthen your conscience, and which protect your soul against satan.'

Melanchthon distinguishes between two categories of loci. The first category, he says, is made up of subjects which are 'altogether incomprehensible' and lead us to 'useless debates, which are alien to Christ'. However, the other category consists of loci 'Christ wanted all Christian people to know very precisely'.

With regard to the first category – God, his unity, the Trinity, the mystery of creation, the Incarnation – he says: 'there is no reason why we should spend much effort on the above mentioned main themes'. With regard to the loci discussing *Peccatum – Lex – Gratia* (sin – the law – grace),[166] however, he says something else. If people do not know about these subjects, he explains, 'I do not know how I might still call them Christians'. *Nam ex his proprie Christus cognoscitur, siquidem hoc est Christum cognoscere beneficia eius cognoscere, non, quod isti (sc. scholastici theologistae) docent, eius naturas, modos incarnationis contueri* (Knowing Christ means to know his benefactions, and not – as the scholastics teach – to contemplate his natures and the different aspects of his incarnation). The loci that truly matter in preaching and instruction are neglected by the scholastics. Melanchthon tells us what these loci are with the words 'This, then, is Christian knowledge. It means to know what the law demands, where you might get the strength to fulfill it, where you can obtain the grace for the forgiveness of your sins, how you may raise your stumbling soul to confront the devil, the flesh, and the world, and how your wounded conscience can be comforted.' This is how Melanchthon in 1521 described the contents of the *practica notitia* of the Reformational *pietatis experientia*. Indeed, all the reformers read the Scripture from the perspective of Paul's letter to the Romans. About what does Paul 'speculate' in this letter? 'He talks about the law, sin, grace. These things alone constitute the knowledge of Christ.'

This is the background to Calvin's *Institutes*, as it was composed up to 1559, following the early Reformation scheme (borrowed from Paul's teachings) of 'Law and Faith'. This original form of Reformation doctrine expressed the 'practical knowledge' of a very specific 'experience of piety'. What this 'experience' meant is expressed by Calvin in the words which we cited from the *Institutes* of 1536:

> 'Although humanity has been depraved from the beginning of time due to Adam's sin, God has taken from this defiled multitude a few sanctified vessels for His glory, so that there would not be a single generation which would not experience His mercy.'[167]

The *electi* (chosen) do not so much experience their election as the mercy of God in their election. The entire preceding chapter showed us clearly to what extent the concept of *misericordia Dei* (mercy of God) was the central concept in the *Institutes* of 1536.

> 'It should be recognized that our salvation is possible through the mercy of God alone, and surely not because of any dignity on our part, or because of anything that originates in us.'[168]

Through the law we are brought to the knowledge of ourselves and 'we are taught to seek God's mercy'.[169] In order to possess a quiet conscience, in which the *libertas Christiana* (Christian freedom) is grounded, we need to be freed from the curse of the law:

> 'We obtain this liberation from the law, this freeing from slavery, when by faith we grasp the mercy of God in Christ. Then we can be assured that our sins are forgiven, and we are no longer held captive to the law.'[170]

This corresponds with what he says in the sixth chapter:

> 'Therefore, as far as justification is concerned, all mention of the law should be abandoned, and every thought of works disregarded. We should only embrace the mercy of God, turning away from ourselves and looking upon Christ.'[171]

Looking back at what was discussed in the first chapter 'The Law', Calvin said at the beginning of the second chapter 'Faith':

'However, we also noticed that there is a way out of this disaster. The mercy of the Lord can restore us. When we accept it with a firm faith we will undoubtedly experience it. It wil give us shelter.'[172]

Here, too, Calvin talks about 'experiencing' the mercy of God.[173] This experience is a *fidei experientia* (experience of faith).[174] Calvin calls the *ordo salutis* (order of salvation) of Romans 8:18-30 the *ordo misericordiae Dei* (the order of the mercy of God).[175] Just as at the conclusion of the previous chapter, we now – at the conclusion of the second chapter – need to mention the 'order' of the way God deals with mankind, as it is reflected in the *ordo docendi* (order of instruction) of the early Reformation doctrines:

'The Lord meant to reveal himself to mankind in this order. Only when we discard all pride in the knowledge of our own misery, reject ourselves completely, and deem ourselves totally worthless, will we begin to taste the sweetness of the mercy that He offers us in Christ.'[176]

We should hardly be surprised that Calvin in the *definitio fidei* (description of faith) of the Catechism of 1537, discussed in this second chapter, is able to summarize the entire promise of the gospel in the single concept of the 'mercy of God':

'Faith is a strong and solid confidence of the heart, allowing us to rest assured in the mercy of God, as promised by the gospel.'[177]

We find the 'practical knowledge' of this very specific 'experience' expressed in all early Reformation doctrines. Based on Paul's letter to the Romans, the conceptual scheme 'Law and Gospel' (first the law and then the gospel) determined the structure of sacred doctrine. Calvin does his utmost to mold the *Institutes,* composed according to this scheme, into the most perfect form, although we can also see how Calvin deviates from this scheme in 1539.

In this second chapter we have described how this form began to manifest itself in the 1537 Catechism. The following chapter will describe what that form looks like in the wonderfully well-proportioned book of 1539.

NOTES

1. OS I, 283.
2. CO I, 230; OS I, 260 ll. 22-23 (Inst. 1536); CO I, 1102 (Inst. 1539-54: XX.,3); CO II, 1094 (Inst. 1559: IV.20.3). It is well known that Calvin, traveling through Geneva, was apprehended by Farel in August 1536.
3. 'Articles bailles par les prescheurs'. 17 Ianuarii 1537. See CO X.1, 5 and XXI (annales Calviniani), 206-207.

4. On 5 September he had begun his 'lecturae' (Bible readings) in St. Peter's church. CO XXI, 204.

5. Doumergue, *Jean Calvin. Les hommes et les choses de son temps*. Tome Second, *Les premiers essais*, Lausanna 1902, 288: 'The Catechism (in the sense where we hear that word) is an invention of the Reformation, neither less important, nor less characteristic'; in 289: 'The word Catechism, in the actual sense, appears to have been employed for the first time by Luther, namely in a letter of February 2, 1525. By composing his large and particularly his small Catechism in 1529, Luther established what a catechism in the Reformed tradition is.'

6. CO X.1, 12-13; OS I, 375 ll. 34-376 l. 19.

7. See above, chap. I §2, the discussion of the opening sentence of the Institutes of 1536.

8. *Instruction et Confession de Foy, dont on use en leglise de Genève*, CO XXII, 25-74; OS I, 378-417.

9. *Catechismus, sive Christianae Religionis Institutio*, CO X.2, 83.

10. See Annales April 27, 1537, CO XXI, 210-211, and CO XXII, 7-8.

11. A comprehensive report concerning the printer Wigand Koeln may be found in Le Catéchisme francais de Calvin, publ. 1537, reprinted for the first time after a new copy was discovered, and followed by the oldest confession of faith of the church of Geneva. With two notes by Albert Rilliet and Théophile Dufour, Geneva, 1878. 'Bibliographic note on the Catechism and the confession of faith by Calvin (1537), and on the other printed books at Geneva and in Neuchatel in the early times of the Reformation (1533-1540) by Théophile Dufour' (XCVIIII-CCLXXXVII); §3 'Wigand Koeln'. CLXIII-CLXXIV.

12. CO V, 313-314: *CATECHISMUS, SIVE CHRISTIANAE RELIGIONIS INSTITUTIO*, communibus renatae nuper in Euangelio Genevensis Ecclesiae suffragiis recepta et vulgari quidem prius idiomato, nun vero Latine etiam quo de Fidei illius sinceritate passim aliis etiam Ecclesiis constet, in lucem edita. Ioanne Calvino Autore. Basileae, Anno MDXXXVIII.

13. CO V, 317-322; OS I, 426-432.

14. See OS III, X-XII, in the 'Descriptio et historia editionum Institutionis latinarum'.

15. OS I, 19.

16. CO X.1, 11-12; OS I, 374 ll. 18 – 375 l. 8.

17. CO IX, 693-700; OS I, 418-426.

18. A.-L. Herminjard, *Corrrespondence des reformateurs* dans les Pays de langue française, Geneva/Paris 1872 (photomechanical reprint, Nieuwkoop 1965). Tome IV, 185 n. 9: '(...), ne pourrrait-on pas conclude, que le *Catéchisme* fut d'abord composé en latin, puis immédiatement traduit et publié en français, dès le commencement de l'année 1537?'

19. CO X.2. (106-109) 107: Conscriptus aliquanto ante Catechismus a nobis fuerat, gallice etiam editus.

20. Cf. above, Introduction §1.

21. Resp. OS I, 369-377: 'Articles;' 378-417: 'Catechisme'. 418-426: 'Confessio Fidei;' 426-432 'Praefatio'.

22. See CO XXII, 6.

23. The desire of the pastors and the City Council that all citizens should take an oath on the Confession in little groups of ten in the St. Peter church met with increasing resistance in the course of 1537. On September 29 we read of a decision of the Council to call up a refuser to testify to the faith (CO XXI, 215). However, on November 25, the entire Council meeting of the local citizens ('le Conseil general') rejected a motion of approval to accept this policy. At the same time the 'lords of Bern' declared that the oath, which the citizens were supposed to

swear on the Confession, was really perjury, because they were forced to accept something which sinful people could not comply with (Calvin discusses this issue elaborately in the preface of the Latin edition of the Catechism). From the moment that the opposition party, after the elections of 1538, acquired the majority in the Council, developments escalated which would result during the Easter season in the banning of the pastors from the city.

24. Albert Rilliet: 'Notice on the first stay by Calvin in Geneva, to serve as a historical introduction to the Catechism and the Confession of Faith of 1537'. loc. cit., V-XCVIII. The second introduction – the one by Théophile Dufour – has been mentioned above (n. 11).

25. 'The servant of the City Hall has brought the order to messieurs Farel and Calvin that they were no longer to preach in the city, and to move a three days' journey away from the city, as was decided in the General Council. The pastors answered: "Alright then! If we had been in the service of men, we would have been rewarded poorly, but we serve a greater master who will reward us." Calvin had his answer. Farel said: "Alright then" and "surely!" Registres au Conseil de Genève, tome 32 fol. 36; CO XXI (Annales Calviniani), 226-227.

26. CO XXII, 74; OS I, 417. This concerns article 33 in the count followed below.

27. Rilliet, op. cit. XCVII-XCVIII.

28. Rilliet, op. cit., LIX.

29. K. Barth, KD IV.3, 883, 887, 892 (CD, 772, 775, 779).

30. See above, the second point in the commentary on the Latin title of the Catechism of 1537.

31. J. Pannier in his book *Jean Calvin, Epitre au Roi*, op. cit., XX.

32. CO and OS do not have any numbering.

33. CO V, XLIV.

34. See above, the Introduction §2, point 2, and see below, Chapter III §1.

35. See above, Chapter I §2.

36. Rilliet, op. cit., XLII-XLIII.

37. Rilliet, op cit., XLVII-XLVIII.

38. On the irregularities in the manner of writing of the French text, Dufour writes (op. cit., CXIII: 'quelques unes, sans doute, pourraient etre attribuées à ses faultes typographiques'. – but that means twenty at the most – 'mais la plupart rappellent d'une manière sensible un état de choses réel, celui d'une langue qui n'était point encore fixée'. Therefore, now and then he adds letters or words in parentheses for clarification of the text.

39. The theme 'vera et falsa religio' is discussed by Barth in paragraph 17 of the KD. What Barth says christologically in KD I.2 §14 on 'The Time of Revelation' corresponds pneumatologically with KD I.2 §17 'Gottes Offenbaring als Aufhebung der Religion'. ('The Revelation of God as the Abolition of Religion').

40. Lat. Catechismus 1538: 'animis insita Dei opinio'; 1539: 'sensus divinitatis'.

41. CO XXII, 35; OS I, 380.

42. Inst. 1539: I.20, CO I, 293. See below Chap. III §3c-A.

43. Inst. 1559: I.6.3, O.S. III, 63 ll. 25-28.

44. This issue had not been thematically dealt with in the Institutes of 1536, which were begun in 1534 in Angouleme. It is briefly mentioned in the explanation of the sixth petition, when Calvin says: 'Let others, if they so eagerly want this, trust their free will and the powers they have in themselves, but it suffices us when we remain standing in the power of God alone, and are strong'. CO I, 98 below; OS I, 114 ll. 29-31.

45. The Latin text here mentions the word 'primum' twice, but the French text first mentions 'premierement' and then 'au commencement.' The French text gives the impression of being a translation of the Latin.
46. See above, Chapter I §4.
47. KD II.2 (title of the second part of the paragraph).
48. KD I.2, 981ff. (CD 878ff.).
49. OS I, 41 ll. 24-41.
50. CO I, 426-438 (Inst. 1539-1554: III.91-105 = Inst. 1559 II.7.3-17). In 1559 this discussion no longer follows the *explicatio legis*, but precedes it.
51. Note here: 'auparavant – maintenant' ; 'antea – nunc'.
52. CO XXII, 50; OS I, 394; Latin: CO V, 335.
53. Inst. 1539-1554: III.101 = Inst. 1559: II.7.12; OS III, 337 l. 23.
54. Cf. the *Heidelberg Catechism*, Sundays II-IV (Taken together, the segment 'Of Man's Misery').
55. CO XXII, 45; OS I, 390; the Latin text (CO V, 332) adds: *patrem:* '(He shows Himself) to be a benevolent and affectionate Father'.
56. For these 'heavenly treasures' and 'riches of the heavenly blessings' see above, Chap. I §2 at the opening of the part 'Faith' from the Introduction of 1536.
57. Inst. 1559: I.2.1. See above, the Introduction §2, n. 28.
58. See above, Chapter I, notes 55 and 165.
59. See above, Chapter I, note 47.
60. CO I, 78; OS I, 92. Also see above, Chapter I, note 163.
61. Compare above, the text of paragraph 7.
62. CO XXII, 46; OS I, 390.
63. The *Loci Communes* of 1521 deal with 1.'the powers of man, in particular free will', 2. 'sin', 3. 'the Law', 4. 'the gospel' and 5. 'grace'. Chiastically ordered, he treats the knowledge of sin and grace (in the framework: chapters 2 and 5) *by Law and Gospel* (in the middle: chapters 3 and 4) as the theme that dominates the entire book. See also, chapter III §1, supplement.
64. See Von Harnack in Gerhard Ebeling, *Wort und Glaube* I, Tübingen 1962, 260, and Otto Weber, *Grundlagen der Dogmatik* II, Neukirchen 1962, 408.
65. See above, Chapter I §3 at the conclusion of the discussion of Chap. II, 'Faith' of 1536.
66. II.2, §34: 'Die Erwählung der Gemeinde' = 'Israel und die Kirche'.
67. Cf. Calvin, *Defensio sanae et orthodoxae doctrinae de servitute et liberatione humani aribtrii adversus calumnias Alberti Pighii Campensus* (1543), CO VI, 225-404; this polemic is continued – because of the case against Jérome Bolsec (who because of his opposition to predestination was banned from Geneva: the *Articles* of 1536/37 in practice!) – in the work *De aeterna Dei praedestinatione quo in saltem alios ex hominibus eligit alios sua exitio reliquit: item de providentia quo res humanas gubernat* (On the eternal election of God, through which He elects some from humanity to salvation and leaves others to damnation; and also on the Providence that governs the human affairs) of 1552: CO VIII, 249-366. Bolsec is not named in this work; he was named previously, however, in Calvin's lecture before the congregation: *Congrégation sur l'élection éternelle de Dieu*, CO VIII, 85-140.
68. KD II.2, §32.2, (36-82) 37-55; CD, (24-76) 34-51.
69. This concerns a reference from Boettner's book, *The Reformed Doctrine of Predestination* (1932; Grand Rapids, 1941, 3), KD op. cit., 37; CD, 36.

70. Barth, KD op cit., 46; CD, 44.

71. Thomas Aquinas, S.Th. I Q. 23 art. 1 corpus. art.

72. In the first of sixteen lectures on *Das Wesen des Christentums* (Leipzig, 1900, 6) Adolf Harnack cites the saying *latet dolus in generalibus* (deception lurks in generalities). We assume that Barth quoted this saying from Harnack and replaced the word *dolus* by *periculum,* which results in a contamination of the two Latin sayings *latet anguis in herba* (an adder is hiding in the grass) and *periculum in mora* (there is danger in procrastination).

73. Barth, KD op. cit., 40-43. Citation 40 below, 41 above; CD, 39-41.

74. The line which follows serves in the OS as the first sentence of a new paragraph; we have joined it with the previous text; FB.

75. Luther, *Disputatio Heidelbergae habita* (April 1518), WA 1 (350) 353-354: thesis 21.

76. CO I, 74; OS I, 88 (Inst. 1536) and CO I, 863 (Inst. 1539-54: XIV.2). This translation read: 'qui scrutator est maiestatis, opprimetur a gloria.'

77. CO II, 681; OS IV, 371 ll. 24-25 (Inst. 1559): III.21.2). The text reads then: 'sicut nimium mellis non bonum est, ita investigationem gloriae non cedere curiosis in gloriam (Prov 25 d. 27.' 'Just as a surplus of honey is not good, so the investigation into glory does not bring honor to the curious.'

78. KD II.2, 68; CD 63.

79. Breukelman refers to the German words in Barths's text, the *Erkenntnisgrund* and *Realgrund.* Barth, op. cit., 98, 366; CD 91, 332-333.

80. For this foundation, see KD II.2, 55-64; CD 51-60.

81. Cf. Paul Tillich about God as 'abyss' in: *Systematic Theology*, I. Chicago, 1951, at the locations mentioned in the index.

82. CO I, 74; OS I, 88 ll. 8-10 and 18-21.

83. See the following (third and final) paragraph of this chapter.

84. CO I, 74; OS I, 87 ll. 35-39. See above, in the cited final part of paragraph 13, the saying: 'They will *experience* how true it is what Solomon says (Prov 25).'

85. Samuël Maresius, *Systema breve Universae Theologiae*, first ed., 1645, [7]Groningen 1673, IV, XIX: 'The general decision of the Council...is called the eternal Providence of God; to deny this, means to deny God Himself.' That was the starting point of orthodox doctrine.

86. CO I, 73; OS I, 86 ll. 26-28.

87. CO I, 73; OS I, 87 ll. 14-16.

88. Inst. 1539: VIII, 1554: XIV; CO I, 861-889 (Predestination) and 889-902 (Providence). The same structure is to be found in the work *De aeterna Dei praedestinatione* (About the Eternal election of God): firstly, 92 columns on predestination (CO VIII, 254-347) to be followed by 20 columns on Providence (op. cit., 347-366).

89. W. Niesel, *Die Theologie Calvins*, op. cit.

90. Niesel, op. cit., 12. Chapter I. The Election in Christ; 2. The Question of Assurance of Salvation.

91. Niesel, op. cit., [1]158-59, [2]168.

92. K. Barth, KD II.2 §32.3: 'The Place of the Doctrine (of Election) in Dogmatics'. 92-93; CD, 86.

93. KD II.2, 98; CD, 91.

94. K. Barth, KD I.1, 438; CD, 417.

95. Book I: CO II, 31-174 = 144 columns; Book II: CO II, 175-392 = 218 columns; Book III: CO II, 393-744 = 352 columns; Book IV: CO II, 745-1118 = 374 columns.

96. The 'modus percipiendae Christi gratiae' appears in the third Book to be a 'modus participiendae' as well. The 'receiving' of grace also means 'participation' in it.
97. CO XXII, 47; OS I, 391 below, 392 above.
98. Augustinus, *Enchiridion*; Migne PL 40, 231-288; CCSL XKLVI, Turnhout 1969 (23) 49-114; Bibliothèque augustinenne 9; Paris 1947, J. Rivière.
99. See above, Chapter I §3, at the end of the discussion of Chapter II of 1536, note 95.
100. 1536: CO I, 79-80; OS I, 93-94; 1539 (1554: V.37): CO I, 475 and 684 = 1559: III.2.42: OS IV, 52 ll. 26-53 l. 11 (points 1 and 2).
101. Thus, this twenty-first paragraph contains the words - from the above mentioned part (in 2) - from 'When faith, as we heard...' through 'by patient hoping and expecting'; see CO V, 343 (Latin) and CO XXII, 59; OS I, 403 (French).
102. OS I, 69 ll. 7-14. Cf. above, Chapter I §3. Note 86.
103. 'Spem omnem ac fidiciam in uno Deo ac Christo reponere.'
104. CO IX, 705 l. 4.
105. E. Bizer, *Theologie der Verheissung. Studien zur theologischen Entwicklung des jungen Melanchthon* (1519-1524), Neukirchen-Vluyn, 1964.
106. J. Moltmann, *Theologie der Hoffnung*, Munich. [1]1964. [3]1966.
107. See above, note 62 of this chapter. In 1539 Calvin prints these words in the Introduction to the *Explicatio symboli* (explanation of the Creed) – 1550 VI.2; CO I, 478 – and in 1559 in the discussion of *Quid sit fides* (what faith is) in III.26; OS IV, 13 ll. 15-16.
108. CO V, 337 (Latin); CO XXII, 52; OS I, 396 (French). Contrary to the Pauline text (1 Cor 1:30) Calvin, looking back at paragraphs 16-19, deliberately poses the words *iustitia – sanctificatio* (righteousness – holiness) at the conclusion.
109. See above, note 94 of this Chapter.
110. CO I, 477-478; 1550 VI.1-2. Cf. above, The Introduction §3, note 25.
111. See above, notes 62 and 107 of this chapter.
112. Institutes, 1541, Pannier, op. cit., 213.
113. Pagination according to the reissue of Pannier.
114. See below, at the beginning of Chapter IV §1, the overview of the editions 1536, 1539, and 1543-1554.
115. See below, Chapter IV of this study.
116. Inst. 1559: III.2; OS IV, 6 ll. 16ff.
117. Inst. 1559: III.2.42-43; OS IV, 52 ll. 26ff.
118. See above, notes 105 and 106 of this chapter.
119. Moltmann, op. cit., 15-16 (Moltmann cites from the 1559 Institutes).
120. See the lengthy citation in part 4 of the passage on faith, hope, and love of 1536 in this chapter, where in 1559 Calvin moved the word *individua*, so that it might not be lost, to the opening sentence on the *spes* as the *comes* of the *fides*.
121. KD IV.3, 1047-48 and 1049; CD, 913. Barth, too, cites the 1559 Institutes: III.2.42.
122. Cf. the basic principle ['Leitsatz'] of §73, op. cit., 1035; CD, 903.
123. KD IV.I, 366; CD, 332.
124. See above, n. 108.
125. We have seen already that Calvin, in connection with his retrospect on paragraphs 16-19, intentionally places the words *righteousness* and *sanctification* at the conclusion, unlike the Pauline text.

126. The issue of the authorship of the Apostolicum (which became relevant at the time of humanist textual criticism) will from 1539 onward be dealt with in the third section of the introduction to the explanation of the Creed; see *Institutes* 1543-54: VI.3 (CO 1.478-79).
127. See above, chapter I, the final part of §3.2.
128. Inst. 1543-54: VI.8, CO I, 481; Pannier, op. cit., 217 ll. 16-17.
129. CO V, 337.
130. Cf. KD I.1 §6.3 'Das Wort Gottes und die Erfahrung'. ('The Word of God and Experience'.)
131. OS I, 75 ll. 5-7.
132. KD I.1, 438; CD, 417.
133. Krusche, op. cit., 2.
134. Calvin read aloud the relevant article of the Catechism (together with the explanation of the *secunda pars symboli*). See CO X.1, 83 (Epistola 49).
135. See Doumergue II, op. cit., 266ff.
136. *Confessio Trinitate propter calumnias P. Caroli*: CO IX, 703-707.
137. See Calvin's own report of the entire controversy with Caroli in the year 1545: *Pro G. Farello et collegis eius, adversus Petri Caroli theologastri calumnias, defensio Nicolai Gallasii*, CO VII, 289ff.
138. Cf. (for the conclusion) OS III, 137 ll. 2-5 = Inst. 1554: VI.6; Inst 1559: I.13.21.
139. CO XLVII, 473.
140. KD I.1, 379ff.; CD, 359.
141. '...fiduciam spemque'; see above, n. 104.
142. CO XLVII, 4.
143. Inst. 1550: VI. 6-25.
144. Inst. 1550: VI.6 beginning, and VI. 17-25.
145. The words cited above appear at the conclusion of VI.15 and at the beginning of VI.16; in the *Institutes* of 1559 that equals the end of I.13.13 and further on in I.13.14; OS III, 127 ll. 8-14 and ll. 25-27.
146. Inst. 1554: VI.18; Inst. 1559: I.13.17, OS III, 131, ll.3-4. Also cited by Barth in KD I.1, 389; CD, 369.
147. CO I, 492 = Inst. 1554; VI.21; Inst. 1559: I.13.3, OS III, 112 ll. 9-10.
148. See above, Chap. I §3, n. 93.
149. CO I, 495 = Inst. 1554: VI.25; Inst. 1559: I.13.5, OS III, 115 ll. 21-116 l. 1.
150. Doumerge II, op. cit., 262.
151. *De voce Trinitatis et de voce personae*: CO IX, 707-708. See also KD I.1, 437-439 (CD, 416-418), where Barth, with regard to the reticence with which Melanchthon and Calvin originally spoke about the Trinity of God, spoke of 'a passing mood'.
152. Inst. 1559: I.13 with twenty-nine sections.
153. This is Calvin's term at the beginning of I.13.6.
154. In 1559 I.13.1-5 of the new *Institutes* we find VI.21-25 of the old version. See the marginalia in the OS.
155. In I.13.6-20 of the new *Institutes* we find the text of VI.8-10 of the old version.
156. Inst. 1559: I.13.21-29; VI.6 of the old *Institutes* = I.13.21 of the new version.
157. CO I, 58; OS I, 70, below.
158. Inst. 1539: V.6; CO I, 480.
159. Inst. 1559 I.13.21; CO II, 107; OS III, 135 l. 26-136 l. 9.
160. Krusche, op. cit., 2-3. With reference to Wernle, op. cit., 36ff.

161. K.D. I. 1, §8.1 'The Place of the Doctrine of the Trinity in Dogmatics'.
162. See above, n. 41.
163. OS III, 63, lines 25-38 (In reference to CO V. 325). Another example is formed by their remarks in the seventeenth and final chapter of Book Two of the Institutes of 1559 (Inst. 1559: II.17; OS III 508-515): 'Recte at proprie dici Christum nobis promeritum esse gratiam Dei et salutem' (rightly and properly it is said that Christ has merited for us the grace of God and salvation). Barth and Niesel remark in OS III. 509 (in section 1), line 20: 'hinc usque ad fin. Sect. 5 ex scripto: *Calvini ad Laelii Socini questiones Responsio* Nonis Iun. 1555 (CO X. I, 160 sqq.) ad primam questionem invenitur' (in the part from here to the end of section 5, one finds Calvin's answer to the first question from the work *Answer by Calvin to the questions of Lelio Sozzini*).
164. OS III, 127, lines 8-12 and ll. 25ff. (see above, n. 145) and OS III, 137, ll. 2-5 (see above, n. 138).
165. OS III, 137, ll. 41-42: 'similem sententiam Melanchthon protulit in Locus 1521' (Melanchthon wrote a similar sentence in his *Loci communes* of 1521), ed. G. L. Plitt (1864). G. L. Plitt-Theodor Kolde, Leipzig ([2]1889, [3]1900), [4]1925, 61-64.
166. We need to distinguish between 'Law and Gospel' as a thematic element (see above, n. 63) and the triad *Peccatum – Lex – Gratia* as a methodical principle, which helps to order the book.
167. OS I, 87 ll. 35-59. See above, n. 84.
168. OS I, 60 ll. 11-13. See above, Chap. I §2 n. 45. Cf. Inst. 12559: II.8.3., OS III, 345, ll. 29-34.
169. OS I, 41, ll. 14-15. See above, Chap. I §2 n. 55.
170. OS I, 58 ll. 40-44. See above, Chap. I §2 n. 38.
171. OS I, 224 ll. 15-18. See above, Chap. I §3 n. 135.
172. OS I, 68 ll. 28-31. See above, Chap. I §3 n. 82. Cf. Inst. 1559: III.2.1, OS IV, 7, ll. 4-10.
173. Cf. OS IV, 26 l. 6 ('misericordia dei') and ll. 17-20 ('sentire et experiri'): Inst. 1539-54: V.VIII.8; Inst. 1559: III.2.15.
174. CO XLVII, 330 and John 14:17.
175. OS I, 86 ll. 31ff.
176. OS I, 92, ll. 34-38. See above, Chap. I §2 n. 47 and §4, n. 163 and this chapter §2, n. 60.
177. CO XXII, 47; OS I, 391. See above, this chapter §2, n. 97. G. C. van Niftrik, *Sola Fide. De rechtvaardigingsleer in de nieuwere theologie*. The Hague, 1940, 19, writes: 'All this, preached to us by the Gospel – forgiveness of sins, reconciliation, substitution – may be summarized in the single word: *gratia*, grace; Calvin prefers to say: *mercy*, in order to better indicate to what people grace applies.' See also the term 'misericordia Dei' in the preface to the commentary on Genesis; CO XXIII (5-12) 11-12.

CHAPTER III

THE *INSTITUTIO CHRISTIANAE RELIGIONIS* OF 1539

§1. THE NEW DRAFT

In 1539, Calvin wanted to give the *Institutes* of 1536 a new form. Almost all of the earlier text would be included in the new book, which was to be three times larger. Calvin did not wish to discard anything that had been well formulated already.

In the 1536 *Institutes*, the entire *summa doctrinae* (essence of doctrine) had been unfolded in its first three chapters, 'The Law', 'Faith', and 'Prayer', just as Calvin had announced in the introduction to that *Institutio*. These chapters were followed by a fourth, 'The Sacraments'. In addition to these four chapters, Calvin included two large polemic chapters: 'The false sacraments' and 'Christian freedom'. We will proceed from this old draft of 1536 to describe the 1539 version, keeping in mind, of course, that Calvin had shown in the 1537 Catechism in what direction his thoughts were moving in his search for a new and better form for his book. The new draft for the book was a result of four decisions:

1. In 1536, 'essence of doctrine' was divided into three chapters, 'The Law', 'Faith', and 'Prayer'. In 1539, Calvin separated the third chapter, 'Prayer', from the other two. He now focused only on the first two chapters (*lex et evangelium*, law and gospel) to describe the 'essence of doctrine'. This decision underpins all decisions to follow. Because of this scheme of law and gospel, Calvin arrives at a very well balanced structure for his book. Indeed, Wernle says that 'this second *Institutes* has become the most complete of all his theological works'.[1]
2. The early Reformation scheme 'The Law → Faith' implies the following. The law gives us knowledge of our misery. This drives us to the knowledge of the grace of God in Christ, which we acquire through the gospel. As a result, the exposition of sacred doctrine moves from the knowledge of self to the knowledge of God. In 1536 this dialectic of law and gospel dominated the *Institutes*. However, in 1539 Calvin turned things around. He now wanted to demonstrate how we, being under the law, are brought from the knowledge of God to the knowledge of ourselves. Thus, the single chapter 'The Law' of 1536 is now divided into three chapters:

I. The Knowledge of God – II. The Knowledge of Man – III. The Law.

In the 1537 Catechism, the first three paragraphs had already given a sketch of the new chapter on the knowledge of God (*De cognitione Dei*). The second group of three paragraphs of that Catechism was used as an outline of the new chapter on the knowledge of man (*De cognitione hominis*).

3. The three chapters on the knowledge of God, the knowledge of man and the law, is followed by the subject of faith. Here, too, the original chapter of 1536 is turned into three separate chapters. In the previous chapter of the present study we saw how Reformational teaching initially concentrated on problems concerning the appropriation of salvation.[2] In 1536 Calvin had introduced these problems in the first chapter, 'The Law' after the *explicatio legis* (explanation of the law, i.e., the Ten Commandments). However, in 1537 he moved the discussion of these problems from 'The Law' to 'Faith'. We partake in salvation through faith. Thus, in 1537 the following classification was given:

Faith (§§14-15)	Justification and sanctification (§§16-19)	Explanation of the Creed (§20)	Hope (§21)

In 1539, the paragraphs 'What is faith?', 'Explanation of the Creed', and 'What is hope?' are put together in chapter 4, 'Faith'. However, Calvin still clings to the idea that faith is about our participation in salvation. Immediately after the fourth chapter, therefore, he adds two chapters in which salvation is described as a 'dual grace' (*duplex gratia*): justification and sanctification. First, he discusses sanctification. He does this in the fifth chapter on repentance (*De poenitentia*). Then, in chapter 6, he discusses justification (*De iustificatione*):

IV. Faith – V. Repentance – VI. Justification.

What had begun to emerge in the 1537 Catechism is now fully realized in the *Institutes* of 1539. This is Calvin's way to develop the 'essence of doctrine' according to the scheme 'The Law – Faith'. Calvin himself tells us at the beginning of the seventh chapter that the first six chapters dealt with the unfolding of the 'essence of doctrine':

> 'Above I have, to the best of my abilities, explained the essence of sacred doctrine. From the true knowledge of God and of ourselves we arrive at the communion of salvation.'[3]

In 1539, this is the main theme of arriving from the law to the gospel, and from the knowledge of self to the knowledge of the mercy of God in Christ. However, in our description of the 1539 *Institutes* we will stumble upon something very remarkable. While it is compositionally entirely dominated by the scheme 'Law → Faith', there is very little mention of this dialectic between law and gospel in the contents of the book. The dialectic of the knowledge of God and of the self has become independent vis-à-vis the dialectic of law and gospel. These two dialectics no longer co-incide.

4. Calvin now adds to these first six chapters as many chapters as he deems necessary to discuss the main aspects of the essence of doctrine. First, he adds two chapters: chapter 7, *De similitudine ac differentia veteris et novi testamenti* (similarities and differences between the Old and the New Testaments) and chapter 8, *De praedestinatione et providentia Dei* (Predestination and Providence of God). The two chapters are mutually connected. From the beginning of the world it has been one and the same doctrine – which Calvin expounded in the first six chapters – by which God saves people. However, he only gave this salvation to his elect. Not all people hear the preaching of the covenant of life. Also, not all who hear it, respond to it. These two chapters are then followed by the four remaining chapters of 1536:

- 'Prayer' (chapter 9)
- 'The sacraments', divided in three parts: 'The Sacraments' (chapter 10), 'Baptism' (chapter 11) and 'The Supper of the Lord' (chapter 12)
- 'Christian Freedom', divided into three parts as well: 'Christian Freedom' (chapter 13), 'Ecclesiastical Power' (chapter 14), and 'Civil Government' (chapter 15).
- 'The false Sacraments' (chapter 16).

The book is concluded by a new chapter: *De vita hominis Christiani* (The Life of a Christian). This is how the 1536 *Institutes*, consisting of six chapters, was expanded into seventeen chapters in 1539.[4]

To summarize, the four decisions that constituted the basis for the new design are:

1. Full concentration on 'The Law → Faith'.
2. 'The Law' is divided into three chapters, 'The Knowledge of God' – 'The Knowledge of Man' – 'The Law'.
3. 'Faith' is divided into three chapters, 'Faith' – 'Repentance' – 'Justification'.
4. Eleven new chapters follow, discussing separately the various aspects of the essence of the doctrine expounded in the first six chapters.

Thus, the book will consist of two parts. In the first part, the essence of doctrine is unfolded in six chapters. In the second part, the various aspects of this essence of doctrine are discussed. These two parts of the book are almost equal in length. In the French edition of 1541 the first parts comes to 432 pages and the second part to 390 pages.[5]

By the time of 1539 the *Institutes* had become a textbook for students and ministers. Nevertheless, Calvin still arranges his material around the explanation of the catechetical main parts: *decalogue, symbolum apostolicum, oratio dominica* (the Ten Commandments, the Creed, the Lord's Prayer), with the sacraments added to it. However, we saw how Calvin in 1535 in Basel, after explaining the main parts of the essence of doctrine, had added two more chapters.[6] In these chapters he discussed issues which in the main part had been insufficiently addressed. In 1539, too, Calvin created separate chapters for issues which demanded a more detailed explanation than could be given in the main chapters. Calvin's *Institutes* thus became a *loci*-theology, used as a textbook by students, while at the same time remaining his 'large Catechism'.

We can distinguish five phases in Calvin's efforts to compose the 1539 *Institutes*. In the first phase, the earlier first chapter 'The Law' evolved into the first three chapters: 'The Knowledge of God' – 'The Knowledge of Man' – 'The Law'. During the second phase, the earlier second chapter evolved into 'Faith' – 'Repentance' – 'Justification'. In the remaining phases, the second part of the *Institutes* came into being. In the third phase, the mutually connected chapters 7 and 8 were written. In the fourth phase, the old chapters 3 to 6 were added, divided into chapters 9 up to and including 16. Finally, during the fifth and final phase, the ethical chapter 17, *De vita hominis Christiani*, was written.

However, Calvin began his work on this new form by replacing the old introduction at the beginning of the book with a new one. In the following paragraph we therefore first need to discuss the new introduction. Then, in §3, we will discuss the first chapter of the 1539 *Institutes*, which originated in the first phase, and which will form the foundation of the first book of the 1559 *Institutes* and simultaneously the foundation of the entire definitive Institutes.[7]

APPENDIX: THE DEVELOPMENT OF MELANCHTHON'S *LOCI*

In the introduction to this study we stated that, in 1539, the *Institutes* were turned into a theological textbook for students following the example of Melanchthon's *Loci communes*.[8] Like the *Institutes*, Melanchthon's book has undergone several editorial stages. These can be classified into three *aetates* (generations).[9] It is interesting to compare these with the development of the *Institutes*.[10] Therefore, on the next page we give an overview of the development of Melanchthon's *Loci*.[11]

§2. THE NEW INTRODUCTION (I.1-3)
    on the dialectic between the knowledge of God and the knowledge of self.

The opening sentence of the old introduction of 1536 read:

'The essence of sacred doctrine consists almost entirely of these two parts: the knowledge of God and of ourselves.'[12]

This sentence is followed by a very elaborate section concerning the law, consisting of three parts:

The knowledge of God – the knowledge of man – the law.

PRIMA AETAS (1521-1525)	SECUNDA AETAS (1535-1541)	TERTIA AETAS (1543-1559)
Dedicatory Letter		Philip Melanchthon to the Pious Reader
Introduction	Preface	Preface
	(1) God	(1) God
	(2) The Creation	(2) The Creation
	(3) The Cause of Sin; Chance	(3) The Cause of Sin; Chance
(1) The Powers of Man, particularly Free Will	(4) The Powers of Man; Free Will	(4) The Powers of Man; Free Will
(2) *Sin*	(5) *Sin*	(5) *Sin*
(3) *The Law*	(6) *The Law of God*	(6) *The Law of God*
(4) *The Gospel*	(7) *The Gospel*	(7) *The Gospel*
(5) *Grace*	(8) *Grace;* Justification	(8) *Grace;* Justification
(6) Justification: Faith	(9) The Good Works	(9) The Good Works
(7) The Difference between the Old and the New Testament	(10) The Difference of mortal sin and venial sin	(10) The Difference between the Old and the New Testament
(8) The Old and the New Man	(11) Predestination	(11) The Difference between Mortal Sin and Venial Sin
	(12) The Difference between Old and New Testament	(12) The Church
(9) The Signs (Sacraments)	(13) The Spirit and the Letter	(13) The Sacraments
(10) Love	(14) Christian Freedom	(14) Predestination
	(15) The Sacraments	(15) The Kingdom of Christ
	(16) The Church	(16) The Resurrection of the Dead
	(17) Human Traditions	(17) The Spirit and the Letter
	(18) The Mortification of the Flesh	(18) Suffering and the Cross and True Comfort
	(19) The Vexation	(19) The Invocation of God or the Petition
(11) The Authorities	(20) The Kingdom of Christ	(20) Civil Authorities and the Dignity of Political Affairs
	(21) The Resurrection of the Dead	(21) Human Ceremonies in the Church
	(22) The Bearing of the Cross or Suffering	(22) The Mortification of the Flesh
(12) The Offence	(23) Prayer	(23) The Offence
	(24) Civil Authorities and the Dignity of Political Affairs	(24) Christian Freedom
	(added later: The Angels)	

By depicting how, from a biblical perspective, the knowledge of God and the knowledge of self should be understood, Calvin spelled out the main theme of sacred doctrine, which is 'the relationship between God and man'.[13] After this section on the law, Calvin moved on to two other much less detailed sections on faith and prayer. Calvin aimed to show how the three main sections of the Catechism are connected. In doing so, the old introduction not only formulated the main theme but also summarized the content of sacred doctrine.

At the conclusion of the old introduction Calvin announced the third chapter 'Prayer' in one sentence. In this sentence the introduction as well a the exposition of doctrine in the ensuing three chapters are summarized.[14] The sentence states that the content of the essence of doctrine in 1536 is about how God guides us from the knowledge of our misery to the knowledge of his mercy in Christ. The movement is from the knowledge of self to the knowledge of God. In that way, the entire summary of sacred doctrine consists of these two *partes* (parts): the knowledge of God and the knowledge of ourselves. The dialectic between these two coincides with the dialectic between law and gospel. With this in mind we are able to understand that Calvin already in 1536 used the expression 'essence of sacred doctrine' in his opening sentence: 'The essence of sacred doctrine consists almost entirely of these two parts: the knowledge of God and of ourselves.'

We now turn to the Introduction of 1539. Here, too, we encounter the same opening sentence, though in a somewhat altered form (1539: I.1):

'The essence of our true and unshakeable wisdom consists almost entirely of two parts: the knowledge of God and the knowledge of ourselves.'[15]

The words *summa sacrae doctrinae* (the essence of sacred doctrine) are thus replaced by the words *sapientiae nostrae summa* (the essence of our wisdom). We shall soon understand why Calvin did that.

The opening sentence is followed by two sentences (in the Latin original) which briefly describe what is to be understood by 'knowledge of God' and 'knowledge of ourselves'.

The knowledge of God:	'Clearly, the first part of our exposition must not only show us that there is one God, who must be worshipped and honored by all. It must also teach us that He is the only source of all truth, wisdom, goodness, righteousness, justice, compassion, power, and holiness, so that we learn to expect and ask from him all things. And then, having received these things from Him with praise and thanksgiving, we should learn to return them to Him.
The knowledge of man:	However, the second part should show us our weakness, misery, emptiness, and ugliness. This leads to true meekness, rejection, uncertainty, and hatred of ourselves. It will then arouse in us the longing to seek God. We realize that, because we are empty-handed and naked, all of our good rests in Him.'

The first of these two sentences describes the theme of the first chapter of the 1539 *Institutes* – 'the knowledge of God' – and the second describes the theme of the second chapter, 'the knowledge of man'. The two parts, which follow the opening sentence in the 1536 Introduction – very briefly, 'the knowledge of God', and in much more detail, 'the knowledge of man' – are thus summarized in these two sentences. However, the two parts are now of equal size.

They are not followed by the three parts that Calvin used in 1536 to announce the content of the first three chapters: 'The Law, Faith, Prayer'. In this new introduction he will only discuss what was mentioned in the two sentences that followed the opening sentence. They are followed by the statement (1539: I.2):[16]

'which of the two precedes and brings forth the other is not easy to discern'.

How these two kinds of knowledge, i.e., the knowledge of God and of ourselves, are interrelated, which of the two precedes and brings forth the other – this is the sole question to be answered in the introduction of 1539.

We now understand the nature of the difference between this new introduction of 1539 and the old one of 1536. The old introduction announced – together with the theme – the entire contents of the ensuing three chapters: 'The Law, Faith, Prayer'. The new introduction exclusively discusses main theme of sacred doctrine, to be discussed more extensively in the first two chapters of 1539: the knowledge of God – the knowledge of man. This allows us to understand why Calvin replaced the words 'the essence of sacred doctrine' in the opening sentence with the words 'the essence of our wisdom'. What will be discussed in the first two chapters of the new *Institutes* is not yet the entire 'essence of sacred doctrine'. It merely focuses on its main theme. In 1539 Calvin will not use the phrase 'essence of doctrine' until he has discussed its content in its entirety in the first six chapters.

Indeed, at the beginning of the seventh chapter – as already mentioned in the previous paragraph – he says: 'Above I have, to the best of my abilities, explained the essence of sacred doctrine. From the true knowledge of God and of ourselves we arrive at the communion of salvation.'[17] Because the new introduction does not announce the contents of the essence of doctrine in advance, limiting itself to expounding its main theme, Calvin moved the words 'the essence of doctrine' from the opening sentence to the beginning of the seventh chapter.[18]

After the two sentences on how the 'knowledge of God' and 'knowledge of ourselves' are to be understood, the introduction is devoted to the question 'which of the two precedes and brings forth the other'. Discussing this question, Calvin takes his cue from what he said about the knowledge of the self in the second sentence. According to Calvin, this knowledge has a dual effect. By showing us who we are, we are first led to humble ourselves, but then it will 'arouse in us the longing to seek God. We realize that, because we are empty-handed and naked, all of our good rests in Him'.

Since the longing to seek God originates in the knowledge of self, we move from the knowledge of ourselves to the knowledge of God. This is the issue Calvin wrestles with after the words 'Which of the two precedes and brings forth the other, is not easy to discern'. He proceeds as follows:

'In man, there exists a world of misery.[19] Therefore, we cannot look at ourselves honestly and not be tormented by the awareness of our own misery. Yet, as soon as we raise our eyes to the Lord, we gain at least some knowledge of him.'

Again, the idea expressed here is that we are led from the knowledge of self to the knowledge of God. This idea is subsequently emphasized and elaborated on in three distinct ways:[20]

(1) 'Because of our own misery, lifelessness, vanity, wrongness, and corruption we come to acknowledge that nowhere except in the Lord our true greatness, wisdom, truth, righteousness, and purity are to be found;

(2) Indeed, what is more, we are stirred by all the evil in us to see the goodness of God. We cannot earnestly try to reach Him, until we have begun to hate ourselves.

(3) For who would not enjoy to find rest in himself? And if someone is unknown to himself, that is, content with his gifts and ignorant of his misery – does he find rest? Not only are we prompted by the knowledge of ourselves to seek God, but also are we led by His hand to find Him.'

The expression *quaerere Deum* (seeking God) from the second sentence quoted above returns at the close of this train of thought. We are dealing here with the core concept of the 1536 *Institutes* ('Man → God'), as stated in the old introduction:

'Because this knowledge of our neediness – indeed, our disaster – by which we are taught to humble ourselves and to cast ourselves down before God and to seek His mercy...does not find its origin in us...'.

Immediately after the question 'which of the two precedes and brings forth the other', Calvin confirms the core concept of the 1536 *Institutes*. It is as though he is saying: 'I stick with that, that idea was correct.' Nevertheless, he continues by saying that, as a matter of fact, we must first move in the reverse direction, the movement leading us from the knowledge of God to the knowledge of self (1539: I.3):

'On the other hand, man can never achieve pure knowledge of himself, if he has not first seen God's face and from there descended to observe himself. For – being born with pride in ourselves – we always appear to ourselves righteous and truthful and wise and holy, unless we are persuaded of the contrary by clear evidence of our unrighteousness, dishonesty, folly, and impurity. However, we are not persuaded if we only look at ourselves, and not at the Lord, who is the only criterion by which this judgment must be measured.'[21]

God compares us to himself, being the measure (Latin: *regula*) of all things. That is the fundamental thought of this entire paragraph. Calvin spends more time on this second thought (that the knowledge of God leads to the knowledge of self) than he does on the first idea (that the knowledge of self leads to the knowledge of God):

'...when we have begun to raise our thoughts to God, and to consider what He is
like, and how perfect His righteousness, wisdom, and power are
– as the measure by which we ought to be measured –,
then, what used to smile upon us under the deceptive excuse of righteousness,
    will soon appear to be defiled by the greatest unrighteousness;
what wondrously bewitched us in the guise of wisdom,
    will disgust us as the most far-reaching folly;
what appeared to be power,
    will be unmasked as the most miserable weakness.
There are so few things which can match with divine purity,
    no matter how high are opinion of it may be!'[22]

This second thought is illustrated by quotes from Scripture. After considering both of
these thoughts, Calvin answers the question 'which of the two precedes and brings
forth the other' in the concluding sentence of the introduction as follows:

'No matter how the connection between the knowledge of God and of ourselves is
to be explained in the end, the proper order of instruction (*ordo recte dicendi*, 1543:
docendi) demands that we first discuss the knowledge of God (in chapter 1. FB).
After this we can descend to discussing the knowledge of the self (in chapter 2,
FB).'[23]

In this new Introduction Calvin is conversing with himself, having begun working on a
new design for the *Institutes*. He has now pointed out the direction he will follow. First,
we move from the knowledge of God to the knowledge of the self (in the first three
chapters 'The Knowledge of God', 'The Knowledge of Man', and 'The Law'). Then
we will move from the knowledge of self to the knowledge of God as knowledge of the
mercy of God in Christ. This will be done in the second group of three chapters 'Faith',
'Repentance', and 'Justification'. In 1539, the essence of sacred doctrine consists in
moving 'from the true knowledge of God and of ourselves' towards 'the communion of
salvation.'[24]

§3. DISCUSSION OF CHAPTER ONE: THE KNOWLEDGE OF GOD[25]

The 1539 title of chapter 1 is 'The Knowledge of God'. The 1543 title of this chapter
gives us a more complete description of what will be discussed in this first chapter:
'The knowledge of God, which is the first basic principle of religion and the question
from which to derive its true rule.'[26]

    We saw that in the new *Institutes* of 1539 we move from the knowledge of God to
arrive at the correct knowledge of ourselves, and then – based on this knowledge of
ourselves – move back towards the knowledge of God again. This leads us to wonder:
are the knowledge of God from which we came and the knowledge of God which we
arrive at the same? Do they both mean: knowing God as the God of the covenant, the
'God-with-us' in the history of his many acts, the YHWH-knowledge of those who are

known by him – and that means: the knowing of God *in Christo suo* (in his Anointed One)? Or are we dealing with a dual knowledge, a *duplex Dei cognitio*?

This question that we put to Calvin concerns the essence of the conversation we wish to have with him from the perspective of Barth's *Church Dogmatics*. Calvin will give us a clear answer to this question in the *Institutes* of 1559, in which all of sacred doctrine, in all its parts and subdivisions, will be unfolded within the framework of the *explicatio symboli* on the basis of the duality of the knowledge of God. Right at the beginning of that edition of the *Institutes*, in the second chapter 'What it means to know God', Calvin formulates this in a very clear way: 'The Lord first appears to us as the creator, both in the making of the world and in the general doctrine of Scripture. Then, in Christ, we meet him as redeemer as well. From this it follows that there is a dual knowledge of God.'[27] This answer does not yet appear in the *Institutes* of 1539. However, in the first chapter of this edition of the *Institutes* we will see how – already in 1539 – Calvin was developing this answer.

Calvin did not only use this first chapter 'The Knowledge of God' of the 1539 *Institutes* as the foundation for the first book of the 1559 edition, 'the Knowledge of God the Creator'. He also uses it as the starting point for the definitive *Institutes* as a whole. The *explicatio symboli* is based on the duality of the knowledge of God. We must now thoroughly analyze this first chapter of the 1539 Institutes.

In the first chapter, Calvin discusses the possibility and the reality of human knowledge of God as *fundamentum religionis* (basic principle of religion). God can be known by man because (1) man, in his entire being, is made to know God (subjective reason) and (2) God lets himself be known in the *mundus* (world) and in his *opera* (works), of which man himself is the most wonderful example (objective reason). Because of man's alienation from God, this possibility *ab initia mundi* (from the beginning of the world) only becomes reality among the *fideles* (believers). For them (3) God has added his Word to the 'works', which are nothing more than *muti magistri* (mute teachers). In the single event of knowing God, these three aspects each have their role.[28]

In the three parts which make up the argument of this chapter, Calvin discusses these three aspects. We may specify them with the titles Calvin himself will formulate in 1559. First, the theme 'That the knowledge of God is implanted in the minds of men by nature' in I.4-10 (in 1559 this is the title of I.3). Second, in I.11-18 we encounter the theme 'That the knowledge of God shines forth in the making of the world and in its continuing government' (in 1559 this is the title of I.5). Finally, in I.19-38 the third aspect is discussed under the heading of 'That Anyone, in order to Come to God, needs the Scripture as Guide and Teacher' (in 1559 this is the title of I.6: 'To come to God the creator...').[29] Each of these three parts will now be discussed.

§3.1 'THAT THE KNOWLEDGE OF GOD IS IMPLANTED IN THE MINDS OF MEN BY NATURE' (I.4-10)

I.4-5

When describing human knowledge of God 'in its fulfillment',[30] Calvin – again – starts from a 'fact of experience'.[31] It is abundantly clear, he says, from countless human acts and from religion in all its manifestations, that 'from the beginning of the world', God has planted a *divinitatis sensus* (a feeling of the Deity) in the hearts of all men, as a *semen religionis* (seed of religion). Here in Inst. 1539 I.4-5, but in other writings as well, Calvin expresses this *sensus divinitatis* or *sensus deitatis* in many ways, as an 'impression of a higher power', 'a certain knowledge of God', 'the conviction that there must be a God', 'a conviction concerning God, from which grows the inclination towards religion as from a seed'.[32] The section opens with the following sentence:

'We do not need to discuss that in the human spirit, by a natural inclination, there is a feeling of the godhead.'

In the second half of the sentence Calvin explains that it is God himself who brings this about in the human spirit:

'To prevent anyone from finding excuses in his ignorance the Lord has given to everyone a certain notion of a higher power.'[33]

When God created man, he created him with this 'sense of the godhead' in his innermost being. He constantly stimulates this God-consciousness 'in the spirits, the souls, the hearts of all men', so that it keeps manifesting itself again and again. Particularly as regards mankind, God is not a *deus otiosus* (a God who refrains from works). He does not leave us alone after creating us.

In the second half of the first sentence, Calvin told us why God deals with us in this way. He does so 'to prevent anyone from finding excuses in his ignorance'. This is powerfully underscored by what Calvin says next, referring to the words 'the Lord has given to everyone a certain notion of a higher power':

'in order that, when all understand that there is one God, and that He is their Maker, they are judged by their own witness, for not having...'

and now Calvin does not proceed by saying 'for not having wanted to know Him', but:

'for not having honored Him, and dedicating their lives to carrying out His will.'[34]

To know God, Calvin writes, is to honor him and serve him by obeying his will. The reformers again heard the biblical witness concerning God's dispute with his people and with mankind, and they particularly heard this witness in Paul's letter to the Romans. They saw mankind as subject to God's judgment. Although people are quite conscious that they exist in the presence of the living God, who never ceases witnessing to them, they ignore him as much as they can. They therefore must testify against themselves in God's judgment and 'will be condemned by their own testimony'.[35]

The opening sentences of the fourth paragraph form the foundation for the ensuing argument of the first chapter 'The Knowledge of God'. In the first section of this argument (paragraphs 4 and 5), Calvin discusses some examples of human conduct as examples of the fact that 'there is always in the souls of all men a certain knowledge of God being powerfully active.'[36] This is the conclusion that matters to Calvin. At the end of the first part of his argument, he soon will, in the tenth paragraph, give us a complete description of this conclusion. Before he does this, however, he first (in paragraphs 6 to 9) describes how this 'knowledge of God naturally implanted in the spirits of man' is – as *practica notitia* (practical knowledge) – the *fundamentum religionis* (basic principle of religion).

I.6-9

We recall how Calvin at the start of the first chapter in the first paragraph described the knowledge of God and then the knowledge of self. He repeats this description at the start of the sixth paragraph in the following words:

§6 (start)   §1

'We have already touched on the idea (in §1) that the knowledge of God should work as follows:

first, it teaches us to fear and re-spect Him,

second, it teaches us that all good things must be asked of Him, and that we should accept them.'[37]

'...must not only show us that there is one God, who must be worshipped and honored by all.

It must also teach us that He is the only source of all truth, wisdom, goodness, righteousness, justice, compassion, power, and holiness, so that we learn to expect and ask from Him all things. And then, having received these things from Him with praise and thanksgiving, we should learn to return them to Him.'[38]

These two sides of the knowledge of God will now be described in some more detail. First, the fear of God is the source of the obedience to his commandments (compare the biblical *yir'at elohim*, the fear of God).[39] Second, trust in God is the source of good-ness. At the conclusion of paragraph 9 Calvin will describe 'pure and real religion' as *fides cum serio timore coniuncta* (faith combined with fear). However, in the middle of the paragraph Calvin states: 'Our astounding vanity and madness come to light both in the one (fear) and in the other (trust).'[40] Indeed, instead of obeying God, we fob him off with a few offerings and a little dutiful service. Instead of trusting in him alone we put our trust in ourselves and in creatures. At the conclusion of this paragraph Calvin pro-nounces his verdict on empirical religion as follows:

'Finally we get ourselves into so many errors and pernicious opinions, that the little spark, which used to shed some light around us so that we could see the majesty of God, is choked and extinguished. It no longer leads us to true knowledge. Yet, the seed remains and in no way can be divorced from the root, that is, the knowledge that there is a God. However, it is corrupted to such an extent that it only brings forth the worst fruit.'[41]

In Calvin's judgment, all empirical religion, proceeding from 'the feeling of the god-head', which is the 'seed of religion', comes down to the 'corruption of the best', which is to say, 'the worst'. In paragraphs 7 and 8 he describes the two ways in which people sin in this regard. The first sin, described in paragraph 7, is that the *miseri homines* (miserable people) want to understand God not as he makes himself known, but as they wish to imagine him, projecting their carnal stupidity on him. 'They pay no attention to the fact that true religion must be in agreement with the good will of God, as with a rule that does not change.'[42]

The second sin, described in §8, is that they only take God into account when forced to do so, not gladly but with aversion, and not out of respect for his majesty, but from fear of his judgment. They shudder because they cannot escape it, but they abhor it at the same time. 'Those who are alienated from God's righteousness hope that the judgment seat, which has been erected to punish their transgressions, will be knocked down.'[43] This is an empty and deceptive shadow of religion, Calvin states. It hardly deserves the name of 'shadow'.

We now need to describe in a few words 'that unique knowledge of God poured out into the hearts of those who believe, and also the piety flowing out from that'.[44] Calvin does not know of any *Dei notitia* (knowledge of God), which is not also *pietas* (piety) and *Dei cultus* (service to God), and becomes *religio* (religion). Therefore, after showing us from paragraph 6 to 8 what *falsa religio* (false religion) is, in paragraph 9 Calvin will show us what the *vera religio* (true religion) looks like.

It is characteristic of true religion, Calvin says, that the two sins described in paragraphs 7 and 8 are not committed. He writes: 'To begin with, the pious soul is content to have God (...) only as He makes himself known. Second, he always makes sure he does not move in overconfident rashness beyond His will.'[45] This is followed by the impressive description of the way in which the *pia mens* (pious soul) in the *vera religio* (true religion) behaves with regard to God, not committing the two sins mentioned above. The passage opens with the words 'The pious soul knows God...'. What this means, is then described in five parts, all of which begin with *quia* (because). Time and again *qualem se manifestat ipse* (how He makes himself known) is described. Then the main sentences follow, which do not cease to tell us that *talem habere contenta est pia mens* (this is the way the pious soul is content to know him). We present this passage here in its even sharper formulation of 1559:[46]

'The pious soul knows God

because   he understands that He governs everything,
          he trusts that God is his keeper and protector
          and therefore entrusts himself completely to God's faithfulness;
because   he understands that God is the author of all good things,
          he will, when something troubles him, or when he lacks something, place
          himself immediately under God's care, from whom he expects his support;
because   he is convinced of God's goodness and mercy,
          he will rest in God with sure confidence
          not doubting that, whatever his disease may be,
          there is healing in store for him, because of God's benevolence;

because   he acknowledges God as Lord and Father,
              he deems God to be worthy of his obedience,
              keeping his commandment at all times,
              indeed, he reveres God's majesty,
              giving Him glory,
              and following His commandments;
because   he sees that God is a righteous Judge,
              armed with sternness to punish misdeeds,
              he keeps God's judgment seat forever in his mind,
              and will, because of his fear of God
              refrain from everything that might arouse God's anger.'

What Calvin says in this final sentence about the relationship of the *pia mens* (pious soul) to God as the *iustus iudex* (righteous Judge) is discussed in more detail in two subsequent comments:[47]

1. God is the 'avenger of the wicked' as much as the 'benefactor of the pious'. The 'pious soul' loves God equally in both manifestations:

   'Indeed, he embraces God
           no less as avenger of the wicked
           than as benefactor of the pious,
   because he understands that He is honored,
           no less when the righteous receive the wages of eternal life,
           than when the godless and evildoers are punished.'

2. Calvin's second comment states that the 'pious soul' does not refrain from sin out of fear for divine judgment, but because he loves God and serves God voluntarily and spontaneously:

   'Moreover he does not refrain from sinning just out of fear of punishment.
   He does so because he loves and worships God as his Father
   and because he respects his Lord and serves Him.
   Even if there were no hell, he would not treat God with contempt.'

This is what Calvin believes to be *pura germanaque religio* (pure and real religion). Indeed, immediately after this description, as a conclusion of the ninth paragraph, he comments:

   'This, then, is what pure and real religion amounts to.
   It is faith combined with an attentive fear of God,
   where "fear" is understood to be
           both an honest love for His righteousness,
           as prescribed by His law,
           and a voluntary respect for His divine majesty.'[48]

It is typical for Calvin to call the 'righteousness' of human action, 'righteousness which is prescribed by the law'. In 1559 he changes the final lines into:

> '(...) where "fear" is understood to be voluntary homage,
> such as the proper service to God demands, as prescribed in the law.'[49]

To this description of the *vera religio* in the ninth paragraph we want to add two more comments.

1. Everything that Calvin says in the five auxiliary sentences beginning with the word *because* was already mentioned in the 1536 *Institutes*. This was done at the very beginning of the *Institutes*, directly following the opening sentence, where the content of the knowledge of God was described. We can understand what Calvin aims at in 1539. He does not want to present the complete content of the knowledge of God right away, as he did in 1536. Rather, he limits himself to the briefest description possible, repeating it – using different words – at the start of paragraph 6. The much more elaborate description of the knowledge of God, which in 1536 had stood at the very beginning, is expanded and placed in paragraph 9 describing 'true religion'. Calvin wants this paragraph to be the climax of chapter 1.

   In 1559 Calvin combines these three passages on the knowledge of God into one single chapter, chapter II of book 1 entitled, 'What it is to Know God, and what Ends this Knowledge serves'. He writes another introduction to the entire *Institutes* at the beginning of this chapter, in addition to the introduction at the beginning of chapter I. In this second introduction, Calvin formulates the thesis of the duality of the knowledge of God, which will be the ruling principle for his explanation of the Creed.[50]

2. What Calvin describes here as the 'knowledge of God' of 'pure and real religion' is the equivalent of what, in the Tanakh, is called the *da'at elohim* (knowledge of God). It describes Israel's relationship with the God of the covenant. Here we recall Hosea 2:21-22 for example:[51]

> I betroth you to Me for ever,
> I betroth you to Me
> in truthfulness and justice,
> in steadfast love and in mercy,
> I betroth you to Me
> in faithfulness.
> You shall acknowledge Me.

Excursus
This is a love story. Thrice we hear: 'I betroth you to me.' Although she had become a prostitute, unfaithful and rejected, the wife is spoken to as though she were a young maiden once again. 'I betroth you to me' is firstly followed by 'for ever', meaning: 'all days'. This is followed by the words 'in truthfulness and justice / in steadfast love and in mercy'. The third time we only read: 'in faithfulness'.

The five phrases 'in truthfulness', 'in justice', 'in steadfast love, 'in mercy', 'in faithfulness' express the qualities by which the man and his wife will be bound together for ever. All of this is his gift to her: 'I betroth you to me'. It will be hers when she obeys him: 'you shall acknowledge Me.'[52]

After the conceptual pair 'truth and justice' we would expect to find the pair 'steadfast love and faithfulness' in the next sentence. However, what follows is: 'steadfast love and *mercy*'. Only then comes 'faithfulness'. The poet accomplishes three things with this:

(1) It allows the lover to express the words 'I betroth you to me' for a third time.
(2) After the four words that follow the expression the second time, the lover can now express his covenantal 'being in the act' for the third and last time in a single word: 'in faithfulness'.
(3) The lover surprises us with the words 'steadfast love and *mercy*'. In this way he expresses the meaning of his steadfast love. This love can be characterized as compassion.

Hosea's preaching is all about love.[53] Contrary to what the religious cult in Hosea's days had become – having been perverted by the influence of Baal – , true love is a story between 'I and thou', to use the words of Martin Buber. 'I betroth you to me – you will acknowledge Me.' The amazing climax of this love story is that God has mercy on the people of Israel, although Israel in the book of Hosea is called *Lo rukhamah*, 'You will not take pity' (Hos 1:2-9; 2:1-3, 6, 25).

'Steadfast love' and 'faithfulness' are relational concepts. However, God's faithfulness is not answered by the side of man. He is not given faithfulness in return. The issue here is what Paul described as: 'Will their unfaithfulness undo the faithfulness of God? Certainly not!' (Rom 3:3).

Let us now connect these thoughts to our discussion on Calvin's concept of true religion. What Calvin is saying is this: Just as Israel knows YHWH as the God of the covenant of grace, so the believers know God in true religion.

I.10

In paragraphs 6-9, Calvin has described the *Dei notitia* (knowledge of God) as the 'fundamental principle of religion'. He has put 'pure and genuine religion' over against empirical religion. In doing so, he has unfolded the theme of the second paragraph of the 1537 Catechism 'What is the Difference between True and False Religion'. Now, in the short tenth paragraph, he concludes the first part on the knowledge of God:

'Therefore, we are to know God, that is the way we are born.
Yet the knowledge of God, when it does not reach the point described above, is
    vain and languishing.
As a result, it is a public fact
that all those who no longer dedicate themselves with their whole life to find this
    knowledge
are estranged from the law of their creation'.[54]

We recognize the title of the first paragraph of the 1537 Catechism: 'All men are born to know God.' To be born to know God is the law of human creation (which did not remain hidden from the philosophers either). This is the only thing which distinguishes mankind from irrational animals. The final sentence of the paragraph containing the second instance of the word *therefore* reads as follows:

'Therefore, the service of God is the only thing which makes man superior to the animals. Only man can strive for immortality.'[55]

In this final line we hear a thought which resonates throughout the *Institutes*. The believers' life is a continuing 'meditation on the future life'.[56] Calvin expressed this in the second half of the first paragraph of 1537 as follows:

'Let the unbelievers try to erase the consciousness of God planted in their hearts. We, who confess our piety, have to consider that this ruined life, which shall soon come to an end, is nothing but a meditation on immortality. Eternal and immortal life cannot be found anywhere except in God alone. Therefore, it must be our first concern and effort in our lives to seek God, to strive after Him with all the inclination of our hearts, and to find rest in Him alone.'[57]

Following on the conclusion of the first part of the argument, conducted in the tenth paragraph, the second part of the argument – in the first sentence of the eleventh paragraph – starts with the words:

'The Lord wants the ultimate goal of life to be the knowledge of Him (John 17:3). Apparently, He does not want anyone to be excluded from this state of bliss. Therefore, He makes himself known publicly to all. He reveals himself.'[58]

Excursus
In the Catechism of 1542 Calvin will no longer take the dialectic of the knowledge of God and of self as his starting point as he did in the first six paragraphs of the 1537 Catechism. In the 1542 Catechism, his point of departure is the conclusion we encountered above, in paragraphs 10 and 11. The first five questions and answers are:

'1. *Minister:*   What is the chief end of human life?
    Student: To know God.
2. *Minister:*   Why do you say that?
    Student: Because he has created us and placed us in this world to be glorified in us. And it is indeed right that our life, of which he himself is the beginning, should be devoted to his glory.
3. *Minister:*   What is the highest good of man?
    Student: The same thing.
4. *Minister:*   Why do you call that the highest good?
    Student: Because without it our condition is more miserable than that of brute beasts.
5. *Minister:*   From this we see then, that nothing worse can happen to a man than to live without God.
    Student: That is true'.[59]

We now turn to the second part of Calvin's exposition on the knowledge of God.

§3.2 'THAT THE KNOWLEDGE OF GOD SHINES FORTH IN THE MAKING OF THE WORLD AND IN ITS CONTINUING GOVERNMENT' (I.11-18)

This title, formulated by Calvin in 1559, tells us that in this second part of his argument Calvin wants to discuss the way in which God makes himself known in the *mundi fabrica* (the making of the world) and in the *mundi gubernatio* (the government of the world). Instead of telling the story of the 'Bundesgeschichte' (history of the covenant) to which the Tanakh testifies, Calvin offers us in this second part of his argument a religious worldview using biblical concepts and images.

I.11

In the first part of his argument Calvin had announced the content of this paragraph. First, in the seventh paragraph, he wrote about 'understanding God as He makes himself known' and in the ninth paragraph about 'having God in the way He reveals himself'.[60]

In this second part of his argument on the knowledge of God, Calvin describes how the act of 'making himself to be known' and 'revealing himself' function. God reveals himself in the universally visible *opera* (works) of the entire *mundus* (world) surrounding us. Calvin begins by describing this theme of I.11-18 in the eleventh paragraph. We will put the 1559 version next to the 1539 version because in the former Calvin improves on the original text by giving an even more precise description of the theme:

1539 (§11 first sentence)[61]	1559[62]
'The Lord wants the ultimate goal of life to be the knowledge of Him (John 17:3). Apparently, He does not want anyone to be excluded from this state of bliss.	'Moreover, the ultimate goal of a blessed life lies in the knowledge of God, and no one is to be excluded from this state of bliss. Therefore, God has not only implanted the seed of religion (as we call it) in the spirits of men, but has also revealed himself in the artifact of the world.
Therefore, He makes himself known publicly to all.	In this way He makes himself known publicly every day,
He reveals himself.'	so that they are not able to open their eyes without being forced to see Him.'

In the first sentence of the eleventh paragraph Calvin proceeds from what he had formulated as the conclusion in the tenth paragraph: the goal of our life is knowing God and this knowing is the access to happiness, that is, the happiness of *immortalitas* (immortality) and of the *vita futura* (the future life). To make sure that this access will not be denied to anyone, God manifests himself to all in a visible way. This is described in more detail in 1559. First, this text says that God reveals himself in 'the artifact of the world'. Secondly, it happens in such a way that people cannot open their eyes without being forced to see God.

Moreover, in 1559 Calvin points to the connection between the subjective side of the knowledge of God, discussed above, and its objective side, which is now to be discussed. He says: 'God has not only implanted the seed of religion (as we call it) in the spirits of men, but has also revealed himself in the artifact of the world'. In what follows Calvin will point out in fuller detail exactly how God reveals himself 'in the artifact of the world'. God, who in his *natura* (nature) and *essentia* (essence) is incomprehensible to us, reveals himself to us in his '*opera*' (works):

1539 (§11 second sentence)[63]	1559[64]
'For though His nature is incomprehensible and to a large degree hidden to human understanding, He has imprinted in all of His works certain distinguishing marks of His majesty. Because of these marks we can come to understand Him, according to the measure of our weakness.	'His essence is indeed incomprehensible, so that His higher power is quite beyond us as humans. Yet in each of His works He has engraved certain signs of His majesty.
Indeed, they are so clear and evident that every excuse of ignorance fails, no matter how blind and obtuse we may be.	These signs are so clear and recognizable that every excuse of ignorance fails, no matter how untrained and obtuse one may be.

(third sentence:)

No matter how hidden His being may be, we constantly perceive His virtues. He makes himself know to us to such an extent as is necessary for our salvation.'

After Calvin has mentioned the 'world' in the first sentence (1559), his next topic, in the second sentence, is 'works'. All speech about the divine 'nature' or 'being' is rejected as *otiosa speculatio* (useless reflection).[65] The 'practical knowledge' of the 'pious soul' is related to God's 'works'. In his works God makes himself known. He has imprinted and engraved (1539: *impressit*; 1559: *insculpsit*) in mankind certain marks of his majesty (1559: of his glory). By means of these marks, he says in 1539, God can be understood according to the measure of our weak cognitive powers. These words are deleted in 1559. He leaves out the concept of accommodation, which is so characteristic of his theological epistemology, at this particular point, because he only wishes to express the thought that God, while being incomprehensible in himself, makes himself known in his 'works'. He has engraved certain signs in us which are so clear and evident that no men, however uneducated and obtuse he may be, has an *ignorantiae excusatio* (excuse of ignorance). At the beginning of the first part of his argument, Calvin wrote: 'To prevent anyone from finding excuses in his ignorance...'.[66] Here, he says the same thing with the words: 'That every excuse of ignorance fails...'.

The thought which follows in the 1539 edition – namely that God's *virtutes* (virtues) are made known to us to such an extent as is necessary for our salvation – is deleted in 1559. In 1539, the knowledge of God in his *opera* (works) and the knowledge of God *in Christo suo* (in his Christ) belong together in the single movement 'from the true knowledge of God and of ourselves to the communion of salvation'. In 1559, this is no longer the case.

In the first three sentences of the eleventh paragraph, Calvin has described the theme that he plans to unfold in all of the second part of his argument on the knowledge of God (I.11-18): the God who is incomprehensible according to his 'essence' and who is hidden to us, makes his 'majesty' shine in all of the visible 'works' of the world. The knowledge of God is not born from hearing about the story of the *debarim*, but in the seeing with our own eyes the visible works of the world surrounding us. In this argument we constantly meet, on the one hand, the words 'world' and 'works', and, on the other hand, words referring to visual observation.[67] In this chapter, Calvin does not speak from the perspective of the covenant or Christ about the way God makes himself known to man. Rather, he speaks about his acts, his *kabod*, *doxa* and *gloria* (majesty), his appearance (*Erscheining*, Buber). Calvin speaks from the perspective of visual observation. The two sentences, following the first group of three sentences of §11, express this concisely:

'In the first place, wherever you turn your eyes, there is no part of the world so small, that you cannot see at least a few sparks of his majesty in. No one can look at this grand and rich work of art, in all its breadth and depth, without being amazed by its immeasurable power and its brilliance.'[68]

Likewise, Calvin says of God's messenger, who in the narrative of Luke 2 stood by the shepherds,[69] that he *fulgore coelestis gloriae instructus* (was equipped with the brilliance of heavenly glory).[70] The unfolding of this theme follows in paragraphs 12-18 after the description of the theme in §11.

I.12-13

In paragraphs 12 and 13 Calvin first gives a summarizing overview of the *opera Dei* by characterizing the *providentia Dei* (Providence of God) as *gubernatio mundi* (government of the world).[71] Calvin distinguishes two sorts of 'works of God'. The first kind is that of the *ordinarius naturae cursus* (the normal functioning of nature) and the other is that of the *opera, quae praeter ordinarium naturae cursus eveniunt* (works which happen outside of the common course of nature).[72]

The first kind, described in paragraph 12, is about natural phenomena (to which also belong the wonders of the human body) while the second kind, described in paragraph 13, is about the ups and downs of human society.[73] In both kinds of 'works' God shows his 'virtues' (I.11). All 'works of God' are 'means of proof', 'information' (I.12; I, 19), 'witnesses' (I.14) of his virtues.[74] However, the multiplicity of 'virtues' all testify to the one glory of the divine majesty, which radiates and glitters in all his works, for 'God's glory is the sum of all divine perfections'.[75] The first kind of *opera* (in paragraph 12) is primarily about divine *sapientia* (wisdom), *potentia* (power), and *bonitas* (goodness). The second kind (paragraph 13) is particularly about divine *clementia* (nobility), *misericordia* (mercy), and *iustitia* (*vindicatrix*) (punishing righteousness).[76]

With this we have indicated all the basic concepts that Calvin uses here. We have also noted how they relate to each other. They are all governed and dominated by the concept of the 'world'. For example, Calvin says in the introduction to his Genesis commentary of 1553, in which he repeats this entire argument about the knowledge of God: 'The world is our school if we wish to know God in a fitting manner' for 'the otherwise invisible God has placed His image in the world – to a certain point – and in that image He shows himself to us'.[77]

I.14-15

After the works have been described in paragraphs 12 and 13, Calvin discusses in paragraphs 14 and 15 two aspects of the knowledge of God concerning these works. In §14 he emphatically underlines the thought already expressed in §11, that we – contrary to scholastic speculations on the divine 'essence' – need to be content with the works. This is because in them all the divine 'virtues' become manifest. They make us experience and feel who God is for us:

'The Lord is, after all, made known to us by His virtues. We feel their power within us and enjoy their benevolences. As a result, knowing these virtues will touch us in a much more powerful way than when we would imagine a God who does not enter our feelings. Hence, we understand that the most direct and suitable way to seek God is via His virtues. We should want to try and to grasp His essence with audacious curiosity. We should worship God instead of examine His essence meticulously.[78] We see Him in His works. Through His works He relates to us in a trustful way, and shares himself with us to a certain degree.'[79]

Excursus
Compare this with answer 25 of the 1542 Catechism:
Minister: Why do you add that he is Creator of heaven and earth?
Student: Since He reveals himself to us by His works, we ought to seek Him in them. Our mind cannot grasp His essence. The world is for us like a mirror in which we may contemplate Him, to such an extent as is fitting for us.'[80]

In the final paragraph of this chapter (§38), this thought is expressed once more. Citing Exodus 34:6 – 'YHWH YHWH God, merciful and gracious', etc. – Calvin says:

'At this place we note that His great name' – YHWH, meaning 'I am who I am', FB – 'is repeated. Hereby His eternity is proclaimed, His self-sufficiency. Then we are reminded of His virtues, by which He is described to us, not as He is in himself' – that is, his being, FB – 'but as He is toward us' – that is, His works, FB – 'so that the knowledge of Him is founded on living experience rather than on empty and floating reflection'.[81]

Next to this first aspect of the knowledge of God in his works, a second aspect is discussed in paragraph 15. Seeing how the godly are oppressed and humbled and how the godless enjoy prosperity, we can conclude 'that there will be another life, in which unrighteousness will be punished and righteousness will be rewarded'.[82] Looking back at what was said so far, Calvin says at the end of §15:

> 'One needs to acknowledge that in the works of God His virtues are portrayed, especially when seen together, like a painting in which many details make up one image. By these virtues the entire human race is invited to the knowledge of Him, and with that knowledge to the possession of bliss.'[83]

Calvin said the same thing in different words at the beginning of this second part of the argument, in the above cited fourth and fifth sentences of paragraph 11.[84]

Excursus
It is interesting to compare this quote to the character of the biblical *tehillah* (hymn). This song of praise is not only about this or that act of God, but about all God's acts taken together. By saving us he has become 'God with us'. This causes his people to praise him. The biblical songs of praise are expressing the total reaction (with all available means) of all of the people (and of all creatures) to all of God's acts for our good. In this way it is the song of the congregation. In Calvin's words we hear an echo of the hymnic ecstasy of the biblical psalms.[85]

I.16-18
Paragraphs 16-18 form the conclusion of this argument about the knowledge of God in his works.

The sixteenth paragraph begins with the word *atqui* (however). No matter how clearly God and his immortal kingdom is placed before our eyes through his works, we are all totally blind and do not see it. This blindness pertains both to the works of the 'normal functioning of nature' and to the works 'which happen outside of the common course of nature'. From the most uneducated folks to the most gifted spirits, we are all cursed without exception with the disease of turning away from the one true God.

The seventeenth paragraph, which opens with the word *ergo* (therefore), formulates this conclusion as follows:

> 'In vain therefore do so many bright lamps cast their light around us in the artifact of the world. In vain do they express the glory of its Author. They do indeed send us their rays from all sides, but in such a way that they cannot possibly lead us towards the right path.'[86]

This being the case, does it make sense, we ask, that God never ceased to make himself known in all of his works so clearly and powerfully?

The eighteenth and final paragraph of the second part of this argument provide an answer to this question. 'Every escape route is cut off for us'.[87] What was said at the beginning of the first part (I.4) and repeated at the beginning of the second part (I.11, the second sentence) is now, at the conclusion of these two parts, emphatically underlined in a separate paragraph, which is the climax of the first two parts. 'We deserve this. Every excuse has been taken away from us.'[88]

We understand by now that this beautifully constructed argument on the knowledge of God in his works (we still need to discuss the third part) is nothing but an exhaustive exegesis of Romans 1:19-23. The early Reformation doctrines as we see them in Melanchthon's *Loci communes* of 1521 and in Calvin's 1539 Institutes, are of one pair with the exegesis of Paul's letter to the Romans (Calvin's commentary on this epistle was published in 1541).[89] It is no surprise that Wernle has entitled the second part of his book on Calvin, in which he discusses the 1539 *Institutes*, 'Die paulinischen Zentraldogmen von 1539'.[90]

Conclusion of the discussion on I.11-18: a conversation with Calvin
We need to ask, however, to what extent the exegesis of Romans 1:19-23 in the first chapter of the 1539 Institutes agrees with the structure of biblical proclamation. Our objections to Calvin's argument concentrate on two points. On the one hand we object to the way Calvin distinguishes 'the essence of God' from 'the works of God', and on the other hand against the way in which he speaks about the 'works of God' in connection with the whole of the visible 'world'. We will briefly indicate in what direction our objections go, as relating to both points:

1. Calvin rightly says that we need to focus on God's works when we want to know who God is for us. All speculations about the divine being, apart from the works, bring us on a dangerous track. However, in the proclamation of prophets and apostles this focus on God's works occurs in a different way than in Calvin's *Institutes*. In three places in the Tanakh we hear the expression 'to tell of God's name' (Ex 9:16; Ps 22:23; Ps 102:22). But we also hear: 'to tell of his *kabod* (glory)' (Ps 96:3; Ps 19:2), 'to tell of his *tehillah* (praise)' (Ps 9:15; Ps 78:4; Ps 79:13; Isa 43:21) and 'to tell of his *gedolah* (greatness)' (Ps 145:6).

The Tanakh talks about God's name and his glory by mentioning his *ma'asim* (acts) (Ps 107:22; Ps 118:17; Ps 40:6, cf. Ps 92:5-6). His acts are those of a divine covenant partner. They are pure *sedaqot* (righteousness), *hasadim* (mercies), *yeshu'ot* (acts of liberation – when people are in mortal fear). The Tanakh tells us to seek God's name in his acts, because who God is, becomes known in what he does. But we should also reverse this sentence. Because of what God does we know who he is, and not only who he is *quoad nos* (in his relationship to us), but also who he is *apud se* (in himself). As the God of the covenant he wanted to become 'for us' what He was in himself. Therefore 'the name of the LORD is a strong tower; the righteous will run to it and be put in a high place' (Prov 18:10).

This, then, is the biblical structure ('God corresponds to himself'):[91] God becomes known in what he does, but also: in what he does, he becomes known as he is in himself. This structure is preserved in the *Church Dogmatics* of Karl Barth (with a discussion in the Prolegomena of the doctrine of the Trinity as explication of the biblical concept of revelation). 'The Doctrine of God' (vol. II.1-2) is about 'the description and explanation of the *subject* of all that is heard and said in the Christian church'.[92]

After the first chapter about '*Die Erkenntnis Gottes*' ('The Knowledge of God'), the second chapter of this locus *de Deo* (God) by Barth does not bear the traditional title '*De essentia Dei et attributis eius*' ('On the Essence of God and His Attributes', thus also again Emil Brunner and Otto Weber),[93] but 'Die Wirklichkeit Gottes' ('The

Reality of God'). In this chapter Barth tries to describe 'Die Lebendigkeit Gottes' ('The living God') as 'Gottes Sein in der Tat' ('Being of God in Act').[94] It is right that the title of the sixth chapter should be 'Die Wirklichkeit Gottes', Barth explains, because 'Wirklichkeit is the combining concept of being and act, while essence is precisely the concept which tears apart being and act'.[95]

In the period of orthodoxy after the Reformation, discussions on the being of God were reintroduced in theology. Indeed, the topic of the being of God became more important than that of his works (according to the logic 'acting follows being').[96] What Calvin (who was an anti-scholastic!) had left open for understandable reasons, though without justification, is now filled in again in the wrong way. God's works were not described as 'God's being in the act'. For example, in Johannes Wollebius's *Christianae Theologiae Compendium* (1626) we read at the very beginning of the first book on the knowledge of God that 'God is known as He is in himself and in His works', as though it were possible to distinguish between 'who God is' and 'what God does', between *shem* and *dabar*, 'person' and 'work'.[97] From this vantage point, it is a pity that Calvin in his opposition against all scholastic speculation has gone too far in his denial (for example when he discusses those who 'raise themselves in a proud flight over the world and seek God in His naked being').[98] Because of this strong denial he could not give an adequate account of what he should have confirmed, on the grounds of the biblical witness: the reality of God, the life of God, the being of God as 'God being in the act'.[99]

In the same *Compendium* of Wollebius mentioned above, the chapter on 'The Works of God and the Divine Decrees in General' begins as follows: 'We have examined how God is in himself. Now we must look at his works.'[100] Then follows the familiar distinction between *opera ad extra interna* and *opera ad extra externa*. The first kind of works are described as: 'Immanent or internally directed are those works, which occur within God's essence; to these belong the divine decrees.'[101] The second category of works concern those works which are directed outside of God's being.

As concerns God's acts within the realm of time, the Reformed dogmaticians spoke of a plurality of *decreta* (decrees). However, in relation to God they spoke of a singular *decretum* (decree). Wollebius's definition of the *decretum Dei* is as follows: 'The decree of God is an internal action of the divine will, by which He from eternity has in complete freedom determined which things would happen within the realm of time.'[102]

Now we need to hear some of Barth's commentary on these points. He gives them at the conclusion of his discussion on 'the steadfastness of God'. As Barth has replaced the concept of the 'essence of God' by the 'reality of God', he has also replaced the concept '*immutabilitas Dei*' (the unchangeableness of God) by 'God's steadfastness'. Barth's commentary is as follows:[103]

> 'One will first have to grant to this doctrine (of the *decretum Dei*) the merit, that it has made the problem and the acknowledgment of it, which is the concern here, visible: In the relationship between God and the creature in all cases, we deal with the one unchangeable God himself, with the *essentia Dei*, but now in this single unchangeable being of God – for this relationship is not simply fixed, but it is determined and ordered by a decree, a decision of the will of God – we have to do with something special in God (*interna voluntatis divina actio*). But in the concreteness

which it has by its relation with the created world, this *actio* cannot be expressly placed in the essence of God and therefore identified with God himself, without involving a notable contradiction [dankenswerte Inconsequenz[104]] of the order of God's absolutely simple and immovable essence'. (...) 'There is after this chapter particularly the orthodox Reformed dogmatics with something special in God: a movement, change and decision, in virtue of which he can be and is the One he is in relation to his creation. We certainly cannot say, according to what is at any rate the embryonic teaching of this Chapter (in contrast with that on the *essentia Dei*), that death is God and God is dead' – formerly Barth had said: 'what is immovable clearly is death!'[105] 'The doctrine of a living God does at least begin to emerge, it does at least become possible. What is difficult to see is how the older dogmaticians could speak, as they did, about the essence of God as if they had never heard of this *actio interna* which is now identified with God's essence.'

The answer to that question by Barth is, that Calvin, concentrating in an anti-scholastic way on the works of God, did not want to discuss the being of God. When it began to be discussed again by Reformed orthodoxy it was not done in a biblical way.

Excursus
In paragraph 11 we heard Calvin say: 'His essence is indeed incomprehensible. Yet in each of His works He has engraved certain signs of His majesty' (text of 1559).[106] As though God's works are not even more incomprehensible! Are not the 'works of God' *nefil'ot* (works of wonder)?[107]

2. The way Calvin distinguishes the works of God from the essence of God is tied together with the way he connects these *opera Dei* (works of God) with the spatial and visible *mundus* (world). This is not in agreement with the structure of the biblical proclamation either. To Calvin, 'seeing' the 'works' in the space of the 'world' comes first. This is followed by 'hearing' the *dabar* when the time was fulfilled as though space is more important than time.[108] God's *ma'asim* in the biblical proclamation are his acts as they happen *in tempore* (in time): 'it happened in those days...'. Regarding the works of God we are dealing with the single history of God's many acts. The eternal God becomes our covenant partner – in 'contingent contemporaneity'.[109] He became our contemporary and constantly wants to become that.[110] In the sphere of influence of God's acts and becoming involved in them, we move from hearing to seeing, just like the shepherds from the story of Luke 2.[111] The shepherds returned, glorifying and praise God because of what they – first – had heard and – then – had seen (v. 20).[112] In the first chapter of the 1539 *Institutes* we move, however, from seeing to hearing. How Calvin understands this movement is demonstrated in the third part of his argument on the knowledge of God through his works.

§3.3 'THAT ANYONE, IN ORDER TO COME TO GOD, NEEDS THE GUIDANCE AND THE TEACHING OF SCRIPTURE' (I.19-38)

This third part of Calvin's argument on the knowledge of God through his works (in the artifact of the world) consists of three parts: A. I.19-20; B. I.21-36; C. I.37-38. In the first part Calvin argues that the Word adequately describes how God makes himself known to man through his works. Here, the movement is from the *verbum Dei* (Word of God) to the *opera Dei* (works of God). In the third part (C. I.37-38), serving as a conclusion of the entire argument, the reverse occurs. Here Calvin argues that those who know God in his works find their knowledge of God confirmed in his Word. The movement here is from the works of God to the Word of God. The development of Calvin's argument from the first to the third part is interrupted by the extensive middle part (consisting of sixteen paragraphs, B. I.37-38), which contains Calvin's doctrine of Holy Scripture.[113]

I.19-20
The word 'therefore' from the end of the second part of the argument[114] is repeated at the beginning of the third part of the argument. 'Therefore (...) He has come to help those whom He has destined to be saved with a more powerful cure for their weakness'.[115] This more powerful cure consists of the Word. Not only does God instruct his people by means of his works as *muti magistri* (mute teachers), he now opens his mouth as well: 'For He does not only use mute teachers for their instruction, but He also opens His holy mouth'. The Word functions as the remedy for our (inherited) disease of blindness. This remedy is comparable to spectacles. In the introduction to his commentary on Genesis of 1553, Calvin has formulated this as follows:[116]

'Because the Lord gets no results when He calls us by means of His creatures (!) – except that there remains no excuse for us':

– Cf. what we heard above at the beginning of the first part (§4) and then at the beginning of the second part (§11) and finally in §18 at the conclusion of the first two parts, FB[117] –

'He has, out of necessity, added another new cure, or at least He has given us another aid to our weak understanding. For under the guidance and the teaching of the Scripture He does not only show us, but even forces us to see what we otherwise would miss, just as weak eyes are aided by spectacles.'

– In the words 'out of necessity' and 'under the guidance and the teaching of Scripture' we already hear the title which Calvin in 1559 will give to this part of the Institutes, 'Scripture is needed as guide and teacher for anyone who would come to God the creator', FB.[118] –

This image of spectacles as remedy is repeated in the *Institutes* of 1559:

'If one holds the most beautiful book in front of elderly people or those who suffer from weak eyes, they have difficulty distinguishing the words from each other, even though they see that there is something written there. However, if they put on spectacles they can read clearly and see the letters distinctly in their context. This is what Scripture does. It gathers the knowledge of God, which otherwise would be dispersed, and drives away the darkness. In a very clear way it shows us the true God.' [119]

Calvin continues by saying that, from the very beginning of the world, God has kept this *ordo* (order). To the works as 'mute teachers' he adds the *adminiculum, subsidium, remedium* (aid, support, cure) of his Word.

'In calling His servants, the Lord has always followed this order. Beside all other information He also used the Word, which is a much more correct and trustworthy sign to learn to know Him. Adam, Noah, Abraham and the other fathers, having been enlightened by His Word, arrived at a more profound knowledge of Him.' [120]

We keep hearing comparative words: a more powerful cure (1559: a stronger aid), a more correct and trustworthy (1559: surer) sign, a more profound knowledge. [121] This is characteristic of Calvin's theology. We will meet it repeatedly in other contexts.

Calvin briefly indicates how God by a special providence has seen to it that the words which he had spoken to all the fathers, beginning with Adam, first orally and later by written tradition, were kept by the people of God. Here follows the complete formulation of the thesis, which he unfolds in the third part of his argument:

'It is clear that God used His Word to instruct those whom He wanted to know Him. He foresaw that His image, which He had imprinted on the composition of the world, would be of little effect. Therefore, if we sincerely wish to attain a true vision of God we need to take this true way.' [122]

Calvin underscores this thesis with the words in which the first three paragraphs of the 1537 Catechism culminated: [123]

'Therefore, one needs to come to the Word of God, in which God is described very adequately by His works, since these works are not valued here according to our failing judgment, but according to the rule of eternal truth.' [124]

In these two sentences Calvin first formulates his thesis and then underscores it. Again we hear the word 'world' and then the word 'works'. In this third part of Calvin's argument about the knowledge of God, this pair of concepts, 'works' and 'world', are now combined with the concept 'Word of God'.

Continuation of our conversation with Calvin.
3. However, we must ask again to what extent Calvin's argument – also as concerns the relationship between the 'works of God' and the 'Word of God' – is in agreement with the structure of biblical proclamation. In the proclamation of the prophets and the apostles, the 'Word' of God is never understood as an appendix, but always as the original. It 'happens', for the history they tell us is a history of *debarim*. A *dabar* happens because someone in his communication with others (in his heart or with his mouth) says what he does and simultaneously (with his hand) does what he says. A *dabar* also con-

sists of being announced and told, affirmed and proclaimed, made known and heard. It is the *dabar* itself which does this. The 'true' history, the history of God with Israel, which was confirmed by the Tanakh, that *particula pro toto* (as the smallest part for the whole) is the history of God with all of us, is 'a history which announces itself' spontaneously. The *nabi'* (Buber translates: 'Der Künder') is the 'announcer',[125] he 'announces' the *dabar* that happens.

Excursus
Compare Luke 2:15, where the shepherds say to one another: 'Let us go then to Bethlehem and see the *word* that has happened', the word 'which the Lord' (Luke 1:37-38) through the *verbi divini ministerium* (the service of the divine word) 'has made known to us'. Cf. Amos 3:7 and passim. The intercourse of those who are involved in the happening of the *debarim* is dialogical. It is 'being in the act' and 'being in community' and as such 'being in conversation' (which, as such, is a 'being in keeping', 'in faithfulness', and 'in the victorious realization of salvation'.)[126]

Here also Karl Barth has shown the right way. We need to hear what he says in a clear formulation at the beginning of his argument on 'the prophetic history of Israel as an adequate prefiguration of the prophecy of Jesus Christ':

> 'The history of Israel *happens*, and while it happens, it also *speaks – not only additional and belated*, but in this and with this, that it happens in that totality and in that context, and happens thus, as it happens. For that it happens, and happens thus, as it happens, has its basis according to the representation of the Old Testament from the beginning and constantly, in a speaking, promises, commanding, ordering, calling of YHWH. "For he, he spoke, and it happened; he commanded and it stood" (Ps 33:9). Even this basis is proven faithful – how could it fail to happen? – in that it, for its part, while it happened, is speaking, calling, prophetic history: history of the Word of God in the flesh. Surely it also happens then that it is authentically interpreted and explained, particularly by chosen and called individual human witnesses: and they are just (in a narrower and wider sense of the concept): Israel's prophets. But not *her* existence and activity causes Israel's history to speak. They *confirm* and *document* only that she *does* that. But because and while Israel's history, grounded in the Word of God, speaks for her part, the saying is – from her abundance as history of the Word of God in the flesh – it comes to the existence and activity of the prophets. They only follow the movement in which the history of Israel not only *happens*, but makes itself, while it happens, *perceptible*, audible, understandable.'[127]

Barth says of this prophetic history of Israel (the covenant history confirmed by the Tanakh) in his 'Doctrine of the Creation': '*This* history is, theologically viewed, *the* history'.[128] The 'creation history' – the *conditi mundi historia* (history of the creation of the world), as Calvin calls it at the beginning of his commentary on Genesis[129] – is the 'prehistory'.[130]

In the narrative concerning the *bara'* (the act of creation) of '*elohim* (God) at the beginning of the Tanakh, we deal with the proclamation of a *dabar* as well. Ten times we hear the words *wayomer 'elohim*, 'and God said'. God said what he wanted to happen and he did what he said. Underneath the protective covering of the *raqiya^c* as his 'heaven', he made the *'erets*, the earth, as the place where he wanted to begin a future (*shalom be'erets*, 'peace on earth') for man.[131] This 'divine gift of the land' makes 'covenantal history possible'.[132] The difference between Calvin's exegesis of the creation story and that of Karl Barth is that Calvin offers us a cosmological explanation of the text (of which the religio-historical explanation of Gunkel does not differ very much)[133] while Barth gives a covenant-historical-Christological explanation (which Brunner unjustly calls 'the allegorical method').[134]

When we discussed the first three paragraphs of the 1537 Catechism in the previous chapter, we said that our conversation with Calvin will particularly deal with the difference between the biblical *ma°asim* as history of God's acts and the *opera*, the 'works', of dogmatic tradition. Now that we have begun with this conversation, we can already say that Calvin's distinction between 'works of God' and 'Word of God' is not in line with the biblical proclamation.

I.21-36

According to Calvin, God has made sure by a *singularis providentia* (special providence)[135] that believers would never be without his word 'in which God is described very well and realistically by his works'.[136] In paragraphs 21 to 36 He develops this though in the locus *De sacra scriptura* (the Holy Scriptures).

'The Holy Scriptures', Calvin says, are a 'witness of God's revelation'. They are 'God's Word for the church'.[137] In these 16 paragraphs (almost a third of the first chapter), Calvin does not speak on Scripture from the perspective of faith in Jesus Christ as the Word made flesh. Rather, he does so from the perspective of the knowledge of God in his 'works', in the 'artifact of the world'. We shall return to this topic in the following chapter with the discussion on the 1559 Institutes.[138]

Against the Romana Calvin appeals to the Spirit to establish the authority of the Word. The words have authority as words of the Spirit. Against the fanatics ('fanatici;' Otto Weber: 'Schwärmer'[139]) he appeals to the Word to safeguard a right understanding of how the Spirit works. The Spirit is active and exercises his power as the Spirit of the Word. Calvin beautifully expresses this correlation of Spirit and Word[140] at the conclusion of this in I.36:

> 'By a reciprocal bond the Lord has mutually connected the certainty of His Word and His Spirit. His aim is to make sure that a well founded obedience to the Word takes hold of our souls, where the Spirit illuminates us and makes us see the face of God. On the other hand, we should embrace the Spirit wherever we recognize Him in His image, that is: in the Word. We can do so without fear of error.'[141]

In 1559 Calvin divides the sixteen paragraphs of this first chapter, in which he unfolds the doctrine of the Holy Scriptures, in three chapters. The titles he gives to the three chapters reflect the three themes which in these sixteen paragraphs are unfolded:

Caput VII ← 1539-1554: I.21-24

Against the   'The Scriptures must be confirmed by the witness of the Holy
Romana   Spirit, so that their authority might be sure. It is a godless illusion
that the credibility of Scripture depends on the judgment of the
church.'

Caput VIII ← 1539-1554: I.25-33

    'Human reason gives sufficient proofs to underscore the credibility
of the Scriptures.'

> – Calvin explains what he means by these *probationes* (proofs) in a sentence
> he adds in 1559: 'Yet those who wish to prove to unbelievers that the Scrip-
> tures are the Word of God are completely off the mark. This knowledge is
> only possible through faith', FB[142] –

Caput IX ← 1539: I.34-36

Against the   'The fanatics who, ignoring Scripture, appeal directly to Revela-
'fanatics'   tion, overthrow all principles of piety.'

In his exposition of the doctrine of the inspiration of the Holy Scriptures, Barth distinguishes between 'the doctrine of inspiration' of the reformers of the sixteenth century,
and the 'doctrine of being inspired' of the orthodox theologians of the seventeenth century'.[143] Concerning the seventeenth century orthodox concept of inspiration, he comments:

'It was (...) perhaps the most meaningful exponent of the great *process of seculari-
zation*, which post-Reformation Protestantism entered next. This new understanding of biblical inspiration certainly meant that the phrase, that "the Bible is God's
Word", now (in the traces of objectionable attempts which we have already met in
the ancient church) from a proposition about God's free grace was changed to a
proposition about the *nature* of the Bible as exposed to human inquiry brought under human control.'[144]

Among Calvin scholars there is a controversy on the question whether Calvin is to be
called the father of the orthodox doctrine of inspiration. Warfield and R. Seeberg do
think so;[145] Doumergue and Clavier do not.[146] In his nuanced argument about 'Die Inspiration der biblischen Zeugen', Werner Krusche concludes: 'we cannot make Calvin
the father of the old protestant doctrine of inspiration. (...) Calvin has not formulated a
doctrine of the Scriptures as being inspired; he taught the inspiration of the biblical
witnesses in their speaking and writing.'[147] Krusche quotes H. Cramer on the seven-
teenth-century doctrine of inspiration: 'This doctrine of inspiration was an absolute
novum'.[148] However, Dowey comments on this by saying, not entirely unfounded:
'There were roots in Calvin and before Calvin for what evolved in that century'.[149]

I.37-38

In the first segment of the third part of Calvin's argument about the knowledge of God
in his works (A. I. 19-20), we moved from the Word of God to the works of God. In

this third and final segment Calvin lets us make the reverse move – not from the Word of God to the works of God, but from the works of God to the Word of God. He asks the remarkable question whether what the Scriptures say about 'the works of God in the making the world' is in agreement with the way God makes himself known to all eyes of all the world. This third segment begins as follows:

'Because we have learned that the knowledge of God, which was clearly placed before our eyes in the world and in all creatures',

> – this is what Calvin wrote in I.11-18, FB –

'is explained still more trustworthily and clearer by his Word',

> – this is what he argued in the first segment, I. 19-20, followed by the locus on the Scriptures in I.21-36, FB –

'it will be worthwhile to consider whether God represents himself in Scriptures in the same way as He is portrayed in His works.'[150]

If this question is to answered in the broad sense, it will be a *longa materia* (it will take a long time). However, Calvin merely wishes to give a brief summary of the entire biblical witness, and then to answer the question whether this witness agrees with the way in which God reveals himself in all of the world. The brief summary of the entire biblical witness concerning the knowledge of God in his 'works' is as follows:

'To begin with, the Lord declares',

> – i.e., in the Holy Scriptures, FB –

'that He is the God who, after having created heaven and earth,
has poured out on all humanity His immeasurable benevolence,
and has also guided them constantly.
Nevertheless, by a special grace He took particular care of the pious.
He nourished, protected and supported them.
Therefore, they know Him and serve Him with a religious attitude.[151]
Moreover, with the aid of all the histories of all centuries,
He has set before our eyes like images
how reliable His goodness toward the believers is,
how alert His providence,
how decisive His benevolence,
how virtuous His assistance,
how fiery His love,
how tireless His patience to tolerate errors,
how fatherly and understanding His discipline in punishment,
and how persistent His faithfulness.
On the other hand, He has shown us
how severe His vengeance against sinners is,
how terrifying (after long tolerance) the inflaming of His anger,
and how powerful His hand to cast them down and crush them.[152]

Here, Calvin gives us another summarizing depiction of what the knowledge of God in his works consists of. It runs completely parallel with the description he gave in paragraph 9 discussing the knowledge of God of believers in 'true religion'.[153] What we noted with regard to that description needs to be repeated here. Calvin gives us a rather complete account of the way the Tanakh 'tells us of the name of the LORD'. He summarizes the witness of the Tanakh concerning the God of Israel, who became 'God with us' in the history of his acts. This covenantal history is 'the presupposition of reconciliation', as the reconciliation is in turn 'the fulfillment of covenant history'.[154]

However, that is not what Calvin is thinking of at all. Calvin does not see the works of God in the Tanakh from the perspective of the covenant, the incarnation of the Word, the outpouring of the Spirit, and 'the sending of the Christian community' in order to be a 'Community for the world' (outside of Israel, in the midst of the *goyim*).[155] Instead, he regards them from the perspective of the visible world surrounding us. The image that the Bible gives us of God in all of his acts, Calvin is asserting, agrees beautifully with the image God gives of himself in all of the world:

> 'We have shown' – in I.11-18, FB – 'how beautifully the depiction of God' – in the biblical witness, FB – 'agrees with the image of God which comes to light in all of the world'.[156]

This *convenire* (agree), this *convenientia* (agreement) of the Bible with the knowledge of God in his works is further highlighted in the thirty-eighth and final paragraph of the first chapter, with reference to some biblical texts. This discussion is introduced as follows:[157]

> 'In certain places we are given clear descriptions of Him, in which His face is shown very realistically in the form of an image. Because of this fact, this agreement may be acknowledged even more clearly.'

After a brief discussion on Exodus 34:6, cited above,[158] Calvin again points to the 'agreement' of the Bible with the revelation of God in his 'works':

> 'In the Bible the same virtues that shine in heaven and on earth are summed up: grace, goodness, compassion, righteousness, justice and faithfulness.'[159]

Calvin does not connect the way God calls out his own name in Exodus 34:6-7 and the way all of the Tanakh tells the name of the Lord by telling his acts.[160] By these acts Israel lives *media morte in vita* (in the midst of death: see, we live!).[161] And therefore the psalmist says in the song of thanksgiving: I shall not die, no, I can live, and tell of your acts (Ps 118:17). The Tanakh speaks of God's *sedaqa* (righteousness) in the doing of *mishpat*. As *sadiq* he is the source of right and stands ready as helper toward liberation in distress, and towards establishing 'peace'. The Tanakh also speaks of his *'emet* or *'emunah*, his 'faithfulness' in doing *hesed* – which constantly very suddenly becomes *rehamim* (mercy). When in Exodus 34:6 and in six additional places[162] YHWH is called 'merciful and gracious, longsuffering and rich in faithfulness', then all of these phrases deal with the *virtutes Dei* (virtues of God). These are descriptions of the covenantal spirit of the divine 'being in the act'. Therefore, when Calvin says that he sees all 'virtues of God' shine in heaven and on earth, we can only agree with him that 'heaven and earth' is the stage where this dramatic communication of God with his humans is played out.[163] After a reference to Exodus 34:6, Psalm 145 is mentioned first, and then Jeremiah 9:23:[164]

> (...) but if someone wishes to boast
> let him boast of this:
> to understand (cf. Ps 14:2),
> and to know Me,
> to know that I am the one
> who assures that there is
> steadfast love, justice and righteousness on earth.
> Indeed, these things delight Me,
> He says.

Calvin's discussion of this text, too, leads to the conclusion that the Bible and the revelation of God in his works agree:[165]

> 'Well then, the knowledge of God which is presented to us in the Scriptures serves no other purpose than the knowledge which is imprinted in creatures and radiates through them. It invites us first to the fear of God and then to trust.[166] As a result, we learn how we are to honor Him in our walk of life with sincere obedience. Moreover, we learn how to fully rely on His goodness.'

In all of the concluding part of the first chapter, 'The Knowledge of God' (§37-38), the biblical witness is compared with the revelation of God in his works (discussed in paragraphs 11-18) to answer the question whether the biblical witness agrees with that revelation. In all of this concluding part we move from the works of God to the Word of God, first in the question which Calvin asks at the beginning:

> 'whether God represents himself in Scriptures in the same way as He is portrayed in His works'[167]

then the question was answered three times:

1. 'How beautifully the depiction of God' – in the biblical witness, FB – 'agrees with the image of God which comes to light in all of the world'.[168]
2. 'In the Bible the same virtues that shine in heaven and on earth are summed up.'[169]
3. 'the knowledge of God which is presented to us in the Scriptures, serves no other purpose than the knowledge which is imprinted in creatures and radiates through them.'[170]

In these texts we see the following unity: in his works = in all of the world = in heaven and on earth = in his creatures.

In 1559 Calvin will give the *Institutes* the form of *Explicatio symboli* (explanation of the Creed). He will posit the thesis of the duality of the knowledge of God as the foundation of the explanation of the Creed. In the formulation of that thesis we will hear the words: 'both in the world and in the general doctrine of scripture' and 'because the Lord first appears as creator and then as redeemer in Christ, there is a twofold knowledge of God'.[171]

All of the argument of the first chapter of the 1539 *Institutes* leads to the 'agreement' of what Calvin in 1559 (in distinction to the 'proper doctrine of faith')[172] will call the 'general teaching of Scripture'[173] with the revelation of God 'in the making of the world' (that is, 'in His works').

When Calvin speaks about 'the work of God in the creation of the world', orthodox theologians speak about *opera naturae* (works of nature) in distinction to the *opera gratiae* (works of grace). What Calvin in 1559 calls the *generalis scripturae doctrina* (general teaching of the Scriptures), the orthodox theologians call *theologia naturalis – insufficiens ad salutem* (natural theology which is insufficient for salvation). Calvin could not have suspected that his comparison between the biblical witness and the revelation of God in his works would eventually lead to a description of the *utilitas* (use) of the *theologia naturalis*. It is a 'preconception' which helps one to recognize the *vera revelatio* (true revelation). This idea was expounded by theologians of the 17th century belonging to the so-called 'rational orthodoxy'.[174]

The final sentence of the first chapter of the 1539 *Institutes* still needs to be discussed:

> 'Nevertheless, the Lord nowhere makes himself known in a more intimate way than in the face of Christ, which can only be seen with the eyes of faith. Therefore, what remains to be said about the knowledge of God can better be postponed to the place where the concept of faith is treated.'[175]

God, then, makes himself known more intimately in the face of Christ than in his works. Here also Calvin uses a comparative.

Now that we have seen Calvin distinguish between the knowledge of God in his 'works' and the knowledge of God 'in the face of his Christ', it would be interesting to hear a few comments from other scholars about this distinction of Calvin. Reinhold Seeberg says the following: 'From Luther he has learned that we may can grasp the essence of God first of all in Christ. Like Luther he also turns his specifically Christian thought into a general metaphysical theory. However, we dare to affirm that Calvin, in contrast to Luther, did not contrast these two elements in the concept of God as strongly as did Luther.'[176] This is visible in Calvin's use of comparative pronouns and in the dialectic relationship between the knowledge of God and the knowledge of self, which in 1539 does not coincide with that of 'law and gospel'.

Wernle says about both of these elements in the concept of God: 'These thoughts' – concerning the knowledge of God in his works, FB – 'are very instructive for Calvin's piety. One does not only enter God's world with Jesus, Calvin claims. Not even with the Bible. One is always, as with Zwingli, already standing in God's world. God's wisdom, power, righteousness, and goodness speak through nature and history in eloquent ways. Calvin, like Zwingli, lacked Luther's sense of God being hidden outside of Christ, or being terrifying, although Luther at times did feel at home in God's natural world, like a child.'[177]

We can only have a genuine dialogue with Calvin if we take him seriously as interpreter of the biblical witness, and also his hermeneutics written down in his *Institutes*.

Nowhere, Calvin says in the concluding sentence of the first chapter, does God give himself to be known as directly as in the face of his Christ. This face, however, can only be seen with the eyes of faith. Therefore, Calvin says, whatever else we have to say on the knowledge of God, we might better reserve this discussion for the section on faith. This section, *De fide*, concerning faith in Jesus Christ, is not yet discussed in this first chapter of the 1539 *Institutes*. At the conclusion of this first chapter we are only halfway with the discussion of the *cognitio Dei* or *Dei notitia* (knowledge of God). The knowledge of God in the face of his Christ has not yet been mentioned. The most important is yet to follow.

But that can *nondum* (not yet) be discussed, Calvin says.[178] First, the second chapter must follow, in which the knowledge of ourselves as sinners is discussed: 'The Knowledge of Man'. In a third chapter, 'The Law', it will be argued that the law is God's way of leading us from the knowledge of God discussed in chapter I to the knowledge of self in the second chapter. And only then, in the fourth chapter, 'Faith', the knowledge of God again comes to the fore, but then as the knowledge of God 'in the face of his Christ', and that means: as the knowledge of faith.

The scheme 'Law → Faith' (or law and gospel) has led to the distinction of a twofold knowledge of God. There is on the one hand the knowledge of God in *operibus suis – in mundi universitate = in creaturis impressa* (in his works, in the whole of the world, imprinted in the creatures). On the other hand, there is the knowledge of God *in facie Christi sui* (in the face of his Christ). Only this second knowledge is called the knowledge of faith. Yet, at the close of paragraph 8 we heard Calvin describing the knowledge of God in his works as that knowledge 'which is only administered to the hearts of those who believe'.[179] (In the summary of the biblical witness in paragraph 37 he also spoke about 'believers'.)[180]

In 1559 Calvin distinguishes the twofold *doctrina* in the Holy Scriptures. There is on the one hand the *generalis scripturae doctrina* (general doctrine of the Scriptures), which refers to the knowledge of God in his works, and there is on the other hand the *propria fidei doctrina* (proper doctrine of faith), which refers to the knowledge of God in the face of Christ (see the title of the second Book, 'The Knowledge of God the redeemer in Christ'. Being received through the Word of God, the knowledge of God in his works will also be faith knowledge. Even so, this knowledge will not be the subject of the proper doctrine of faith. The proper doctrine of faith only deals with the knowledge of God as redeemer in Christ.

The discussion on the knowledge of God in the face of his Christ, given in the fourth chapter 'Faith' of the 1539 *Institutes*, is a continuation of the discussion on the knowledge of God in the first chapter. The 1539 Institutes are built up according to the scheme 'God → man → man → God'. They first move from the knowledge of God to the knowledge of self, and then from the knowledge of self to the knowledge of God. As a result, in these *Institutes* the second knowledge of God is both the extension of the first knowledge of God and firmly separated from it.

At the beginning of the discussion on this first chapter of the 1539 *Institutes*, in the third paragraph, we asked: 'Are the knowledge of God from which we came and the knowledge of God which we arrive at the same? Or are we dealing with a dual knowledge, a *duplex Dei cognitio*?' We announced that Calvin would give us a clear answer to this question in 1559 as he unfolds all of the sacred doctrine within the frame of the explanation of the Creed, basing himself on the thesis of the duality of the knowledge of God. In our analysis of the first chapter of the 1539 *Institutes* we have seen how Calvin already in 1539 was on the way to give us this answer. What we see happening here, is what Karl Barth has called 'The division of God into a God in and a God outside of Christ'. This division occurs 'because the knowledge of God has been severed from the Word of God'.[181] In the 1539 *Institutes*, constructed according to the scheme 'God → man → man → God', this division begins to take shape. In 1559 it will also be evident in the composition of the entire *Institutes*.

NOTES

1. Wernle, op. cit., 166.
2. See above, chap. II, the scheme with the discussion on paragraphs 16-19 of the 1537 Catechism.
3. CO I, 801: '*Summam doctrinam*, qua ex vera Dei nostrique notitia, in salutis communionem pervenimus, supra, ut potui, exsequutus sum.' Italics added.
4. See above, the overview of the contents in the Introduction §2, point 2.
5. Cf. the new edition of Pannier (mentioned above) and others of 1911, in two volumes.
6. See above, Chapter I §3.5.
7. And also the foundation for the doctrine of the 'twofold knowledge of God' in the 1559 *Institutes*.
8. See above, the Introduction, §2, the opening words of point 2.
9. 1. *Prima Aetas*. 1521-1525. In the edition of the *Corpus Reformatorum* 148 columns (CR XXI, 81-228): *Loci Communes Rerum Theologicarum seu Hypotheses Theologiae*. 17 editions (three published at Wittenberg in 1521, 1521, 1522, and twelve in other places, of which four in Basel and five in Strasbourg, see op. cit., 71-72).
    2. *Secunda Aetas*. 1535-1541. 226 columns (CR XXI, 333-558): *Loci communes theologici recens collecti et recogniti a Ph. Melanchthone*. 14 editions (see op. cit., 241-242).
    3. *Tertia Aetas*. 1543-1559. 450 columns (CR XXI, 601-1051): *Loci praecipui theologici nunc denuo cura et diligentia summa recogniti, multisque in locis copiose illustrati*. Twenty-five editions till 1559, and an additional nine other editions between 1559 and 1595, as well as eight editions in the *Corpus Doctrinae Christianae* (1560-1580), in total forty-two editions. In the sixteenth century as a whole, a total therefore of 17 + 14 + 42 = 73 editions, not counting translations. The influence of this work was great in the Reformed world. Already in Calvin's *Institutes* of 1536 one notes its influence (perhaps Calvin read the *Loci* of 1521, but certainly the one of 1535). Though Calvin differed in his opinion with Melanchthon with regard to the doctrines of predestination and free will, in 1546 a French translation of the *Loci* was published with a preface by Calvin (*Préface de la Somme de theologie, ou Lieux Communs, par M. Philippe Melanchthon*, CO IX, 848ff.).
10. It would not only be worthwhile to compare the *Loci* of Melanchthon (in their different aetates) with Calvin's *Institutes* of 1539, but also with the expanded *Institutes* of 1543 (still in the form of a loci-theology). See below, the beginning of Chapter IV.

11. The table of contents of the *prima aetas* does not belong to the printed text of Melanchthon's book. Following H E. Bindseil (CR XXI) and Hans Engelland (*Melanchthons Werke*. Studienausgabe II.1, Gütersloh 1952) we have expressed the articulation of the composition of the Loci of 1521 in the table of contents given here (what G. I. Plitt and Th. Kolde have not done in their edition). The tables of contents of the *secunda* and the *tertia aetas* have been derived from CR, with italics added.

12. OS I, 37. See above, Chap. I, the beginning of §2.

13. Karl Reuter, op. cit., 208: 'Calvin's theological conception does not have a scientific principle, but rather a scientific theme: God and man in their mutual relationship.'

14. OS I, 41 ll. 12-23. See above, Chap. I §2.4

15. CO I, 279 (1539: I.1) tota fere sapientiae nostrae summa, quae vera demum ac solida sapientia censeri debeat, duabus partibus constat: cognitione Dei et nostra; cf. OS III, 31 ll. 6-8 (1559: I.1.1).

16. CO I, 279 (1539: I.2): utra autem alteram praecedat ac ex se pariat, non facile est discernere; cf. OS I, 31 ll. 9-10 (1559: I.1.1).

17. See above, n. 3.

18. In Reuters's study, referred to above, we read about the term *summa doctrinae* (1536, 9ff.) the following comment: 'The concept of the doctrine partly corresponds to the further content of the book and shows the support to the theological conception of the Wittenberg Reformation with Melanchthon. But precisely this concept is replaced in later editions of the Institutes since 1539 by the concept of *wisdom*. Since that time the sentence reads as follows...' (after this follows a quotation of the opening sentence of 1539). 'With this exchange of concepts Calvin gave up his passing support to the more intellectualizing Melanchthonian shaping of the Wittenberg theology and opened himself in its basic disposition ultimately to an understanding of theology which was more akin to his.' (then follows a consideration of Calvin's concept of wisdom). Reuter would not have needed this theory if he had noted how Calvin did not tend to discard words from former editions (as here the word *doctrina*) but that he carefully found a new place for it.

19. For these words compare OS III, 31 ll. 21-22 (1559: I.1.1).

20. CO I, 279-280 (I.2); cf. (with some variants) OS III, 31 ll. 26-32 l. 9 (1559: I.1.1).

21. CO I, 280 (I.3); cf. OS III, 32 ll. 10-18 (with variants; 1559: I.1.2).

22. CO I, 281 (I.3); cf. OS III, 33 ll. 4-12 (1559: I.1.2).

23. CO I, 181 below – 282, above (I.3): utcunque tamen Dei nostrique notitia mutuo inter se nexu sint colligatae, ordo recte dicendi (1543: docendi) postulat ut de illa priori disseramus loco, tum ad hanc tractandam postea descendamus; cf. OS III, 33 ll. 38 – 34, l. 3 (1559: I.1.3).

24. In his book *The Knowledge of God in Calvin's Theology* E. A. Dowey Jr. discusses 'The Correlative Character of the Knowledge of God and Man' (op. cit., 18-24). In a footnote he remarks: 'I first heard this term applied to Calvin in a seminar by Professor Paul Tillich at Union Theological Seminary. I shall use this language repeatedly' (op. cit., 18, n. 62). In the following paragraph, however, 'The Existential Character of All Our Knowledge of God' (op. cit., 18-24) Dowey shows that the 'correlation' of Calvin is different from the one of Tillich (though he does not say that that is the case). In Tillich's case, the 'questioning' relates to human 'existence', and 'revelation' is the 'answer.' But in Calvin's case, it is exactly the reverse. 'The knowledge of God (...) is never separated from the answer that man gives through worship and obedience when God reveals himself' (op. cit., 24). We see how Dowey reverses it: God asks and man is called to answer. But man also asks and expects a divine answer (for example in the Lamentations: 'How long?') That Tillich made all of this into one-direction traffic 'man asks God' is perhaps a symptom of the Lutheran climate, in which 'The Law → The Gospel' meant the direction of knowledge of ourselves to the knowledge of God in his revelation.

25. CO I, (279) 282-304.
26. De Cognitione Dei, quae primum est religionis fundamentum; et unde vera eius regula sit petenda.
27. OS III, 34 ll. 21-24 (1559: I.2.1). See above, Introduction, n. 28.
28. Cf. above, Chap. II §2, the discussion of the first three paragraphs of the 1537 Catechism.
29. Inst. 1559: I.3: Dei notitiam hominum mentibus naturaliter esse inditam; Inst. 1559: I.5: Dei notitiam in mundi fabrica et continua eius gubernatione lucere; Inst. 1559: I.6: ut ad Deum (creatorem) quis perveniat, opus esse Scripture duce et magistra.
30. K. Barth, KD II.1 §25: 'Die Erkenntnis Gottes in ihrem Vollzug' (CD II.1 §25 'The Fulfillment of the Knowledge of God').
31. Cf. above, chap. II §2, the discussion of §13 of the Catechism of 1537 on predestination and §3, the discussion of §20 of the Catechism on the 'experience' of the trinity.
32. 'De numine impressio' ; 'aliqua Dei notitia' ; 'persuasio aliquem esse Deum' ; 'de Deo persuasio, ex quo velut semine mergit ad religionem propensio.' This final formulation in Inst. 1539: I.5, CO I, 282; cf. OS III, 38 ll. 28-30 (1559: I.3.2).
33. CO I, 282 ll. 3-7 (I.4); cf. OS III, 37 ll. 16-21 (1559: I.3.1). In 1559 Calvin changes the words 'universis Dominus *installavit*' (...that the Lord *has administered* to all) to: 'universis Deus ‖ ipse *indidit*, cuius memoriam assidue renovans, novas subinde guttas ‖ *instillat*' (that God himself *has added* this concept in all and, in order to constantly renew the memory of it, repeatedly *administering* new drops). The text of 1539 thus contained only the perfect *instillavit*. In 1559 he changes this perfect into perfect *indidit* so that it might be followed the present *instillat*, preceded by the participle *renovans*. That Calvin in 1559 after the perfect indidit, changed the perfect *instillavit* into the present *instillat*, Barth-Niesel have neglected to mention in the apparatus. The signs ‖ ... ‖ in their edition point to an addition of 1559 in the 1554 text. They do mention the change from *Dominus* to *Deus* before these vertical lines.
34. CO I, 282 ll. 7-11 (I.4); cf. OS III, 37 ll. 21-24 (I.3.1).
35. In 1559 Calvin turns the first two sentences into one, by a change of the interpunction: in 1539 he had put a period after the word *instillavit* and had written the following word *Ut* with a capital. In 1559, after the word *instillat*, he changed the period to a colon, and writes the word that follows, *ut*, in lower case.
36. CO I, 283, the final sentence of I.5; cf. OS III, 39 ll. 18-20 (1559: I.3.2).
37. CO I, 283, the beginning of I.6. The sentence is partly to be found in OS III, 35 ll. 17-20 (1559: I.2.2) and further in the crit. app. on ll. 32-35.
38. See above, §2, the discussion on the second sentence of I.1 (*the knowledge of God*).
39. See e.g., Eccl 12:13-14; Ps 112:1; 103:17-18; Job 1:1-9; 2:3; Prov 8:13; 9:10; 14:2; 31:30.
40. CO I, 283 ll. 41-42 (I.6). The sentence does not appear in 1559.
41. CO I, 283 below, 284 above (I.6); cf. OS III, 44 ll. 39-42 (crit. app.) and 16-18 (1559: I.4.4).
42. CO I, 284 ll. 17-19 (I.7); cf. OS III, 42 ll. 27-29 (1559; I.4.3).
43. CO I, 284 below (I.8); cf. OS III, 43 ll. 19-21 (1559: I.4.4).
44. CO I, 285, the conclusion of I.8: qualis sit illa singularis, quae solis *fidelium* pectoribus instillatur, Dei notitia; qualis etiam, qui inde consequetur, pietatis affectus; this sentence has dropped out in 1559, cf. OS III, 44, ll. 32-34 (crit. app. with I.4.4).
45. CO I, 285, the beginning of I.9; cf. OS III, 36 ll. 5-9 (with alterations; 1559: I.2.2).
46. OS III, 36 ll. 10-23 (1559: I.2.2).
47. OS III, 36 ll. 23-37, l. 7 (1559: I.2.2).
48. Thus in the version of 1539: CO I, 285 below, the conclusion of I.9. Only the beginning corresponds with OS III, 37 ll. 7-8 (1559: I.2.2).
49. OS III, 37 ll. 8-10 (1559: I.2.2). The accommodation is related to Calvin's new definition of the law in Inst. 1559: II.7.1 as *forma religionis per manum Mosis a Deo tradita* (the form of religion which was delivered by the hand of Moses from God), OS III, 326 ll. 29-30.

50. See in OS III, 34-37, the marginalia on the inside of the pages: I.1; I.6; I.9.
51. See also F. H. Breukelman, *Biblische Theologie II. Debharim*, op. cit., 82-83 and 214-215.
52. Cf, Hos 4:1,6; 6:6: 'knowing in Hosea is actually the concept of mutuality in relationship between God and the people', Buber, in *Der Glaube der Propheten*, Zurich, 1950, 165; also in: *Werke* II, Munich, 1964, 357.
53. Buber, *Werke II*, op. cit., 352; we find in the book of Hosea a form of the root *'ahab* nineteen times.
54. CO I, 285 below – 286 above (I.10); cf. OS III, 40 ll. 14-18 (with alterations; Inst. 1559: I.3.3).
55. CO I, 286, the conclusion of I.10; cf. OS III, 40 ll. 27-28 (Inst. 1559: I.3.3).
56. Inst. 1559: III.9.
57. CO XXII, 33; OS I, 378.
58. CO I, 286 at the beginning of I.11; cf. OS III, 45 ll. 31-34 (crit. app.) the sentence at the beginning of Inst. 1559: I.5.1 has been strongly altered. See below, the discussion of paragraph 11.
59. See the edition of Ernst Pfisterers in W. Niesel, *Bekenntnisschriften und Kirchenordnungen der nach Gottes Wort reformierten Kirche*, Zurich, 1938, 3. T. F. Torrance, *School of Faith. The Catechisms of the Reformed Church.* London 1959, 5, 6.
60. CO I, 284 (beginning I.7): Deum, talem apprehendere qualem se cognoscendum exhibet; cf. OS III, 41 ll. 40-41 (crit. ap. ad 1559: I.4.1.; ll. 13-14: apprehendunt qualem se offert); CO I, 285 (beginning I.9): Deum talem habere qualem se manifestat.
61. See above, n. 58.
62. OS III, 44 ll. 30-45 l. 4 (1559: I.5.1).
63. CO I, 286 ll. 22-32 (I.11); cf. OS III, 45 ll. 34-41 (crit. app.).
64. OS III, 45 ll. 4-8 (1559: I.5.1).
65. See above, chap. II in §2 in connection with paragraph 13 of the Catechism of 1537 on predestination and in §3 in connection with the Trinity.
66. See above, n. 33 (the beginning of I.4).
67. For example, *conspicere, adspicere, contemplare, considerare.*
68. CO I, 286, ll. 32-38 (I.11); cf. OS III, 45 ll. 19-23 (1559: I.5.1).
69. Luke says, that 'the glory of the Lord' shone about the shepherds when they were told about 'the word that had happened', the *dabar* which happened at the birth of the Savior as 'fulfillment of the covenant history'. See F. H. Breukelman, ' "and it happened..." A brief discussion of the overture of the gospel according to Luke' (1960), reprinted in: *Bijbelse Theology II/1. De ouverture van het evangelie naar Mattheüs*, Kampen, 1984, 179-225.
70. CO XLV, 74 (ad Luke 2:9).
71. See the concept providentia Dei in I.12, OS III, 46 l. 19 (1559: I.5.2) and in I.13, OS III, 51 l. 33 (1559: I.5.7).
72. CO I, 287 below – 288 above (beginning 1539: I.12; I.13), OS III, 51 ll. 31-32 (1559: I.5.7).
73. Wernle speaks in reference to these two kinds of 'opera' about 'Nature and History', op. cit., 170, 172.
74. Resp. 'argumenta', 'documenta', and 'testimonia.'
75. K. Barth, KD II.I, 725, cf. 364-368; CD 643, cf. 324-327.
76. See e.g.: sapientia OS III, 53 l. 2 (1559: I.5.8); potentia OS III, 51 ll. 3-4 (1559: I.5.6); bonitas OS III, 51 l. 25 (1559: I.5.6); clementia OS III, 51, l. 35 (1559: I.5.7); misericordia OS III, 52, l. 9 (1559: I.5.7), iustitia OS III, 52 l. 1 (OS 1559: I.5.7). The three-part sapientia – potentia – bonitas may also be found in OS III, 46 l. 54 – 47 l. 1 (I.5.3, a part added in 1559) and 'Argumentum in Genesin', CO XXIII (5-12) 7.
77. CO XXIII, 7-8.

78. Here also Barth-Niesel might have referred to the beginning of the *Loci* of Melanchthon, which we cited above, Chap. II §3.

79. CO I, 289 above (I.14); cf. OS III, 53, ll. 14-23 (1559: I.5.9).

80. CO VI, 16 cf. OS II, 77 ll. 23-27 (Latin). Pfisterer, op. cit, 5 (French). Cf. also the third paragraph of the 1537 Catechism, CO V, 324, the 'Argumentum in Genesin', CO XXIII, 8 and the 'Sermons sur le livre de Job', CO XXXIII, 709-710 (ad Job 31:34) et passim.

81. CO I, 303 below – 304 above (I.38); cf. OS III, 86 ll. 14-19; 1559: I.10.2. In 1539 we read 'describatur' (was described), in 1559 'describitur' (is described).

82. CO I, 289 (I.15): alteram vitam fore, in qua et sua iniquitati vindicta, et merces iustitiae reposita sit – Calvin uses a chiasm here; cf. OS III, 54 ll. 11-13 (1559: I.5.10).

83. CO I, 289 below (I.15); cf. OS III, 54 ll. 19-24 (with alterations; 1559: I.5.10).

84. See above, n. 68.

85. See F. H. Breukelman, 'Psalm 113', op. cit., 212-250, particularly 216-217.

86. CO I, 290 (beginning of I.17); cf. OS III, 58 ll. 35-59 l. 1 (1559: I.5.14).

87. CO I, 291 (beginning of I.18); cf. OS III, 59 ll. 26-27 (1559: I.5.15).

88. CO I, 291 (I.18); cf. OS III, 59 ll. 34-35 (1559: I.5.15).

89. Similarly, §34 of Barth's KD, his dogmatic argument about 'The Election of the Community' runs fully parallel with his exegesis of Romans 9-11 (KD II.2, 222 below).

90. Wernle, op. cit., 166-354. Dieter Schellong (op. cit., 192-193) comments: 'Paul Wernle indicates but *one* moment when he points to the profound exegetic labor in Romans, and subsumes the new teachings under the superscription: the Pauline central dogma's of 1539.' He then points to Calvin's struggle with the Anabaptists, to the role which the concept of the covenant plays, to 'the large-scale defense of infant baptism', and to the interpretation of the law. 'Thus, the reference to Calvin's occupation with the epistle to the Romans by itself does not give a satisfactory explanation of the new edition of the Institutes in Strasbourg'.

91. Karl Barth calls God's revelation 'the self interpretation of God', KD I.1, 329 and 364 (CD, 311 and 345). Eberhard Jüngel has indicated the tendency of this 'revelation as self interpretation of God' in his book *Gottes Sein ist im Werden* (Tübingen ²1967) with the words 'Gott entspricht sich'; 'in der Tat ist die Barthsche Dogmatik im Grunde eine ausführliche Exegese dieses Satzes'. Op. cit., 36.

92. KD II.2,3; CD, 3 (italics in the text); cf. KD II.1, 28; CD, 257.

93. Emil Brunner, *Die christliche Lehre von Gott. Dogmatik, Band I*, Zurich 1946, 'Das Wesen Gottes und seine Eigenschaften', 121-322; Otto Weber, *Grundlagen der Dogmatik. Erster Band*, Neukirchen-Vluyn, ³1964, 2. Kapitel, 'Gottes Wesen und Eigenschaften:' 439-508.

94. This is the title of the first section of this chapter, §28.I; KD II.1, 288-305; CD, 257-272.

95. KD II.1, 293; CD, 262.

96. *Operari sequitur esse*. Barth turns this around: *esse sequitur operari*, KD II.1, 91; CD, 83.

97. Wollebius, op. cit., Libri primi, Cap. I §1.2.

98. 'Argumentum in Genesin', op. cit., CO XXIII, 8.

99. In Barth's opinion, Melanchthon was already guilty by giving 'all of Protestant orthodoxy a fatal example', by wrongly filling in what initially had been left open, in the later editions of the *Loci* (those of the second and the third *aetas*). Cf. KD II.1, 290f.; CD 259f. Cf. KD I.1, 437ff.; CD 416ff. See above, in the appendix of §1 of this chapter, which offers an overview of the table of contents of Melanchthon's *Loci* in the three *aetates*. It shows us how from the second *aetas* loci which originally had been rejected – God (including the Trinity) and Creation – come first again.

100. Wollebius, op. cit., chap. III §1.

101. Wollebius, op. cit., Chap. III §2: 'opera Dei ad extra sunt *emmenousa*, immenentia seu interna, vel *metabainousa*, transeuntia seu externa'; and: 'Immanentia sei interna opera sunt, quae intra Dei essentiam fiunt; atque huc pertinent Dei decreta'.

102. Wollebius, op. cit., cap. III §3: Decretum Dei est interna voluntatis divinae actio, qua de iis, quae in tempore fieri debebant, ab aeterno liberrime et certissime statuit.

103. KD II.1 (583-587) 584ff.; CD, (519-522)519f. Italics by Barth.

104. Here Barth calls the way in which the locus *De Decreto* (the decree) of Reformed theology, the 'inward act of the divine will', was identified with the being of God, a 'notable contradiction'. In most other places of the *Church Dogmatics* he speaks of a 'happy inconsistency'. See for this concept 'notable contradictions' the following places: KD I.2, 5, 9, 10, 584 (CD, 4, 8, 9, 526); KD II.1, 140, 194ff. (CD, 127. 172ff.); KD II.2, 85 (CD, 79); KD IV I, 406, 409 (CD, 367, 370); 'Das erste Gebot als theologisches Axiom' (1933), in: *Theologische Fragen und Antworten*, Gesammelte Vorträge III, Zurich 1957, 140.

105. KD II.1, 555; CD, 494.

106. See above, n. 64.

107. In the Psalms, this plural occurs twenty-seven times. In Job 9:10 Jerome translates this plural not with '*mirabilia*' (wonderworks) but with '*incomprehensibilia.*'

108. As in the 'transcendental esthetics' of Kant. See Immanuel Kant, *Kritik der reinen Vernunft*, Riga, [1]1787, I. 'Transcendentale Elementarlehre', Erster Theil. 'Transcendentale *Aesthetik*', 1. Abschnitt 'Vom Raume', 22-29; 2. Abschnitt 'Von der Zeit', 30-49.

109. KD I.1, 150-155; CD, 145-149.

110. This is the reason why Barth never ceases to describe the theological concept of time, in his KD: KD I.1, 150-155; CD 145-149; KD I.2, §14; KD II.1, §31.3; KD II.2, §33.2; KD III.1, 72-82; CD, 67-76; KD III.2, §47; KD III.4, §56.l; KD IV.1, §62.3; KD IV.3, 57-78; CD, 52-72.

111. See in the third part of that story the word 'see' occurring three times; 2:15-20. F. H. Breukelman, 'En het geschiedde…' op. cit., 183ff.; 206ff.

112. The original translation of the *Bible de Jérusalem (La sainte Bible, traduite en francais sous la direction de l'école biblique de Jérusalem*, Paris 1956), 'Puis les bergers s'en retournèrent, glorifiant et louant Dieu pour tout ce qu'ils avaient *vu et entendu*' (italics added) was incorrect. In the 'new edition, reviewed and expanded' of 1974 this has been corrected. There we read: 'entendu et vu.'

113. At least the first part of that doctrine. In 1559 Calvin will also explicitly introduce a duplicity in the doctrine of Scripture. See below, Chapter IV §2-III with the discussion of Inst. 1559: II.9.

114. At the beginning of paragraph 17, 'In vain therefore do so many bright lamps cast their light around us in the artifact of the world…'. See above, n. 86.

115. CO I, 292 (beginning I.19); cf. OS III, 60 ll. 36-39 (crit. app. Ad 1559: I.6.1).

116. 'Argumentum in Genesin', op. cit., 9 ll. 13-16.

117. See above n. 88.

118. Inst. 1559, I.6

119. OS III, 60 ll. 25-30. This image of the book, which can be read with the aid of spectacles, had led to the fact that the second article of the *Confessio Belgica* speaks about Creation as a Book, 'in which all creatures, great and small, are like letters', next to which Scripture is laid, 'in which God gives himself to know ever clearer and more perfectly.' See Niesel, *Bekenntnisschriften*, op. cit., 120, ll. 8-17.

120. CO I, 292; cf. OS III, 61 ll. 4-0 (see also below, Chap. V §I.1).

121. Resp. *effecacius /melius: rectior et familiarior / certior; interior*. The same comparative we also heard in the cited art. 2 of the *Confessio Belgica*: 'God gives himself to be known still clearer and more perfectly in his holy and divine Word.'

122. CO I, 292 below – 293 above (I.20); cf. OS III, 63 ll. 20-25 (with alterations; 1559: I.6.3).

123. Cf. above, Chap. II, n. 41.

124. CO I, 293 above (I.20); cf. OS III, ll. 25-28 (1559: I.6.3).

125. Buber, *Die Bücher der Kundung*, the third volume of the 'Verdeutschung der Schrift'.
126. Cf. F. H. Breukelman, *Bijbelse Theologie II. Debharim*, op. cit., the titles of paragraphs 1, 2, and 3 (and in parentheses 4, 5, and 6).
127. KD IV.3 (56-78) 57-58; CD, (52-72) 53. Italics by Barth. Italics of '*not only additional and belated*' added.
128. KD III.I, 63; CD, 59. Italics by Barth.
129. 'Argumentum in Genesis', op. cit., 5, l.4.
130. German: 'Vorgeschichte' KD III, I, 67; CD, 63.
131. See F. H. Breukelman, 'Im Anfang schuf Gott den Himmel und die Erde. The Story of the Creation in Genesis 1:1-2:3 as proclamation of an act of God', in: *Om het levende Woord* I/2-3 (1968), 129-198.
132. See this concept of 'Ermöglichung der Bundesgeschichte' (making covenantal history possible), KD III.I, 44; CD, 42 (the 'Leitsatz' of §41) and further, op. cit., 50 and 107 (CD, 47 and 97).
133. Cf. F. H. Breukelman, 'Psalm 113', op. cit., 246-250.
134. Emil Brunner, *Die christliche Lehre von Schöpfung und Erlösung*. Dogmatik Band II, Zurich, 1950, 47.
135. CO I, 292 (I.20); cf. OS I, 63 l. 13 (conclusion 1559: I.6.2).
136. See above, n. 124.
137. K. Barth, KD I.2 §19.
138. See below, Chap. IV §2.I (the passage about chapters I.7-9 [1559] and §2.III (1559: II.9).
139. The title of 1559: I.9 in the German translation of Otto Weber: 'The *Schwärmer* appeal unjustly to the Holy Spirit'.
140. Cf. *The Heidelberg Catechism*, Answer 54.
141. CO I, 302 ll. 29-35 (I.36); OS III, 84 ll. 14-20.
142. CO I, 300 below; cf. OS III, 81 ll. 28-29 (1559: I.9.13). See also Barth's commentary on this chapter in KD I.2, 596ff.; CD, 536-537.
143. German: 'Inspiriertheitslehre'. KD I.2 (557-598)571-585; CD, (502-537) 514-526.
144. Barth, op. cit., 580 (CD, 522). Italics by Barth.
145. See R. Seeberg, op. cit., 566, 569.
146. See Doumergue, *Tome IV La pensée religieuse de Calvin*, op. cit., 72-73.
147. Krusche, op. cit., 161-184, particularly 184 (Krusche makes the same distinction between 'inspiration' and 'being inspired' as does Barth).
148. PRE[3], Vol. 9, (183-203), 192 l. 7.
149. E. A. Dowey Jr., op. cit., [2]1964, IX.
150. CO I, 303 (beginning I.37); cf. OS III, 85 ll. 7-12 (Inst. 1559: I.10.1).
151. Cf. 'I betroth you to me…you will know me;' see above, n. 51.
152. CO I, 303; OS III, 85 ll. 29-41 crit. app. In 1559 this passage is deleted.
153. 'Ita cognitum quia…'; see above n. 46.
154. K. Barth, KD IV.I, §57.1, 2, 3.
155. KD IV.3, §72.
156. CO I, 303 (the last sentence of §37); OS III, 85 ll. 42-43 (crit. app.)
157. CO I, 303 (beginning I. 38); cf. OS III, 86 ll. 6-8.
158. See above, n. 81.
159. CO I, 304 ll. 5-8 (I.38); cf. OS III, 86 ll. 19-22 (1559: I.10.2).
160. The divine 'being in the act' is as a 'being in community'. He is also a 'being in conversation', a 'being in covenant', a 'being in righteousness' (in the doing of *mishpat, justice*) and a 'being in faithfulness' (in the doing of *hesed,* steadfast love). He is a 'being in the history of His acts, in the victorious realization of salvation in space'. He brings *yeshu^cah*, liberation in

distress. In this way He gives us *shalom* (peace)'. F. H. Breukelman, *Bijbelse Theologie II. Debharim*, op. cit., passim.

161. Reversing the medieval antiphon: 'media vita in morte sumus', 'In the midst of life, we are surrounded by death' (Luther).

162. Joel 2:13; Jon 4:2; Ps 86:15; Ps 103:8; Ps 145:8; Neh 9:17.

163. See e.g., Deut 32:1; Ps 36:6-7; Ps 103:10-14; Isa 1:2; Jer 2:12; Hos 4:3, and passim.

164. CO I, 304; cf. OS III, 86 l. 30ff. Colometry by Buber.

165. CO I, 304 ll. 39-44; cf. OS III, 87 ll. 14-19 (the conclusion of 159: I.10.2).

166. Cf. 'timor – fides' (fear – faith) at the beginning of §6 and 'fides cum timore coniuncta' (faith, connected with fear) at the conclusion of §9.

167. See above, n. 150 (beginning I.37).

168. See above, n. 156 (conclusion I.37).

169. See above, n. 159 (I.38).

170. See above, n. 165 (the conclusion of I.38).

171. OS III, 34 ll. 21-24 (1559: I.2.1).

172. OS III, 61 l. 10 (1559: I. 6.1).

173. OS III, 34 l. 23 (1559: I.2.1) and 87 l. 20 (1559: I.10.3)

174. German: 'Vernünftige Orthodoxie'. See below, Chap. V §1.10 and §1.11: of the Lutheran Johannes Franciscus Buddeus de *Institutiones Theologicae Dogmaticae* (Lipsiae 1723). I.I, XVI-XXII and of the Reformed theologian Jean Alfonse Turretin the 'Theses de Theologia Naturali in genere' (§2: 'on the excellence and the usefulness of natural theology:' Theses XX-XXVIII).

175. CO I, 304 below (conclusion I.38): verum, quia se Dominus propinquiore intuitu contemplandum non exhibet, quam in facie Christi sui, quae ipsa fidei tantum oculis conspicitur: quod de notitia Dei dicendum restat, in eum locum melius differetur, quo tractabitur fide intelligentia; cf. OS III, 87 ll. 36-40.

176. Seeberg, op. cit., 570.

177. Wernle, op. cit., 172.

178. In the new edition of this first chapter in the 1559 Institutes, Calvin, in the first ten chapters on 'the knowledge of God the creator', repeats the word *nondum* (not yet) several times. See below, chap. IV §2.I with the discussion of Inst. 1559: I.X.

179. See above, n. 44.

180. See above, n. 152.

181. KD IV.1,400f. (CD, 363f.); cf. KD II.1, 86-92 (CD, 79-84) and KD II.2, 69 (CD, 64). Barth also uses terms like 'double system of bookkeeping' (KD III.1, 476; CD, 414), 'strange duality' (KD III.3, 38; CD, 33), 'two-tracked' (KD I.1, 354; CD, 335), 'the construction of sub-centres alien to its content' (KD I.2, 135; CD, 123), and 'elliptic' ('Nein!', op. cit., 40, 44).

CHAPTER IV

CALVIN'S *INSTITUTIO* IN ITS FINAL FORM

The Latin edition of 1559 and the French edition of 1560

§1. CALVIN'S WORK ON THE DEFINITIVE NEW VERSION OF HIS MAIN
DOGMATIC WORK DURING THE WINTER OF 1558/59

In the winter of 1558/59 Calvin started to work for the last time on a new version of
his *Institutes*. He had the book in front of him, which had been divided into seventeen
chapters in 1539 and into twenty-one chapters in 1543-1554. The following overview
shows us what the book looked like in these previous editions.

1536	1539	1543-1554

SUMMA DOCTRINAE

	1. The Knowledge of God.	1. The knowledge of God, which is the first basic principle of religion and the question from which to derive its true rule.
	2. The Knowledge of Man and Free Will.	2. The knowledge of man; dealing with original sin, the corruption of man by nature, the impotence of free will, the grace of being born again, and the aid of the Holy Spirit.
I. The Law. Including an explanation of the Ten Words.	3. The Law.	3. The law; firstly determining the function and use of that law and subsequently discussing the true service to God, images, oaths, ecclesiastical feasts, and monastic vows.
		4. The vows; on monasticism.

1536	1539	1543-1554
II. Faith. Including an explanation of the Apostles' Creed.	4. Faith. Including an explanation of the Apostles' Creed.	5. Faith. Including an explanation of the Apostles' Creed.
		6. Explanation of the first part of the Creed; discussing the object of faith, the trinity, the omnipotence of God, and the creation of the world.
		7. Explanation of the second part of the Creed; dealing with incarnation, death, the resurrection of Christ, and the entire mystery of salvation. Also the explanation of the third part of the Creed; discussing the Holy Spirit.
		8. Explanation of the fourth part of the Creed; discussing the church, its government, organization, power and the imposition of discipline; the power of the keys (to the kingdom of heaven), the forgiveness of sins, and the final resurrection.
	5. Repentance.	9. Repentance.
	6. Justification and the merit of works.	10. Justification and the merit of works.

Aspects

	7. Agreement and difference between the Old and the New Testaments.	11. Agreement and difference between the Old and the New Testaments.
		12. Christian freedom.
		13. Human traditions.
	8. Predestination and the providence of God.	14. Predestination and the providence of God.
III. Prayer. Including an explanation of the Lord's Prayer.	9. Prayer. Including an explanation of the Lord's Prayer.	15. Prayer. Including an explanation of the Lord's Prayer.

IV. The Sacraments.	10. The sacraments.	16. The sacraments (in general).
	11. Baptism.	17. Baptism.
	12. The Lord's Supper.	18. The Lord's Supper.
		19. In which the other five sacraments are revealed not to be sacraments at all, although they are commonly held to be so. Their true nature is shown.'
VI. Christian Freedom, Ecclesial Power, and Civil Government.	13. Christian freedom.	
	14. Ecclesiastical power.	
	15. Civil government.	20. Civil government.
	16. In which the other five sacraments are revealed not to be sacraments at all, although they are commonly held to be so. Their true nature is shown.'	
	17. The life of a Christian man.	21. The life of a Christian man.

Excursus

In the French edition of 1541, the chapter on 'The five false sacraments' followed immediately after the three chapters 10-12 on the sacraments. In 1543, the newly written chapter 'The vows; on monasticism' was inserted as a fourth chapter after the third chapter 'The law'. Given the considerable increase in material – especially concerning the church – the fourth chapter 'Faith' was divided into four chapters. These are chapters 5-8 in the *Institutes* of 1543. The material of the chapter on 'Ecclesial power' was largely incorporated into the eighth chapter on the church. The chapter 'Human traditions' was rewritten in 1543. Together with the chapter 'Christian freedom' it was placed between the chapters 'Agreement and difference between the Old and New Testaments' and 'Predestination and the providence of God' (as chapters 11-14). Consequently, from 1543 onward the *Institutes* did not count seventeen (as in 1539), but twenty-one chapters. In 1550 all paragraphs of every chapter were numbered.

In the winter of 1558/59 Calvin wanted to give this book – conceived in 1543 – a new form. We recall the words he added to the old preface in 1559: 'I was never satisfied, until I arrived at the order and arrangement in which the *Institutes* are presently offered.[1] The definitive new form of the *Institutes* emerged by dividing all the material of the doctrines into four books following Calvin's division of the Creed into four parts:

(Father:)	(Son:)	(Holy Spirit:)	(Church:)
Creation	Redemption	Dual Grace	Community of Saints

First book:	The knowledge of God the Creator.	18 chaps.
Second book:	The knowledge of God the Redeemer in Christ, which was first revealed to the fathers under the law, and then to us as well in the gospel.	17 chaps.
Third book:	The way in which the grace of Christ is received, the fruits that flow from this to us, and the effects that follow.	25 chaps.
Fourth book:	The external resources, used by God to invite us to the community of Christ and to keep us there.	20 chaps.
		80 chaps.

In the old *Institutes*, Calvin referred to his division of the Creed into four parts in the Introduction to the whole of the explanation of the Creed (*explicatio symboli*).[2]

This chapter will show how the trinitarian division of the *explicatio symboli* in Calvin's 1559 *Institutes* was not quite displaced, but still forcefully pushed back because of the scheme of the *historica series* (see below, §2.4 of this chapter) and the thesis of the duality of the knowledge of God (*duplex cognitio Dei*). Taking into account all that we need to discuss now, it would be good to bear in mind the words of the old Introduction to the whole of the *explicatio symboli*[3] and in particular the words of the last paragraph already mentioned. This final paragraph of the old Introduction reads as follows:

1539*[4]
(1536 I,70)

1539

'(…) As far as the classification of the Creed is concerned: three of its parts describe the Father, the Son and the Spirit, on which depends the entire mystery of our faith.[5] The fourth part indicates what our salvation consists of. This disposition is not to be neglected. That is to say, if we wish to come to knowledge of our salvation,[6] we need to consider these three issues on which the entire matter rests: (1) the most gracious goodness of the Father and His most abundant love for the human race, expressed in the fact that He did not spare His own Son but has given Him over to death for us all, in order to bring us back to life (John 3:16; Rom 8:32); (2) the obedience of the Son, being the fulfillment of divine mercy in order to accomplish our salvation; (3) the power of the Spirit, through which we have a share in the fruits of God's goodness in Christ. This is what Paul had in mind when he wished the Corinthians 'the love of God, the grace of Christ and the communion of the spirit' (2 Cor 13:13). For all that is good flows to us from God's love; it is shown to us in Christ as the source of all grace; and by the power of the Spirit we share in all that is offered to us by God's benevolence. From this follow the doctrines of the church, the forgiveness of sins, the resurrection of the dead, and life eternal, to which the fourth part of the Creed is dedicated.'[7]

In the final form of the *Institutes*, the scheme 'The Law → Faith' is no longer the framework within which the 'summary of doctrine' is developed. The framework now consists of the *explicatio symboli*.

Excursus

Under (2) in the paragraph quoted above Calvin speaks of *Filii obedientia, quae est divinae misericordiae complementum...* (the obedience of the Son, which is the fulfillment of divine mercy...). We remember that *misericordia Dei* (the mercy of God, LXX: *eleos*) was the core concept of the *Institutes* of 1536.[8] For example, the first chapter 'De Lege' told us the following: 'Faith rests on the mercy of God alone. It is assured because it knows that mercy and truth have come together and that God will faithfully fulfill all that He promises out of mercy. And this firm faith is followed by a firm promise that cannot remain unfulfilled for those who believe (Ps 85:11)'[9] – Calvin, who was well trained in Hebrew by Vatables, one of the royal lecturers in Paris, correctly explains the expression *hesed we-'emet*. Calvin now continues as follows: 'It needs to be recognized, therefore, that our salvation exists by the mercy of God alone, and certainly not by any dignity of ourselves...'. We come across the words *sola Dei misericordia* (the mercy of God alone) twice.

We now must contrast this passage from the 1536 *Institutes* with Calvin's definition of faith from the Catechism of 1537, which was influenced by Melanchthon: 'Faith is a strong and firm confidence of the heart, allowing us to rest securely in the mercy of God promised to us in the gospel.'[10] Let us now compare these two texts by Calvin to excerpts from Melanchthon's *Loci*:

1. Aetas (1521-1525), at the beginning of the fourth paragraph of the chapter 'On justification and faith':[11]

'Faith is therefore nothing but trust in divine mercy, promised to us in Christ and even in a single sign. This trust in the benevolence or the mercy of God first brings peace to the heart, and then sets it aflame, as if to thank God for His mercy, in order that we perform the law spontaneously and joyfully. Whereas if we do not believe, we have no sense in our hearts of the mercy of God. Where there is no sense of the mercy of God, there is either contempt or hatred towards God. Whatever great works may be achieved without faith, it still is a sin. (...) Therefore, people should not take notice of their works, but rather of the promise[12] of the mercy of God.'

2. Aetas (1535-1541), in the chapter 'Grace and Justification':[13]

'A soul, thoroughly frightened by the knowledge of his sins, must firmly put in mind that his sins are forgiven for nothing because of Christ, by mercy, not because of the dignity of repentance, of love, or other works (...). Having a firm and strong comfort does not depend at all on the state of our dignity, but on mercy alone, which is promised because of Christ (...). We gather witnesses for the belief that we achieve the forgiveness of sins and reconciliation for nothing, because of Christ, by faith, not because of the dignity of our works. (...) For Paul, "faith" undoubtedly means trusting in the promised mercy because of Christ (…). We truly do not exclude the history regarding Christ, as some are saying. When we say "trusting in the promised grace because of Christ" we embrace all the articles of faith. We relate the history of Christ to that one article, which brings to mind the *beneficium Christi* (the benevolence of Christ),[14] i.e, the forgiveness of sins.'

In the first form of the *Institutes* (1536), consisting of six chapters, and also in the 1539 *Institutes*, consisting of seventeen chapters, the *explicatio symboli* covered only the content of a single chapter. In 1536, it was the second chapter and in 1539 the fourth. Because of a large increase of material, Calvin divided the fourth chapter (Faith) of the 1539 version into four chapters in 1543.

In the final edition of his book, Calvin planned to turn these four chapters (V to VIII) of the 1543-1554 Institutes into the four books of the new version. Nevertheless, he did not start from these old four chapters containing the *explicatio symboli* when he started his work. When he took up the old book with its twenty-one chapters, he began with the first chapter of this book of the old *Institutes*. Beginning with that chapter, he continued through the old book from chapter to chapter, until he had placed all twenty-one chapters of the old book in the four books of the new *Institutes*.

When Calvin began his work, he knew precisely how he wished to divide all of the material over the four books. One is therefore inclined to assume that he first divided this material over the four books and then started to thoroughly edit the four books. Our depiction of Calvin's work on the *Institutes* in the winter of 1558/59 will show, however, that this was not the way Calvin worked on the final form of his book.

We see how Calvin assembles his first two books ('The Knowledge of God the Creator' and 'The Knowledge of God the Redeemer') out of the material of the first three chapters of the old *Institutes* (The Knowledge of God – The Knowledge of Man – The Law), being guided by his thesis of the duality of the knowledge of God (first phase). Then, when Calvin reaches the four chapters on 'faith', in the old *Institutes*, he divides the four *partes* (segments) of the old *explicatio symboli* among the four books of the new *Institutes* (second phase). Finally, we see the completion of the four books of the new *Institutes* one after another in their definitive form (third phase).

We now wish to trace the way Calvin went about to shape the final edition of his book. This is how we get the best access to the structure of his entire theology. In the three phases mentioned above we count a total of *eight steps*. These eight steps will be described in the paragraphs to follow. First, in paragraph 2 the 'first phase' will be analyzed. Then, in paragraph 3, we will give a brief indication of the 'second' and the 'third phase' of Calvin's activities.

First phase   First phase
Calvin creates his first two books ('The Knowledge of God the Creator' and 'The Knowledge of God the Redeemer'), being guided by his thesis of the duality of the knowledge of God.

    I. First Step
The old first chapter, 'The Knowledge of God', becomes the basis of the new first book, 'The Knowledge of God the Creator', in the first ten chapters of this book.

   II. Second Step
The old second chapter, 'The Knowledge of Man', becomes the starting point of the new second book, 'The Knowledge of God the Redeemer', in the first five chapters of this book (= the doctrine of sin).

  III. Third Step
By assembling the old chapter III, 'The Law' (= II.7-8) and XI, 'Agreement and Difference...' (= II.10-11), the structure of the chapters 6-11 of the second book of the new *Institutes* comes into being, with the theme 'Law and gospel as witness to Christ'.

Second phase   Second phase = Fourth step

  IV. The division of the four *partes* of the old *explicatio symboli* among the four books of the new *Institutio* (the old chaps. V-VIII).

Excursus
The scheme of the *historica series* and the thesis of the duality of the knowledge of God had acquired a leading role. Therefore, the old introduction to the *explicatio symboli* (Inst. 1550: VI:1-5) could no longer be determinant for the form of the new Institutio. Hence, this old Introduction was omitted.

Third phase   Third phase
The division of the old chapters IX-XXI among the new third and fourth books. The final editing of each of the four books of the new *Institutes*.

   V. Fifth Step
The completion of the first book.

  VI. Sixth Step
The completion of the second book.

 VII. Seventh Step
The composition of the third book.

VIII. Eighth Step
The composition of the fourth book.

§2   THE FIRST PHASE. The work on the first two books, being guided by the thesis of
the duality of the knowledge of God

§2.1 THE FIRST STEP: THE KNOWLEDGE OF GOD (I.1-10)

As we said above, Calvin began with the old first chapter. In 1539 the heading of this
chapter was very briefly: 'The Knowledge of God'. In 1543-1554 it became: 'The
knowledge of God, which is the first basic principle of religion and the question from
which to derive its true rule'. Calvin now made this first chapter with its division in
thirty-eight paragraphs the foundation for the first book of the new *Institutes* ('The
Knowledge of God the Creator').

In the previous chapter of our study we discussed the *Institutes* in its second edition, and analyzed the composition and the train of thought of this chapter as completely as possible. The chapter opened in I.1-3 with an introduction, in which the
opening sentence of the Institutes 'almost the entire summary of our wisdom (...) consists of two parts: the knowledge of God and of ourselves' was clarified. Inspired by
the Wittenberg theology, Calvin unfolded the doctrine according to the scheme 'The
Law → Faith' (Wittenberg: law and gospel). From the knowledge of sin through the
law, we arrive at knowledge of God's grace through the gospel. This means: from the
knowledge of self man arrives at the knowledge of God. However, Calvin wished (already in 1536) to go in the opposite direction, from the knowledge of God to the
knowledge of self. The concluding sentence of the introduction said:

'No matter how the connection between the knowledge of God and of ourselves is to
be explained in the end, the proper order of instruction (*ordo recte docendi*) demands
that we first discuss the knowledge of God. After this we can descend to discussing
the knowledge of the self'.[15]

Excursus
That Calvin wished to think from the knowledge of God to the knowledge of self is a characteristic trait of his theology (and of his 'piety'). We may compare this with what Barth has often
called 'the slope'.[16] Undoubtedly this means the rejection of any anthropologization of theology.
In the French edition of the *Institutes* in 1560, Calvin expresses this as follows: 'The entire sum
of almost all of our wisdom, which merits to be called true and total wisdom, is given in two
parts: *c'est qu'en cognoissant Dieu, chacun de nous aussi se cognoisse*' (by knowing God, everyone of us also knows himself).[17] In all previous editions (1541-1557) the sentence ended with:
'la congnoissance de Dieu et de nousmesmes' (the knowledge of God and of ourselves').[18]
Noteworthy in this connection are the headings of chapters 4-7 in the book by Wilhelm Maurer,
Der junge Melanchthon, Band 2.[19] As a commentary on Melanchthon's *Loci* of 1521, these
headings form the heart of Maurer's book:

   4. Toward an understanding of man
   5. Man under sin
   6. Man under the law
   7. Man under grace.

Maurer comments on Melanchthon's famous phrase 'to know Christ is to know his benefits'[20] in the following way:

'What matters to Melanchthon is the redemptory effects of incarnation and crucifixion. He was not interested in idle speculations about how the divine and human nature can co-exist in Christ or how the incarnation should be understood. (...) We should not put the essential anthropological feature of the *Loci* over against the theological-Christological interest. Rather, the reverse should be the case. Melanchthon's understanding of man is determined by the salvific acts of God in Christ.'[21]

Compare this to the following statement by Ernst Wolf:[22]

'In Luther's view, the formula's "law and gospel" and "gospel and law" are not to be put in opposition to each other. On the other hand, they are not identical either. "Law and gospel" involves the danger of an anthropological version of the doctrine of justification. "Gospel and law" seeks to safeguard the Christological character of the commanding, creating and redeeming Word of God. This corresponds to two sayings of Luther. First, the law should "remain under the Lord Christ" and second, "Christ has all from Moses, but Moses not all from Christ" (*habere Christum omnia Mosi, sed Mosen non omnia Christi*).'[23]

During the description of the third phase we shall see how Calvin explains the theme 'law and gospel' during the winter of 1558/59.

The heading of the first chapter in the year 1543 announces that after the introduction (I.1-3), two parts will follow:

First Part (paragraphs 4-18):
The knowledge of God, which is the first basic principle of religion.

This first part deals with man's knowledge of God (§§4-10) and of God, who makes himself known to man in his 'works' ('in the world') (§§11-18).[24]

Second Part (paragraphs 19-38):
The Knowledge of God (...) and the question from which to derive its true rule.

This second part deals with the authority of the Holy Scriptures. In the first ten chapters of the new *Institutes*, which include a total of fifty-five paragraphs, we meet this old first chapter again:

Chap. I	Introduction
Chap. II-VI	The Knowledge of God
Chap. VII-IX	The Holy Scriptures
Chap. X	God

Chap. I contains in three paragraphs the old introduction, to which Calvin now gives the heading: 'The knowledge of God and that of ourselves are mutually connected. How do they relate to each other?'
= 1539 (1550) I.1-3; French 1541, 1 ll. 1 - 4, 1. 2.[25]

Chap. II contains in two paragraphs the newly composed second introduction with the heading: 'What does it mean to know God, and what purpose does this knowledge serve?'[26]

Using parts of the old paragraphs 1, 6, 9 and 38, Calvin has newly composed this second chapter. In the first paragraph of this chapter he formulates the thesis of the duality of the knowledge of God: 'The Lord first appears to us as the creator, both in the making of the world and in the general doctrine of Scripture. Then, in Christ, we meet him as redeemer as well. From this it follows that there is a dual knowledge of God. The former will be treated presently' – in book I, FB – 'and the other will follow in due time' – in books II, III and IV, FB.[27] Basing himself on this main thesis, Calvin works writes the first two books of the new Institutes.

Next follow the chapters on man's knowledge of God (Chap. II-IV) and God's revelation in his *opera* (works) in chaps. V-VI.

Chap. III in three paragraphs
'That the knowledge of God is implanted in the minds of men by nature.'
= 1539 (1550) I.4-5-10; French 1541, 4 ll. 3-5 1. 39; 9 ll. 24 - 10 1. 3.[28]

Chap. IV in four paragraphs
'That this knowledge is corrupted, partly by ignorance, partly by malice.'
= 1539 (1550) I.7-8-6; French 1541, 6 ll. 1 - 8 1. 26.[29]

Chap. V in fifteen paragraphs
'That the knowledge of God constantly shines forth in the artifact of the world and in its continuing government.'
= 1539 (1550) I.11-18; French 1541, 10 ll. 4 - 17 1. 14.[30]

Chap. VI in four paragraphs
'That anyone, in order to come to God the creator, needs the guidance and the teaching of the scripture.'
= 1539 (1550) I.19-20; French 1541, 17 ll. 15 - 19 1.16.[31]

The theme of the sixth chapter (= 1539 I.19-20) was arranged by Calvin in such a way that in this place he could discuss the authority of the Holy Scriptures in the ensuing three chapters:

Chap. VII   in five paragraphs (against the Roman theologians)
'The Scriptures must be confirmed by the witness of the Holy Spirit, so that their authority might be sure. It is a godless illusion that the credibility of Scripture depends on the judgment of the church.'
= 1539 (1550) I.21-24; French 1541, 19 ll. 17 - 21 l. 39.[32]

Chap. VIII   in thirteen paragraphs
'Human reason gives sufficient proofs to underscore the credibility of the Scriptures.'
= 1539 (1550) I.25-33; French 1541, 22 ll. 1 - 24 l. 32.[33]

Chap. IX   in three paragraphs (against the Anabaptists):
'The fanatics who, ignoring Scripture, appeal directly to Revelation, overthrow all principles of piety.'
= 1539 (1550) I.34-36; French 1541, 24 ll. 33 - 27 l. 29.[34]

In his 'answer to cardinal Sadoleto' (1539) Calvin says: 'We are opposed by two parties, which seemingly differ as much as is possible. For what does the Pope have in common with the Anabaptists? And yet...'.[35] And yet, they both separate the Spirit from the Word. We may compare Karl Barth's description of the two basic forms of heresy (conceived of as 'a different faith'): 'If the being of the church is identical with Jesus Christ (...), then the starting point of dogmatic knowledge can be neither a prior anthropological possibility nor a subsequent ecclesial reality, but only the present moment of the speaking and hearing of Jesus Christ himself, the divine "creation of light" in our hearts (1 Cor 4:6).'[36]

When Calvin writes about the Holy Scriptures in the three chapters mentioned above, he refers to what he calls in the 1559 *Institutes* the *generalis scripturae doctrina* (the general doctrine of the Scripture).[37] In the second book of the new *Institutes* he also comes to talk about Scripture, but here he does so from the perspective of Christ, referring to what he calls the *propria fidei doctrina* (the proper doctrine of faith).[38] Contrary to this dualism, however, Karl Barth in the Prolegomena of his Dogmatics – 'The Doctrine of the Word of God' in its threefold form – simply talks about the Holy Scriptures as witness of the revelation of the triune God in the Word made flesh through the Holy Spirit.[39]

In this first phase, Calvin was beginning to turn the conclusion of the old first chapter (I.37-38) into a locus *de Deo* ('God').

Chap. X   in three paragraphs
'That Scripture, to correct all superstition, has set the true God alone over against all the gods of the nations'.
= 1539 (1550) I.37-38; French 1541, 27 ll. 30 - 29 l. 39.[40]

The theme of the last two paragraphs of the old first chapter (I.37-38) was: 'whether God represents himself in Scriptures in the same way as He is portrayed in His works'.[41] At the end of the first chapter Calvin did not wish to say that we must start from God's revelation in Scripture and then see whether He reveals himself in the same way in creation. Rather, he does the reverse, asking whether God is the same in Scripture as we can see Him in His 'works'.[42]

However, in the heading which Calvin assigned to the tenth chapter of the first book, he does tell us that he wishes to start with Scripture. For him the decisive factor was that we must view God in his 'works' as he speaks of himself in Scripture.

To give the tenth chapter of the first book the content which was announced in the heading, Calvin first copies the old paragraphs 37-38 (= I.10.1-2). He then removes the final sentence of this section. In its place he puts a newly written third paragraph.[43] In agreement with the heading of the chapter, this final paragraph begins as follows: 'But the intention here is' – i.e., in this first book of the *Institutes*, FB – 'to summarize the essence of the general doctrine of Scripture. The first thing readers will note is that Scripture, to lead us to the true God, clearly rejects all the gods of the heathen. Indeed, religion has committed adultery almost always and everywhere.'[44] In this first book of the *Institutes,* Calvin does not speak of the *summa totius doctrinae* (the essence of the entire doctrine), but of the *summa generalis scripturae doctrinae* (the essence of the general doctrine of Scripture). This is about that part of doctrine, 'which is not grounded in Christ.'[45]

Apart from a few rearrangements in the first ten paragraphs, the text of the entire first chapter of the old *Institutes* has been moved to the first ten chapters of the new *Institutes*. It has been left unchanged. We do see Calvin add smaller and now and then also larger passages, mainly to emphasize or apply thoughts which had already been referred to. However, the series of thoughts in chapters 2, 6, and 10 concerning a biblical-theological grounding of the new, and this time final, form of his *Institutes*, are entirely new. I speak *nondum* (not yet) of the knowledge of God the redeemer, but I speak *tantum* (only) of the knowledge of God the creator, Calvin writes.

Excursus
'Here I speak not yet of Christ, (...) not yet of the proper doctrine of faith, (...) not yet of that part of doctrine which has always been unknown by the unholy heathen, because it was grounded in Christ.' This word *nondum* (not yet) is seen three times in this passage[46] and then once more also in an insertion in the first paragraph of the tenth chapter: 'I do not yet speak about that particular covenant, by which He has distinguished the generation of Abraham from the other nations. For in that covenant He received His enemies as His children and showed himself to be a Redeemer. Here, we are concerned with the knowledge arising out of creation, which and does not ascend to Christ, the mediator.'[47]

Contrary to Calvin, Karl Barth in the first paragraph of his doctrine of creation says 'already!' instead of 'not yet'. Already in the doctrine of creation we are dealing with faith in Jesus Christ, 'because all parts of the doctrine are grounded in Christ'. The basic principle of the first, introductory paragraph in Barth's doctrine of creation, is: 'The insight that we owe our presence and essence to God can only be gained in the context of divine self-revelation, Jesus Christ. Indeed, it can only be gained by seeing that in Christ, creator and creature are united. Our present life under the justice and in the experience of the good Creator is mediated by Christ.' (Note how in this leading motif the *particula exclusiva* of Reformation theology – 'only' – occurs twice.)[48]

In the three steps of the first phase Calvin has sketched the draft of the first two books of the 1559 *Institutes*, basing himself on the duality of the knowledge of God. At this point we must, again, briefly describe how Calvin arrived at the formulation of this thesis in the newly composed second chapter of the first book 'What it is to know God'. The final sentence of the old first chapter 'The Knowledge of God' read:

'Nevertheless, the Lord nowhere makes himself known in a more intimate way than in the face of Christ, which can only be seen with the eyes of faith. Therefore, what remains to be said about the knowledge of God can better be postponed to the place where the concept of faith is treated.'[49]

In the first chapter of the old *Institutes* Calvin discusses the content of the knowledge of God 'in His works, in the fashioning of the world'. The knowledge of God 'in the face of His Christ' was not yet on the agenda in that chapter. He wishes to postpone that subject, so he says in the final sentence of the first chapter, until he would discuss the concept of faith in the fourth chapter. From the knowledge of God the knowledge of ourselves as sinners through the law is derived.[50] This theme had to be unfolded in the first three chapters of the 1539 *Institutes* ('The Knowledge of God – The Knowledge of Man – The Law'). Only then the 'mercy of God', the knowledge of God 'in the face of Christ' could be discussed in the *explicatio symboli* of the fourth chapter, 'Faith'.

Thus, the scheme was:

God	→	Man	→	Man as Sinner	→	God

God in his works (in the making of the world)	→	Man as Sinner	→	God in the face of Christ

I. The Knowledge of God / II. The Knowledge of Man / III. The Law / IV. Faith

Calvin did not drop this scheme in 1559. To the contrary, he made this scheme the foundation of his *Institutes* as *explicatio symboli*, for:

God in his works	→	Man as Sinner	→	God in the face of Christ

in 1559 became:

God the Creator	→ Man →	Man as Sinner	→	God the Redeemer

Because of the changed *ordo docendi* (order of instruction), Calvin had to drop the cited final sentence of the old first chapter of 'The Knowledge of God'. In its place he put, as we have seen, the newly written third paragraph of the tenth chapter. Yet he did not delete the words 'in the face of his Christ' of that sentence. He inserted these words in the newly composed second chapter of the first book (as second introduction at the beginning of the new *Institutes*) in the formulation of the thesis of the duality of the knowledge of God:

'The Lord first appears to us as the creator, both in the making of the world and in the general doctrine of Scripture. Then, in Christ, we meet Him as redeemer as well. From this it follows that there is a dual knowledge of God. The former will be treated presently and the other will follow in due time'.

Contrary to Calvin, Karl Barth bases his *Kirchliche Dogmatik* (also conceived as an *explicatio symboli*) on the thesis: God in his works = God in the face of Christ; God's appearance in the single history of his many covenantal acts is identical to the appearance of God in the face of Jesus Christ.

Calvin's thesis of the duality of the knowledge of God is derived from his old scheme (God in his works → Man as Sinner → God in the face of Christ). He shapes the first two books of the new *Institutes* on the basis of this main thesis. The material for the first book was mainly taken from the old first chapter 'The Knowledge of God'. Likewise, the material for the second book stems from the old second chapter, as we shall see in the description of the second step. The locus on 'sin' serves as a starting point for the new second book, 'The Knowledge of God the Redeemer'.

And what happens to the old third chapter, 'The Law'? Well, that would be one of the novelties of the new *Institutes*. After the locus on 'sin' Calvin will speak in the second book about the Law as witness to Christ. We will only be able to see that in the description of the third step. First we need to discuss the second step.

§2.2 THE SECOND STEP: THE KNOWLEDGE OF MAN (II.1-5)

In 1539 the heading of the second chapter read: 'The Knowledge of Man and Free Will'. In 1543 this was changed into a more extensive indication of content: 'The knowledge of man; dealing with original sin, the corruption of man by nature, the impotence of free will, the grace of being born again, and the aid of the Holy Spirit' (1550: 94 paragraphs).[51] This old second chapter Calvin made his starting point for the new second book, and with that at the same time the starting point for books II-IV. The word *foundation* would not be the right word. In our description of the third step we will see what Calvin uses as a foundation for books II-IV (namely: 'law and gospel' as witness to Christ in the six chapters II.6-11).

In the first five chapters of the second book of the new *Institutes* (with a total of seventy-nine paragraphs) consist of the old second chapter. The headings, which Calvin gave to these five chapters in the winter of 1558/59, are as follows:

Second book: 'The knowledge of God the Redeemer in Christ,
               which were first revealed to the fathers under the law,
               and then also to us in the gospel.'

Chap. I   in eleven paragraphs
'That by the fall and revolt of Adam the whole human race is subjected to the curse and degenerated from its original condition; and in which original sin is described.'
= 1539 (1550) II.1-15; French 1541, 30 l. 1–39, l. 15.[52]

Chap. II   in twenty-seven paragraphs
'That man is now deprived of his freedom of choice and is bound to miserable servitude.'
= 1539 (1550) II.16-46; French 1541, 39 l. 16–67 l. 13.[53]

Chap. III   in fourteen paragraphs
'That from man's corrupt nature comes forth nothing but damnable things.'
= 1539 (1550) II.47-60; French 1541, 67 l. 14–85 l. 16.[54]

Chap. IV   in eight paragraphs
'How God works in human hearts.'
= 1539 (1550) II.68-75; French 1541, 85 l. 17–92 l. 11.[55]

Chap. V   in nineteen paragraphs
'Refutation of the objections commonly put forward in defense of free will.'
= 1539 (1550) II.76-94; French 1541, 92 l. 12–111 l. 21.[56]

Of the ninety-four old paragraphs, eleven are taken and removed into another context:
II.6-7 + 18-19 → book I, chap. XV.6-7 (in the doctrine of man, I.XV)
II.61-67   → book III, chap. III.10-14 (in the doctrine of repentance, III.III-V).[57]

In the later editions, published after Calvin's death, each of the four books is opened with an Argumentum. These Argumenta stem from Olevianus. The Argumentum to the second book begins as follows:

'Having discussed the first part of the Creed on the knowledge of God the creator, a second section follows on the knowledge of God the redeemer in Christ.

First he discusses the fall of Adam, which occasioned redemption. Secondly, he discusses redemption itself. The first five chapters are assigned to the treatment of the first, the rest to what follows.

As to the occasion for redemption, he does not only treat the fall in general, but also its effects: original sin, the bondage of the will, the corrupt nature of man and God's work in human hearts, in respectively chapters 1, 2, 3 and 4. In chapter 5 he adds a refutation of the objections adduced to defend free will'.[58]

In 1550 Calvin had already given a sketch of how he would structure his explanation through the way he numbered the paragraphs. As we saw, the first chapter counted thirty-eight paragraphs. The more detailed second chapter contained 94 paragraphs.

When Calvin in the winter of 1558/59 inserted the material of the twenty-one chapters of the old *Institutes* in the four books of the new *Institutes*, he arranged his explanation in a new way, dividing each of the old twenty-one chapters into several chapters. These new chapters he divided in several paragraphs, mostly in agreement with the division of paragraphs in the old Institutes. Thus he divided the old second chapter into five chapters with a total of (11 + 27 + 14 + 8 + 19 =) seventy-nine paragraphs. These five chapters he organized as a *dissertatio de Adae lapsu et eius effectis* (discourse about Adam's fall and its effects). This locus on 'sin' at the beginning of the second book deals with the *redemptionis occasio* (the occasion of redemption), as the later Argumentum correctly explains. The new structure is very clear:

I. Generally, the fall (of man), but also in particular its effects, that is, original sin.
II. The Bondage of the Will.
    §§1-11   The concept of *liberum arbitrium* (free will).
    §§12-27 *Intelligentia et voluntas* (understanding and will) of man after the fall.
III. The corrupt nature of all men.
IV. God's working in the hearts of men.
V. Refutation of the objections defending free will.

The heading of the fifth chapter shows that the discussion of the *liberum arbitrium* in the second chapter is the main topic of the entire explanation. First, however, we need to discuss the introduction to this explanation, because it shows the principle of Calvin's editorial work in the winter of 1558/59. In the old *Institutes*, the introduction to the entire second chapter was given in the first five paragraphs (1559: II.1-5). In the new *Institutes* we find this introduction again at the beginning of the second book in the first three paragraphs of the first chapter (1559: II.1-3 ← 1550: II.1-5).

In this introduction Calvin contrasts philosophical to Christian knowledge of the human self. The first is characterized as *superbia* (pride), the second as *humilitas* (humility). At the end of this introduction he tells us how he wanted to unfold the knowledge of the human self in the old second chapter:

'Let us therefore, if you please, divide the knowledge which man needs to have of himself. First, he needs to consider for what purpose he was created with so many gifts. Reflecting on this he is encouraged to serve God and to meditate on the future life.[59] Only then should he consider his powers, or rather his lack of these. Having realized that, in the end, he is nothing, he lies down in utter despair. The first consideration teaches him what his duty is. The second what he needs to have in order to fulfil this duty. Both of these points will be explained at different places, in the order which the instruction demands.'[60]

Calvin says that in the locus on the knowledge of man of the old *Institutes* both the theme 'man as God's creature'[61] and the theme 'man as sinner'[62] had to be discussed,[63] '*prout series docendi poscet*' (in the order which the instruction demands) and *sparsim* (at different places).

After this introduction Calvin began his explanation as follows:
'Before we turn in earnest to the description of the miserable state of man',

> – that description is the real theme of the entire chapter, FB –

'it is worthwhile to remember in which state man was created.
For we need to watch out that we do not, by pointing out the natural evil of man, appear to ascribe this to the author of nature'.[64]

It was only to avoid the impression that he was ascribing the natural wickedness of man to the originator of nature that Calvin, in the second chapter of the old Institutes, spoke also of man as God's creature. He did this only in two passages in four of the total of ninety-four paragraphs, namely II.6-7 and II.18-19. In 1558/59, Calvin took these four paragraphs out of their original context of the old second chapter and inserted them in the newly written fifteenth chapter of the first book of the new *Institutes* entitled 'How man was created; in which are discussed the faculties of the soul, the image of God, free will and the original state of integrity'.[65]

In order to understand what Calvin in the winter of 1558/59 is doing with the old introduction of the locus 'The knowledge of man', we must begin with the first three sentences of the old Institutes:[66]

Opening sentence:	'The essence of our true and unshakeable wisdom consists almost entirely of two parts: the knowledge of God and the knowledge of ourselves.'
Second sentence, The knowledge of God	'Clearly, the first part of our exposition must not only show us that there is one God, who must be worshipped and honored by all. It must also teach us that He is the only source of all truth, wisdom, goodness, righteousness, justice, compassion, power, and holiness, so that we learn to expect and ask from Him all things. And then, having received these things from Him with praise and thanksgiving, we should learn to return them to Him.'
Third sentence, The knowledge of man	'However, the second part should show us our weakness, misery, emptiness, and ugliness. This leads to true meekness, rejection, uncertainty, and hatred of ourselves. It will then arouse in us the longing to seek God. We realize that, because we are empty-handed and naked, all of our good rests in Him.'

Calvin took the two sentences about the knowledge of God and of ourselves out of the context of the old introduction to the entire *Institutes*. He inserted the first sentence on the knowledge of God at the beginning of the newly composed second chapter in the first book, 'What it is to Know God'. We find it again in Inst. I.2.1.[67] But now Calvin has placed his thesis of the duality of the knowledge of God in the middle ('...first simply as creator, then in the face of Christ as redeemer...').

Likewise, he inserted the sentence concerning the knowledge of man in the first paragraph of the second book. And here also he formulates a *primum – deinde* (first – and then). To gain a clearer understanding of this matter, let us look at the entire first paragraph of the old introduction and then at the form Calvin gave it in 1558/59.[68]

1539	'It is not without reason, that the self-knowledge of man is so strongly recommended by an old proverb (i.e., 'Know thyself'). For if we make a bad impression when we are not aware of the things which belong to human life, it is still more shameful if we do not know ourselves. Because we lack this knowledge we commit miserable blunders and are very much blinded. But the more useful this advice is, the more careful we need to see that we do not use it wrongly, which, as we see, has happened to some philosophers. They encourage people to know themselves so that they would always be aware of their dignity and excellence. They do not wish that they should discover something other than those things which make them boast in their idle self confidence and proud (Gen 1:27).'	2.1

Note the insertion	1559	'The knowledge of ourselves consists *first* of this. Considering what has been given to us in creation and how mercifully God holds fast to His grace toward us, we realize how great the excellence of our nature might have been, if only it had remained unharmed. At the same time we realize that we do not possess anything of our own. Everything we have has been given to us by the grace of God, so that we might always cleave to Him.

Then when we become conscious of our miserable state after the fall of Adam, we are covered with shame, since all glory and confidence is ruined. This truly makes us humble. God formed us in His image in the beginning, and raised our spirits both to striving after virtue and to meditating future life. This is what distinguishes us from irrational animals. We should not forget the nobility of our species. We are gifted with reason and understanding, so that by leading a holy and honorable life we could stretch ourselves toward the goal held before us of a blissful immortality.'

The sentence on	1559*	'Further, the moment we realize our dignity, we	1.1
cognitio sui	(1539)	become aware of the sad drama of our shame, which	
(knowledge of		began with the first man, having fallen from his ori-	
self) from the be-		gin. And from this arises hatred and displeasure	
ginning of the old		toward ourselves and true humility. A new striving	
Institutes.		is fired up in us to seek God. In him we hope to find	
		the goods we were robbed of, having become	
		empty-handed and naked.'[69]	

What has happened? In I.2.1 Calvin formulated a *primum – deinde* (first – and then) concerning the knowledge of God. It was the *primum – deinde* of the *ante et post hominem lapsum* (before and after the fall of man). This formed the basis for his thesis about the duality of the knowledge of God. Now, in II.1.1, he formulates a *primum – deinde* again, this time concerning the knowledge of man. Here again there is an *ante et post hominem lapsum*, but this time it forms the basis for Calvin's thesis about the duality of the knowledge of man.

Both the knowledge of God and the knowledge of self, then, are characterized by a duality. During the three steps of the first phase of his editing of the *Institutes* in 1558/59, Calvin builds the first two books of the new *Institutes* on this duality.

Indeed, this scheme of the *historica series* and the duality of theological knowledge gains predominance in Calvin's *explicatio symboli*. At the same time, the trinitarian organization is pushed back, as we shall see.

Excursus
In the 1559 *Institutes* Calvin speaks *primum* (first) of man as God's creature (I.15) and *deinde* (then) of man as sinner (II.1-5). Thus, he does not speak anymore of man as creature and as sinner in the same chapter *sparsim* (here and there). Because of this *primum – deinde* also relative to the knowledge of man, he must delete the word 'sparsim' from the close of the introduction.[70] The French text has kept 'çà et là', however.[71]

§2.2.1 THE DUALITY OF 'BEFORE AND AFTER THE FALL OF MAN'

We already heard how Calvin in the old second chapter after the introduction discussed the theme 'in which state man was created', so as not to create the impression that he ascribed the natural wickedness of man to the Author of nature. We also saw that he took this passage out of this context in the 1558/59 edition, to insert it in the chapter 'How man was created...' of book 1.[72] In its stead he now placed a passage on the history of the fall.[73] Following this history of the fall, he speaks in the whole of the first chapter of the second book about original sin (*peccatum originale*) as inherited sin (*peccatum haereditarium*).[74] The *corruptio naturae*, the destruction and corruption of nature, continues to have an effect in all generations on human nature, which was created good by God.[75]

Excursus
Concerning the roll of the fall in Calvin's theology, Paul Wernle notes the following:

> 'Calvin elaborates far more extensively' – already in the introduction of the 1536 *Institutes*,
> FB – 'on self-knowledge. From there he reaches his first theme, the law. Reformation ex-
> perience should really begin with the law – in our language with the absolute ideal – and
> then arise to the knowledge of moral need and guilt. But Calvin's thought is no longer free at
> this point. Following the examples of Melanchthon and Zwingli he traces the knowledge of
> sin historically to the original state, the fall of Adam and inherited sin as the result of this
> mythical history. In this respect Calvin is orthodox…'.[76]

Indeed, in Calvin's theology the scheme of the 'historica series', that is, the *ante et post hominem lapsum* (man before and after the fall, 'we against God'), precedes in the unfolding of doctrine. Then only the *ante et post Christum natum* (before and after the birth of Christ, 'God with
us') follows. Unfortunately, this unbiblical scheme was later seen as being truly 'orthodox'.[77]

Paul Wernle was not aware of the fact that the Neo-Protestant theology which he represents
was the direct result of the 'orthodox' doctrine sketched above. The historicizing, anthropologizing, and religionizing tendency in Neo-Protestant theology was the unavoidable consequence of
'orthodoxy', as orthodoxy was already, as regards the structure of its teaching, an inconsistent
form of modernism.[78]

Karl Barth has pointed out that neo-protestantism in the period of the so-called rational orthodoxy around 1700 originated directly and consistently from orthodoxy and old Protestantism.[79] In this process the factors of contemporary culture have only worked as catalysts. They
were not the cause of these developments. The cause was a 'potential heresy' in the entire structure of old Protestant doctrine.[80]

After the discussion of the *corruptio naturae* (the corruption of nature) the detailed
second chapter follows with a discussion on *natura corrupta* (corrupted nature). Here,
the 'bondage of the will' as the cause of the entire 'discourse about Adam's fall and its
effects' are discussed.

In the Reformation locus on 'man' as locus about 'sin' the *servum arbitrium* (the
enslaved will) is contrasted to the lost *liberum arbitrium* (free will); *liberum arbitrium*
was called by the Greek fathers *autexousía*. Luther's thirteenth thesis of the Heidelberg
Disputation of the year 1518 was:

> '*Post peccatum* (after the fall), free will is but an empty name, and when it does
> what it wants, it commits mortal sin.'[81]

Among the forty-one theses of Luther, borrowed from seventeen of his writings from
the years 1517-1519, which were condemned by the papal bull *Exsurge Domine* on
June 15, 1520, the thirty-sixth thesis was the thirteenth thesis of the 'Heidelberg disputation' on the *liberum arbitrium*.[82] On November 17 of the same year Luther's defense
Adversus execrabilem Antichristi bullam[83] was published, to be followed by the German version, *Wider die Bulle des Endchrists*.[84] Since Luther in this writing defended
only a few of the condemned phrases, the electoral prince through Spalatin requested
him to publish a justification of all phrases.[85] In the beginning of 1521 the Latin writing *Assertio omnium articulorum M. Lutheri per bullam Leonis novissimam damnato-
rum*[86] was published and a German translation also followed at this time, 'Grund und

Ursach aller Artikel D. Martin Luthers, so durch römische Bulle unrechtlich verdammt sind':[87]

> Number 36. Free will / after the fall of Adam / or after the first sin / is but an empty name / and when it does its own will / it commits mortal sin.'[88]

In the Latin text Luther says:

> 'What is the matter, you pathetic pope, that you growl like this? It is necessary therefore to recall this article. I have indeed spoken an evil word, that free will *ante gratiam* (before grace) would be free only in name...'.[89]

Thus, the issue is about *liberum arbitrium post peccatum ante gratiam* (after sin, before grace).[90] In the *Praefatio* of his *Loci communes* of 1521, Melanchthon announced that he wished to discuss the triad *peccatum – lex – gratia* (sin – Law – Grace) in this book.[91] He was both a baccalaureus in theology in the studies of the *Libri quattuor* of Peter Lombard and a student of Paul's Letter to the Romans.[92] He did not announce in advance the chapter 'The Powers of Man, in Particular Free Will', with which the book opened in 1521. Wilhelm Maurer comments as follows:

> 'In the polemic treatis which Luther published in the middle of January 1521' – i.e., his *Assertio omnium articulorum*, FB – 'the reformer had confirmed all articles which the pope had condemned in his bull. With much passion he had fought against the scholastic teaching of free will. He had already called the acts of free will a mortal sin in number 13 of the Heidelberg theses of April 26, 1518. In doing so, he agreed with Wycliffe's thesis that everything happened with absolute necessity. This thesis had been condemned at the Council of Constance. Melanchthon puts this thesis almost verbatim in the center of his first chapter, in which he rejected free will (...). He defends Luther's controversial teaching and explains it for those who were able to follow the theological arguments. Erasmus belonged to these people, as the Wittenbergers knew. In *De servo arbitrio* (1525) Luther had praised him for that. Going beyond his original concept, Melanchthon put this chapter on free will up front in his work. He did so as an act of loyalty to the banned Luther and his rejection of Christian humanism, which Erasmian adhered to. To publicly and theologically document this assent to Luther and denial to Erasmus was the main occasion for the origin of the *Loci communes*.'[93]

Calvin also stood entirely on Luther's side and remained there, as is shown by Jean-Daniel Benoit in an important footnote on the heading of the second chapter of the second book of the French edition:[94]

> 'It is on the question of free will, and consequently, on justification, that Calvin most decidedly opposed the theology of his time. "This is," he said, "the greatest difference between us and the papists" (*Sermons on the book of Job*, CO XXXIII, 526). Luther was of the same opinion: "Is our will in some way active in the mat-

ters regarding eternal salvation, or is it only passive under the action of grace? (...) That is the heart of all our discussion." (*De servo arbitrio*, WA 18, 611, 614). Denying free will, Calvin knew himself to be faithful to the doctrine of Luther: "As far as the principal point of the whole matter is concerned," he recognized, "we still maintain it today in the same way Luther and others have expounded it from the beginning. And the same is true with regard to other points I made, of which I have said that they are not absolutely necessary for our faith. Nothing has changed from what Luther had taught, except that we have softened the manner of speaking, so that no one can justly take occasion of scandal" (*Response to calumnies of Pighius*, CO IV, 251). Calvin admits that Luther sometimes used "hyperbolic and excessive" language, but he explains that the circumstances had imposed it on him: "He used such language for good reason. He saw how the world was lured into that that false and dangerous alliance of works. It was a mortal lethargy. To awaken people, not only words were needed, not even cries, but blowing trumpets, thunder and lightning" (CO VI, 249).'

§2.2.2 FINAL CONSIDERATION OF THE SECOND STEP: 'WE AGAINST GOD' AND 'GOD WITH US' IN THE STRUCTURE OF SACRED DOCTRINE

Calvin placed the second chapter 'The Knowledge of Man' of the old *Institutes* at the beginning of the second book of the new *Institutes*, under the heading 'Discourse about of the fall of Adam and its effects' or as a teaching on 'sin' (as 'occasion to redemption'). He could do so because originally the doctrine of 'man' and the doctrine of 'sin' practically fell together in Reformation theology. In the 'Gifford lectures' on the Confessio Scotica of 1560 Karl Barth affirms this in 1937/38: 'If there were a particular Reformation doctrine of man, then it could indeed only exist in the doctrine of sin.'[95]

Karl Barth
We will see the change of the structure of sacred doctrine in the theology of Karl Barth when we note the position of the doctrine of 'sin' in his *Kirchliche Dogmatik*.[96] Here this locus is not put after the doctrine of creation, but in the doctrine of reconciliation, after Christology, in correlation with soteriology.[97] 'The doctrine of sin belongs in the context of the doctrine of reconciliation. When one speaks of sin, one should always do so in the context of reconciliation,' Barth says already in the doctrine of creation.[98] In the doctrine of reconciliation, the same is said: 'The doctrine of sin cannot be grounded, established and developed independently of the doctrine of reconciliation. It is rather in itself an integrating element of the doctrine of reconciliation.'[99] When Barth in his overview of the doctrine of reconciliation announces that he will, deviating from the common tradition, speak of sin in the framework of the doctrine of reconciliation, he says: 'The old theology and the new almost universally have kept it this way: between the doctrine of creation and that of reconciliation, one used to and still does (logically quite enlightening and didactically very clear) insert a particular teaching *De peccato*: a doctrine of the fall, of original sin and its results, of the status and state of mind of man in sin, of individual and active sins.'[100] However, to construct a locus on sin in the empty space between the doctrines of creation and reconciliation, 'would that not be viewing past the grace of God?' (...) 'Would that not again – and this time calculated theologically! – mean to sin?'[101]

In each of the three paragraphs which Barth devotes to 'sin', he first discusses the position of this doctrine in the structure of dogmatics.[102] After he has done this for a third time, an important comment follows in small letters: 'These phrases and particularly the concept of gospel and law which they carry and hold together (...) belong to the iron structure of the dogmatics presented here.'[103]

In Protestant theology, the 'before and after the fall of man' ('we against God') came up front in the unfolding of doctrine, followed by the 'before and after the birth of Christ' ('God with us').[104] Between that first and second 'before and after' the theme of 'law and gospel' was discussed. In retrospect to the 'before and after the fall of man' there was talk of law and looking ahead at 'before and after the birth of Christ' of the gospel. With the 'before and after the fall of man', 'nature' now became in Protestant theology 'nature before the fall', and 'grace' became 'grace after the fall'. In the reformed tradition, 'nature before the fall' became the 'covenant of nature before the fall' (law) and 'grace after the fall' became the 'covenant of grace before and after the birth of Christ' (gospel). That means that also in the Protestant dogmatic tradition 'nature and grace' again became, be it in this historicized form, the main theme of theology. Speaking about God's 'works' a distinction was made between the 'works of nature' and the 'works of grace'. Speaking about God's dealing with man, a distinction was made between the 'covenant of nature' – also called the covenant of the 'law', or of 'works' – and the 'covenant of grace' – also called the covenant of the gospel and/or of faith.

The law was generally known, so it was said, whereas the gospel was not. Theology was done in a permanent combination between the two. What was generally known – the law – could just as easily and even in a more developed way be found among the philosophers. However, the reformers with their *particula exclusiva* (faith, grace, Scripture alone), should have rejected the scholastic scheme of 'nature and grace' as totally unbiblical. They should have based themselves on the anti-pagan witness of the Tanakh. However, because of the scheme 'law and gospel' the scheme of 'nature and grace' was not thrown overboard, but only historicized. In that form it later became the central theme in Protestant theology.

There is not much difference between 'nature' in the framework of a hierarchically ordered universe in which it forms more or less the solid 'underground' of all of doctrine, as in the cosmic theology of medieval scholasticism, and 'nature' understood as the 'background', as in the more historicizing Protestant theology. These are only different variations of the same theme: 'Grace does not cancel nature, but presupposes and perfects it.'[105]

The origin of 'nature and grace' in historicizing Protestant theology was the scheme 'law and gospel', whereby *lex* (law) as moral law was identified with the *lex naturalis* (law of nature).[106] Exactly that with which one wished to say 'no' to the medieval synthesis of 'nature and grace', was itself the origin of a new Protestant combination of 'nature' and 'grace'.

Karl Barth
In contrast to this, Karl Barth, being well aware of the anti-pagan witness of the Tanakh, refused any synthesis of 'nature and grace' with a loud and relentless 'No!'[107] In the Kirchliche *Dog-*

matik there is no twofold 'before and after', no twofold 'first and then', but only one 'first – and then', which ordered the *tempora* because it was the gracious choice of God's eternal will to become 'God with us' in the history of his covenant. The covenant is facilitated by creation, fulfilled by reconciliation, and completed by redemption. And in this one history of his many covenantal acts are contained all *opera Dei*, the works of God, which include the so-called *opera naturae* (works of nature) and the *opera gratiae* (works of grace: *hasadim and sedaqot*, works of mercy and of justice).[108]

In the first part of our biblical theology (*toledot*, begettings) we claim that talking about man *post peccatum ante gratiam* (after sin, before grace) in a historicizing way cannot be grounded in biblical theology. This is explained in the section on 'The biblical locus de homine et de peccato' in which we shall discuss the structure of the narratives about *'adam* on the *'adamah* (the man on the field) in Genesis 2:4–4:26.[109] From the perspective of the *bene yisra'el* on the *'erets* (the sons of Israel on the land) Genesis speaks about *'adam* on the *'adamah* (the man on the field). The particular is at the same time the general, the universal.[110] The Bible does not speak humanistically about Israel, but Israelite about humanity, also and first of all in the context of the narratives about *ha-adam* on the *'adamah* in Genesis 2:4–4:26.[111]

Unfortunately we cannot say that the theologians of the sixteenth century in their struggle about *liberum arbitrium* (free will) – e.g., Calvin in chap. 15 of the first book of the *Institutes* of 1559 – held an Israelite discourse of humanity as a common presupposition.[112] Neither can it be said, however, that the reformers had wanted to advocate the old- and neo-protestant synthesis of nature and grace and of reason and revelation. It must be said, however, that

'the reformers made use of the possibility to have a "natural theology". Sometimes this happened in a careful hypothetical way (as Calvin did in the first chapters of his Institutes), but at other times in a careless and bold way (e.g., Luther and Calvin in their teaching on the law)'.[113]

A bit more nuanced, Barth said the same thing in the section 'Dogmatics as Ethics' of the *Kirchliche Dogmatik:*

'Dogmatics is ethics at the same time.' – That is, in the teaching of the reformers, FB. – 'This is all the more noticeable because both Calvin and Luther did not basically reject the idea of the law of nature inborn in man, and the recognition of it as something prior to faith. They agreed with the scholastics in giving this point of view their assent. In practice, however, they did not make any systematic use of the idea. The reason for this was that they focused so strongly on the insight of Col 3:3 that they could not lose sight of Jesus Christ as the one object of faith. They were thus prevented from trying to construct an independent system of ethics. They were also safeguarded against the temptation to exploit this scholastic survival of natural theology.'[114]

One has to say that what happened in post-Reformation protestant theology was precisely what the reformers had not wanted to happen. With the *particula exclusive* they refused, disputed, and rejected this. Yet, ironically enough, it was exactly these particulars that formed the impetus toward the development into natural theology. The reformers allowed the 'before and after the fall of man' to go first in the unfolding of doctrine. Only then did they begin to describe how the gracious God deals with sinful man by 'law and gospel', so that he from the knowledge of his sin might arrive at the knowledge of God's grace.

To what extent Calvin, too, would not have wanted what happened afterward, will become clear to us when discussing the third step of his work on the final edition of the *Institutes*. We will see there that his theology comes to be dominated by a radical (and yet also not wholly radical) Christological concentration.

For now we have seen by way of a hint that in the final form of the *Institutes* the scene of the *historica series* has pushed back the trinitarian structure of the *explicatio symboli*. During the first two steps, Calvin spoke twice of 'first – and then'. Nevertheless, the Christological concentration dominated Calvin's *explicatio symboli*. How this could come about will be shown during the third step.

Karl Barth
The scheme of the old- or neo-Protestant *historica series* no longer dominates the unfolding of doctrine as *explicatio symboli* in Karl Barth's *Kirchliche Dogmatik*. Barth's dogmatics has a trinitarian structure. In the final three paragraphs of the section on the doctrine of the trinity,[115] Barth speaks of God the Father, the Son, and the Holy Spirit as creator, reconciler, and redeemer. Chapters V-VIII on the doctrine of God in the second volume[116] constantly speak of God as creator, reconciler, and redeemer, because it is in what he does that the triune God makes himself known (in the sixth chapter about 'The Reality of God' the heading of the first section reads 'The Being of God in the Act').[117] After the doctrine of God, all of God's 'works' are described as creation (volume III), reconciliation (volume IV), and redemption (volume V), no longer as *creatio et redemption* (creation and redemption), as in Calvin.

§2.3 THE THIRD STEP: LAW AND GOSPEL AS WITNESS TO CHRIST (II.6-11)

We have seen how Calvin made the old first chapter, 'The Knowledge of God', a foundation for the new first book, 'The Knowledge of God the Creator', and how he placed the old second chapter, 'The Knowledge of Man', at the beginning of the new second book 'The Knowledge of God the Redeemer'. We have now come to the third chapter of the old *Institutes*. In 1539 it was very briefly called *De lege* (the Law). But in 1543 this heading also became a detailed indication of content: 'The Law. In which first the function and use of that law are indicated, and then the true service to God, images, the oath, church festivals, monastic vows are treated'.[118] In 1550 the chapter has 105 paragraphs.

In the old *Institutes* the chapter 'The Law' comes after the chapter 'The Knowledge of Man'. By the law God gives the knowledge of sin. In the new *Institutes* as well, the old chapter 'The Law' comes after the 'exposition of Adam's fall and its results' (II.1-5) in chapters 7 and 8 of the second book (II.7-8). Yet, the chapter does not have the same function anymore in this location as it had in the old *Institutes*.

In order to understand how this old third chapter functions in the new *Institutes* (in II.7-8 after II.1-5), we must first pay attention to the brief sixth chapter of the second book, newly written in 1558/59, which comes after the 'discourse of Adam's fall and its effects'.

Second book:
Chap. VI   in four paragraphs
                    'That fallen man must seek his redemption in Christ'.[119]

The 'fallen man', who must seek *redemptio* in Christ, is 'man before and after the birth of Christ', the 'man who is fallen since the beginning of the world to the end of the ages', because – Calvin says in the first paragraph –:

'after the fall of the first man, no knowledge of God has had the strength to raise us toward salvation. We need a mediator. Christ does not only speak of His own life time, but includes all history, when He says: "this is life eternal: to know the Father, the only true God, and him whom he sent, Jesus Christ" (John 17:3)'.[120]

In the fourth paragraph, to which Otto Weber gave the heading 'Faith in God is Faith in Christ', Calvin says:

'We said that salvific knowledge of God does not exist outside of Christ. Therefore He is presented from the beginning of the world to all the elect, as the one to whom they might look and put their trust in...'
    'Many in times long ago have praised the highest being, and claim to have honored the maker of heaven and earth. Nevertheless, since they had no mediator, it was not possible that they truly tasted the mercy of God and were convinced that He was their Father. They did not know the head, which is Christ, their knowledge of God was in vain. That is why it happened that they finally, fallen to coarse and scandalous superstitions, revealed their own ignorance...'.[121]

Seen from the sixth chapter of the second book, therefore, one can say that the biblical concentration on the 'knowledge of God and of ourselves' expressed in the opening sentence of the *Institutes*, is at the same time 'Christological concentration'. The headings of books II-IV testify to this in the following way:

Book II   The knowledge of God the redeemer *in Christ*, which was first revealed to the fathers under the law, then also to us in the Gospel.
Book III   The way in which the grace *of Christ* is received, the fruits which they bring forth to us and what effects follow from this.
Book IV   The external means or aids by which God invites us into the community *of Christ* and keeps us there.

The series of newly written passages of the first book on the duality of the knowledge of God (in I.2.1, I.6.1-2, I.10.1) and the corresponding addition from the year 1559 (in

Inst. II.1.1) on the duality of man's knowledge of himself culminates in the newly written sixth chapter of the second book and must be understood from the perspective of this chapter.

Here we must again pay attention to the phrase (in the second chapter of the first book 'What it is to know God') in which Calvin formulated his thesis of the duality of the knowledge of God. In this phrase he does not say:

'because the Lord appears *primum simpliciter* (first, simply) as Creator
both in making of the world and in the general doctrine of Scripture
deinde dupliciter (and then twofold)
in His works and in the face of Christ'

– that is, as creator and as redeemer, FB –

there follows a twofold knowledge of God'.

Sadly, the overall tradition has interpreted Calvin's theology this way, and has consistently developed his theology along these lines. But in the formulation of his thesis of the duality of the knowledge of God, Calvin, quite consciously, does not say:

| *primum simpliciter* | – | *deinde dupliciter* |
| first simply | – | then twofold |

but:

| *primum simpliciter creator* | – | *deinde in Christi facie redemptor* |
| first simply as Creator | – | then in the face of Christ as Redeemer. |

The word *simpliciter* in the first half of the clause is not followed in the second half of the clause by the word *dupliciter* (which really would have been logical), but by *in Christi facie*. Instead of *dupliciter* Calvin says *in Christi facie*. This way of putting it fully agrees with the composition of the first two books of the 1559 *Institutes*. Or, seen from the other way around, the entire composition of these two books agrees fully with this thesis formulated at the beginning of the new *Institutes* in the second chapter. The entire series of newly written passages of the first book on the duality of the knowledge of God (in I.2.1, I.6.1-2, I.10.1) must be interpreted from the perspective of this newly written sixth chapter of the second book. This prevents us from understanding Calvin in the way later protestant tradition did, saying things Calvin actually never did say and certainly would not have wished to say.

Calvin's biblical concentration is at the same time Christological concentration, we said. This means that, from this chapter on, the entire Bible is read by Calvin as 'testimony of Christ'. It is precisely this what he wished to present next in the five chapters on law and gospel following the sixth chapter of the second book. In the words of the heading of the second book the theme of the newly composed (1558/59) chapters II.7-11 is rightly described in the Argumentum as follows:

'How this Christ is revealed to the world, namely, in a twofold way, first under the law..., and then under the gospel.'[122]

Here we encounter a second duality in the Institutes of 1559 and this duality is also grounded in a *primum – deinde* (first – and then). The twofold duality of the knowledge thus determines in 1558/59 the structure of Calvin's theology in his unfolding of sacred doctrine. First there is the 'first – and then' of the 'before and after the fall of man' and the duality of the knowledge of God. Then there is the 'first – and then' of 'before and after the birth of Christ' and the duality of the knowledge of Christ. First there are the promises of the Old Testament, then there is the *exhibitio* (display) of him in the Gospel.

Excursus
As we said above, the basic form of the historicizing theology of Protestantism looked like this from the beginning. The 'before and after the fall of man' preceded ('we against God'), followed by 'before and after the birth of Christ' ('God with us'). In between there was the section on law and gospel (knowledge of sin and grace through law and gospel). The whole of early Protestant dogmatics shows us nothing but variations of this basic form.

In the next chapter we will describe briefly the most important variations in the period of orthodoxy (1560-1720), demonstrating how from this basic form early Protestantism was to develop into neo-Protestantism aroud 1700 in the period of rational orthodoxy. At this point we should already say that Calvin's desired Christological concentration in the *explicatio symboli* was impossible. It could not be achieved, as long as the scheme of the 'historica series', the scheme of 'before and after the fall of man' and the duality of the knowledge of God dominated the unfolding of sacred doctrine. On the basis of this scheme it was unavoidable that later protestant theology developed the way it has. Calvin's intended Christological concentration could only be implemented if his fatal scheme was replaced by the scheme of trinitarian structure, which has happened in the *Church Dogmatics* of Karl Barth.

We now have to explain how Calvin composed the structure of the five chapters about 'law and gospel as testimony to Christ' in Inst. II.7-11. First, we need to describe how Calvin, during the first half of the third step, composed the third chapter *De lege* (the law).

After the doctrine on sin in chapters 1-5 the theme of the newly written sixth chapter was briefly enunciated: 'That fallen man must seek his redemption in Christ'. In the heading of the second book Calvin had said about the 'Knowledge of God the redeemer in Christ' that it is 'a knowledge which *primum* (first) is revealed under the law'. Consequently after the sixth chapter he wished next to speak about the law as testimony to Christ. He therefore needed to ask: How can I insert the old third chapter, 'The Law', in the new *Institutes*, so that it receives the function of a 'testimony to Christ' after the sixth chapter in the new *Institutes*? The old third chapter counted (since 1550) 105 paragraphs. After the explanation of the Decalogue in paragraphs 1-90 there followed in paragraphs 91-105 the discussion of the *triplex usus officiumque legis* (threefold use and function of the law) as a description of the function of the law. Calvin separated this description of the function of the law from the old chapter, so that it might precede as an independent chapter:

Chap. VII in 17 paragraphs

'That the law was given, not to keep the people of the old covenant in bondage, but to foster the hope of salvation in Christ until his coming.' = 1539 (1550) III.91-105; French 1541, 173 ll. 9 - 186 l. 20.[123]

The law points beyond itself.[124] It was given in order to keep alive in *vetus populus*, in the people of the old covenant, the hope of salvation in Christ till his coming. To say that, Calvin includes two newly written paragraphs (1559: II.7.3-17 ? 1550: III.91-105) in II.7.1-2, in which he explains the 'office' of the law. These two paragraphs begin as follows:

'From this uninterrupted series of Old Testament witnesses which we have shown, one can conclude that the law was not given four hundred years after the death of Abraham to keep the chosen people away from Christ, but rather to keep their hearts alive until his coming, to encourage their longing for him and to strengthen their expectation so that they might not succumb under too much delay. By the law I understand not only the Ten Commandments which prescribe the rule of a reverential and righteous life, but also the form of religion which was delivered by the hand of Moses from God.'[125]

Excursus

In his conversation with the Lutherans about 'law and gospel' Calvin twice indicates in the ninth chapter these *forma religionis per manum Mosis a Deo tradita* (form of the religion which was delivered by the hand of Moses from God), as *tota lex* (the entire law).[126]

After Calvin has informed us in the seventh chapter how his meaning of 'law' must be understood, he will tell us in the ninth chapter how the biblical witness of 'gospel' is to be understood. We may compare this to the insertion of the year 1559 in I.6.2:

1559*   '...In order that the truth of doctrine should remain present in an uninterrupted pro-
(1539) gress, He wished that the divine sayings, which He had given to the Fathers, would be fixed on public tablets.'[127]

1559   'With this intent the law was published, and the prophets were given as its interpreters.[128] For even though the use of the law has been manifold, as will be see more clearly in due time' – e.g., in Inst. II.7, FB – 'it was above all committed to Moses and to all the prophets to teach the way of reconciliation between God and men (for which reason Paul also calls Christ "the end of the law", Rom 10:4). Yet I repeat once more, Scripture not only portrays the proper doctrine of faith and repentance concerning Christ as mediator. It also portrays the one and true God, who created the world and rules it, with unmistakable marks and tokens. This it does so that He may not be confused with all the false gods' – cf. the heading of Inst. I.10, FB.[129]

In the law as 'form of religion delivered by Moses from God' everything points to Christ, says Calvin in the two newly written paragraphs at the beginning of the seventh chapter. After this seventh chapter, Calvin continued with the old paragraphs 1-90, which contain the explanation of the Decalogue:

Chap. VIII   in 59 paragraphs
              'Explanation of the moral law'
              = 1539 (1550) III.1-90; French 1541, 113 ll.1 - 173 l. 8.[130]

From this structure of the old paragraphs 1-90, Calvin removed 27 paragraphs, to insert them in other places of the new Institutes. The explanation of the first commandment:

3.20-23   → book I, chap. XII
           'That God is distinguished from idols, so that He alone may be worshipped';[131]

The second commandment (according to Calvin's account):

3.24-39   → book I, chap. XI
           'That it is unfitting to assign a visible form to God. Those who erect images of idols deviate from the true God'.[132]

These two parts from the explanation of the Decalogue Calvin inserts in the first new book after chapter X, so that he might offer something like a doctrine about 'God' in three chapters (book I chaps. X-XII).[133]

The explanation of the seventh commandment (according to Calvin's account):

3.67-72   → book IV, chap. XII.23-28
3.66[134]   → book IV, chap. XIII.3

These two parts, which he removed from the explanation of the seventh commandment and inserted in IV.12.23-28 and IV.13.3, are the parts in which celibacy of priests and monks is discussed.

Excursus

In the footnote on the heading of the seventh chapter in his edition of the French text, Jean-Daniel Benoit says: 'Calvin insists on the fact that the law is totally oriented toward the Christ: "Without Christ, the law is an empty object and has no power at all".'[135]

We have seen how also in the new *Institutes* the presently divided chapter 'The Law' in II.7-8 comes after the chapter 'The Knowledge of Man' as doctrine of 'sin' in II.1-5. After the newly written sixth chapter, 'That fallen man must seek his redemption in Christ', the dominating viewpoint in the new *Institutes*, where the law is discussed, differs, however, from the old *Institutes*. The law is now *praesertim* (above all) testimony to Christ.

Calvin has, however, apart from the fact that he placed the old paragraphs 91-105 at the head of the seventh chapter, to be followed by paragraphs 1-90 in the eighth chapter, changed practically nothing in the entire chapter, and added very little, apart from the above quoted first two paragraphs of the seventh chapter. We cannot say, therefore, that he indeed unfolded thematically in chapters 7 and 8 what he programmatically announced in the first two paragraphs of the seventh chapter. We have to think here about what Karl Barth remarked concerning Calvin's doctrine of the *unio cum Christo* (union with Christ) in the first chapter of the third book of the 1559 *Institutes:*[136]

'In the *Institutes* of 1559 the breakthrough which occurred is visible in the way the *unio cum Christo* became a common basis, on which Calvin' – namely, in the third book of the *Institutes*, FB – 'wanted to place his entire doctrine of the appropriation of salvation that revealed and made possible in Christ.' (...). 'Yet we cannot really say that his whole theology was worked out in the light of this. The 1559 *Institutes* were not a reconstruction in this sense. In this final edition as in the preceding ones his editorial work was for the most part that of a pair of very skillfully and carefully handled scissors.[137] He took over all the main parts of his earlier texts, but enriched and illumined them by all kinds of major and minor alterations and additions. One such addition (though in detail it incorporates earlier features) is this first chapter of the third book – reminiscent to some extent of the 'new patches' of Mark 2:21. Because of its position the *unio*-doctrine serves unambiguously as an introduction to the whole. Yet one is still a bit surprised that it is not expounded more openly in the remainder of the book. It is hidden by passages of earlier provenance'.

What Barth says here of the *unio*-doctrine in the third book goes for Calvin's doctrine of law as witness to Christ in chapter 7 and 8 of the second book as well. Nevertheless, with regard to this doctrine we cannot say that it was something like a breakthrough. What role this doctrine played for Calvin has been demonstrated by Krusche. He discusses Calvin's concept of the pneumatic unity of the Holy Scriptures as interpretative correlation, of which the law is the foundation.[138]

After we have seen how Calvin dealt with the old third chapter 'The Law', we have only gone halfway on the third step. In the old *Institutes* there was already an entire chapter in which Calvin spoke about the fathers of the old covenant. They had lived by the same promises, by the same hope of eternal life, by the same mercy and by the same faith in the mediator, as 'we' do in the new covenant, Calvin wrote. The heading of this chapter both in 1539 and in 1543 (-1554) read *De similitudine ac differentia veteris et novi testamenti* (agreement and difference between the Old and the New Testaments). Both in 1539 and in 1543 Calvin this chapter comes after the six chapters unfolding the 'essence of doctrine'.[139] Presently, in the winter of 1558/59, this chapter was removed by Calvin from its place and during the third step it was moved forward and connected with the old third chapter 'The Law'. Moreover, he divided the chapter of the old *Institutes* (in 1539 the seventh, in 1543 the eleventh) into two:

Chap. X   in 23 paragraphs
    'The agreement between the Old and the New Testaments'
    = 1550 XI.1-23; French 1541 (Chap. VII), 433 l. 1–453 l. 35.[140]
Chap. XI   in 14 paragraphs
    'The difference of the Old Testament from the New'
    = 1550 XI.24-41; French 1541 (Chap. VII), 453 l. 36–466 l.19.[141]

Calvin wants to speak about the Holy Scriptures as testimony to Christ in the second book of the new Institutes, after the sixth chapter, 'That fallen man must seek his redemption in Christ'. With this aim, Calvin has, as we have seen, first arranged after that newly written sixth chapter, during the first half of the third step, in chapter II.7-8 the divided third chapter 'The Law' of the old *Institutes*. Then, during the second half of the third step, in chapters II.10-11 he divided the eleventh chapter of the old *Institutes*, 'Agreement and Difference between the Old and New Testaments', into two. However, in order to clarify the meaning of this arrangement, Calvin wrote a new chapter as a connecting link between chapters II.7-8 and II.10-11.[142]

Chap. IX   in 5 paragraphs
    'That Christ, though He was already known to the Jews under the law, was fully revealed under the Gospel'.[143]

The heading of the entire second book read, as we heard, 'The knowledge of God the redeemer in Christ, which was first revealed to the fathers under the Law, and then also to us in the Gospel'. After the words 'redeemer' and 'Christ' were repeated from this heading in the heading of the newly written sixth chapter – 'that fallen man must seek his redemption in Christ' – then in the heading of the newly written ninth chapter the words 'Christ', 'under the Law', and 'Gospel' were repeated: 'That Christ, though He was known to the Jews under the law, yet ultimately is presented (*exhibitum*) in the gospel.'[144] At the conclusion of our description of the third step, we now need to discuss briefly this ninth chapter of the second book of the *Institutes*.

§2.3.1 THE NINTH CHAPTER OF THE SECOND BOOK AS CONNECTING LINK BETWEEN CHAPTERS II.7-8 AND II.10-11

In the winter of 1558/59 Calvin wrote the ninth chapter of the second book not so much as 'a new detailed introductory chapter to the section on covenantal theology',[145] but rather, to let it be the brief[146] connecting link between the two old chapters 3 and 11, which were now joined together and thus between chapters II.7-8 and II.10-11 of the new *Institutes*.

As law and gospel, the entire Bible is a testimony to Christ. This is the theme of the entire structure of chapters 7-11 of the second book of the 1559 Institutes. This theme in the newly written ninth chapter must therefore be briefly touched upon. Because of the proclamation of the *iustificatio impii sola gratia sola fide* (the justification of the godless by grace alone, by faith alone) knowledge of nature and grace by reason and revelation was no longer the theme of sacred doctrine in Reformation theology, but the knowledge of sin and grace by law and gospel. As we saw in Melanchthon's *Loci* of the first aetas, 'law and gospel' was the scheme by which initially the entire doctrine was unfolded in Wittenberg as well.[147] We also saw in the first chapter of the present study how Calvin in 1536 unfolded his 'essence of sacred doctrine' entirely in the spirit of the Wittenberg theology according to the scheme 'Law → Faith'. And in the third chapter of our study we saw that Calvin precisely because of this scheme gave his *Institutes* in 1539 a very beautifully proportioned and balanced form, so that Paul Wernle called 'this second *Institutes* the most perfect of all of his theological works'.[148] We saw there also, however, that there were then already elements in Calvin's unfolding of the doctrine which did not fit well in this scheme of 'The Law → Faith':

First: Calvin moved from the knowledge of God to the knowledge of self;
Second: in clear deviation from Melanchthon's *Loci* of the second aetas (1535), Calvin did not say of the *usus elenchticus* (the accusing use) of the law, but of the *usus renatis* (use among the reborn) that 'it is the principal use and it reveals most clearly the real purpose of the law';[149]
Third: Calvin moved from faith to repentance (1539, chaps. IV-VI: 'Faith – Repentance – Justification'), not from repentance to faith (though this was also said by Calvin).

Such elements of his doctrine combined with weighty formal grounds made Calvin say in the preface of the *Institutes* of 1559: 'I was never fully satisfied, until the work was arranged in the order in which it is now offered.' Calvin did not wish to persist with the scheme 'The Law → Faith' or unfold the doctrine in this way. Therefore, for his final new form of the Institutes he chose the form of the *explicatio symboli* in four books. While previously the *explicatio symboli* was given within the frame 'The Law → Faith', in 1558/59 he discusses the theme 'law and gospel' within the framework of the *explicatio symboli*. As an expression of the Christological concentration of his theology, 'law and gospel as testimony to Christ' became the dominant theme in the structure of chapters 7-11 of book two. The way in which the Wittenberg theology spoke about 'law and gospel' was emphatically subordinated to this theme (II.9.4). To clarify all of this, Calvin wrote the ninth chapter of the second book as a connecting link between chapters II.7-8 (= the old third chapter) and chapters II.10-11 (= the old eleventh chapter).

Because of his thesis of the duality of the knowledge of God, Calvin made a distinction in Holy Scripture between the 'general doctrine of the Scriptures' in the first book of the Institutes and the 'particular or proper doctrine of faith' in the remaining three books.[150] The fact is that Calvin during the first phase of his work on the 1559 *Institutes* based the first two books on this thesis. This produced the result that we find the locus *de sacra scriptura* in two places in the 1559 *Institutes*. In connection with the 'general doctrine of Scripture' of the first book Calvin in chapters 7-9 discussed the authority of the Holy Scripture. In connection with the 'proper doctrine of faith' of the remaining three books, Calvin in chapters 7-11 spoke of the Holy Scriptures as testimony to Christ.

Excursus
Because of the fact that Calvin discusses in *Institutio* I.7-9 the authority of Holy Scripture in the context of the 'general doctrine of Scripture', Köstlin says:

'First of all – and this is again precisely characteristic for Calvin – he deals with the doctrine of the divine origin and the divine authority of Scripture and of the testimony of the Spirit as a coherent unit as such. He handles the presentation in such a way that the Spirit first and foremost should bring forth mature faith through this character of Scripture. The Christian infers the contents of Scripture as divinely true. This inference is not at all only a matter of reason. It happens under continual illumination and incessant sealing by the Holy Spirit in the heart. Also when he mentions the "truth" of Scripture, which we are convinced of by the power of the Spirit, he means with this in the present section an absolute character of truth. This is found in Scripture as a whole, and which within us is experienced in and with the divine nature of Scripture. Thus the issue is already put in the second edition.' – i.e., the 1539 edition, FB – 'With Dorner we must comment in spite of everything: "In Calvin, the formal side of the protestant principle is more important than the material side. He sees in Holy Scripture chiefly the revelation of the will of God, which He has dictated to man through the sacred scriptural author." And this direction is seen even stronger in the continuing editions of his *Institut*.'[151]

Werner Krusche reacted to these statements of Köstlin as follows:

'The *Institutes* indeed might raise the impression as if the *testimonium* (internal witness)' – i. e. of the Holy Spirit, FB – 'only convinces us of the divine origin of Scripture, and not of the salvation witnessed to in Scripture, or that at least the first precedes the other, or is independent of it. (…) In view of the *Institutes* one might well arrive at such a judgment. But the commentaries show a different picture (so that it is not well advised to interpret Calvin only from the *Institutes*).[152] The *testimonium* does not only assure us of the divine origin of Scripture, but also and simultaneously of the content of Scripture. Indeed, it assures us of the death and resurrection of Christ, the truth of the gospel, the validity of the promises, of divine benevolence, of our *adoptio* (adoption), of the entire evangelical doctrine. The *testimonium spiritus sancti* is related both to the authority of Scripture and its content. They are not two witnesses, but it is a single witness: "It is therefore a true conviction which those who believe possess concerning the Word of God, salvation, all of religion. It is not based on the feeling of the flesh, not on human or philosophical reasoning, but on the sealing of the Spirit (CO 51, 153; comm. Eph. 1:13)." And indeed the *testimonium* not only assures us of the objective truth of the promise, but also of the content of the promise. Calvin did not tear asunder Scriptural certainty and the certainty of salvation – as happened in orthodoxy. The *testimonium* does not convince us first of the divine origin of the Scriptures, apart from its content of promise, and then finally also of this content. In the end, both are inseparably one'.[153]

At the beginning of our description of the second step we said: 'Calvin made the old second chapter the starting point (as *redemptionis occasio*, occasion for redemption) for the new second book and at the same time the starting point for books II-IV and the "actual doctrine of faith" unfolded in it.' Indeed, 'foundation', as we said, 'would not be the right word here. Later we will see what Calvin will use as the foundation for books II-IV.' This has happened in the description of the third step. We have now seen the basis for the entire 'proper doctrine of faith' in books II-IV. The structure of chapters 6 to 11, established by the compilation of the third step, forms the foundation of the entire unfolding of the 'proper doctrine of faith' in books II-IV.

In the beginning of the description of the third step we said: 'The series of newly written passages of the first book on the duality of the knowledge of God (in I.2.1, I.6.1-2, I.10.1) culminates in the newly written sixth chapter of the second book and must be understood from the perspective of this chapter. In the *Institutes* in its final form we first meet this sixth chapter of the second book, from which we arrive at all that follows in books II-IV.'[154]

Well, that certainly was not wrong. We have convincingly seen what happened during the third step of Calvin's work on the *Institutes* in the winter of 1558/59. We have seen the connection between the newly written sixth chapter and the newly composed structure of chapters 7-11 about the Holy Scriptures as testimony to Christ. We now need to say that this series on the duality of the knowledge of God in the first book of the *Institutes* of 1559 culminates in the newly composed structure of chapters 6-11 of the second book about Scripture as testimony to Christ, and must be understood from the perspective of the entire structure. In the *Institutes* in its final form we first meet the entire structure of chaps. II.6-11 about Scripture as testimony to Christ, before we continue with all that follows in books II-IV.

It is because of his thesis of the duality of the knowledge of God that Calvin during the three steps of the first phase of his work created the first two books of the final

Institutes. It was thus the content of a *Dei cognitio* (knowledge of God), and indeed of a *duplex Dei cognitio* (*twofold* knowledge of God), which Calvin wished to unfold in his 1559 *Institutes*. But in chapters 6 to 11 of the new second book Calvin told us that this entire *Dei cognitio* points to and concentrates on the *cognitio Dei in Christi facie* (knowledge of God in the face of Christ). In the 1559 *Institutes* we move from the theocentric to the christocentric. As Calvin unfolded the 'general doctrine of Scripture' in the first book of the *Institutes* in a christocentric mode, he also unfolded the 'proper doctrine of faith' of the remaining three books of the *Institutes* from a christocentric perspective. Dieter Schellong says: 'Calvin's theology was theocentric, but his piety was christocentric.'[155] From the perspective of Karl Barth's *Dogmatics* we will need to have a conversation with Calvin on the relationship between the theocentric and christocentric in the structure of his doctrine.

We have now come to the conclusion of the first phase of Calvin's work with its three steps on the final form of his *Institutes* during the winter of 1558/59. During the first and the second step we saw how the scheme of the *historica series* – namely: the 'first and then' of the previous 'before and after the fall of man' and the duality of the theological knowledge dominated Calvin's *explicatio symboli*. During the third step we saw how, in spite of this, the duality of the knowledge of God was not really the dominating element in Calvin's unfolding of doctrine or what he actually wished. He wished to have a Christological concentration.

In the scheme of the *historica series* on the one hand, and in the Christological concentration on the other, we have to do with two entirely different structural elements of Calvinian doctrine. They do not fit together and form a *complexio oppositorum* (joining of contradictions).[156] The provenance of these two elements is also quite different. The Christological concentration stems from the *explicatio symboli* in the old Institutes. To understand this one needs to read the entire introduction to the *explicatio symboli* in the old Institutes in chap. VI.1-5 of 1539.[157] In this introduction Calvin likewise shows how the Christological concentration is indissolubly connected to a trinitarian structure in explaining the symbols of faith. At the end of the first paragraph Calvin notes this with the words:

> 'By the Spirit of the Father we should be urged to seek and embrace Christ. We should also understand that we cannot find the Father anywhere else but in Christ, who is his image.'[158]

In the fifth paragraph on the meaning of trinitarian structure for the explanation of symbols of faith, at the conclusion of his introduction, Calvin emphatically points to the words which we have already indicated.[159]

In the second chapter of our study we have heard how in the 1537 Catechism, the introduction to the *explicatio symboli* begins as follows:[160]

> 'It was stated above that we receive Christ by faith; *now* we need to be told what our faith must behold and consider in Christ in order to be confirmed.[161] This is explained, however, in what is called the *Symbolum* (Creed), that is, in what way

Christ was created for us by the Father into wisdom, redemption, life, righteousness, and sanctification (1 Cor 1:30).'

The structural element of the Christological concentration in the 1559 *Institutes* thus stems from the *explicatio symboli* in the old *Institutes*. What about the *historica series*? Well, that does not stem from the old *explicatio symboli* but from the ordered series of the chapters in the old *Institutes*, in which the doctrine is unfolded according to the scheme 'Law →? Faith'

The scheme

The Knowledge of God   →   The Knowledge of Man   →   the Law → Faith

or:

God in his works   →   Man as sinner   →   God in the face of his Christ

in 1558/59 was changed into the scheme:

God   →   Man   →   Man as Sinner   →   God the Redeemer in Christ

First book   Second book[162]

Undoubtedly, Calvin chose the form of the *explicatio symboli* for the final form of his *Institutes*, because, entirely in the style of the *explicatio symboli* of the old *Institutes*, he wished to express the Christological concentration as strongly as possible. First, in the final version of the *Institutes*, as we saw during the third step, we are going in the direction of the six chapters II.6-11 on Scripture as testimony to Christ. First, therefore, we meet in the unfolding of the so-called general doctrine of Scripture the radical christocentricism. Calvin wanted to unfold the ensuing 'proper doctrine of the faith' from within this christocentricism.

But now something had happened with the final new form of the *Institutes*. The results were fatal and had to be fatal. In the final form of the *Institutes* Calvin, in his explanation of the Creed, separated the Christological concentration from the scheme of trinitarian structure and connected it with the scheme of the *historica series*. As a result, Calvin's *Institutes* of 1559 as a grandiose summary of Reformation theology, also became the starting point – at least pertaining to its structure – for the development of the entire later evangelical theology in its Reformed characteristics.

§2.4 PROVENANCE AND SIGNIFICANCE OF THE *HISTORICA SERIES*

We said above that in the *Institutes* of 1559 Calvin no longer expressed the Christological concentration in the framework of a trinitarian scheme, but in the framework of the Creed. On this he founded the scheme of the *historica series* in the first phase of his work. This gains predominance in Calvin's *explicatio symboli* and unfortunately pushes back the trinitarian structure.[163] The concept of the *historica series,* to which we have often referred, stems from the preface of the *Loci* of Melanchthon, from the third *aetas* (1543-1559). What this concept means for the structure of dogmatics must be briefly outlined here.

Initially the entire doctrine in Reformation theology[164] was practically identical to the doctrine of justification. Once the characteristic Reformation decision for the *particula exclusive* was made,[165] Melanchthon naturally had to attempt to give a broader and more complete representation of doctrine that would be based on this decision. That required, however, a new reflection on the problem of dogmatic method.[166] The preface of the *Loci* from the third *aetas* therefore begins as follows:[167]

> 'Human beings are created by God in such a way that they understand numbers and have an idea of an "ordo", a sequence. They are greatly helped by this faculty. Therefore, in the study of the "artes" (arts, sciences) particular attention is paid to the sequence of the parts. In philosophy, this way of explanation is called method. However, church dogmatics is different than the method of the "artes", which are constructed along the road of argumentation. Philosophy proceeds by way of the senses and primary concepts, which are called "principles". In church dogmatics, however, we do not use this method of argumentation. The teaching of the church is not derived from proofs, but from the words of God. God has given these words to humanity by sure and excellent witnesses. He has revealed himself and his will because of his enormous goodness.'[168]

In the description of theological method it was the *ordo partium* (sequence of the parts) which needed to be addressed. After Melanchthon, in the preface referred to above, had pointed to the difference between philosophical and theological method, he continues as follows:

> 'Something must now be said about the sequence of the parts of doctrine. The books of the prophets and apostles themselves are written in the best possible order, as are the articles of faith. There is, after all, a historical line in the prophetic and apostolic books. They first begin with the creation of things and the founding of the church. The series is continued from the creation of things to the kingship of Cyrus. The many renewal movements of the church are told along this line. The narratives of the teaching of the law and the promise of the gospel are woven within this framework. Then the apostles appeared as witnesses to the Christ who was born, crucified and raised from the dead. These are the historical facts. In the preaching of Christ the articles of faith, i.e., the explanation of law and gospel, are contained. Added to this are the explanations of Paul, who as a true master has constructed an exposition, in the epistle to the Romans, about the distinction between law and gospel, and sin and grace or (to put it differently), reconciliation, by which we are restored to eternal life.'[169]

To unfold the *doctrina ecclesiae* Melanchthon chose the scheme of the *historica series* (the historical line). The triad 'sin – law – grace' from the preface of the *Loci* of the first *aetas* has become the *historica series* in the preface of the *Loci* of the third *aetas*.

More thoroughly than ever, the Bible was read in evangelical theology in an unbiblical fashion. It was read in a linear-historically way, as the history of the church, 'from the beginning of the world to the end'.[170] Again and again, from the time of Adam onwards, there were *instaurationes ecclesiae* (renewal movements of the church) and repeatedly, God raised up a Luther with the preaching of law and gospel.

This linear-historical reading of the Bible (and its corresponding historicizing of the works of God in the unfolding of doctrine) does not first show itself in the dynamics of federal theology from the baroque era[171] but also in the more static loci-theology of the Renaissance.[172] The result was that in the *ordo partium doctrinae* (sequence of the parts of doctrine) of evangelical theology, the 'before and after the fall of man' preceded, followed by 'before and after the birth of Christ'.

Excursus

The reason why it is unbiblical to read the Bible linear-historically in this way is expounded in our *Biblischen Theologie*. In the narrative of the biblical proclamation we also have to do with something like a *historica series*. However, in the biblical *historica series* we do not go from the general to the particular, or from the universal to the particular, let alone from *natura* to *gratia*. The *historica series* of the biblical narrative deals equally with the very particular and the altogether particular, which forms the one subject of all of the biblical witness. This particular is, however, at the same time the general and the universal. Humanity is described from the perspective of Israel. The cosmos is described from the perspective of humanity, and not the reverse. The history of God with the people of the sons of Israel on the '*erets* given to them is the history of 'God with us' all, on the whole earth.

From here on we need to have a conversation with Calvin on the 'three circle scheme', to put it in the words of Werner Krusche, who also talked about an 'impressive closed concept' in his dissertation.[173] The three circles are: general providence of God (the world), particular providence (humanity), and most particular providence (the congregation of the elect). These form together 'the three areas of the reality of the Spirit'.

Chapter I: Foundation: the theology of the trinity
Chapter II: The Holy Spirit and the cosmos
Chapter III: The Holy Spirit and man
Chapter IV: The Holy Spirit and the church

Our description of the development of the *Institutes* has shown that the problem of the *ordo docendi* has constantly occupied Calvin. Because the proclamation of 'justification of the ungodly by grace alone' formed the foundation of his theology no less than the Wittenbergers,[174] he also unfolded the totality of doctrine in the old Institutes according to the scheme 'Law → Faith'. For Calvin, too, the 'most important pillar on which religion rests' remains the doctrine of justification.[175] Yet he did not want the scheme 'Law → Faith', indissolubly connected with the doctrine of justification, to form the scheme for the unfolding of all of sacred doctrine. He wanted to arrive at a broader, more complete, and better arranged representation of sacred doctrine. Therefore, he gave up the scheme 'Law → Faith' in the final form of his book. Instead of the *historica series* he chose the form of the *explicatio symboli*.

But alas, as we have seen in the description of the first phase of his work on the final *Institutes*, the scheme of the trinitarian structure was pushed back in the explanation of the Creed by the scheme of the *historica series*, which he made the foundation of his explanation of the Creed. The 'first – and then' of the 'before and after the fall of man' and the duality of the knowledge of God grounded on this came first. Then only came the 'first-and-then' of the 'before and after the birth of Christ' with the duality of the knowledge of Christ grounded on it.

§3 BRIEF OVERVIEW OF THE FOURTH TO THE EIGHTH STEP

We conclude this chapter with a brief overview of how Calvin shaped the definitive new form of his *Institutes*. This is the 'second phase' and 'third phase', or the 'fourth step' up to and including the 'eighth phase'.

§3.1 SECOND PHASE

The fourth chapter of the old *Institutes*, 'The vows; in which monasticism is discussed', was written in 1543. Calvin inserted it at a new place in the context of his fourth book on 'The Church'. Here it forms the conclusion of the first half of that book in IV.13. Chapters 5-8 of the old *Institutes* (1543-1554, Latin text) formed a single chapter in 1539 entitled 'Faith. Containing an explanation of the Apostles' Creed'.

In 1543 this chapter, 'De Fide', is divided in four parts. The definitive new Institutes of 1559 began to emerge. The *fourth step* of the work on the formation of the definitive new *Institutes* is that Calvin divides these four chapters among the four books of the new *Institutes:*

– The *old fifth chapter*, 'Faith. Containing an explanation of the Apostles' Creed' (the same title as the fourth chapter of 1539), is now located in the second chapter of book III with the title: 'Faith. In which a definition of faith is offered and its qualities are explained'.[176]

> 1559: III.2   Faith (43 paragraphs)   ← 1550: 5.1-38

Calvin inserts the conclusion of the old seventh chapter (7.38-39: 'The Holy Spirit') at the beginning of the third book, in the brief first chapter (4 paragraphs) entitled 'That the things which are said of Christ' – i.e., in the previous second book, FB – 'are wrought in us by a secret working of the Spirit'.[177]

– Except for the first five sections (the introduction to the explanation of the Creed!) we rediscover *the old sixth chapter* ('Explanation of the first part of the Creed. In which the object of faith, the trinity, the omnipotence of God and the creation of the world are treated'. 1550: Chap. 6, 53 sections) in chapters 13-14 of the new first book:

1559: I.13.1-29	The Trinity	← 1550: 6.6-25
1559: I.14.1-22	The Creation	← 1550: 6.26-48
1559: I.16.1-9	The Government of the World	← 1550: 6.49-53

- Except for the two final sections (7.38-39: about the Holy Spirit, see above) we find *the old seventh chapter* ('Explanation of the second part of the Creed, in which the incarnation, the death, the resurrection of Christ, and the entire mystery of salvation are discussed. Also the explanation of the third part in which the Holy Spirit is treated'. 1550:7.1-39) in the third main part of the new second book, chap. 12-16 on Christ as the mediator.

1559: II.12-14	Christ's Two Natures	← 1550: 7.8-17
1559: II.15	Christ's Threefold Office	← 1550: 7.2-7
1559: II.16	Christ's Twofold State	← 1550: 7.19-37

- The *old eighth chapter* ('Explanation of the fourth part of the Creed. In which are discussed the church, its government, organization and power and exercise of discipline; also the power of the keys, the forgiveness of sins and the final resurrection' [1550:8, no less than 224 sections]) is found in the first half of the new fourth book, chapters 1-9 and 11-12.

1559: IV.1-2	The Church	← 1550: 8.1-33
1559: IV.3-7	Its Government and Organization	← 1550: 8.34-136
1559: IV.8-9	Its Power	← 1550: 8.137-168
1559: IV.11-12	Its Jurisdiction and Discipline	← 1550: 8.169-205

§3.2 INTERMEZZO

Before Calvin separated the material of the old four chapters among the four books of the new *Institutes*, two preliminary decisions had been made.

During the first step:	The first 'first and then':
	The 'before and after the fall of man'
	The sequence: 'Creation – Fall – Redemption'
During the second step:	The second 'first and then':
	The 'before and after the birth of Christ'
	Law and Gospel as 'witnesses to Christ'
	The titles of books II-IV (Redemption, Sanctification, Church)

During the fifth, sixth, seventh, and eighth steps, the first, second, third, and fourth books of the new *Institutes* are successfully completed.

§3.3 THIRD PHASE

Fifth step: completing the first book
We describe this step as a separate step for the sake of providing an overview. In reality, the first book was probably already completed by Calvin during the fourth step, when he placed the material of the old sixth chapter in the new first book (chapters 13-14):

a. Chapters 1-10 are there already; cf. the first step (the old first chapter)
    After chapter 10, Calvin adds two chapters by inserting material from the old third
    chapter 'The Law':

      Chap. 11   ← 1550: 3.24-39
      Chap. 12   ← 1550: 3.20-23[178]

    Thus Calvin now also has a doctrine 'of God' in chapters 10-12 of the first book of
    the new *Institutes*.

b. Then follows the material of the old sixth chapter.

      Chap. 13   The Trinity   ← 1550: 6.6-25
      Chap. 14   Creation   ← 1550: 6.26-48

c. Starting from some passages from the old second chapter 'The knowledge of man'
    (1550:2.6-7 and 2.18-19) Calvin now also writes about the doctrine of 'man' in:

      Chap. 15   How man was created...[179]

d. From the old fourteenth chapter (1539: the eighth chapter), 'Predestination and the
    Providence of God', the second part, 'The Providence of God', is placed at the con-
    clusion of the new first book:

      Chap. 16-18   Providence   ← 1550: 6.27.4 + 14.38-54

Sixth step: completing the second book
Here also we need to say: this is described as a separate step, for the sake of conven-
ience. In reality, however, the second book was probably already completed by Calvin
during the fourth step, when he placed the material of the old seventh chapter in the
new second book (chap. 12-16).

All of the book with its three chapters is complete:
a. Chap. 1-5   Discussion of Adam's fall
b. Chap. 6-11   Law and Gospel as Witness to Christ
c. Chap. 12-16   Christ as the Mediator

There is a newly written chapter added to it:
d. Chap. 17   Of Christ it may be rightly said that he merited God's grace
                        and salvation for us.[180] (See hereafter the words 'grace of
                        Christ' in the title of the third book).

Seventh step: completing the third book
Chapter 1,'The Holy Spirit', and chapter 2, 'Faith', are already there.

This seventh step is a new step and a very important one. It shows Calvin as theologian of the Holy Spirit. And the *duplex gratia* (twofold grace) of justification and sanctification are treated here.

The first eight chapters of the old *Institutes* are already divided among the four books of the new *Institutes*. Calvin has thus arrived at the ninth chapter of the old *Institutes*. To be able to understand what Calvin now does during this seventh step (and which important decisions are made during this step) we need to bear in mind what the old Institutes looked like from the ninth chapter on:

Chap. 9	*Repentance*
Chap. 10	*Justification* and the Merit of Works
Chap. 11	Agreement and Difference between the Old and New Testament (see above, the 'third step')
Chap. 12	*Christian Freedom*
Chap. 13	Human Traditions
Chap. 14	*Predestination* (with Providence; see above, the 'fifth step')
Chap. 15	*Prayer.* Containing an explanation of the Lord's Prayer.
Chap. 16	The Sacraments
Chap. 17	Baptism
Chap. 18	The Lord's Supper
Chap. 19	The Five So-Called Sacraments
Chap. 20	Civil Government
Chap. 21	*The Life of a Christian Man*

The following chapters offer the material for the new third book, after the already existing two chapters:

a. 'Repentance' (in 1550, 65 sections) is combined with 'The Life of a Christian Man' (in 1550, 37 sections); we find this material again in chapters II.3-5 and III.6-10.
b. 'Justification by faith' (in 1550, 87 sections) is combined with 'Christian Freedom' (in 1550, 16 sections). This material recurs in chaps. III.11-18 and 19.
c. 'Prayer' (in 1550, 51 sections) follows in chapter 20.
d. Subsequently, 'Predestination' (in 1550, 37 sections) in chapters III.21-24.
e. Finally, from the eighth chapter 1550: 8.220-224 chapter III.25, 'The Final Resurrection' is included.

Thus, the third book describes in its totality the life of a Christian man. This is a life in faith, in trust in the *misericordia Dei* (mercy of God), in repentance, in self-denial, in the bearing of the cross. This life of a Christian is the life of the godless who is justified by grace. As such, it is a life in freedom. It is the life of the elect under the rule of free grace, in the hope of eternal life.

During this seventh step Calvin shows that all of sacred doctrine is nowhere about empty speculation. In all of its parts it is about what we need to know in order to lead the life of a Christian.

Eighth step: completing the fourth book

a. Chap. 1-13   'The Church'. Most of the material for this part had already in the fourth step been assigned to this fourth and final book. The old thirteenth chapter, 'Human Traditions', is taken over in chapter IV.10. It is closed with the old fourth chapter on monastic vows, which is now placed in IV.13.

b. Chap. 14-19 The Sacraments

c. Chap. 20   Civil Government

During this 'eighth step' Calvin shows that the scope of the instruction is the church. The *Institutes* must therefore be read as an unfolding of sacred doctrine in the service of the church.

NOTES

1. See above, Introduction, n. 20.
2. Inst. 1550: Chap. VI.5. CO I, 479 = OS III, 506 footnote n). *507,22-41.* Cf. Inst. 1536 CO I, 57 below – 58 = OS I, 70 ll. 27-31, and see in the 1542 Catechism Questions 17 and 18 (according to the numbering of Ernst Pfisterer in W. Niesel, *Bekenntnisschriften*, op. cit., 4).
3. 1550 VI. (1-)5.
4. Notes in margin according to OS III, 507.
5. Cf. the heading of the seventh chapter of the *Institutes* of 1543-1554, the words 'the entire mystery of salvation' (cited above).
6. Compare, how in 1539, after the first six chapters, the seventh begins with the words: 'Above I have, to the best of my abilities, explained the essence of sacred doctrine. From the true knowledge of God and of ourselves we arrive at the communion of salvation.' CO I, 801. See above, Chap. III §1.
7. This is followed, in paragraphs 6-25 (Inst. 1550: VI.6-25, by the doctrine of the Trinity (see above, Chap. II §3) as a second Introduction to the whole of the *explicatio symboli*, as in the Catechism of 1542, the Questions 19-20 following 17-18.
8. See above, Chap. I §4 and also the citations given in the closing part of Chap. II §3. Cf. the biblical expression 'the great mercy' in Exod 34:6; Joel 2:13; Jonah 4:2; Ps 86:15; 103:8; 145:8; Neh 9:17 and 1 Peter 1:13. The title of the second volume of sermons by Karl Barth and Eduard Thurneysen, *Die grosse Barmherzigheit*, Munich, 1935, was borrowed from the latter passage.
9. OS I, 60 ll. 5-10, and what follows after ll. 10-11.
10. OS I, 391-92.
11. CR XXI, I63: Plitt-Kolde, op. cit., 168-169; St. A. II.1, op. cit. On the three 'aetates' of the Loci, see above, Chap. III, n. 9.
12. On the concept 'promissio' see the young Melanchthon (1519-1524), the book by Ernst Bizer, *Theologie der Verheissung*, op. cit., particularly 56-66.
13. CR XXI, 410-428. Cf. with this the Loci of the third *aetas* (1543-1559), St.A. II.2, ed. by Hans Engelland, Gütersloh 1953, 358 ll. 22-27; 360 l. 34-36; 363 ll. 5-9.
14. Justification is *the* 'beneficium Christi' in Lutheranism; cf. K. Barth, KD IV.3,4 (CD, 6).
15. CO I, 281 below – 282 above; cf. OS III, 33 ll. 38 – 34 l. 3. See above, chap. III, n. 23.

16. German: 'das Gefälle'. See e.g. KD I.1, 318 and the study by W. Schlichting, *Biblische Denkform in der Dogmatik. Die Vorbildlichkeit des biblischen Denkens für die Methode der Kirchlichen Dogmatik Karl Barth*, Zurich 1971.

17. Jean Calvin, *Institution de la religion chrestienne*, 1560, edition critique avec introduction, notes et variantes, publiée par Jean-Daniel Benoit, vol. I, Paris, 1957, 50.

18. E.g., in the *Institutes* of 1541 according to Pannier (1911), op. cit., 1: Toute la somme de nostre saigesse, laquelle mérite d'estre appelée vraie et certaine saigesse, est quasi comprinse en deux parties: à scavoir la congnoissance de Dieu et de nousmesmes. T. H. L. Parker speaks of Calvin's 'subordination of self-knowledge to the knowledge of God' in the *Institutes* of 1559: 'now the concept of the knowledge of God predominates' (Parker [2]1969, op. cit., 5).

19. W. Maurer, *Der junge Melanchthon zwischen Humanismus und Reformation. Band 2. Der Theologe*. Göttingen, 1969.

20. St.A. II.1, 7 ll. 10-12. See above, chap. III §3.

21. Maurer, op. cit., 233. Compare W. Maurer's description of the *Loci* of Melanchthon from the first *aetas* with R. Bultmann's description of the theology of Paul in his *Theologie des Neuen Testaments*, Tübingen [4]1958: 'A. Man before the revelation of *pistis* (faith).' B. Man under the *pistis*.' In the spirit of Ritschl, Bultmann placed his presentation on 'the Christology of the New Testament' within the framework of the words of Melanchthon (S. R. Bultmann, *Glauben und Verstehen* I, Tübingen 1933, 246 and 267). Karl Barth has therefore spoken of a 'certain relationship between Bultmann's undertaking and the original composition of the Loci of Melanchthon' (K. Barth, 'Rudolf Bultmann: ein Versuch, ihn zu verstehen', Th.St. Heft 34, [1]1952, 12 and 46). In various places he has spoken about the question to what extent the neo-Protestant appeal to Melanchthon's words might be legitimate. See KD I.1, 437f. (CD, 416f.); KD IV.1, 404 (CD, 366); KD IV.2, 89f. (CD, 82f.); KD IV.3, 4 (CD, 6); *Dogmatik im Grundriss*, Munich 1947, 81, 82. Th. St. Heft 27 ('Die Wirklichkeit des neuen Menschen', 1950), 19; Th. St. 34, op. cit., 12 and 46f.' Th. St. Heft 49 ('Evangelische Theologie im 19. Jahrhundert', 1957), 15.

22. The essay by Ernst Wolf 'Habere Christum omnia Mosi' was first published in the Festschrift for Johannes Reckel, *Für Kirche und Recht*, Cologne/Graz/Böhlau 1959, 287-303; then in *Peregrinatio*, Gesammelte Aufsätze Band II, Munich, 1965, 22-37; and finally in the book *Gesetz und Evangelium*, edited by Ernst Kinder & Klaus Haendler, Beiträge zur gegenwärtigen theologischen Diskussion; Wege der Forschung, Band CXLII, Darmstadt 1968, (166-186) 186.

23. Resp. Kirchenpostille, EA Bd. 9, 251 (For the Twelfth Sunday after Trinity. Epistle 1 or. 3,4-11) and An Justus Jonas, Coburg, June 30, 1530, WA Br., 5, 409, l. 28.

24. Compare Paul Wernle's judgment of this part (Wernle, op. cit., 172 and 182f.) with that of Werner Krusche (Krusche, op. cit., 67-85: 'Die Nichtkenntnis Gottes'). We should pay particular attention to what Krusche says about Wernle on p. 84, n. 300. This is about the question whether Werne was well advised when he claimed that Calvin lacked 'Luther's fear before God, hidden for those outside of Christ, or only the terrible God' (Wernle, op. cit., 172) The following passage may decide: '...that one seeks God in vein unless Christ goes before: for God's majesty is too great for human senses to apprehend it. Indeed, that knowledge of God which is thought to exist outside of Christ, will be a pathetic *abyss*. When he [Christ] says, that the Father is only known to him, he indicates thereby that this task is his most appropriately, to make visible to man which is *hidden* to the rest', Comm. J. 6, 46, CO XLVII, 150, Italics by Krusche. T. H. L. Parker says also (in the section 'Knowledge and Revelation' of the first chapter, 'The Self-revelation of the Creator', Parker, op. cit., 27): 'The concept of

Deus absconditus is as native to Calvin's theology as it is to Luther's, with which it is usually associated'.

25. 'Dei notitiam et nostri res esse coniunctas / Et quomodo inter se cohaereant'; French 1560: Comment la cognoissance de dieu et de nous sont choses conioinctes, et du moyen et liaison (1566 et ss.:... et due moyen de ceste liaison); French 1541 according to Pannier (1911).

26. 'Quid sit Deum cognoiscere / et in quem finem tendat eius cognitio'; French 1560: 'Que c'est de cognoistre dieu, et a quelle fin tend ceste cognoissance'.

27. OS III, 34 ll. 21-25. Cf. above, the Introduction, n. 28.

28. 'Dei Notitiam hominum mentibus naturaliter esse inditam'; French 1560: 'Que la cognoissance de Dieu est naturellement enracinée en l'esprit des hommes.'

29. 'Eandem notitiam partim inscitia, partim malitia vel suffocari vel corrumpi;' French 1560: ' que ceste cognoissance est ou estouffée our corrompue, partie par la sottise des hommes, partie par leur malice.'

30. 'Dei notitiam in mundi fabrica et continua eius gubernatione lucere'; French 1560: 'Que la puissance de Dieu reluit en la création du monde et au gouvernement continuel.'

31. 'Ut ad Deum creatorem quis perveniat, opus esse scriptura duce et magistra' French 1560: 'Pour parvenir a dieu le créateur il faut que l'Escriture nois soit guide et maistresse.'

32. 'Quo testimonio scripturam oporteat sanciri, nempe Spiritus: ut certa constet eius authoritas: atque impium esse commentum, fiden eius pendere ab ecclesiae iudicio'; French 1560: 'Par quels tesmoignages il faut que l'Escriture nous soit approuvée, à ce que nous tenions son authorité certaine, assavoir due saint Esprit: et que c'a esté une impiété maudite de dire qu'elle est fondée sur le jugement de l'Eglise.'

33. 'Probationes, quatenus fert humana ratio, satis firmas suppetere ad stabiliendam Scripturae fidem'; French 1560: 'qu'il y a des proeuves assez certaines, entant que la raison humaine le porte, pour rendre l'escriture indubitable.'

34. 'Omnia pietatis principia evertere fanaticos, qui posthabita scriptura, ad revelationem transvolant'; French 1560: 'Comme aucuns esprits escervelez pervertissent tous les principes de religion en quittant l'Escriture pour voltiger après leurs fantasies, sous ombre de révélations du S. Esprit.'

35. 'Responsio ad Sadoleti Epistolam', CO V, 393; OS I, 465.

36. KD I.1, 41 (CD, 41).

37. Inst. 1559: I.2.1 (OS III, 34 l. 23) and I.10-3 (OS III. 87 l. 20).

38. Inst. 1559: I.6.1-2 (OS III, 61 ll. 10-11).

39. KD I.2, 505ff. (CD, 457ff.): Third Chapter: Holy Scripture.

40. 'Scripturam, ut omnem superstitionem corrigat, verum Deum exclusive opponere Diis omnibus Gentium'; Fren ch 1560: 'Comment l'Escriture, pour corriger toute superstition, oppose exclusivement le vray Dieu à toutes les idoles des payens.'

41. OS III, 85 ll. 10-12.

42. See above, chap. III §3.c.C.

43. See OS III, 87 ll. 36-40 (the reference to the text of 1539-54 in the crit. app.).

44. OS III, 87 ll. 20-24.

45. Cf. I.6.1; OS III, 61 ll. 22-25. Cf. our critique of the translation of O. Weber above, the Introduction, n. 29.

46. OS III 61, 10-28 (1) l. 10: nondum loquor de propria fide doctrina; (2) l. 20: nondum ad mundi lapsum et naturae corruptionem ventum est; (3) l. 22: nondum de foedere illo disserere, quo sibi Deus adoptavit Abrahae filios: et de illa doctrinae parte qua proprie segregati semper fuerunt fideles a profanis gentibus: quia in Christo fundata fuit: sed tantum...

47. OS III, 85 l. 16<21: *Nondum* attingo peculiare foedus quo genus Abrahae a relinquis gentibus distinxit. Nam gratuita adoptione recipiens in filio qui hostes erant, *Redemptor iam tunc apparuit* (cf. I.2.1): nos autem *adhuc* in ea notitia versamur quae in mundi creatione subsistit, neque ascendit ad Christum Mediatorem.

48. KD III.1, 1; CD, 3 (§40 'The Faith in God the Creator').

49. See above, chap. III, n. 175. What Calvin really meant in this closing sentence of the first chapter he has expressed more precisely in the French text than in the Latin. The French text reads as follows: 'Toutesfois pource que Dieu *ne* se baille *point* droictement et de pres à contempler, *sinon* en la face de son Christ, laquelle ne se peut regarder que des yeulx de la foy. Ce qui reste à dire de la congnoissance de Dieu se pourra myeulx differer jusques au lieu, où nous aurons à dire de l'intelligence d'icelle foy' (French, 1541, Pannier I, op. cit., 29 ll. 35-39). Italics of 'ne...point, sinon' (God shows himself *on the whole* nowhere more rightly and closer than...) added.

50. See 1536 OS I, 39 below – 40 l. 12 = 1539-1554 chap. III.3-4 (CO I, 372-373) = 1559 II.8.2-3 (OS III 344 l. 27–345 l. 34). The text of 1536 ends: '*After* we have descended to this humiliation and subjugation, *then* the Lord will let His face shine toward us and show himself accommodating, obliging, merciful and mild.' (For a further analysis of this citation see above, chap. I §2.2). This is about the '*postquam – tum*' (after – then) of the scheme 'the law - faith'.

51. 'De cognitione hominis, ubi de peccato originali, de naturali hominis corruptione, de liberi arbitrii impotentia, item de gratia regenerationis et auxilio Spiritus sancti disputatur.'

52. 'Adae lapsu et defectione totum humanum genus maledictioni fuisse addictum, et a prima origene degenerasse; ubi de peccato originali'; French 1560: 'Comment, par la cheute et révolte d'Adam, tout le genre humain a esté asservy a malédiction, et est decheu de son origine, ou il est aussi parlé du péché originel.' In this heading the word *defectio* (apostasy) is translated in French as 'révolte'. Cf. in the Tanakh beside the words *hat'at* and *'awon* the word *pesha'* (apostasy, revolt, rebellion).

53. 'Hominem arbitrii libertate nunc esse spoliatum, et miserae servitute addictum'; French 1560: 'Que l'homme est maintenant despouillé de Franc arbitre, et misérablement assuietty a tout mal.' See regarding this heading the important footnote by Jean-Daniel Benoit in his edition of the French text, Paris 1957 (below, n. 94).

54. 'Ex corrupta hominis natura nihil nisi damnabile prodire'; French 1560: 'Que la nature de l'homme corrompue ne produit rien que ne mérite condamnation.'

55. 'Quemodo operetur Deus in cordibus hominum'; French 1560: 'Comment c'est que Dieu besongne aux coeurs des hommes.'

56. 'Obiectionum refutatio quae pro defensione liberi arbitrii afferi solent'; French 1560: 'Combien les objections qu'on ameine pour défendre le franc-arbitre sont de nulle valeur.'

57. Otto Weber has put the following heading over Inst. III.3-10-14: 'Fourth Section: The Faithful in Battle against their Sins'.

58. 'Absoluta primae partis *symboli* Apostolici, de Cognitione Dei Creatoris, tractatione, sequitur altera de Cognitione Dei Redemptoris in Christo, quam hic liber secundus explicat. / Primum vero *de Redemptionis occasione*, hoc est, de lapsu Adae disserit. Seundo, de Redemptione ipsa. Dissertationi priori priora quinque capita, posteriori reliqua assignantur. / Quod ad *Redemptionis occasionem*, non tantum in genere de lapsu agit, sed etiam speciatim de eius effectis, id est de peccato originali, de arbitrii servitute, de corrupta omnium hominum natura, de Dei in hominum cordibus operatione, cap. I, II, II, IIII, quibus subiungit refutationem obiectionum, quae pro defensione liberi afferri solent, cap. V.' See the Schipper edition, op. cit., Volume IX, 57.

59. See in the final chapter of the old Institutes *De vita hominis Christiani* (The life of a Christian man), the section *De meditatione futurae vitae* (the meditation of the future life): Inst. 1550 XXI.26-31 = 1559 III:9, and also note how the thought of the *meditatio vitae futurae* dominates the entire chapter 'Agreement and Difference between the Old and the New Testament': CO I, 803 (Inst. 1550: XI.2) = OS III, 404, ll. 13-28 (Inst. 1559: II.10.2). OS III, 405 ll. 2-6 (II.10.3) Calvin says: 'the gospel does not tights the hearts of the people to the joy of the present life, but leads them upward toward the hope of immortality: it does not attach them to earthly enjoyments, but, as it announces hope stored for them in heaven, it brings them there already, in a certain sense.'

60. CO I, 307; OS III, 231 ll. 5-13. The final sentence is in Latin: '*De utraque*, prout series docendi poscet, *sparsim* a nobis disseretur.'

61. Thus the heading of KD III.2 of §44.

62. In KD IV.1 the heading of the first section of §60 is '*The Man of Sin* in the Mirror of the Obedience of the Son of God.'

63. In the doctrine of creation (KD III.2: Chapter ten) Barth speaks about man as creature and as sinner in the second section of the introductory paragraphs (§43.2 'Man as Subject of Theological Knowledge'). This section deals with the answer to the question: (op. cit., 30) 'When we know man (...) only in the reversal and the corruption of his being, how shall we take the first step toward answering the question of his creatureliness?'

64. Inst. 1550: II.6; CO I, 307.

65. Qualis homo sit creatus: ubi de animae facultatibus, de imagine Dei, libero arbitrio, et prima naturae integritate disseretur.

66. Inst. 1550: I.1; CO I, 279. See above, chap. III §2.

67. OS III, 34 ll.28-29 + 34 l. 37–35 l. 2.

68. Inst. 1559: II.1, according to OS III, 228 ll. 9-229 l. 8.

69. For how the sentence about the 'cognitio sui' from the beginning of the old *Institutes* sounded originally, see Barth-Niesel in footnote a) p. 229 ll. 31-35.

70. See OS III, 231 l. 41, footnote a) ad l. 13. Calvin does not use the phrase 'duplex cognitio hominis' (twofold knowledge of man) here (Inst. II.1.1). However, he did use it in I.15.1: 'etsi autem ea duplex est: nempe ut sciamus quales nos prima origine simus conditi, et qualis nostra conditio esse coeperit post Adae lapsum (...) nunc tamen integrae naturae descriptione contenti erimus' (This knowledge of man is twofold. We know how his being was created originally, and we know our condition had begun to be after the fall of Adam. Nevertheless, we content ourselves now with a description of our intact nature)'. OS III, 173 ll. 31-37.

71. CO III, 285: Pannier I, op. cit., 32 ll. 27-29; J.-Benoit, *Institution de la religion chrestienne* (1560), Livre second, Paris 1957, 10: 'nous dirons de l'un et de l'autre ca et la, comme le portera l'ordre de la dispute.'

72. I.15; see OS III, 173 l. 37 and 179 l. 19

73. Otto Weber added the heading: 'The History of the Fall shows us, what Sin is' (Inst. 1559: II.1.4).

74. On the concept 'Erbsünde' (original sin as hereditary sin) see KD IV.1, 556-558 (CD, 499-501), 'This is certain, however one imagine this and make it intelligible, that the concept of an inherited sin, inherited by human procreation, is a most unhappy one, because it is a most misunderstood concept' (KD, 557; CD, 500). 'Erbsünde' is – when both components of the concept are taken seriously – a *contradictio in adjecto*, in face of which there is no help for it but to juggle away either the one part or the other' (KD, 558; CD, 501).

75. Inst. 1559: II.1.5-11 = 1550 II.7-15.

76. Wernle, op. cit., 4f.
77. Wernle called the biblical narrative of Genesis 2 a myth. Karl Barth rightly deems it incorrect to designate the biblical historical narrative as myth. KD I.1, 345ff. (CD, 327ff.); KD III.1, 91 (CD, 84); KD IV.l, 182 (CD, 166-7). *Credo. Die Hauptprobleme der Dogmatik dargestellt im Anschluss an das Apostolisches Glaubensbekenntnis*, 1935, 163; Th. St. Heft 34, op. cit., 31f.
78. Neither does Dieter Schellong is aware of it yet. In his dissertation about Calvin's harmony of the gospels, he has opposed on the one hand 'Bible + Calvin' and on the other hand 'modern historical thought', first in the final section of the second chapter ('Calvins Verhältnis zum Geschichtlichen Denken der Neuzeit', op. cit., 108-113: 'Das synoptische Problem'). And then in many passages of his book (e.g., on pp. 155, 165, 200, 208f., 260, 273, 293f., 302). He should have contrasted the old Protestant *historica series* and the Neo-Protestant so-called historicist thought with the biblical narrative of 'history' [Geschichte] on the other hand.
79. See below, chap. V §1.11.
80. The concept of 'potential heresy' was introduced above, at the beginning of the Introduction.
81. 'Liberum arbitrium post peccatum est de sole titulo, et dum facit quod in se est, peccat mortaliter'; WA I, 353-354. Cf. MA (Band I, *Aus der Frühzeit der Reformation*, ³Munich 1963) I, (125-139) 130.
82. Sf. Denzinger-Schönmetzer, *Enchiridion symbolorum definitionum et declarationum de rebus fidei et morum.* Barcinone/Fribourgi/Grisgoviae/Romae ³⁶1976 nr. 1486, formerly nr. 776.
83. WA 6, (595-612) 595.
84. WA 6, (613-629) 613.
85. Otto Clemen, *Luthers Werke in Auswahl*, 2. Band, ¹1912, ⁶1967, 60.
86. WA 7, 94-151.
87. WA 7, 308-457.
88. WA 7, op. cit., 445; Clemen 2, op. cit., 127: 'Der sechs und dreyssigst. Der frey wille / nach dem fal Ade / odder nach der gethanen sund / ist eyn eytteler name / und wenn er thut das seine / szo sundigt er todlich.'
89. WA 7, 146, ll. 3-5: Habes, miserande Papa, quid hic ogganias? Unde et hunc articulum necesse est revocare. Male enim, quod liberum arbitrium ante gratiam sit res de solo titulo.
90. See Luther's letter to Georg Spalatin dated April 13, 1520, for the problem of grace and free will. WA Br. 2, 80 ll. 3ff.
91. See above, chap. II, notes 63 and 166. In the *Loci* of the second and the third aetas this triad became 'historica series'. See below in this paragraph, part IV.
92. See the collection *Texte aus der Anfangszeit Melanchthons*, published by Ernst Bizer (Texte zur Geschichte der evangelischen Theologie, Heft 2), Neukirchen 1966.
93. Maurer, 2. Band, op. cit., 141.
94. See Benoit, r. II, op. cit, 21. See above, n. 53 of this chapter.
95. K. Barth, *Gotteserkenntnis und Gottesdienst nach reformatorischer Lehre*, Zurich 1938, 77. Ten years later, however, Barth would publish in the framework of the doctrine of creation almost 800 pages of his doctrine of man as creature. KD III.2 (1948), chap. X.
96. See in the context of the question of the *series docendi* or the *ordo recte docendi* which always engaged Calvin, Karl Barth's expression 'The Place in Dogmatics', first in the heading of the first section of his doctrine of revelation: 'The Place of the Doctrine of the Trinity in Dogmatics' (KD I.1 §8.1) and then in the first paragraph of his doctrine of the Election of Grace as doctrine of the beginning of all of God's ways and works of God, in the heading of the third section of this paragraph, 'The Place of the doctrine [of Election] in Dogmatics' (KD II.2 §32.3). It was meaningful that Barth did not use this expression with each beloved

part of his dogmatics, but exclusively in the locus 'The Trinity' and in the locus 'The Election'. However, what must very definitely be said of these two loci in Barth's Dogmatics – namely that from its 'position in Dogmatics' one can make visible the entire structure of Barth's dogmatics – that also pertains to the locus 'sin' in Barth's Dogmatics. Nevertheless, Barth has avoided speaking with good reason of its 'position in dogmatics' in the locus 'sin'. Sin is a gushing in of the nothingness and in the nothingness we have to do with a *foreign body* [Fremdkörper] among the objects of God's Providence (KD III.3, 327; CD, 289), the beginning of §50 'Gott und das Nichtige').

97. KD IV.1 §60; KD IV.2 §65; KD IV.3 §70.

98. KD III.2, 39; CD, 34 (§43.2).

99. KD IV.3, 426; CD, 369.

100. KD IV.1, (152-159) 152; CD (138-144) 139.

101. KD IV.1, 155; CD, 141. 'Sinning theologically' is a good label for the potential heresy of all And-theology. It is a secret and hidden rebellion against grace. In view of the possibility of potential heresy in the proclamation of the church (among the goyim) dogmatics calls the teaching church to a new hearing of the Word of God of the revelation attested in Scripture (see the leading sentence of KD I.2 §21). Theological sinning is not immediately a sin *beyad ramah* (with a raised hand; Num 15:30, etc.). Always in its beginning it is a sin *bishgagah*, as an erroneous act (Lev 4:3 etc.; 'they do not know what they do...', Luke 23:34).

102. KD §60.1, §65.1, §70.1.

103. KD IV.3, 427; CD, 370 (§70.1).

104. Karl Barth always takes his cue from the 'Emmanuel-fact.' See e.g., KD I.1, 110f., 118f., 123, 136, 155, 166, 247, 324, 333 (CD, 108, 115, 120, 132, 149, 160, 235, 307, 316); KD I.2, 180, 186, 226 (CD, 165, 170, 207); KD II.2, 821 (CD, 735); KD III.1, 25 (CD, 24); KD IV.1 §57.1; KD IV.4, 148 (CD, 134); Th.Ex.H. Heft 25 ('Das Evangelium in der Gegenwart', 1935), 10.

105. 'Gratia non tollit naturam, sed *praesupponit* eam et perficit eam'; Thomas Aquinas, S.Th. I q. 1 a. 8 ad sec. In Barth, 'nature' is no longer the presupposition of the grace of reconciliation, but the covenant that was made possible in creation, the one covenant of grace attested in the Tanakh in its multiplicity of forms. The heading of the first of two introductory paragraphs of the doctrine or reconciliation express this (KD IV.1 §58): 1. God with us; 2. The covenant as presuppositon of reconciliation; 3. The fulfillment of the broken covenant.

106. 'Intelligo appellatione Decalogi universam Legem naturae' (I understand by the naming of the Ten Words the general Law of nature): Melanchthon *Examen ordinandorum* (1554), CR XXIII, (1-102), 85. See also below, Chap. V, n. 23.

107. If, however, the 'Nein!' against 'nature and grace' in the year 1934 was to be well-founded, then a year later the traditional order of the historicizing (and psychologizing) Protestant theology had to be reversed, as also happened in the speech at the Barmen theological week in the fall of 1935 'Evangelium und Gesetz'.

108. The expression 'opera naturae' is, judged by the witness of the Tanakh, a contradiction in terms. As covenantal acts they are all God's *ma'asim* (actions) as such *hasadim* (works of mercy) and the *berit* (covenant) as such deals with the doing of *hesed* (mercy).

109. Provided by F. H. Breukelman, *Bijbelse Theologie I/3, Ouvertures van Genesis.*

110. Cf. KD I.2, 69 (CD, 62); KD II.2, 6 and 56 (CD, 7 and 53); 'for the sake of this particular, there is that general...', KD IV.I, 182 (CD, 166); 'The Christian kerygma directed to the *world* with this core of his saying about Israelite man means no less than the drawing of the world into the sphere of the acts of God with *Israel*..., his universality in the form of this par-

ticularity.' Cf. *Dogmatik im Grundriss*, op. cit., 87. Also KD IV.2, 588 (CD, 520): 'The teaching of Calvin of the *participatio Christi* (Inst. 1559: III.1, FB) has a *weakness* which is not lamented enough. (…) It consists in this, that precisely because of the knowledge of the *universal* range of the existence of the man Jesus, that the complete sanctification of *all* men had closed – because they had to be excluded on account of the characteristic doctrine of predestination (…)'.

111. Because the Bible speaks not Jewish about the Messiah, but Messianic (i.e., the Messiah Jesus) about Israel and the church, therefore also not humanistically of Israel, but Israelite of humanity, and not cosmically about man, but human about the cosmos.

112. Also for that reason it was necessary that KD III.2, 'The Doctrine of Creation' was written as anthropology. In the five paragraphs of this volume the attempt was made to speak covenant-historically-Christologically about man as a member of the covenant, for 'just as there is no God but *the God of the covenant*, there is no man but *the man of the covenant*' (KD IV.1, 45; CD, 43).

113. K. Barth, *Gotteserkenntnis*, op. cit., 46.

114. KD I.2, 876; CD, 783 (§22).

115. KD I.1 §§10-12.

116. KD II.1 (chaps. V and VI) and KD II.2 (chaps. VII and VIII).

117. KD II.1 §28.1

118. De lege, ubi primum ostenditur officium ususque ipsius legis; tum de vero cultu Dei, de imaginibus, de iuramento, de feriis, de votis monasticis tractatur.

119. Homini perdito quaerendam in Christo redemptionem esse; French 1560: Qu'il faut que l'homme, estant perdu en soy, cherche sa rédemption en Jesus Christ.

120. OS III, 320 ll. 37 – 321 l. 4 (Inst. II.6.1.).

121. OS III, 325 ll. 38-41 and 326 ll. 8-15 (Inst. II.6.4)

122. Quomodo hic ille Christus mundo patefactus sit, nimirum duplici ratione: *Primum* sub Lege (…) *deinde* sub Evangelio (…). See the 'Schipper edition', op. cit., 57. Italics added.

123. Legem fuisse datam, non quae populum veterem in se retineret, sed quae foveret spem salutis in Christo usque ad eius adventum; French 1560: Que la Loy a esté donnée, non pas pour arrester le peuple ancien a soy, mais pour nourrir l'espérance de salut qu'il devoit avoir en Iesus Christ, iusques a ce qu'il vint.

124. This is the heading by Otto Weber to paragraph Inst. II.7.1.

125. OS III, 326 ll. 22-30. See also above, chap. III, n. 49.

126. Inst. II.9.4, OS III, 401, l. 32 and 402 l. 10. In the first passage Otto Weber rendered the concept of 'tota lex' simply as 'the law', but in the second passage as 'the whole law'. 'The terminus technicus for the law in this wider sense is the concept of *tota lex*, by which the Torah of the Old Testament canon (the *tota doctrina Mosis*) is materially indicated.' W. Krusche, op. cit., 191.

127. OS III, 62 ll. 7-10 (Inst. 1550: I.20).

128. See on this W. Krusche, op. cit., 184ff.

129. OS III, 62 ll. 10-20.

130. Legis moralis explicatio; French 1560: L'exposition de la Loy morale.

131. Deum ab idolis discerni, ut solus in solidum colatur.

132. Deo tribuere visibilem formam nefas esse, ac generaliter deficere a vero Deo quicunque idola sibi erigunt.

133. See above, the 'first step', the discussion of chap. I.10.

134. The opening is removed; see OS III, 383 ll. 1-9 and then the continuation of 3.66 in OS V, 240 ll. 23ff.

135. Benoit, op. cit., second volume, 115.

136. KD IV.3, 634f.; CD, 552f.

137. Referring to 'the scissors' and the overall method of working, see the preface by Colladon of his edition of the *Institutes* from the year 1576 (Lausanne) in the form of a letter to Marquard ('doctissimo viro Blasio Marcuardo, Bernensi Theologo') CO I, XLI; OS III, XLII; Benoit, vol. I, 10.

138. Krusche, op. cit., 184ff.

139. See above §1 of this chapter and see Chap. III §1.

140. De similitude veteris et novi testamenti; French 1560: De la similitude du vieil et nouveau Testament.

141. De differentia unius testamenti ab altero; French 1560: De la différence entre les deux Testaments.

142. Of the chapters of the new edition, 77 could be put together on the basis of the text of the old edition. Three chapters were newly written, so that the number of chapters of the 1559 edition comes to 80. This concerns the chapters discussed here, II.6 and II.9 and II.17.

143. Christum, quanvis *sub lege* iudaeis cognitus fuerit, tamen *evangelio* demum exhibitum fuisse; French 1560: Que combien que Christ ait esté cognu des Iuifs sous la Loy, toutesfois il n'a point ésté pleinement révélé que par l'Evangile.

144. See on this concept of the 'exhibitio' (performance of the promised) as a kind of terminus technicus, Schellong, op. cit., 201.

145. Schellong, op. cit., 199.

146. It is briefer yet than the newly written sixth chapter.

147. In Wilhelm Maurer's beautiful study *Der junge Melanchthon (II)* the commentary on the Loci of 1521 in chapters 4-7 forms the heart of the book. The first of this four chapters (Chap. 4 'Toward Understanding Man'; see above, n. 19 of this chapter) begins with a brief section (I) 'Toward Understanding the Loci of 1521' (op. cit., 230-232). At the end of this section Maurer announces how he will discuss Melanchthon's book. 'We will attempt', he says on page 232, 'to express the unity of the work in the triad of sin, law and grace'. (...) 'The triad of *Sin, Law* and *Grace* has remained decisive for the Reformation theology of the young Melanchthon from his first groping attempt which he undertook in the *Institutes* of 1519. It lies also at the basis of the original concept of the Loci of 1521. And when Melanchthon, in the course of his depiction, changed this triad [sin, law, and grace] to the twofold relationship between law and gospel, formally reducing the dialectical tension and at the same time extending it materially, this happened as a consistent continuation of the Pauline base which he unfolded completely in the Loci.' Since Maurer limited himself to the description of the theology of the young Melanchthon, he could not show how this triad of the Loci from the first *aetas* in the second and the third *aetas* became the scheme of the *historica series*. In the later *Loci* the theme of *iustificatio impii* as 'proprium Christi beneficium' (actual benefit of Christ) and the dialectic of law and gospel as nucleus of the doctrine were unfolded within the framework of this *historica series* (see below, part 4 of this paragraph).

148. Wernle, op. cit., 166. See above, Chap. III n. 1. But see what Tjarko Stadtland says about Calvin's letter to Sadoleto (Stadtland, op. cit., 78f).

149. Inst. II.7.12, OS III, 337 ll. 23-24. Cf. what Melanchthon says in his *Loci* of the second *aetas* in the section 'de usu Legis divinae' (on the use of the divine law): 'by virtue of its office it is the most *characteristic* and the *principal* [function] of the Law, to point to sin, to accuse, to

frighten and to judge consciences'. Melanchthon, St.A. II.1, op. cit., 321, note 33). Italics added.

150. See above, notes 37 and 38 of this chapter.

151. Köstlin (1868), op. cit., 416-418.

152. Cf. the comment by Schellong (op. cit., 36), 'One might also ask how he places the accent in the interpretation of Scripture, what to him appears worthwhile in his striving for brevity of the unfolding and what not. Answering these questions will help one gain a clear knowledge on where, according to his real intention, the center of gravity lies in the confusing, rich comments of the Institutes'. And T. H. L. Parker (op. cit., 12, in the 'Introduction' of the second British printing of his book of 1969): 'Calvin will be best understood by cross references between the *Institutio* and the commentaries.'

153. Krusche, op. cit., 216ff. (in the section 'The authority of Scripture and the testimony of the Spirit'). We have cited Werner Krusche in such detail because we might like to point out how right Schellong was when he, in his dissertation on Calvin's *Harmony of the Gospels,* praised Krusche's book as follows (op. cit., 37): 'From the perspective of pneumatology the dissertation by W. Krusche covers the entire field of Calvin's theology with only a few exceptions. It is so rich in material, so profound in the critical incorporation of the literature, so penetrating in the interpretation (moreover, written in a lively style), that all further work on Calvin can build on this work.' In the Preface of the second edition of his book *The Knowledge of God in Calvin's Theology,* Dowey also appropriately refers to Krusche's book: as 'one of the ablest monographs in the entire Calvin literature' (Dowey, op. cit., XIII). Like Günter Gloede, Dowey also studied with Brunner in Zurich. Krusche did not mention Dowey's study in 1952. As he rejects the interpretations of Calvin by Hans Engelland, Emil Brunner, and Günter Gloede, he would likewise not approve of the thesis defended by Dowey of a 'dialectical relationship between the Knowledge of God the Creator and the Knowledge of God the Redeemer' in Calvin. To grasp that, one should read in Krusche's book the section 'The Loss of the Gifts of the Spirit' (55-95) and particularly the conclusions on pages 83-85 and 94-95.

154. Cf. Krusche, op. cit., 83: 'God the Creator is not the object of a general knowledge of God, he is only known in the Mediator, Jesus Christ. And assuming that there was such a general knowledge of God the Creator, it would not benefit us at all; for we no longer live in the original state. *One can only claim something else than this, if one has overlooked Inst. II.6.1.'* Italics added.

155. Schellong, op. cit., 283; cf. 248 and 260.

156. In his book *Die Probleme der Theologie Calvins* (Leipzig 1922) Hermann Bauke mentioned, in addition to rationalism and biblicism, the 'complexio oppositorum' as a 'characteristic feature of the theology of Calvin' (op. cit., 16-19). About this book, see (Calvin the Frenchman!) Wilhelm Niesel, *Die Theologie Calvins,* op. cit. [1]1938, 8f., [2]1957, 10f., as well as Otto Ritschl, op. cit., 172ff.

157. CO I, 477-480; CO I, 478 (cf. OS IV, 13 ll. 30-44 in footnote d); Inst. 1559 III.2, 'Of Faith'); French 1541, ed. Pannier, op. cit., 213, ll. 17-29. See above, the Introduction, n. 24 and Chapter II, n. 110.

158. CO I, 477; OS IV, 8 l. 15–9 l. 3; French 1541, ed. Pannier, op. cit., 213 ll. 5-9.

159. See above, at n. 7 in §1 of this chapter.

160. CO V, 337; French CO XXII, 52. See above, chap. II, notes 108 and 124.

161. 'Ad eius confirmationem' (toward its confirmation), from the 1539 text (as also n. 157 above).

162. See above, the conclusion of the discussion of the 'first step.'

163. See above (§1 of the present chapter).

164. On the concept of 'doctrina' see Werner Krusche, op. cit., 218, in the section 'Doctrine und Geist', which begins as follows: 'In the area of the problem "Word and Spirit" we have treated the scriptural problem separately, because a few questions take precedence. From now on we turn particularly to the relationship between Spirit and the proclaimed Word (doctrina).' With the footnote: 'Peter Brunner has rightly remarked, that doctrine in Calvin is "praedicatio verbi divini" (preaching of the divine Word), the gospel preached, kerygma.' See also K. Barth, KD I.1,72 (CD, 71): 'Calvin called the preaching (*doctrina*) the *anima ecclesiae* (Inst. IV.12.1 etc.).' See also Hans Joachim Kraus, *Die biblische Theologie. Ihre Geschichte and Problematik.* Neukirchen-Vluyn 1970, 309: 'Admittedly, we must call attention to the fact, that "doctrina" in ecclesiastical speech further has the meaning of "preaching." In CA (Confessio Augustana) VII, this understanding has now become static. It is the "consentire de doctrina evangelii" (the unity concerning evangelical doctrine). This clearly is related to the saying: "in qua evangelium pure docetur" (in which the gospel is purely taught = preached). Not until orthodoxy (and completely in the period of rationalism) does the rational-intellectualistic teaching concept assert itself in its static definitive form.'

165. Cf. the lectures by Karl Barth, 'Reformation als *Entscheidung*' (1933, Th.E.h. 3) and 'Die Souveränität des Wortes Gottes and die *Entscheidung* der Glaubens' (1939, Th.St., 5; italics added), and see the concept 'Entscheidung' in KD I.2, 386, 751, 785ff., 790f. (CD, 351f., 669, 700ff., 705f.).

166. See also in KD the final section of the Prolegomena, KD I.2 §24.2 'The Dogmatic Method' in connection with the material task of dogmatics as function of the teaching church. He also discusses in this section the *ordo partium* (sequence of the parts) – no 'system' (KD I.2, 963-973; CD, 861-870), but record [Bericht] about this one event: 'the work and action of God in his Word': the four main loci (God, Creation, Reconciliation, Redemption, KD I.2, 973-988; CD, 870-883). For the concept 'record' see also KD I.1, 333 (CD, 315).

167. Melanchthon, CR XXI, 603-604; St. A. II.1, op. cit., 167 ll. 21-168 l. 14. Italics added.

168. For this last sentence see the treatment by Immanuel Kant, 'Der Streit der Fakultäten' (1798), the beginning of the section 'Eigenthümlichkeit der theologischen Facultät'; That there is a God, biblical theology proves in that he has spoken in the Bible...'. Cf. I. Kant, *Werke*, Akademie-Textausgabe, Band VII. Berlin 1968 (¹1902), (1-116) 23; cited by K. Barth, *Die protestantische Theologie im 19. Jahrhundert. Ihre Vorgeschichte und ihre Geschichte.* ¹Zurich 1947, 277f.

169. Melanchthon, CR XXI, 605-606; St.A. II.1, op. cit., 170 ll. 6-23.

170. See the Heidelberg Catechism, Question and Answer 54.

171. In his book *Gottesreich und Bund im älteren Protestantismus, vornehmlich bei Johannes Coccejus*, Gütersloh 1923, the historian of federal theology, Gottlob Schrenk, repeatedly designates federal theology as the theology of the baroque era. 'We have here the stylistic character of the baroque era as distinct from the clear classicism of a Calvin' (page 13; see also 29; VIII and XI). Cf. also Barth, KD IV.I.58; CD, 55.

172. Cf. KD IV.1, 57-70 (CD, 54-66), the conclusion of section §57.2 'The Covenant as Presupposition of Reconciliation', the discussion of federal theology. 'Can one *historicize* God's acts and revelation?' (op. cit., 58). See also on the distinction between biblical 'narrating Geschichte' and 'Historie' KD I.1, 342-351 (CD, 324-332); KD III.1, 83-91 (CD, 76-83); KD III.2, 535 (CD, 446); KD IV.1, 331 (CD, 300).

173. Krusche, op. cit., 13-14 and 338-343.

174. See Inst. 1536, OS I, 92, ll. 21-42 (*remissio peccatorum* as *salutis cardo*); Institutes 1539, Chap. VI (1550 chap. X.I), CO I, 737; Inst. 1559 III.11.1; CO II, 533; OS IV, 181 l. 35–182 l. 21.

175. This is how he puts it in the first paragraph cited in the previous footnote of his teaching on justification ('praecipuus sustinendae religionis cardo', OS IV, 182 ll. 15-16). See in the KD, the introductory sections of the two soteriological paragraphs §61.1 and §66.1. In §61.1 (KD IV.I, 585; CD, 524, we read the sentence: 'One thing is certain, that the center of Calvin's theology (if it indeed has one) is not to be found in the doctrine of justification.' But in §66.1 we read: 'If one takes everything (…) into account, then one might well ask, whether Calvin might not primarily be a theologian of *justification*' (KD IV.2, 577, below; CD, 510). See also Stadtland, op. cit.

176. Inst. 1559, Chap. III.2: De fide; ubi et definitio eius ponitur, et explicatur quae habet propria.

177. Inst. 1559, Chap. III.1: Quae de Christo dicta sunt, nobis prodesse, arcana operatione Spiritus.

178. See above, §2.III of this chapter, with the discussion of I.8 in the context of the 'third step'.

179. See above, §2.II of this chapter in the context of the 'second step', n. 65.

180. Recte et proprie dici Christum nobis promeritum esse gratiam Dei et salutem. See also above, n. 142 of this chapter.

CHAPTER V

THE TRADITION OF THEOLOGICAL DUALISM AND THE STRUCTURE OF SACRED DOCTRINE (FRAGMENTS)

§1. THE REFORMED DOCTRINAL TRADITION AS DEVELOPMENT OF CALVIN'S DUALISM

§1.1 CALVIN

We saw that, on the one hand, the duality in the 'knowledge of God and of man' determines the structure of the 1558/59 *Institutes*. (Also, in the 'second step' we saw the remarkably isolated place of the doctrine of 'sin', which divides creation and redemption, before and after the fall.) On the other hand, this duality is cancelled again by the strong Christological concentration in *Institutes* II.6-11, where law and gospel are read as 'testimony to Christ'.

Two times we met a 'first – and then'. First, there was the 'first – and then' of the 'before and after the fall of man'. Second, there was the 'first – and then' of the 'before and after the birth of Christ'. The second 'first – and then' was most decisive for Calvin.[1] However, in Calvin's exegesis and unfolding of doctrine the first 'first – and then' always continued to be of fatal influence. All of the later development of Reformed theology has gone further in the direction of this fatal 'first – and then'. Yet the power of the second 'first – and then' slowed down the potential heresy which was enclosed in the first 'first – and then'. From 1560 onwards, it took some 150 years before this potential heresy began to be an obvious heresy.

Why did it take so long before this tendency came to its full development? The 'by grace alone' and the 'Christ alone' and the 'by Scripture alone' of the sixteenth century have slowed down the process. We have seen this in a beautiful way in the 1559 *Institutes*. One needs to have a good understanding – such as we now have, on the basis of the present study – of the 1539 *Institutes* and the Catechism of 1542 (1545) to be able to evaluate how much weight this dualism in the 1559 *Institutes* does and does not have.

In the Catechism of 1542, 'the Law' does not precede 'Faith' anymore, but 'the Law' follows after 'Faith':

Faith   →   The Law   →   Prayer

This makes us realizes that Calvin in the Institutes, too, will not stick to his original scheme.[2]

We also point here to the Heidelberg Catechism, in which both schemes are related to each other:

The Law   →   The Gospel
Misery   Redemption   Gratitude
                      Faith   →   The Law + Prayer

Calvin's students, however, only paid attention to the *Institutes* of 1559, which so strongly expresses the dualism.

Excursus
This is clear from what happens in the same year (1559) with the Confession of Faith, which Calvin had proposed to the French. They changed the beginning. Calvin had simply wished to say: we know God from his Word (and that Word is to be understood as 'testimony to Christ'). However, the *Gallicana* (the French Confession of Faith) and likewise the *Belgica* (the Dutch Confession of Faith) state: we know God in two ways.[3] A comparison between the first five articles of the *Confessio Gallicana* with the first article of the draft Calvin had sent to the brethren in La Rochelle shows us how the later development of Reformed theology has continued in the direction of the fatal first 'first – and then'. Although this played a role for Calvin in the theological reflection of the *Institutes*, he did not use it in the confessing of the ecclesia.[4] Indeed, if Calvin would have had his way, the *duplex cognitio* would not have played a role in the confession. The same may be said of the catechetical literature.[5]

Law and gospel together are a witness of Christ (Inst. II.6-11). At the same time the idea that the dualism of law and gospel originated historically is fundamental. Before the fall the law alone sufficed. After the fall, the gospel was added to it. At present, therefore, the Word of God consists of two elements.[6] We find this thought in all reformers and in all post-Reformation theology of Protestant scholasticism. To Calvin it was fundamental as well. It contributed toward the definitive form of the 1559 *Institutes*.

For the definitive editing of his main work, Calvin chose the form of *explicatio symboli*. He wanted to express as powerfully as possible his Christological concentration in the unfolding of sacred doctrine. However, the dualistic understanding of the knowledge of God (which, as we saw in chapter III, originated from the scheme 'law and gospel' in 1539) now forms the point of departure for the *explicatio symboli* in the *Institutes* of 1559. Calvin has expressed this in a clear way in a series of insertions, which we meet in the *Institutes* I.2.1, I.6.1, and I.10.1. We have heard the hermeneutical 'basic sentence' in I.2.1 repeatedly. Here, we give the text of I.6.1. In particular, we wish to hear what Calvin says after the words: 'This order He has kept with regard to His church from the beginning onwards':

Institutes 1539: I.19[7]	*Institutes* 1559: I.6.1[8]
'In order to instruct those to whom He gladly wants to give the knowledge of His salvation, He does not only use mute teachers. He also opens His holy mouth. He tells them not only that they should worship this or that God, but that He is the God whom they should worship. He instructs them not only to look to God, but He shows himself to be the one they should look upon. This is the order which the Lord has kept from the beginning onwards, whenever He called His servants. In addition to all other information, He also used the Word, as a far more accurate and trustworthy way to get to know Him.'	'This, then, is an exceptional gift. For the instruction *of His church* God not only uses mute teachers, but also opens His holy mouth. He tells them not only that they should worship this or that God, but that He is the God whom they should worship. He instructs them not only to look to God, but He shows himself to be the one they should look upon. This is the order which the Lord has kept from the beginning onwards *towards the church*. In addition to all other information, He also used the Word, as a far more accurate and trustworthy way to get to know Him.'
'Thus Adam, Noah and the other fathers have come to a more intimate knowledge of Him, enlightened by the Word (...).'	'And there is no doubt that Adam, Noah, Abraham and the other fathers by means of this aid had learned to know God in an intimate way (...).'

Now hear the insertion of 1559:

'(...), which distinguished them from the unbelievers to a certain degree. I do *not yet* speak of the proper doctrine of faith, by which they (the fathers) were enlightened to the hope of eternal life; for in order to move from death to life, they needed not only to know God as creator, but also as redeemer – as they undoubtedly also acquired from the Word. First they came to know God as the one who created and governs the world. Then they came to that other, more intimate knowledge, by which alone dead souls are resurrected. Here, God is not only known as creator of the world and as the only author and judge of all. He is also known as a redeemer in the person of the mediator.

But because we have *not yet* touched upon the fall of the world and the corruption of nature, I will not speak about the cure at present. The readers will understand that I am not yet dealing with that covenant[9] by which God had adopted for himself the children of Abraham. Nor am I talking about that part of doctrine, according to which believers are forever elected out of the ungodly nations, because it was grounded in Christ.[10] I am exclusively dealing with the issue of how one needs to learn from Scripture that the God who is the creator of the world, is to be distinguished by means of unambiguous signs from the entire crowd of lying gods. We will come to the theme of redemption in due time.[11]

Though indeed we will refer to many passages in the New Testament, and also others from the law and the prophets, which explicitly mention Christ, I do so only to show how God reveals himself in Scripture as the maker of the world and also to show what we can know of Him, so that we need not take any detour to find an uncertain divine being.'

Institutes 1539	*Institutes* 1559: I.6.2
'(…), whether they were informed of this by means of direct oracles and visions, or that they had heard it from their leaders, as it were from hand to hand. For it does not make much difference how they actually became participants of His Word. Both ways, they understood that it had come to them from God. God has undoubtedly made them trust His Word, as often as He wished its revelation to be received.'	'Whether God became known to the fathers through oracles and visions, or through the work or ministry of men, there is no doubt that they had a firm assurance in their hearts concerning the doctrine and the preaching. They were convinced that what they had learned had come to them from God. For God always created in them an unshakeable trust in His Word, which exceeded all mere opinion.'

In this way, Calvin's readers could hear him say: after the fall, God added the Word to the *muti magistri* (mute teachers) of the *opera* (the works), so that he might be known by man as creator. And so that man might also know God as redeemer, God has added that 'other, more intimate kind of knowledge, by which God (…) might be known as redeemer in the person of the mediator'. Thus, in Calvin's opinion Scripture contains a *duplex doctrina* (twofold instruction). On the one hand, there is the 'general doctrine of Scripture', by which God is known as 'creator and ruler of the world'. On the other hand, there is the 'proper doctrine of faith', by which God is known as redeemer. His readers have found abundant evidence for this view in Calvin's writing.

§1.2 MELANCHTHON

Loci 1521 (prima aetas)
We turn now to a passage in the *prima aetas* of Melanchthon's *Loci communes* in which we hear how Melanchthon formulated all of this in 1521. It is the passage with the heading *De evangelio* (the gospel):[12]

'Having treated the judgment and the curse of man, we now turn to the renewal or the blessing of man. Holy Scripture consists of two parts: the law and the gospel. The law tells of sin, the gospel of grace. The law points to the sickness, the gospel to the medicine. The law is a servant of death – to use the words of Paul – the gospel serves life and peace. "The law is the power of sin" (1 Cor 15:56), the gospel is "the power of salvation to all who believe" (Rom 1:16).'

First, the sickness is indicated by the law and then the gospel passes on the medicine, which creates healing. This is what Luther said in the preface of the *Betbüchlein* of 1520.[13] And as we have seen, this is also the basic pattern of Calvin's 1536 *Institutes*.

> 'The Scriptures have not handed down law and gospel in such a way that only what Matthew, Mark, Luke and John have written could be viewed as gospel, and as if the books of Moses contain nothing but law. Rather, both the doctrine and the promises of the gospel are dispersed among the books of the Old and New Testament. Neither are – as is commonly assumed – the times of law and gospel distinguished, although at one time the law, and another time, immediately afterward, the gospel is revealed. Looking at our hearts, each time is the time of both law and gospel. At all times men are justified in the same way. Sin became public by the law, and grace by the promise of the gospel.'

Almost every author dealing with the subject of 'law and gospel' speaks about 'dialectics'. Law and gospel do not represent two eras, so they say ('before and after the birth of Christ'; Old and New Testament); neither are they about two phases in a history of conversion. Rather, they are about the dialectic of the way God deals with his people. He makes them approach him by law and gospel. Originally, in his booklet of 1536, the dialectic of law and gospel was also for Calvin 'the formal principle of all of dogmatics'.[14] However, later he renounced this view.

> 'The times of revelation change. Scripture tells us that at one time the law and at another time the gospel is revealed. In addition to the law of nature, which in my opinion is imprinted into the hearts of men, God has charged Adam also with laws: "you shall not enjoy the fruit of the tree of the knowledge of good and evil" (Gen 2:17). And to Cain He commanded: "you shall not be angry with your brother" and "the one who kills (the brother), sins" (Gen 4:5ff.; 4:9ff.). In this way the Spirit of God has renewed the knowledge of the law of nature, which had been quickly darkened, by constant preaching. The human hearts had become blinded by sin. On the basis of that I would be tempted not to assert that the law of nature were implanted and by nature written in the hearts of men. I would rather speak of laws, which were received by the fathers and passed on continually to later generations. As Adam instructed his descendants about the creation of things and about the worship of God, thus Cain was admonished not to kill the brother, etc.'

On the one hand, early Reformation speaking about law and gospel is dialectical: each time is seen as the time of both law and gospel. By the Word of God as law, man is charged and accused and led to repentance. At the same time he is acquitted, comforted and raised by that same Word of God as gospel. On the other hand, the way in which *lex et evangelium* is spoken about in early Reformation doctrine is closely related to the way Scripture is read linear-historically. The result has been that, because of the scheme of law and gospel, the scholastic scheme of 'nature and grace', which the reformers had rejected as unbiblical, was in fact not thrown away but only historicized.

While the distinction between law and gospel meant for Luther that God in his Word by law and gospel brings man to the knowledge of sin and grace, this distinction is soon understood by Melanchthon – as *praeceptor Germaniae* (educator of Germany) and reformer of the arts faculty (Aristotle) – as the distinction between 'nature and grace' (ontically) and 'reason and revelation' (noetically). Much stronger than in the *Loci* of the *prima aetas*, the distinction between law and gospel serves for Melanchthon in the later *Loci* of 1535[15] as the viewpoint from which the relationship between philosophy (*artes liberales*) and theology is seen. We hear this for example in the following pronouncement of the *Loci* of 1535 (of the *secunda aetas*, in the part 'Why the promise of the gospel is necessary'):[16]

'There is one law and this is known to all people and at all times by nature. There is also one gospel, but that is not known by nature but only by divine revelation.'

The order of this scheme 'nature and grace' is now expressed in the fact that the Bible was read more thoroughly linear-historically than ever before, as church history *ab initio mundi ad finem usque* (from the beginning of the world to the end).[17] The beginning of the world is simultaneously the beginning of the human race and the end of the human race is simultaneously the end of the world. Because of what happens in the acts of the Son of God, all of world history is essentially church history.[18] The proclaiming narrative and the narrative proclamation of the biblical text were read as reports of all that had happened *ab initio mundi* in this church history.[19] Of course all of the narrative was also read Christologically from the middle of the fulfillment and eschatologically from the end. It was well known that believing in a biblical sense is much more and really something very different than only maintaining the truth of a historical report. All the same, the Bible was read primarily historically from beginning to end. As an example[20] we note here a few passages from Melanchthon's *Examen ordinandorum* from the year 1552:[21]

'But this segment of doctrine, with the weak name of "moral law", is not a perishable law which first began with Moses. Rather, it is the eternal, unchangeable wisdom in God himself and the eternal rule of righteousness in His divine will, which He formed in rational creatures[22] out of His unspeakable goodness. And *from the times of Adam*, He has repeatedly explained and refreshed it in His churches with His preaching, so that we might know what He himself is like, namely wise, good, truthful, righteous, clean. He also did this, so that we might know that He wants the rational creature to be like Him. For this reason He has shared this high wisdom with created beings, and is terribly angry with all that is an abomination in the light of His unchangeable wisdom, and He destroys it. This law is commonly called the Ten Commandments.'

Thus we see that the Decalogue is understood as *lex aeterna* (the eternal law).[23]

Karl Barth

Melanchthon rightly says that the relationship between God and man is about 'how He himself is' and 'that He wants the rational creature to be like to Him'. In the view of Melanchthon, however, this relationship is primarily seen as a matter of the *lex aeterna*, which precedes the gospel. The correction, which Barth has made at this point in the unfolding of sacred doctrine, is this. He describes this relationship as being the relationship between 'God's gracious choice' and 'God's command' in chapters VII and VIII of Part Two of the Doctrine of 'God' (KD II.2: gospel and law). It is from this perspective that he speaks about 'creation, reconciliation and redemption' as 'facilitation, fulfillment and completion of covenantal history', in volumes III, IV (and V). Each of these three loci is closed with a chapter on ethics.[24]

> 'Therefore at all times this eternal law, the moral law, with its judgment on sin, is preached in God's churches *from the times of Adam* onwards. The Lord Christ himself has often revitalized this knowledge.'

> 'This great comfort has been preached *from the times of Adam* in the churches, after the wondrous promise (of which no creature had known before) was revealed: "the seed of the woman will bruise the head of the serpent" (Gen 3:15). And by this comfort, Adam and Eve were saved from eternal death.'

Thus, in each of these three citations we hear (in the law as well as in the gospel): 'from the times of Adam'.[25]

The later 'historical-critical' reading of the biblical texts was the consistent continuation of this naïve pre-critical 'historical' reading. This later historical-critical reading of the biblical texts was beneficial in a certain way. It made it totally clear that what we hear in these texts is not about 'history' or 'historians', but about prophetic and apostolic testimony and 'poetic memory'. Reading the biblical texts along linear-historically lines, from the beginning of the world to its end (the Bible functioning as a 'source of direct information',[26] as 'source-literature')[27] is not in agreement with the tendency of these texts.

§1.3 URSINUS

Zacharias Ursinus (born 1534) was the man who circa 1560 – while Calvin was still alive – coined the term *foedus naturale* (covenant of nature). With short interruptions, Ursinus studied seven years (from 1550-1557) with Melanchthon in Wittenberg. The distinction between law and gospel was, as we have seen, the heart of the theology taught in Wittenberg, as interpreted by Melanchthon the systematician in the *Loci communes*. After Wittenberg, Ursinus went to Switzerland and France (in the years 1557-1558) and was influenced by Calvin, Beza, Bullinger, and Peter Martyr. He then returned to Breslau, his place of birth. Here he taught Melanchthon's *Examen ordinandorum* of 1552 (the Latin text of 1554) at the Elisabeth gymnasium. He had to leave Breslau because of his doctrine of the Lord's Supper and went to Zurich in 1560. Here he must have heard the doctrine of the covenant from Bullinger. In 1561 Frederick III of the Paltz invited him to come to Heidelberg to become the rector of the 'Collegium Sapientiae', a seminary for future ministers. As syllabus for his instruction at this Collegium, Ursinus then wrote his large Catechism.[28]

The Zurich doctrine of the covenant tied all parts of this Catechism together. It was, however, at the same time Melanchthon's above mentioned distinction of law and gospel which dominated this textbook.[29] We find this combination of the Zurich doctrine of the covenant with Melanchthon's description of the distinction between law and gospel expressed in Question and Answer 36 of Ursinus's Large Catechism. It reads as follows:[30]

> 'What is the distinction between law and gospel?
>
> The law contains the covenant of nature, which God signed with man at the creation. That is to say, its nature is known to man and demands our perfect obedience toward God. It promises eternal life to those who accomplish it. Those who do not accomplish it are threatened with eternal punishment.
>
> The gospel contains the covenant of grace. That is to say, it is not at all known by nature. It shows us how the righteousness which the law requires is fulfilled in Christ and is restored in us by the Spirit of Christ. It promises eternal life for free, because of Christ, to those who believe in him'.[31]

Here the concept of *foedus naturale* or *foedus naturae* (covenant of nature) has made its entry into Reformed theology. August Lang comments: 'Bullinger and Melanchthon are therefore the patrons, the one for the covenant idea in general, the other for its peculiar coloring.'[32] Basing himself on Melanchthon's concept of the law as *lex naturalis* (law of nature), Ursinus spoke of a *foedus naturale* (covenant of nature). Polanus and Wollebius subsequently called this *foedus naturae* the *foedus operum* (covenant of works).[33]

Thus we see how the distinction between law and gospel has led to the distinction between a *foedus naturae* (covenant *of nature*) before the fall and a *foedus gratiae* (covenant of grace) after the fall. In this way, circa 1560, the covenant of nature (before the fall) made its entry in the landscape of sacred doctrine. Originally this covenant of nature did not make much of an impact. But it was there. And being there, it began to do something. In the course of the seventeenth century it increasingly began to function as background, model, and framework for the covenant of grace. In the period of rational orthodoxy, which functioned as a transitional phase from orthodoxy to neo-Protestantism, all of the *natura* came to function as measure and criterion. With the of the covenant of nature the truth of the *vera religio* (true religion) could be indicated. The theology of the churches of the Reformation, which in the sixteenth century had begun with the *sola gratia* (grace alone) of the doctrine of justification, ended in the eighteenth century in a pitiful *sola natura* (nature alone).

§1.4 GOMARUS

Franciscus Gomarus (1563-1641) was pastor of the Dutch (refugee)-congregation at Frankfurt-am-Main from 1587 onwards and became professor of theology in Leiden in 1594. On May 8 he gave his inaugural lecture there, *De foedere Dei* (on the covenant of God).[34] In this lecture he says:

> 'Because there is not just one kind of covenant of God, it must be defined and classified, and more closely distinguished by us, so that we may realize more profoundly what must be understood by the name "new covenant" or "new testament".

The covenant of God is a mutual agreement of God and humans concerning eternal life, which He grants them on a certain condition. It has two sides: the promise of God, which is eternal life, and the promise of men to fulfill the condition which God has ordained.

This covenant has two further sides, the natural and the supernatural. It is natural because it is known by nature. God promises eternal life and demands complete obedience as a condition from man. This is properly called natural, because it is written on the hearts of men by nature (Rom 2:14,15).[35]

In itself the covenant is simple, but it varies on the basis of the added qualities. On the basis of these additions it is not so much divided as distinguished....'

Gomarus is talking about the one 'covenant of nature' (known by nature)[36] in two forms: before and after the fall of man. God gave it *primum* (first) immediately to our first parents at the creation and simultaneously to the human race. *Deinde* (then), when our nature was corrupted and had become the enemy of God, He gave it again to the Israelites by Moses the mediator on two tablets. At the beginning, man had complete knowledge of this covenant and had been able to fulfill it. Then, however, that knowledge had been lost, and man became incapable of fulfilling it. As test and touchstone of obedience, the yoke of ceremonies was now added:

'The supernatural covenant, in which God offers Christ to man and receives perfect obedience in return is truly unknown by nature. In this covenant, God not only gives mankind reconciliation and eternal life, but also, by his Spirit, gives the condition of faith and of conversion. The covenant formula in Jer 31:31ff., Heb 8:8 ff. and the preaching of Christ in Mk 1:15 testify to this. We call it supernatural, because it cannot be known and maintained by the understanding nor by the powers of nature, but exclusively by the supernatural grace of the Spirit.

This covenant also is unique in itself, and eternal, yet it is distinguished at certain times and circumstances.

It first began in paradise, after the fall of the human race, with the promise of the coming of the Messiah and of the crushing of the head of the serpent (Gen 3:15). It was then confirmed to Abraham and the Israelites....

This covenant was later repeated by Moses and confirmed by ceremonies. Its administration was twofold. On the one hand it was the proclamation of the legal covenant, or the covenant of nature (...). On the other hand, it served as a reminder to the covenant which was supernatural and for free, the covenant which had been given to Abraham and the Israelites, as the Mosaic promises prove (Deut 18:15 and elsewhere) and as Christ and the apostles testify (Joh 5:46, Acts 3:21 etc.)...'.[37]

The *foedus supernaturale* (the supernatural covenant) deals with one covenant in two forms: before and after the birth of Christ. In connection with this *duplex foedus* (twofold covenant) Gomarus now also speaks of a *duplex ministerium Mosis* (twofold administration of Moses). The very characteristic and original nature of the Tanakh is thus prevented from exercising its validity. The Tanakh is a framework for the apostolic *kerygma*; without it, the apostolic *kerygma* cannot be explained. It does not, by way of a *duplex ministerium*, hold the dualism of 'nature and grace'. On the contrary, the anti-pagan testimony of the Tanakh serves to show us the entire structure of biblical theology, and as soon as that occurs, all talk about 'nature and grace' automatically ceases. The question whether the structure of the dualism in theological knowledge is biblical or not can only be answered in the exegesis of the Tanakh.

It would be illuminating to carefully read and discuss this lecture by Gomarus, at the beginning of his professorial career, on the *duplex ministerium Mosis*, because it forms the background for his exegesis.[38]

§1.5 Gerhard

When we compare the *Loci theologici* by Johann Gerhard with the Leiden *Synopsis purioris theologiae*, to be discussed in the following sub-paragraph, we learn how the subject of 'law and gospel' was discussed during the time of confessional orthodoxy both by the Lutherans and the Reformed.

Excursus
The point of departure of the theology of all reformers, including and particularly Gerhard, is masterfully formulated at the beginning of the fifth article of the 'Solid Declaration' of the *Formula Concordiae* of 1580:[39]

'1. The distinction between Law and Gospel is an especially brilliant light which serves the purpose that the Word of God may be rightly divided and the writings of the holy prophets and apostles may be explained and understood correctly. We must therefore observe this distinction with particular diligence lest we confuse *the two doctrines* and change the Gospel into law. This would darken the merit of Christ and rob disturbed consciences of the comfort, which they would otherwise have in the holy Gospel when it is preached purely and without admixture, for by it Christians can support themselves in their greatest temptations against the terrors of the law.
2. On this point, too, there has been a controversy among some theologians of the Augsburg Confession.'[40]

This fifth part, '*De lege et evangelio* of the Solid Declaration, consists of twenty-seven paragraphs. In paragraphs 23 and 24 we read:

'23. Since the beginning of the world these two kinds of proclamation have continually been set forth side by side in the church of God with the proper distinction....
24. We believe and confess that these two doctrines must be urged constantly and diligently in the church of God until the end of the world, but with the due distinction....'

Indeed, sacred doctrine is about what is valid and true *ab initio mundi* (from the beginning of the world) *usque ad novissium diem* (to the Last Day).

The *Loci theologici* by Johann Gerhard (1582-1637) were written 1610-1622 and published in nine volumes.[41] Loci 12-14 (of the 31 loci in total) deal with *De lege Dei – De evangelio* (the law of God – the gospel). In the fourteenth locus, second paragraph, we read:

'If the first human ancestor had remained in the righteousness in which he was created, one kind of heavenly doctrine (i.e., the law) would have sufficed for his salvation. By perfectly fulfilling it with absolute obedience he might have merited the triumph of eternal life.

But after falling into sin, he was not able to keep the law any longer. He needed another aid toward life and salvation. The richness of the promises of the gospel consists in this. Out of compassion toward Adam and us all, God left the secret abode of his majesty. Immediately after the fall in paradise (Gen 3:15), He revealed "the first gospel" about the seed of the woman that would crush the hellish head.

Since that time, the preaching of law and gospel were always connected in the ecclesia. This connection of a twofold doctrine was confirmed in the example of God preaching "the first gospel".

According to the suitable sequence, the doctrine (preaching) of the gospel is preceded by the explanation of the divine law.[42]

And in such a way, that those who were crushed by the hammer of the law, who were terrified at the thunderclap of the law, are cured and cheered up by the preaching of the gospel as by a very sweet balm. For the gospel proclaims that the obedience which is required by the law has been completed by Christ in our place.

Let us therefore go from Moses to Christ, from Mount Sinai to Mount Zion, from the diagnosis of the sickness to its medicine.'

Concerning the sequence in which the concepts 'law and gospel' are introduced – first 'the law' and then 'the gospel' – Gerhard says: originally 'only one kind of heavenly doctrine sufficed for salvation,' namely the law. After the fall, the knowledge of the law was no longer sufficient to become a participant of eternal salvation. As 'another aid toward life and salvation' the *promissiones evangelii* (promises of the gospel) were added. Since the fall, there were two kinds of teaching: 'the teaching of the gospel is preceded by the explanation of the law'. The *conveniens ordo docendi* (suitable order of instruction), according to which the *ecclesia* goes from the instruction of the law to the gospel, is founded in this 'historical' order. The 'principle' of all of orthodox doctrine – here with the Lutherans, but no different with the Reformed – is therefore, historicizing:

'*Dominus primum (ante lapsum) simpliciter (in lege),*
deinde (post lapsum) dupliciter (in lege et evangelio) apparet.'

'The Lord appears first (before the fall) only in the law
and then (after the fall) in both law and gospel.'

§1.6 THE LEIDEN SYNOPSIS

The Reformed doctrinal tradition was more varied than the Lutheran tradition in speaking historically about church history, which was supposed to have begun in paradise. In the old-Protestant loci-theology 'historical' (or: historicizing) speaking was originally static (in the Reformed tradition as well): first creation, then the fall, then grace for sinners and finally the end. We see this in a classical way in the *Leiden synopsis purioris theologiae* (overview of pure theology) of 1625.[43]

In its structure the Leiden Synopsis reflects the stance of infralapsarianism. The basic pattern of Protestant theology resulted in their being the majority in the Synod of Dordt (1618-1619). In their description of the *ordo decretorum* (order of the decrees of God) – with the *homo creatus et lapsus* (created and fallen man) as *objectum praedestinationis* (object of predestination) and not (as in the opinion of the so-called supralapsarians) the *homo creabilis et labilis* (man before creation and fall) – we find the historicizing tendency of this theology. The Leiden Synopsis also shows this in the sequence of its fifty-two disputations. Disputations 7-9 on *De Deo uno en trino* (the one and triune God) are not immediately followed by a disputation *De decretis* (the decrees), but by *De mundi creatione* (the creation of the world: disputatio 10). We are therefore not offered a view of the whole of doctrine from the perspective of God's eternal counsel, but from the perspective of God's being, that is, the sixth disputation on *De natura Dei et divinis Attributis* (the being of God and the divine attributes).

In the seventeenth thesis of this disputation we find the *Dei descriptio* (description of God). As in every Reformed dogmatics, here also we first hear: *Deus non potest definiri* (no definition can be given of God). Indeed, *Deus non est in genere* (God does not fall under a *genus*, as a specimen of a certain kind of being).[44] This is followed by the table of contents of the remainder of the disputation:

'That God is a spiritual being, simple and infinite,
namely eternal, immeasurable and unchanging,'

> – this is commented on in theses 19 and 20, FB –

living and immortal, understanding, knowing and all-knowing'

> – these *attributa incommunicabilia* (incommunicable attributes) are discussed in thesis 22-29, FB –

'and also goodness, love, benevolence, mercy, longsuffering, righteousness, holiness, etc.'

> – these *attributa communicabilia* (communicable attributes) are discussed in thesis 30-42, FB –

'He is one being and three persons: the Father, who eternally generates the Son, the Son, who was born of the Father,
the Spirit who is from the Father and the Son
and who proceeds from the Father through the Son:
the creator, who maintains and rules all,
the redeemer, who saves and glorifies the elect.'

The following chapters are thus indicated:

De natura Dei	–	*De trinitate*	–	*De operibus*
God's being and attributes		The trinity		The works of God (creation, redemption)

This final scheme:

Creator universi –	*Redemptor electorum*
The creator who	The redeemer who
maintains and rules all	saves and glorifies the elect

is strongly influenced by Calvin's *Institutes*, particularly the *Institutes* of 1539-1554 (the 'second basic form').[45] First, creation and fall are mentioned, then the law (disputations 18-21) and the gospel (disputation 22). Then the Old and New Testaments are mentioned (disputation 23), followed by predestination (disputation 24). Then follows Christology, soteriology, ecclesiology, politicology, and eschatology.

We can briefly summarize the structure of doctrine, as it is unfolded here from the perspective of the *Dei descriptio* (description of God), as follows: *de Deo – de universo – de electis* (God, the universe, the elect). A dangerous tendency comes to the fore. First the *universum* is described in a historicizing way. Then the *electi* are described in a psychological-biographical way. Through calling, justification, and sanctification, they meet the eternal *gloria* (glory). Next, the data of the biblical 'covenantal history' are placed within this framework: Christology, predestination, law and gospel, Old and New Testaments, creation and redemption. Such a dogmatics does not narrate the biblical *debarim* (the one *dabar* in a multitude of *debarim*), but reveals a series of *veritates* (truths). The connection between these truths is determined by the (very un-biblical) structure: *deus – universum – electi*.

Excursus
In addition to the scheme:

God –	The universe	–	The elect

we also find the following scheme in the Reformed doctrinal tradition:

God –	The decrees of God in general	–	Predestination in particular

Thus, in the thought of Franciscus Turrettini[46] the fourth locus, *De decretis in genere et de praedestinatio in specie'* (the decrees in general and predestination in particular), comes immediately after the third locus, *De Deo uno et trino* (God one and triune). Here the general 'world' events are mentioned first. The biblical 'covenantal history' is seen within that framework, instead of the reverse. Here, too, we have to do with a 'potential heresy', which became a manifest heresy after 1700 and which urgently requires a correction.

The orthodox fathers in the Reformed doctrinal tradition have this in common, that in their theology, predestination forms only one of the many *decreta* (decrees). Yet it can be very biblical to discuss (in this second line, not in the line of the Leiden synopsis), in direct connection with the doctrine of 'God', the *decretum divinum* (divine decree), and then unfold all of doctrine from this perspective. The supralapsarians[47] applied this *decretum praedestinationis* (decree of predestination) to the 'man before creation and fall'. In their view, this *decretum* dominated all other decrees. Barth took over this supralapsarianism (in a critical way).[48]

We said that within the scheme *universum – electi* (the universe – the elect) the scheme law and gospel also finds a place. That is a variation on the early Protestant basic scheme. After the disputations *De lege Dei* (the law of God, 18-21), the disputation *De evangelio* (on the gospel) begins as follows (disputation 22, thesis 1):

> 'The law, which we have discussed above, shows us the corruption and ruin of our spiritual sickness, which is sin. The medicine for it is shown by the gospel.'[49]

Here we find the same basic pattern as with the Lutheran Johann Gerhard.

§1.7 THE COCCEIAN FEDERAL THEOLOGY

If this 'historical' talk was at first very static, in the Cocceian variant of federal theology[50] it becomes active and dynamic:

> 'The "loci" are not "loci" anymore, that is to say, fixed places to which other doctrines can or cannot be linked. (...) They are now the different stages in a series of events, the individual moments in a *movement*. This movement as such is now understood as Christian truth. Christian doctrine records this movement. This theology is concerned with the bold review of a *history* which unfolds itself from creation to the day of the last judgment....'[51]

This movement and mobility about which Barth speaks is superbly expressed by the greatest systematician of the Cocceian federal theology, Franciscus Burmann (1628-1679; from 1662 to 1679 professor and pastor at Utrecht) in his main work, the *Synopsis theologiae et speciatim oeconomiae foederum Dei ab initio saeculorum usque ad consummationem eorum* (Synopsis of the theology and particularly of the economy of salvation of the covenants of God from the beginning to the completion of this world), written in the year 1671.[52] After he has spoken in the first introductory chapter about the *oeconomia temporum* (successive eras of salvation) and the *oeconomia foederum* (the succession of the covenants in the economy of salvation), he says in §XIII:

> 'We shall begin therefore with God and his eternity and we shall subsequently walk through all ages until we end in eternity again' – then follows a quote from Romans 8:29-30, FB – 'as the Creed also, in the Apostolic summary of the faith, begins with the Almighty God, then moves to the work of creation and of redemption, and ends with eternal life.'

Thus Burmann also finds a place for the *explicatio symboli* (explanation of the Creed) in the scheme of the *historica series*. As the Cocceian federal theology with its 'mobility', as Barth called it, made its entry into old-Protestant loci-theology, the historicizing tendency in all of this theology was being emphasized much more strongly.[53]

In his *Summa doctrinae de foedere et testamento Dei* (Summary of the doctrine of the covenant and the testament of God)[54] of 1648, Johannes Cocceius (1603-1669) has tried to hold fast to the original concern of the proclamation of the Reformation. He did so by means of the doctrine of the *gradata antiquatio foederis operum* (the gradual aging of the covenant of works, §58), which dominates his entire book. This original concern was the 'dialectic of law and gospel'. In his opinion, the history of salvation is nothing but a progressing *antiquatio* (aging) of the *foedus operum* (covenant of works), in the form of five successive *abrogationes* (abolitions).

Barth has justly evaluated Cocceius's aim in a very positive way.[55] However, Cocceius's attempt has been in vain. His powerful relativizing of the covenant of works could no longer battle the every enlarging liberation of the original *foedus naturae* (covenant of nature) and the ever strengthening historicizing of theology (promoted by Cocceius himself), by which we ever more intensively make the movement from the beginning to the end. That was the result of the fact that the more balanced Renaissance Loci-theology had been turned into the dynamic and movable federal theology of the baroque. Already in the theology of Cocceius's student Burmann we see how the thought of the aging of the covenant of works shifts to the background. The 'walking through all the ages from the beginning to the end of the world' gains the upper hand in Burmann. For him, the early Reformation proclamation is no longer the heart of the matter.

§1.8 WITSIUS

When Herman Witsius (1636-1708)[56] in 1677 published his *De oeconomia foederum Dei cum homine* (The economy of salvation of God's covenants with man)[57] he did not intend to oppose Cocceius and his followers. He had two motives:

1. He, too, wished to offer a federal theology and a biblical theology in an anti-scholastic sense. Therefore, his main work does not consist in a loci-theology, but in a description of the *foedera Dei* (covenants of God).
2. The conservatism of Witsius consists in this, that he wished to maintain the static aspect of the loci-theology. He therefore removed the dynamics of federal theology in both forms. He rejected both the 'aging of the covenant of works' with the five *abrogationes* (abolitions),[58] and the division of the times in the 'walking through all ages'.

The *Oeconomia foederum* of Witsius consists of four books, which have no titles, but show agreement with the four books of Calvin's *Institutes* (in the final version): The Father – The Son – The Holy Spirit – The Church. The characteristic part of Witsius comes to the fore most emphatically in the third book, when he describes the *ordo salutis* (order of salvation). The historical process, which may be indicated with the aid of the Bible, becomes the biography of the predestined believers.[59] In an entirely new way, a *cantus graduum* (song of the steps) is sung with this.[60]

The movement and dynamics of Cocceius has disappeared in Witsius. As a result the 'covenant of nature before the fall' strongly asserts itself again. *Lex* has become to Witsius a complete *doctrina legis* (doctrine of the law) and that means: a complete *doctrina foederis legalis (operum, naturae) ante lapsum* (doctrine of the covenant of the law – i.e., of works, of nature – before the fall). This is discussed in the first book.

Evangelium has become a complete *doctrina evangelica* (evangelical doctrine), which means: a complete *doctrina foederis evangelicae (fidei, gratiae) post lapsum* (doctrine of the covenant of the gospel – i.e., of faith, of grace – after the fall). This is discussed in books II-IV. Thus we see the old scheme of *natura – gratia* return again, but in a historicized way this time.

The first of the nine chapters of book I is entitled: *De foederibus Dei in genere* (the covenants of God in general). It forms the introduction to the entire work (covenant of nature plus covenant of grace). After an introduction in the first paragraph, paragraphs 2-8 give a discussion of the *vox* (the etymology and meaning of the Hebrew and Greek word for 'covenant'). Paragraph 9 offers a definition of *foedus* (covenant, note the singular) and paragraphs 10-14 provide an explanation of the constitutive elements of the definition. If we should only pay attention to this *explicatio definitionis* (explanation of the definition) we would have to say that Witsius might better have entitled this first introductory chapter *de foederis Dei cum homine natura* (the covenant between God and man by nature). The *foedus* in paragraph 9 would then have to be explained on that line. Why did he not choose this title, but the title *de foederibus Dei in genere* (the plural *foedera*, covenants)? This becomes clear to us when we read the fifteenth and final paragraph of this chapter, of which the content is indicated in the margin as follows:

'The covenant is twofold: of works and of grace.'[61]

The content of this paragraph consists in this. First the *formula foederis operis* (the formula of the covenant of works) and the *formula foederis gratiae* (the formula of the covenant of grace) are given, with an appeal to respectively Romans 10:5 – 'the man who does these things, will live by the law' – and Romans 10:11 – 'no one who believes in him, will be ashamed'. After this both covenants are compared. First, the agreements[62] between them are listed, in four points:

1. In both covenants there are parties who make an agreement, God and man;
2. In both there is the promise of eternal life;
3. In both there is the same condition, namely the fulfillment of the law;
4. In both there is the same goal, namely the 'glory of God's holiest goodness'.

The covenants differ[63] in six ways:
1. In the first covenant God acts as the supreme giver of the law with regard to his creature. His creature lives in the state of righteousness. In the later covenant God acts as the merciful one toward the elected sinner;
2. 'In the covenant of works, there was no mediator. The covenant of grace has Christ as mediator';
3. 'In the covenant of works, the condition of perfect obedience was to be accomplished by man himself as covenant partner. In the covenant of grace this same condition is accomplished or completed by the mediator. In this lies the chief and essential difference of the covenants. In the latter, another person replaces the first covenant partner';[64]

4. In the covenant of works, man works for wages, and would have received wages if he had completed the works. In the covenant of grace, men in themselves are godless, but by grace receive eternal life because of the mediator;

5. The covenant of works is conditional; the covenant of grace exists purely by faith and perseverance in the promises;[65]

6. In the covenant of works God's virtues of holiness, goodness, and righteousness come to the fore (as they appear from his law). In the covenant of grace the glory of God's grace and wisdom (toward sinners) is shown.

In virtually all constitutive elements the two covenants appear to agree; they only appear to differ in what Witsius calls the *substitutio personae* (the one person takes the place of the other). That means: the mediator – who did not appear in the covenant of nature – puts himself in man's place, to do in the power of his divinity what man cannot do any longer. This is the *satisfactio* (satisfaction).[66] Witsius himself says that this is 'the chief and essential difference'. By this emancipation of the 'covenant of nature before the fall' this *foedus naturae* became a dominating background, a basis, a framework, indeed, one would have to say: a model for the later covenant of grace.

§1.9 À MARCK

The final phase of Reformed orthodoxy in The Netherlands, except from *De oeconomia Foederum* by Witsius, can also be seen very clearly in the *Compendium theologiae christianae* of his student and Leiden colleague, Johannes à Marck (1656-1732).[67] His *Compendium* became in two forms (in an elaborate and in an abbreviated form, both in Latin and in Dutch, in many editions) the orthodox textbook for eighteenth-century congregations in the Netherlands.[68] The book is structured as a conservative, static loci-theology in thirty-four chapters. Each chapter contains an average of about 30 paragraphs. There are a thousand paragraphs in total. Each one of these paragraphs consists of the *explicatio* (explanation) of a single thought. At the conclusion of the book, all of the material is summarized once more in a thousand *positiones* (theses). À Marck's *Compendium* begins of course with a chapter on 'theology' (Chap. 1), of which paragraph 27 gives a definition. Theology is:

'the doctrine which true religion delivers to sinful man on the basis of God's revelation, for man's salvation and for the glory of God'.[69]

Starting from the (Aristotelian) sentiment concerning a definition which needs to consist of the *genus proximum* (generic name) and the *differentia specifica* (specific characteristic) à Marck continues as follows:

'Thus we have the generic name (the doctrine)
and the principle (God's revelation in the Scriptures),
the object which it treats (true religion),
the subject which receives instruction (fallen man)
and the subordinate and the ultimate goal (man's salvation and God's glory).'[70]

The final paragraphs (§28-36) conclude the first chapter with the explication of this definition, by successively discussing the five components of which they exist (generic name – principle – object – subject – goal). In the final sentence of this chapter à Marck gives an overview of the whole of his *Compendium*:

> 'Starting with the principle, we shall move on with a discussion on object and subject, and finally round of our work with a discussion on the goal. We will then also reach the end and the goal of this Compendium.'[71]

À Marck is an excellent teacher (though he misses the elegant style of Witsius). As announced, the work consists of the following parts:

(1) Chapter 2: The Principle of Theology, or the Holy Scriptures

Here we find a direct identification between Scripture and revelation, 'as it were a freezing of the relationship between Scripture and Revelation'.[72] Also, because of the *infallibilitas* (infallibility) of the Scriptures (§22) under the authorship of the Holy Spirit, they are seen as absolutely reliable with regard to the *res naturales* (matters of nature) as well. This must lead to the complaint, that 'the critical philosophy and science of the world' must serve the congregation in bringing it to a new hearing of the words of Scripture in order to understand, to explain and to apply them according to their true kerygmatic intention.[73]

(2) Chapters 3-12: The Object of Theology: Religion

Religio is defined as follows (chap. 3 §4): 'The true concept to know and serve God' (*recta ratio Deum cognoscendi & colendi*). According to à Marck, then, true religion is about the *cognitio Dei* (knowledge of God) and the *cultus Dei* (the service to God).

Chapter 3 is the introduction to chapters 4-10, which deal with the knowledge of God: God (4), the trinity (5), the decrees of God: in general (6), predestination: in particular (7), creation (8), the angels (9), providence (10). Chapters 11-12 deal with the service to God: the law as norm of religion (11) and the explanation of the Decalogue (12).

We have seen that à Marck, beginning with Chapter 1, composed his book in four main parts. However, he has not expressed that in the outward form. Taking the book in hand and glancing at the table of contents, one would think this is an ordinary orthodox loci-dogmatics.[74] Certainly, à Marck also intended it that way. As a good teacher he only arranged the dogmatic material somewhat more conveniently for his students. He therefore moved the doctrine on 'man' somewhat to the back. This locus – *de hominis creatione et natura* (creation and nature of man, chapter 13) – has been taken out of the context where this locus always appears: creation, angels, and providence. It is but a small thing. However, though he did not notice what he actually did with that – neither did Bernardinus de Moor in his commentary – we need to notice what happened when this was done.

À Marck moved the locus about 'man' somewhat to the back because he first wished to discuss everything concerning God in chapters 3-12. Here, he talks about the God of the eternal decrees and of the *opera naturae* (works of nature) of the law as the eternal and temporal 'presupposition' of the *historia hominis* (history of man). In chapters 13-34 – that is, in the remainder of the *Compendium*, almost two-thirds of the entire book – he exclusively discusses the subject of man and everything relating to man.

(3) Chapters 13-33: The Subject of Theology: Man

As the object of theology was introduced in the third chapter, 'Religion,' so the subject of theology is introduced in the thirteenth chapter, 'Man'. At the beginning of this chapter we read in the margin: *transitus ad hominum* (transition to man). The first sentence of this chapter (and thus of this entire subject) reads:

'The consideration concerning God, the knowledge of him and the service to him, is followed in theology the knowledge concerning man himself as the one who needs to know and serve God.'[75]

In paragraph 2 we now hear the definition of man:

'A creature,
consisting of a well functioning and upright walking body
and a rational soul united with it,
and which is made for the knowledge and praise of the divine glory,
first created by God in a most happy state,
then fallen by sin into the greatest misery,
however, from that was redeemed by Christ,
and beatified for eternity.'[76]

In the first three lines this definition announces what will be discussed in the thirteenth chapter (in §§3-18); in the final four lines this definition announces all that will follow in all of the *Compendium*, namely:

Status integritatis:	man in the state of righteousness	chapter 14
Status lapsus:	man in the fallen state	chapters 15-16
Status gratiae:	man in the state of grace	chapters 17-33
Status gloriae:	man in the state of glory	chapter 34.

With this, the fourth and final main part of the book is mentioned as well:

(4) Chapter 34: The Goal of Theology: the Beatification of Man

Thus, this whole section on man deals with *De homine in quadruplici statu*, man in his four stages.[77] To properly grasp the situation, we need to hear the words of chapter 14 §1:

'To man, whose creation and nature we have heretofore discussed, theologians on the basis of Scripture assign a threefold or a fourfold state: [1] that of the first righteousness in which he was created; [2] that of the misery in which he fell by sin; [3] that of grace, in which he is restored by God; and [4] that of glory, when he finally arrives by God's favor to the state of grace. According to some, this fourth state belongs in fact to the third. In order to follow the thread of history and of the matter itself, we begin this discussion with the first state, which is often called the "state of innocence," but more frequently and properly it is called the "state of righteousness," which more clearly expresses its character.'[78]

Even if we do not see the Voetian à Marck 'walking through all the centuries' in a Cocceian fashion with Burmann, he still follows the *historiae filus*, the thread of history, and in his view this thread is the *rei ipsius filus*, the thread of the thing that matters. The thread of the thing that matters is simultaneously the thread of the historical sequence.

And only now that à Marck begins to speak in all of this material about 'man in his fourfold state' as 'covenant man,' he also speaks – which he did not do in the discussion on 'the object of theology' – about God, as 'the covenant God'. All of God's acts as the God of the Covenant, all of the *oeconomia foederum* (economy of salvation of the covenants), which à Marck had learned from Witsius, now find its place within the framework of *de homine*, man. And particularly all of the *foedus gratiae* (covenant of grace) – i.e., all of Christology,[79] soteriology, pneumatology, ecclesiology, and eschatology, in short: all of Christian faith – all of these are found in the framework of 'man in his recreated state'.[80]

We can now see the true concern of this *Compendium* of Voetian orthodoxy circa 1700: the *vera religio* (true religion) of *homo* (man) in *historia* (history) in its fourfold state. Historicizing, religionizing, and anthropologizing of theology – all of this is done. Sacred doctrine in this *Compendium* is a religious worldview (chapters 3-13) and a science of human history of religion (chapters 13-34). Thus, all neo-Protestantism is already enclosed in this Compendium, this final form of Reformed 'high orthodoxy'. Orthodox 'history' of 'man in his fourfold state' in 'true religion' could become the 'human history of religion'. Theology became (before and after Schleiermacher) 'science of religion'.[81] Protestant 'modernism' is nothing but consistent 'orthodoxy', and 'orthodoxy' after 1700 is inconsistent 'modernism'. Only a few things still needed to happen, only a few more labour pains needed to come, only a few more nudges were needed for the collapse of the orthodox building which appeared so intact and then – neo-Protestantism was born. The 'critical philosophy of the world' would take care of those few things, those few labour pains, those few nudges.

§1.10 BUDDEUS

Neo-Protestantism was born from the inside out. It was the logical outcome of old-Protestant theology. It was in the transitional period of the so-called rational orthodoxy when this birth took place.[82] One may think of theologians like Joh. Franz Buddeus (1667-1729), Christoph Matthäus Pfaff (1686-1760) and J. L. von Mosheim (1694-

1755) in Germany, and Samuel Werenfels (1657-1740),[83] Joh. Friedrich Osterwald (1663-1747) and Jean Alphonse Turrettini (1671-1737) in Switzerland.[84] The fathers of these theologians were all still fully 'orthodox'. So were their pietist-rationalist sons. At the same time they were no longer totally so. A symptom of the enormous difference between these two generations is what happened in Geneva with the Swiss *Formula Consensus* of 1675 (directed against the theology of Saumur), composed by Heidegger of Zurich, by request of a number of Swiss cities. Franciscus Turrettini (1623-1687) took much trouble to have this orthodox *Formula consensus* used in Geneva as well in 1679. About twenty-five years later his son Jean Alphonse Turrettini does his utmost in 1706 to put this *Formula* out of use.[85] The tendency which in all of the development of the old-Protestant theology had been secretly at work and which began to manifest itself openly in the theology of 'rational orthodoxy' consisted in this: something which can be known generally came to function as a 'presupposition', 'criterion', and 'framework' for the understanding and explanation of the particulars of revelation.[86] To see how this happened, we will now focus on two theologians of the time of rational orthodoxy: Johannes Franciscus Buddeus and Jean Alphonse Turrettini, though not all of them spoke as drastically as these two.

The main work of Joh. Fr. Buddeus was the *Institutiones theologiae dogmaticae* (1723), which was divided into five books.[87] As a somewhat younger Lutheran contemporary of à Marck,[88] his work agrees in many respects with the latter. He, too, is predominantly conservative in attitude.[89] He gives a modest place to the federal-theological method, but without letting it becoming determinative for the structure of his dogmatics.[90] With him the anthropologizing of theology was completed while he did not seem to be aware of it at all.[91] It is precisely in the work of Buddeus and his generation that we see the transition from 'potential heresy' to obvious heresy. He is taking but a small step perhaps, but it is a decisive one. The first book consists of two chapters:

First chapter: On Religion and Theology
Second chapter: On Revelation and the Holy Scriptures.[92]

With à Marck the sequence was:

1. Theology – 2. The Holy Scriptures (= Revelation) – 3. Religion.

This traditional sequence was already dangerous, in that there was mention of *theologia* already before Scripture was referred to, as on the one hand *naturalis* (natural) and on the other hand *revelata* (revealed). Buddeus takes a further step: *de religione* (religion) precedes, and *de revelatione* (revelation) follows afterward. In connection with this preceding *religio, theologia* is mentioned, and in connection with *revelatio* discussed afterward, *Scriptura sacra* is the topic. The general *notiones* (concepts) of the *religio naturalis* (natural religion) function here as criterion. Religion determines what is revelation.[93] The possibility determines what is real.[94]

In the first chapter 'On theology' the old orthodoxy first described the *theologia naturalis* (natural theology) and then claimed that it was *insufficiens ad salutem* (insufficient for salvation) after the fall. Yet, it had remained of great significance and was presupposed by the *theologia revelata* (revealed theology). This is how Buddeus also proceeds in the first chapter, the difference being that he not only speaks of a natural and revealed theology, but about natural and revealed religion. Only then does he speak about theology:

§§1-15: description of the content of natural religion (*cognitio et cultus Dei*, knowledge of and service to God) as the *recta ratio* (properly functioning reason) teaches it;

§§16-18 'after the fall' this 'natural religion' is 'insufficient for salvation'. Our 'properly functioning reason' teaches us this (§§16-17). Holy Scripture also confirms it (*quod et Scriptura Sacra confirmat*, §18). *Ratio docet, scriptura confirmat* (reason teaches, Scripture confirms). We see this pattern return time and again in his work.

§19-22 Though insufficient for salvation, natural religion is still of great benefit. It contains – and this is what the orthodox fathers had never said this way – the criteria for distinguishing the *vera revelatio* (true revelation).

These final four paragraphs are of the greatest importance for the understanding of Buddeus. They read as follows:

'XIX. Natural religion is not rejected to such a degree that it does not still prove its worth. Its theoretical concepts form the pillars and the foundations of every religion. For this reason, anyone who rejects one of these concepts must be regarded as someone who has no religion at all, or someone who embraces the ugliest and most despicable superstition. It is fitting, after all, that natural religion shows us the characteristics to recognize religions which are derived from revelation in the proper way. Those who reckon with something which is diametrically opposed to these concepts either err despicably, in that they hold a revelation for divine when it is not, or they fail to properly understand the spirit and the meaning of divine revelation.

XX. Natural religion shows itself moreover to be a more than excellent pedagogy, by stimulating investigation of true revelation, and to recognize it in the proper way. The natural light, compared to the highest goodness of the Supreme Being, is insufficient for salvation. Nevertheless, it shows us the necessity of its revelation. It also helps us to distinguish between true and false revelation.

XXI. For the name of true and divine revelation, which we must adhere to, contains nothing which contradicts the most evident insights of natural religion. It perfects them by providing for this things which natural religion lacks and which even stand in our way, so as to keep us from searching for eternal salvation. For if divine revelation is compared to natural religion, and the other marks of divine origin show themselves, the truth of the revelation needs no longer be in doubt.

XXII. And by this same reason is understood that true and divine revelation must be universal: it has begun with the first origin of the human race, as long as there were at least people in this state, and it stretches all along the whole line, no one excepted. After all, there cannot be proposed any reason why God would share of himself more benevolently to some and would refuse the same to others; or, if such a reason could be adduced, it is not difficult to see, why it would be unworthy of God.'

Indeed, here we see the birth of neo-Protestantism.

§1.11. JEAN ALPHONSE TURRETTINI

In his *Theses de theologiae naturali in genere* (theses on natural theology in General) Turrettini writes as follows:[95]

Thesis I

'Theology is the discipline which deals with God and divine matters.'[96]

Here, Jean Alphonse repeats the description of his father Franciscus. In his *Institutio theologiae elencticae* (1679-1686) the description of the concept 'theology' is as follows:

Locus primus, Quaestio I.vii:

'The concept of "theology" is used in a threefold way in literature: 1. In a broad sense; 2. In a narrow sense; 3. According to the proper range of its significance. In the first sense it is found ... in Aristotle ... (as a part of metaphysics). In the second ... in the Fathers ... (as a contemplation of all that concerns the deity of Christ, in contrast to the economy of salvation). In the third and most appropriate sense it is conceived of as a *syntagma*, that is, as a well ordered whole of doctrines concerning God and divine matters, revealed by God to his glory and for the salvation of human beings. In this last meaning it will be dealt with by us.'[97]

Thesis II

'Since God reveals himself in two ways to men – first by natural light, to all mortals in common, then by documents of men who have been inspired by God – a twofold theology appears: *a natural and a revealed*.'[98]

J. A. Turrettini tells us here how the words, by which Calvin in 1558/59 form the perspective of biblical theology motivated the definitive form in section I.2.1 of his *Institutio Christianae religionis* were explained a little more than 150 years later. After all, Calvin did not say: 'Because the Lord first reveals himself simply and then in a twofold way', but: 'Because the Lord appears first' – before the fall, FB – 'simply as creator, and then' – after the fall, FB – 'in the face of Christ as redeemer – there follows a twofold knowledge of God.'[99]

When Brunner in his plea for a Christian *theologia naturalis* in his little book *Natur und Gnade* appeals to Calvin to demonstrate that his vision is 'good Reformation,' Barth reproaches Brunner as follows: 'Brunner has made Calvin into someone like a Jean Alphonse Turrettini.'[100] When can you call something 'good biblical' or 'good Reformation'? That is the question we are trying to answer.

Thesis III

'No one should think that these two kinds of theology – which, after all, have the same author, namely God – should be in conflict. To the contrary, they work together in a most friendly way and assist one another. For the revealed theology presupposes the natural *and cannot be known and explained in any other way than with the first principles which were borrowed from natural theology.* On the other hand, natural theology is restored, perfected and clarified by revealed theology.'[101]

In the italicized words we hear Jean Alphonse say what is the difference between him and his orthodox father. The formulations of the father are as follows:

Locus primus Quaestio IX: 'Does reason have any judgment in matters of faith? Or does it serve no use at all?'

I.IX.V. 'Though human understanding is utterly blinded, a few rays of natural light have remained. Certain first principles of truth are undoubted: that the whole is more than its part, that the effect presupposes a cause, that being and non-being at one and the same moment cannot be united, etc. If this were not so, not a single science or art could exist, neither would anything in the nature of things be certain. 2. These first principles should not only be held to be certain in nature but also in grace and in the mysteries of faith. Faith, far from destroying them, to the contrary borrows from reason, using it to confirm its own dogma's. 3. No matter how much reason and faith differ in order – the one natural, the other supernatural –, yet they are not contradictory, but find themselves in a mutual relationship and they are subordinated to each other: reason is perfected by faith, and faith presupposes reason to add the mysteries of grace to it.'

Locus primus Quaestio XIII: 'Can philosophy be used in any way in theology? The answer is affirmative.'

I.XIII.III. 'Though not everything that is true can be proven by reason (truth knows many wider perimeters that those of the limits of reason), yet a lie can never find support in reason against the truth. Neither can one truth ever be cancelled by another truth, no matter how much the one may transcend and supersede the other. For no matter what truth is involved – a [truth] *infra rationem* (below reason), as observed in feeling; a [truth] *juxta rationem* (on the level of reason), as observed in understanding; a [truth] *supra rationem* (above reason) as observed in faith –: it does not originate anywhere else than from God who is the Father of truth. Thus grace does not destroy nature, but perfects it and does not cancel supernatural revelation, but purifies it.'[102]

'Grace does not cancel nature, but presupposes and perfects it' (Thomas). That has now also become the basic principle of Protestant dogmatics. However, father Franciscus does not yet express the words, which were italicized in the third thesis of Jean Alphonse.

Thesis XXII

'Natural theology is the basis and foundation of revealed theology. Revealed theology cannot exist without the natural in any way. Things which we are taught by nature do not need confirmation from the outside; they prove themselves. We are born with them, because we are born as men gifted with reason. Therefore, they cannot be rejected by anyone with full understanding. The revelation, however, is contained in a certain few books. It must be made acceptable to us before it can be granted admission. But it can only be made acceptable by way of first principles, derived from natural light.'[103]

The difference between the two generations lies also in this, that Franciscus, the father, still favored Aristotle, but the son Jean Alphonse on the other hand favored Descartes.[104] It is not we who, wishes and thinking, speaking, and acting, exist within the scope of revelation, as Scripture says and the church proclaims, but the other way round. The revelation contained in Scripture exists within the space of our own self-consciousness. For our own self-consciousness is indisputable and unassailable. It is given directly and does not need any outside proof and confirmation. Revelation must first be proved by reason, before we can accept it. This fatal reversal characterizes all of neo-Protestantism. In the following thesis we hear how radical Jean A. Turrettini intended this reversal to be:

Thesis XXIII

'How can I be sure that the things which God revealed must be believed, when I have not learned from the natural light that God is true and that therefore He cannot deceive me? How can I be sure that this or that revelation truly has God as its author, when the natural light has not taught me, what is worthy or unworthy of God and what therefore are the characteristic qualities of divine revelation? How can I be moved to display a certain devotion to God, fulfill duties for Him, engage myself toward observing respect and virtue, if I have not learned from the natural light what a task is, what it is to be obligated to something, what the fundamentals of duty are and what distinguishes the righteous from the unrighteous, the reverent from the ungodly? If indeed "righteous" and "unrighteous" are nothing but empty words (as the poet says) and if something like a natural duty should not exist, then not a single revelation could move me to do or not to do something. Therefore, these natural concepts must necessarily be laid as a foundation. Tertullian rightly says: "God has sent nature ahead so that he might send out prophecy only later. As a student of nature you will more easily accept the prophecy in faith".'[105]

Three times we hear first the word 'how?' (*quomodo*) and then follows: 'therefore' (*itaque*). We now understand that Jean Alphonse Turrettini might be called 'the local liberal theologian' of Geneva.[106]

The theologians of 'rational orthodoxy' at the beginning of the eighteenth century thought they could appeal to the apologetes of the second century. In the twenty-seventh thesis, not only Tertullian of the second century, but all the Fathers of the early church are called to witness in favor of Turrettini's thoughts on the relationship between natural and revealed theology:

Thesis XXVII

'Those early doctors, who are called Church Fathers, particularly those who lived in a very early and besides very favourable era, had been brilliantly sensitive to natural theology, and they came very close to identifying natural and revealed theology.'[107]

In a lecture we hear Barth say in 1939:

> 'One does not need to dispute with a great many people today, that in the history of modern Protestant theology a very deep-seated error has played a disastrous role which we should avoid in the future if possible. Where is this error?'[108]

Our study was dedicated to answering this question.

§2. KARL BARTH'S *CHURCH DOGMATICS* AS A PROPOSAL TO THE HEARING AND TEACHING CHURCH

Ultimately, Barth has addressed only one question in his *Church Dogmatics* to all other theologians.[109] It is a very definite, unambiguous and decisive question. It is the one which we have to formulate here at the conclusion.

Barth asks: Have I seen rightly and understood correctly, have I heard well, when I say: in my *Kirchliche Dogmatik* I have tried to express the consequence of Reformation theology – when one look at the heart of this doctrine – in a radical renewal of all of doctrine? Have I heard rightly, when I say that the revelation of God is identical with the grace of God in Jesus Christ and thus with reconciliation? Am I right that therefore the doctrine of reconciliation has to be the material center of all of dogmatics? Have I seen and understood correctly, when I say that the reformers (and later 'orthodoxy') remained caught up in an unbiblical tradition (*natura – gratia*) with regard to their doctrine of the *duplex dei cognitio*? Am I right to say that – when one looks not the heart of their doctrine, but at their thesis of the *duplex Dei cognitio* – neo-Protestantism (in the eighteenth century its pre-history, in the nineteenth century its history till Troeltsch)[110] is not only the consequence of the 'orthodoxy' of the seventeenth century, but already of Reformation theology in the sixteenth century itself? Have I seen and understood correctly when I say that we therefore in the twentieth century cannot simply continue the line from Calvin via 'orthodoxy' (albeit it in a modernized form) without letting eighteenth and nineteenth neo-Protestantism asking us some decisive questions, from Schleiermacher for instance, but also and precisely from Feuerbach? Am I right, therefore, to say that we should say *everything* differently ('aliter'), basing ourselves on the hermeneutical and dogmatic presupposition 'because of a simple appearance of God, therefore also a simple knowledge of God' (Cf. Inst. 1559 I.2.1) – precisely as a consequence of what is at the heart of Reformation doctrine? Not for the sake of saying it otherwise, but for the sake of the truth we need to proclaim, for the sake of salvation and comfort of man, whom we have to proclaim the truth.

We ask: Does the *aliter* of Calvin (i.e., *the duplex cognitio Dei*) – when we compare him to Barth – form a (the!) potential heresy, because via his *duplex Dei cognitio* natural theology had already secretly begun its victorious march? Or does the *aliter* of Barth – when we compare him to Calvin – form a (the?) potential heresy, because his thesis of the *simplex Dei cognitio* has forced him to conform everything to his own system (*Systemzwang*) and to deduce everything from the principle of grace?

Karl Barth stands over against all other theologians. Karl Barth says: your hermeneutical and dogmatic foundation – 'because of a twofold appearance of God, therefore also a twofold knowledge of God' – means, even if you have a strict and exclusive doctrine of Scripture, that in your teaching and proclamation you continually also pursue 'natural theology' (and it is only thanks to the 'happy inconsistency'[111] that your doctrine is to such a degree pure doctrine in spite of this).

All other theologians say to Barth: your hermeneutical and dogmatic foundation – 'because of a simple appearance of God, therefore also a simple knowledge of God' – means, in spite of all your appeals to Holy Scripture, that you do not do justice to the riches of the Holy Scriptures. Your Christological concentration means forcing everything into one system, it is a monism, an narrowing a priori. (Of course, we do not wish to deny that your theology is of immeasurable significance for the whole church and will remain so for the time being.)

We cannot of course conclude with a mere opposition, Karl Barth versus all other theologians. We – and that means: all of the church – are required and challenged to decide. The question, which Karl Barth has placed before us, demands an answer.[112]

NOTES

1. See, in addition to Inst. 1559: II.6 also the Argumentum (the foreword) of his commentary on Genesis (CO XXIII, op. cit., columns 9-10, the passage about 1 Cor 1:21).

2. Already in the *Institutes* of 1539, Calvin had called the 'third use of the law', namely, its function in the life of believers under the rule of the Holy Spirit, the 'principal use' (see above, chap. IV, n. 149). He wishes to express this also in the Catechism by discussing the Decalogue no longer before, but after the Creed. He therefore chooses an entirely different composition for this catechetical booklet.

3. CO IX, 739-741; W. Niesel, *Bekenntnisschriften*, op. cit., 65ff. and J. N. Bakhuizen van den Brink, *De Nederlandsche Belijdenisgeschriften*. Vergelijkende teksten, Amsterdam 1940, 58 (continued on 70).

4. Cf. K. Barth, KD II.1, 141 (CD, 127).

5. Precisely as in the *Institutes* of 1536 (= a catechism!), in the catechism of 1542 the *duplex cognitio* does not play a role. Neither does it do so in the previous and following catechetical literature. See M. A. Gooszen, *De Heidelbergse Catechismus*. Textus Receptus met toelichtende teksten, Leiden 1890. Here it may be said what Barth, KD IV.1, 92 (CD, 88) says of the Catholic doctrine of grace: one did not *live* by this doctrine (of the 'duplex cognitio').

6. In an 'utriusque doctricae conjunctio', see below, n. 42 (J. Gerhard).

7. CO I, 292.

8. OS III, 60 l. 31–62 l. 7. Italics added.

9. We do not yet hear Calvin speak of a 'foedus naturale' (covenant of nature). However, G. Schrenk (op. cit., 45) remarks: 'Indeed, a passage in the *Institutes* of 1559 comes close to this distinction (foedus naturale – foedus gratiae)' and then refers to a footnote from Inst. I.6.1 where this sentence occurs.

10. Thus, with Calvin not each part of doctrine is 'in Christo fundata' (grounded in Christ).

11. In the original text, Calvin speaks of a 'sequence': opportune deinde series ipsa ad redemptionem nos deducet. This 'series ipsa' is the 'series historica' of Melanchthon. See above, chap. IV §2.4.

12. CR 21, 139 l. 17–140 l. 14; Ed. Plitt-Kolde, op. cit., 140-141; St.A. II.1, 66 l. 13–67 l. 14.

13. See above, Chap. I §1, particularly note 8.
14. Term by H. Berkhof in his contribution to the volume by E. Kinder and K. Haendler, *Gesetz und Evangelium*, op. cit. (58-75) 71: 'Not the order law-gospel or gospel-law, about which we might do battle with our Lutheran brothers (...) but the extrapolation of the dialectic relationship between law and gospel in general, and the exclusive claim of the law-gospel scheme in particular as the formal principle of all of dogmatics, seem to us inadmissible.'
15. Cf. G. Schrenk, op. cit., 49: 'The Loci (in their later form, FB) exercised a great influence in the circles of the German Reformed.'
16. CR 21, 417; The entire part 'Quare opus est Evangelii promissione' was verbally taken over from the Loci of the second *aetas* in the third *aetas*. See CR 21, 735; St. A. II.1, 348 ll. 11-14.
17. Heidelberg Catechism answer of Question 54; Latin text with Bakhuizen van den Brink, op. cit., 172.
18. Still in the nineteenth century was published in twenty-seven parts (by M. l'Abbé J. P. Migne): *Histoire Ecclésiastique depuis la création jusqu' au pontificat de Pie IX*, Paris 1858-1883.
19. Calvin said in Inst. 1559: I.6.1: 'this order God has maintained for his church since the beginning.'
20. Another example: Heinrich Bullinger, a writing from the year 1537 with the title: *Der alte Glaube, das ist klarer Erweis, dass der christliche Glaube von Anfang der Welt gewährt habe und dies der rechte, wahre, alte und ungezweifelte Glaube sei.*
21. St.A. VI (Bekenntnisse und kleine Lehrschriften, herausgegeben von Robert Stupperich, Gütersloh 1955), 184 l. 35 – 185 l. 13, 185 ll. 27-29 and 187 ll. 16-21 for the German text. For the Latin text, see above, Chapter IV n. 106.
22. Cf. the 'creatura rationalis' of Thomas Aquinas.
23. Compare with this citation the words of Calvin from the Institutes of 1539: 3.80 = Inst. 1559: II.8.51: 'It will not be difficult now to judge which purpose entire law serves. It serves the fulfillment of righteousness, so that human life be formed according to the example of the divine purity. *For God had portrayed his nature in the law* so that, if anyone in his acts represents something of the law, he will express the image of God in one way or another in his life'; OS III, 390 ll. 15-20, italics added.
24. 'The Command of the God of Creation' (KD III.4, Chapter XII); 'The Command of God the Reconciler' (KD IV.4, Chapter XVII), 'The Command of God the Redeemer' (not written).
25. The reference to Genesis 3:15 is about the so-called protevangelium (or the 'mother's promise'): semen mulieris conteret caput Serpentis (the seed of the woman will crush the head of the serpent).
26. K. Barth, KD I.2, 562 (CD, 507).
27. K. Barth, KD I.2, 546 (CD, 493).
28. *Catechesis, summa theologiae per questiones et responsiones exposita: sive capita religionis Christianae continens* (Catechism, containing the essence of theology, expounded by means of questions and answers, or chapters from the Christian religion): the so-called Catechismus Major.
29. The way in which the scheme of law and gospel was historicized, which Ursinus had learned from Melanchthon, is also to be found in the Heidelberg Catechism (as a 'Catechismus minor', drafted also by him). It appears from Question and Answer 19 (as the conclusion of the complex of questions 3-19: 'Law and gospel'). Question 19: 'How do you know this? Answer. From the holy gospel which God revealed *in the beginning* in Paradise, and which was *afterwards* proclaimed by the holy patriarchs and prophets, and foreshadowed by the sacrifices and other ceremonies of the law, and *finally*, fulfilled by his well-beloved Son.' (Italics added.)
30. See August Lang, *Der Heidelberger Catechismus und vier verwandte Katechismen (Leo Juds*

und Microns kleine Katechismen sowie die zwei Vorarbeiten Ursins), mit einer historisch-theologischen Einleitung herausgegeben von A. Lang, Leipzig, [1]1907, Darmstadt [2]1967, (152-199) 156.

31. Quid est discrimen Legis et Evangelii? *Lex* continet *foedus naturale*, in creatione a Deo cum hominibus initum, hoc est, natura hominibus nota est; et requirit a nobis perfectam obedientiam erga Deum, et praestantibus eam, promittit vitam aeternam, non praestantibus minatur aeternas poenas. Evangelium vero continet foedus gratiae, hoc est, minime natura notum existens: ostendit nobis ejus justitiae, quam Lex requirit, impletionem in Christo, et restitutionem in nobis per Christi Spiritum; et promittit vitam aternam gratis propter Christum, his qui in eum credunt.

32. A. Lang, op. cit., LXV.

33. Cf. K. Barth, KD IV.I, 62 (CD, 59).

34. Francisci Gomari Brugensis viri clariss. *Opera Theologica omnia*, secundis Curis emendatiora, Amstelodami anno MDCLXIV. Prolegomena. I. 'Oratio de Foedere Dei'. Quae est instar praefationis in Novum Testamentum, habita Lugduni Batavorum Anno 1594, octavo die Junii. Because it forms the background for his exegesis of the New Testament, the publishers of his *Opera Theologica omnia* put it up front under the 'prolegomena'. In the dissertation by G. P. van Itterson, *Franciscus Gomarus. Met portret, een fascimile en 57 onuitgegeven bijlagen*, 's Gravenhage 1930, we do find a very precise transcript of this 'oratio' (48-50), but not a discussion. A theological conversation with Gomarus is lacking.

35. *Hoc porro foedus est duplex, Naturale et Supernaturale.* Naturale est foedus Dei natura notum, quod Deus vitam aeternam promittit tantum, & conditionem perfectae obedientiae ab hominibus requirit. Eoque naturale rite vocatur, quia pectoribus humanis natura insculptum, Rom 2.14, 15. Italics added.

36. In this formulation (the distinction between 'natura notum' and 'non natura notum') we clearly note the influence of Melanchthon and Ursinus.

37. Repetitum est postea hoc foedus & ceremoniis etiam obsignatum per Mosen, *cujus ministerium fuit duplex*, primarium quidem legem seu foedus naturale promulgare (...) secundarium vero fuit renovare memoriam foederis supernaturalis & gratuiti cum Abrahamo et Israëlitis olim initi, ut promissiones Mosaicae probant, Deuter. 18. v. 25. & alibi, & Christus Apostolique testantur, Joh. 5.46. Actor. 3.21. &c....

38. We might compare Gomarus's oration on his entry as professor of dogmatics in Leiden (1594) with the inaugural oration by K. H. Miskotte also as professor in Leiden on Friday, 26 October 1945 on 'The Practical Sense of the *Simplicity* of God'.

39. *The Book of Concord*, ed., Theodore G. Tappert. Philadelphia 1959, 558.

40. The beginning of point 1 reads as follows in the Latin text: 'Cum discrimen legis et evangelii magnam et clarissimam lucem sacris litteris adferat, cuius adminiculo verbum Dei recte secari et prophetica atque apostolica scripta dextre explicari atque intelligi possunt: accurata diligentia illud est in ecclesia conservandum atque retinendum, *ne haec duo doctrinarum genera* inter se commisceantur, aut evangelion in legem transformetur.' Italics added. Ottto Weber remarks in his *Grundlagen der Dogmatik* II, op. cit., 416, n.3, as follows: 'When the FC SD V.1 lifts up the distinction between lex and evangelium to a hermeneutical criterion, we should not overlook that the same 'Word' might be Law or also Gospel. Indeed, *every* "Word" might become "Law" but also "Gospel" to us. The difference cannot by quantified.'

41. A reissue of the *Loci theologici* in the nineteenth century in Leipzig: volumes 2 through 9 in the years 1864-1875, vol. I in a second printing in the year 1885. The loci 12-16 may be found in the third volume, the cited paragraph in columns 140-141.

42. These sentences read in Latin: Ex eo tempora in ecclesia semper conjuncta fuit legis et evangelii praedicatio, quam utriusque doctrinae conjunctionem ipsius Dei *prooteuaggelistos* exemplum comprobavit. Convenienti igitur ordine legis divinae explicationi succedit doctrina

evangelii.

43. *Synopsis purioris Theologiae*, comprehensa ac conscripta per Johannem Polyandrem, Andream Rivetum, Antonium Walleaum, Antonium Thysium, SS. Theologiae Doctores et Professores in Academia Leidensi, Lugduni Batavorum 1625, Leiden [6]1881.

44. Thomas Aquinas, *S. Th.* I Question 3 a 5. In the following, the colometry was added.

45. See above, Chap. III §1.

46. Franciscus Turrettini, *Institutio Theologiae Elencticae*, Pars prior, [1]Geneva 1679, [9]Geneva 1688. English translation by George Musgrave Giger in three volumes, published by James T. Morrison Jr., Phillipsburg, NJ: I. First Through Tenth Topics, 1992; II. Eleventh through Seventeenth Topics, 1994; III. Eighteenth through Twentieth Topics, 1997.

47. To which Fr. Turrettini does not belong, however: he allowed the order of the decrees to dominate but arranged them in an infralapsarian way.

48. K. Barth, KD II.2 §33.1: 'Jesus Christ, Electing and Elected'. On Barth's judgment of the Reformed doctrine of the decrees, see also above, Chap. III, n. 103.

49. Quemadmodum per legem, de qua supra disputavimus, *morbi* nostri spiritualis, nimirum peccati, contagium ac labes, sic ejus *remedium* per Evangelium cognoscitur. Italics added.

50. The term 'federal theology' indicating the theology of Cocceius and his followers is somewhat misleading. With virtually all theologians of the second half of the seventeenth century, we find the distinction between the *foedus naturae* (ante lapsum) and the *foedus gratiae* (post lapsum); yet not all theologians who speak of the 'duplex foedus' (twofold covenant), are called federal theologians.

51. K. Barth, KD IV.1, 58 (CD, 55).

52. We use the Dutch translation: Franciscus Burmannus, *Synopsis dat is Kort Begryp der heilige God-Geleertheit, en voornamelijk van de Huishouding der Verbonden Gods. Van het begin toe tot aan het einde der Wereldt.* Translated by Dirk Smouth, Utrecht 1688.

53. To this we add a saying by Burmann's father-in-law, Abraham Heidanus (1597-1678, professor at Leiden from 1648 to his dismissal in 1676): the Holy Scriptures were 'not written by way of a system, but they describe the history of the church which has taken place from the beginning of the world to the end'; non scripta ut systema quoddam, sed *historica nobis facta Ecclesiae ab initio mundi ad finem* describet. Abraham Heidanus, *Corpus theologiae Christianae in quindecim locos digestum*, Lugduni Batavorum 1686; cited by Barth, KD I.1, 15 (CD, 16). Italics added.

54. Johannes Cocceius, *Summa doctrinae de foedere et testamento Dei*, 1648. Newly published in the Opera Omnia Tom. VI, Amstelodami 1673. Cocceius, originally primarily philologian and Hebraist, was professor at Bremen since 1630, at Franeker since 1636, and at Leiden since 1650.

55. K. Barth, KD IV.1, 57-70 (CD, 54-66).

56. From 1675-1680 he served as professor and pastor at Franeker, 1680-1698 at Utrecht as successor of Burmann.

57. Hermanni Witsii, *De oeconomia foederum Dei cum hominibus libri quator*, Leovardiae [1]1677.

58. *De oec. Foed.,* op. cit., 1 Caput 9.

59. In his dissertation *Herman Witsius*. Bijdrage to the kennis der gereformeerde theologie, 's Gravenhage 1953, 147, J. van Genderen opens his description of the third book of Witsius's *De Oeconomia Foederum* with the words: 'We now come to the heart of the dogmatic work of Witsius.' Voetians and Cocceians will find each other more and more in the pietism of Witsius.

60. In medieval scholastics, 'gratia' is an intermediate sphere between 'natura' and 'gloria'; 'gratia' is 'something', by which 'natura' rises by steps toward 'gloria' (Thomas, also Dante). Cf. Windelband-Heimsoeth, *Lehrbuch der Geschichte der Philosophie*, Tübingen 1935, §25,

267-276: 'Das Reich der Natur und das Reich der Gnade'.

61. Duplex foedus est, operum et gratiae.

62. Coveniunt haec foedera in eo, quod...

63. Differunt vero in hisce:...

64. Points 2 and 3 are in the Latin text: 2. In foedere Operum nullus fuit Mediator. Foedus Gratiae Mediatorem habet Christum. 3. De foedere Operum conditio perfectae obedientiae exigebatur, ut praestanda ab ipso homine foederato. In foedere Gratiae *eadem conditio* proponitur ut praestanda vel praestita a Mediatore, Et *in hac substitutione personae princeps ac essentialis foederum differentia est.* Italics added.

65. On this fifth point à Marck (see in the following paragraph) will differ from Witsius. In addition to 'beneficia' (benefactions) he also wishes to hear of 'officia sive conditiones foederis gratiae' (duties or conditions of the covenant of grace). See *Comp. Theol. Christ.* XXII.1-2.

66. Cf. The Heidelberg Catechism, Questions 12-19.

67. Professor at Franeker (1676-1682), at Groningen (1682-1689) (as a colleague and fierce opponent of the Cocceian Braunius), at Leiden (1689-1731). Van Genderen, op. cit., 54 calls him 'a devoted follower of Voetianism at the transition from the 17th to the 18th century'.

68. The *Compendium Theologiae Christianae didactico-elencticum* was published for the first time in Groningen in 1686 (⁴Amsterdam 1727). An abbreviated form for students, the *Christianae Theologiae Medulla*, was published in a first printing in Amsterdam in 1690 (⁵Amsterdam 1721). *Het Merch der christene Gotgeleertheit* (Rotterdam ¹1705, ⁴1741) is a Dutch translation and editing of the *Compendium* by à Marck himself, the *Kort Opstel der christene Got-Geleertheit* was a translation of the *Medulla* by Joh. Wilhelmius (Rotterdam ⁶1750). The Leiden professor Bernhardinus de Moor published, in seven large volumes, a detailed *Commentarius Perpetuus* (Leiden 1761-1771).

69. Doctrinam, quae veram Religionem ex Dei Revelatione homini peccatori tradit, ad hominis salutem Deique gloriam.

70. Ut habemus *Genus* (sc. *doctrinam*), Differentiamque, petitam à / *Principio* unde hauritur (sc. *Dei revelatio in Scriptura*) / *Objecto* quod tractat (sc. *vera religio*) / *Subjecto* quod instruitur (sc. *homo lapsus*) / *fine* denique subordinato (sc. *hominis salus*) et supremo (sc. *Dei gloria*).

71. A *Principio* inchoantes, *Objecto* et *Subjecto* pertractato, in hoc *Fine* finem quoque Compendii huius faciemus.

72. K. Barth, KD I.1 127 (CD, 124); also KD I.2, 576 (CD, 518). Cf. about the direct and indirect identity, KD I.1, 321 (CD, 304).

73. K. Barth, KD I.1, 128 (CD I.1, 124): 'The catastrophic crash of orthodoxy in the 18th century, the consequences of which we still have to carry to this day, is no more puzzling than the collapse of a house whose foundations are giving way. Responsibility for the disaster must be borne, *not by the philosophy of the world which had become critical*, but by the theology of the Church which had become too uncritical, which no longer understood itself at the centre.' Italics added.

74. As e.g., De veritate religionis reformatae seu evangelicae libri VII, Trajecti ad Rhenum 1688 of the militant follower of Voetius, Melchior Leydecker (1642-1721; from 1679 Professor at Utrecht).

75. Post *Deum* tractatur in Theologia etiam de *Homine*: utpote a quo Deus *agnosci et coli* debet.

76. Creatura / ex corpore organico erectoque et anima rationali illi unita constans, / ad Divinae gloriae agnitionem et praedicationem facta, / in statu primum felicissimo a Deo creata, / in summam miseriam hinc per peccatum lapsa, / ex ea secundum magnam partem per Christum restituenda, / et aeternum beanda.

77. Cf. Joh. Wollebius, *Chr. Theol. Comp.*, op. cit., Lib I Caput VIII §1: 'Hominus gubernatio tum in statu innocentiae et miseriae tum in statu gratiae et gloriae elucescit'; Lib. I Cap. XIII §1: 'Hactenus de statu innocentiae et miseriae; sequitur status gratiae et gloriae.' What the

Christianae theologicae compendium by the Basel professor and pastor, Johannes Wollebius, was to the theology of Reformed orthodoxy in the first half of the seventeenth century, the *Compendium Theologiae Christianae* by Johannes à Marck was – in a more comprehensive form – to the theology of circa 1700, namely a very concise and orderly, but also a complete summary of all of the doctrinal content of this theology.

78. 'Hominis, de cujus Creatione & Natura modo egimus, *Triplicem* vel *Quadruplicem* Theologi ex Scriptura tradunt *statum*; – institutum, qui alias Integritatis; – destitutum, qui lapsus; – restitutum, qui Gratiae; – & constitutum, qui Gloriae dicitur, ac sub Restituto à quibusdam comprehenditur. Historiae vero & rei ipsius filum secuti, à Primo nunc Statu inchoamus, qui frequenter *Innocentiae*, frequentius vero et melius *Integritatis*, vel *Rectitudinis*, dicitur, quod positiva ejus Conditio clarius sic innuatur.'

79. À Marck, *Comp. Theol. Christ.* Cap 18. See also the identical title of Locus XVII in H. Heppe, *Die Dogmatik der evangelisch-reformierten Kirche*. Dargestellt und aus den Quellen belegt ([1]1861, [2]1935). Neu durchgesehen und hrsg. von Ernst Bizer, Neukirchen 1958, 323ff. Something strange is going on here: at the conclusion of Chap. 18, in §§17-18, the appearance of the mediator suddenly – as in the *Doctrina de Foedere ad Testamento Dei* by Cocceius (op. cit., §§88-89) – turns out to be grounded in God's eternal Council by the 'pactum salutis patrem inter filiumque' (covenant of salvation between the Father and the Son), before §19 discusses the 'executio pacti salutis in tempore' (the execution of the covenant of salvation *in time*).

80. We are here reminded of R. Bultmann: 'Properly, therefore, Pauline theology is best developed, when it is presented as the doctrine of man,' *Die Theologie des Neuen Testaments*, op. cit., 188.

81. K. Barth, *Die christliche Dogmatik im Entwurf*, op. cit., 86.

82. Cf. K. Barth, KD I.1, 128 (CD, 124; cited above, n. 73); cf. KD I.2 (CD, 288, 313: 'It was (…) the modern movement of the so-called "rational orthodoxy," at the beginning of the 18th century, in which the catastrophe occurred and when Neo-Protestantism experienced its actual and public birth.' In 1934 Barth counseled Brunner to study this 'interesting intermediate stage' thoroughly; see 'Nein!,' op. cit., 46. Cf. already 'Abschied von *Zwischen den Zeiten*' (1933), Th.E.H. 7, 33.

83. See K. Barth, 'Samuel Werenfels und die Theologie seiner Zeit', Inaugural address held on Wednesday, May 6, 1936, in the Assembly Hall of the Basel University, in: *Evangelische Theologie* 1936, 180-203. Barth says here, op. cit., 184: 'Something old in the history of theology has ended here, something new has entered the plan, and all the further new, that since then and has entered deeply into the beginning of our century, is finally (…) only the lengthening and repetition of what then became the plan.' We need to note that Barth does not say: 'Something old in the history of Protestant theology here came to an end.' This is about 'something old in the history of theology in general'.

84. Karl Barth had already spoken about them in his lectures on Protestant theology. See *Die Protestantische Theologie,* op. cit., 118-135.

85. See G. Keizer, *Francois Turrettini. Sa vie et ses oeuvres et le consensus*, Kampen-Lausanne 1900, 96-219: 'Turrettini et le Consensus'; the article on the 'Helvetic Consensus Formula' in the PRE[3] 7, 647-654 (F. Trechsel); E. F. K. Müller, *Die Bekenntnisschriften der reformierten Kirche*, Leipzig 1903, LXIV ff., 861-870; K. Barth, KD I.2, 582 (CD, 524); KD IV.I, 407 (CD, 368); *Vorträge* I, 196.

86. K. Barth, KD I.2, 315 (CD, 289).

87. Franciscus Buddeus, *Institutiones Theologiae Dogmaticae*, Leipzig 1723 (1320 pp.), published again (with the *Institutiones Theologiae Moralis*, 706 pp.) [2]1724.

88. From 1693 Buddeus was professor of philosophy in Halle, from 1705 professor of theology at

Jena.

89. For example, it is amazing how faithfully Buddeus sets forth the traditional angelology (Book II, Chapter II §§19-39). All of the great doctrines of the old dogmatics still occur in his work and he broadly discusses them, *although* he is for a long time busy with something else, which may be seen in his presenting of the old dogmatics as he still presents it. With Buddeus this new material only peeks out every once in a while in his work. This is what makes it so interesting. The old system is presented in a full-blown way, yet at the same time, rationalism is creeping into it on all sides.

90. Like a Fr. Turrettini and virtually all Reformed theologians of the second half of the seventeenth century, the Lutheran Buddeus now also adds the thought of the covenant of works before, and the covenant of grace after the fall in the framework of the old loci theology. Cf. K. Barth KD IV.1, 58 (CD, 55; without naming Buddeus): 'At the beginning of the 18th century it [federal theology] also had an occasional influence amongst Lutherans....'

91. See how the second book ends with the third chapter: 'The blessedness of man and about all those other matters which contribute to this' and how this chapter subsequently forms the starting point for all of the content of the three following Books.

92. Caput primum: de Religione et Theologia / Caput secundum: de Revelatione et Scriptura Sacra.

93. Cf. on the other hand K. Barth, KD I, Chapter I: 'The Word of God as the Criterion of Dogmatics.' See also the excursus in KD I.2 §17.1, 'The Problem of Religion in Theology', 313-318 (CD, 288-290), where he discusses and evaluates the Lutheran Buddeus with the Reformed Salomon van Til (1643-1713).

94. Cf. on the other hand K. Barth, KD I.2, §13.1: 'The Objective Reality of Revelation' and also §16.1: 'The Subjective Reality of Revelation', and only after that §13.2: 'The Objective Possibility of Revelation' and §16.2: 'The Subjective Reality of Revelation'.

95. We cite from the *Opera Omnia*, Leeuwarden 1774, Tomus Primus, 40-51.

96. Theologia ea Disciplina dicitur, quae de Deo & rebus Divinis agit.

97. Franciscus Turrettini, op. cit., pars prima, Locus Primus, in the first edition Quaestio I.VII, in the ninth edition Q. I.VIII.

98. Cum vero duplici via sese Deus Hominibus notum faciat, primum quidem Naturali Lumine, Mortalibus omnibus communi, deinde Virorum divinitus adflatorum documentis, hinc duplex Theologia exsurgit, *Naturalis & Revelata.*

99. See above, Chapter IV §2.III in the discussion of the 1559 Institutes, Chapter II.6.

100. E. Brunner, *Natur und Gnade,* op. cit., 22-36; K. Barth, 'Nein!,' op. cit., 41.

101. Duae illae Theologiae species, cum eundem habeant auctorem Deum, haudquaquam inter se pugnare existamandae sunt. Contra amicissime inter se conspirant, & mutuas sibi suppetias ferunt. Nam Revelata Naturalem supponit, *nec nisi principiis e Naturali dictis dignoscitur atque explicatur.* Naturalis vicissim a Revelata restituitur, perficitur, atque illustratur. Italics added.

102. The concluding sentence reads: Ita gratia non destruat naturam, sed perficit, nec revelatio supernaturalis naturalem abrogat, sed repurgat. Cf. Thomas Aquinas, as cited above, Chapter IV, note 105.

103. Quid, quod Theologia Naturalis Revelatae basis veluti & fundamentum est, nec sine Naturali Revelata ullo modo consistere potest. Nam quae a Natura docemur, externa confirmatione non indigent; per se ipsa demonstrantur; cum iis nascimur, dum nascimur Homines, & ratione praediti, neque a quoquam rationis compote rejici possunt. *Sed Revelatio, certis quibusdam Libris comprehensa, probari nobis debet, antequam admittatur; nec nisi principiis e Lumine Naturali desumptis probari potest.*

104. Cf. K. Barth, *Die christliche Dogmatik im Entwurf.* Erster Band. Die Lehre vom Worte Gottes. Prolegomena zur christlichen Dogmatik, Munich 1927, 302; KD I.1, 203f. (CD I.1,

195f.).

105. Enimvero, *quomodo* certus esse possum, quaecunque Deus revelavit credenda esse, nisi ex Lumine Naturali didicero, Deum esse veracem, meque proinde fallere non posse? *Quomodo* certus esse possum, hanc vel illam Revelationem vere Deum auctorem habere, nisi me Naturale Lumen docuerit, quid sit Deo dignum, quidve indignum, & quinam proinde sint Revelationis Divinae Characteres? *Quomodo* etiam adduci potero, ut Cultum aliquem Deo exhibeam, ut quaedam officia ei persolvam, ut pietati & virtuti operam dem, nisi ope Luminis Naturalis didicero, quid sit officium, quid sit obligari ad aliquid, quae sint fundamenta obligationis, & quod Justum ab Injusto, Pium ab Impio, re vera distinguantur? Nam, si Justum & Injustum nihil sunt, si 'Virtutem verba vocas', ut habet Poëta, neque ulla detur naturalis obligato, sane nulla Revelatio ad aliquid agendum vel fugiendum me poterit adigere. *Itaque* notiones illae naturales tanquam fundamentum necessario praestruendae sunt. Recte Tertullianus (De Resurrectione carni, cap. 12): 'Praemisit Deus Naturam magistram, submissurus & Prophetiam, ut facilius credas Prophetiae, discipulus Naturae.' Quotes which are in italics in Turrettini's work are here given between quotation marks.

106. In the PRE^3 7, 653 l. 3.

107. Veteris illi Doctores, qui Patres Ecclesiae vocantur, illi praesertim, qui antiquissima adeoque optima vixerunt actate, de Theologia Naturali magnifice admodum senserunt, *parumque abfuit quominus illam Revelatae aequipararent.*

108. 'Die Souveränität des Wortes Gottes und die Entscheidung des Glaubens' (1939), *Th. St.* Heft 5, op. cit., 5. In his discussion of Emil Brunner's book on Schleiermacher, Barth indicates this event as 'the great catastrophe' ('Brunners Schleiermacherbuch', *Zwischen den Zeiten,* 1924, 60). Also, in his inaugural address on Werenfeld he spoke about 'eine völlige Katastrophe' ('Werenfeld', op. cit., 199); see also the cited references KD I.1, 128 ('katastrophale Zusammenbruch'; CD, 124: 'catastrophic crash') and KD I.2, 313 (CD, 288). In the *Einführung in die evangelische Theologie* (Zurich 1962, 127) he speaks about 'jene verhängnisvolle Wende vom 17. zum 18. Jahrhundert' as well.

109. On the first page of his brochure 'Natur und Gnade' of 1934, Emil Brunner speaks about Barth's 'Farewell to *Zwischen den Zeiten*' as about a 'letter of refusal [Absagebrief] to – let us say it briefly, to all other theologians'.

110. In the foreword of his book *Die Protestantische Theologie im 19. Jahrhundert*, Barth writes in 1946: 'I had hoped to pursue the history to the era of Troeltsch' – if there had been more time for the lecture series in 1933.

111. For this term, see above, Chapter III, n. 105.

112. This study was originally intended for the volume *Antwort* (Answer); E. Wolf (hrsg.), *Antwort. Karl Barth zum siebzigsten Geburtstag.* Zurich, 1956.